Psychology at Work

Peter Warr was educated at Cambridge and Sheffield Universities, and is currently a Research Professor in the Institute of Work Psychology at Sheffield University. He has also taught at Princeton University and the Universities of Colorado and California in the USA, at Canterbury University in New Zealand and at Curtin University in Australia. He has received all the awards made by the British Psychological Society for outstanding contributions to psychological knowledge: the Spearman Medal (1969), the Presidents' Award (1982) and an Honorary Fellowship (1997).

Professor Warr has carried out investigations in several areas of applied psychology. His research publications mainly concern interpersonal judgement, job characteristics and other factors linked to high or low well-being, psychological aspects of unemployment, processes of learning and training, age patterns in cognition and motivation, associations between personality and behaviour, and the development of instruments for measurement in those areas. He has served on many national committees and on editorial boards for journals to promote the understanding of psychology.

Peter Warr has published twenty-five books, including *Psychology and Collective Bargaining* (1973), *Work, Unemployment and Mental Health* (1987), *Training for Managers* (1993) and *Work, Well-Being and Effectiveness* (1999). He is the editor of *Thought and Personality* (1970) and *Personal Goals and Work Design* (1976), and a co-author of *Work and Well-Being* (1975), *The Experience of Work* (1981), *People and Computers* (1988) and *Measures of Job Satisfaction, Mental Health and Job-Related Well-Being* (1999).

Psychology at Work

Fifth Edition

Edited by Peter Warr

PENGUIN BOOKS

PENGUIN BOOKS

Published by the Penguin Group
Penguin Books Ltd, 80 Strand, London WC2R 0RL, England
Penguin Putnam Inc., 375 Hudson Street, New York, New York 10014, USA
Penguin Books Australia Ltd, 250 Camberwell Road, Camberwell, Victoria 3124, Australia
Penguin Books Canada Ltd, 10 Alcorn Avenue, Toronto, Ontario, Canada M4V 3B2
Penguin Books India (P) Ltd, 11 Community Centre, Panchsheel Park, New Delhi – 110 017, India
Penguin Books (NZ) Ltd, Cnr Rosedale and Airborne Roads, Albany, Auckland, New Zealand
Penguin Books (South Africa) (Pty) Ltd, 24 Sturdee Avenue, Rosebank 2196, South Africa

Penguin Books Ltd, Registered Offices: 80 Strand, London WC2R 0RL, England

www.penguin.com

First published in Penguin Books 1971
Second edition 1978
Third edition published in Pelican Books 1987
Reprinted in Penguin Books 1991
Fourth edition 1996
This edition published 2002
4

Set in 9.5/12 pt Adobe Minion
Typeset by Rowland Phototypesetting Ltd, Bury St Edmunds, Suffolk
Printed in England by Clays Ltd, St Ives plc

To the memory of Sir Frederic Bartlett and Dr Donald Broadbent

Contents

Introduction   ix
Peter Warr

1 The Study of Well-being, Behaviour and Attitudes   1
Peter Warr, Institute of Work Psychology, University of Sheffield

2 Human Performance in the Working Environment   26
Robert Hockey, Department of Psychology, University of Leeds

3 Shiftwork: Body Rhythm and Social Factors   51
Simon Folkard and Joanne Hill, Department of Psychology, University of Wales, Swansea

4 People and Computers: Emerging Work Practice in the Information Age   77
Ken Eason, Department of Human Sciences, Loughborough University

5 Personnel Selection and Assessment   100
Ivan Robertson, Manchester School of Management, University of Manchester Institute of Science and Technology; Dave Bartram, SHL Group plc, Thames Ditton; and Militza Callinan, Manchester School of Management, University of Manchester Institute of Science and Technology

6 Learning and Training   153
Peter Warr, Institute of Work Psychology, University of Sheffield

7 Careers and Career Management   178
Jennifer M. Kidd, Department of Organizational Psychology, Birkbeck College, University of London

8 Job-related Stress and Burnout 203

Michael P. O'Driscoll, Department of Psychology, University of Waikato, New Zealand; and Cary L. Cooper, Manchester School of Management, University of Manchester Institute of Science and Technology

9 The Experience, Expression and Management of Emotion at Work 229

Rob B. Briner, Department of Organizational Psychology, Birkbeck College, University of London; and Peter Totterdell, Institute of Work Psychology, University of Sheffield

10 Occupational Safety 253

Julian Barling, School of Business, Queen's University, Canada; E. Kevin Kelloway, Faculty of Management, St Mary's University, Canada; and Anthea Zacharatos, School of Business, Queen's University, Canada

11 Designing Jobs to Enhance Well-being and Performance 276

Sharon K. Parker, Australian Graduate School of Management, University of New South Wales, Sydney, Australia

12 Leadership 300

Beverly Alimo-Metcalfe, Nuffield Institute for Health, University of Leeds; and Robert J. Alban-Metcalfe, Trinity and All Saints' University College, Leeds

13 Team Working 326

John Cordery, Department of Organisational and Labour Studies, University of Western Australia, Perth, Australia

14 Human Resource Management and Business Performance 351

Stephen Wood and Toby Wall, Institute of Work Psychology, University of Sheffield

15 Organizations as Psychological Environments 375

Roy Payne, Institute of Work Psychology, University of Sheffield

16 Organizational Change and Development 399

Jean Hartley, Warwick Business School, University of Warwick

Author Index 427
Subject Index 445

Introduction

Peter Warr

Paid employment has long been a cornerstone of society. It is a source of social cohesion and material welfare; and for the individual it is often crucial to both mental and physical health. The majority of adults spend much of their life at work, and they are affected by it in multiple and sometimes conflicting ways. It warrants study by psychologists for its enormous social and personal importance, and also for the contribution that increased understanding of work processes can make to the development of psychology itself.

'Work' is usually defined to indicate that it is an activity directed to valued goals beyond enjoyment of the activity itself. That does not mean that work cannot be enjoyed; merely that immediate enjoyment is not part of the definition. In addition, definitions often suggest that work is required and that it involves the expenditure of effort.

PATTERNS OF WORK

People work in many different settings. The focus here is upon *paid* work, although many of the issues raised also apply to non-paid activities in housework, voluntary work, do-it-yourself work, and so on. Paid work is often 'full-time', with a job taking on average between thirty-five and forty hours a week. Travelling to and from a place of employment on average adds more than four hours a week, with jobs in large cities requiring substantially longer travel time (Anon, 2001a). 'Part-time' jobs of course vary in their duration, but thirty hours a week is often taken as their upper limit for statistical and survey purposes.

Recent years have seen many changes in the nature of paid work and in people's relationships to that work. For instance, there has been a general trend away from agriculture and production industries into service work. Within Europe, job losses have occurred principally in farming, textiles, iron and steel and the wood industry. The main growth sectors in the past decade have been health and social services, business services, hotels and restaurants, education and recreational activities (European Commission, 2000). Most developed countries now have approximately three-quarters of their jobs in service sectors.

Considerable expansion has occurred in technical, professional and managerial work, and more than two-thirds of British employers report that their jobs now require higher skill-levels than previously. That shift is particularly pronounced in larger organizations, and is widely attributed to greater use of technology, more complex working processes, multi-skilling, more international competition, and increased emphasis on customer requirements.

Men have traditionally sought paid employment throughout most of their adult lives, whereas labour market participation by women has tended to decline after they acquire child-care responsibilities. However, there has recently been a marked increase in the number of women remaining in jobs. For example, around 60 per cent of women of conventional employment age in Europe as a whole are now economically active, making up some 42 per cent of the workforce. (The percentages for the United Kingdom are 72 and 48 respectively.) Further information is set out in the table at the end of this Introduction.

Many women are employed part-time (44 per cent of all female workers in the United Kingdom, comprising more than three-quarters of the part-time workforce). Most of those prefer part-time to full-time work. For example, in 2000 94 per cent of part-time British women employees with dependent children (and 65 per cent of women without dependent children) reported that they did not want a full-time job. Most of those indicated that they prefer to have time for domestic and family activities (Anon, 2001b).

Men are less likely than women to work part-time (nine per cent of male workers in the UK), both through preference and because of aspects of national welfare schemes. (Welfare legislation in most countries has been designed with the full-time worker in mind.) The majority of men who work part-time are at the extremes of the labour-force age-range, being either students or those moving into retirement. Of part-time British male employees in 2000, 43 per cent did not want a full-time position, often because they reported not needing additional money (for example, since they also received a pension) or because they were studying (Anon, 2001b).

The labour force participation rate for older men has declined in recent years in many countries, so that the proportion of men who may be termed 'retired' has increased accordingly. However, in many cases retirement does not mean a complete cessation of paid employment; it is often partial, especially at relatively young ages. In the United States of America, between one-quarter and one-half of retired people at some point take up either full-time or (more usually) part-time work, possibly on a temporary or intermittent basis (Myers, 1991).

Other recent developments include a shift to more short-term and temporary jobs, more so in Europe than in the USA (Delsen, 1995). In 1999, some 13 per cent of European employees were on fixed-term contracts. About one-third of temporary employees in the United Kingdom indicate that they do not want a permanent job, preferring flexibility of choice and variation between roles (Department for Education and Employment, 2000). Temporary workers are mainly grouped at either end of the skill spectrum, tending to be either low-skilled or highly educated professional people (European Commission, 2000).

Self-employment has also increased recently, accounting for 15 per cent of employment in the European Union in 1999. This increase is partly because of the intrinsic attraction of working for oneself, but also because of the difficulty experienced by some people in finding an employed position (for instance, if displaced from a manufacturing job). In addition, self-employment serves to provide a second job for some temporary or part-time workers.

TYPES OF PSYCHOLOGY

The subject matter of psychology is wide-ranging, and some specialization has naturally occurred. The branch of the discipline that deals with people at work has been variously labelled as 'industrial', 'occupational', 'work' and 'organizational' psychology. Each of those terms has merit, but each has its limitation.

'Industrial' excludes the large number of non-industrial settings in which people are employed (hospitals, schools, government departments and so on), and is somewhat old-fashioned in the light of expansion in the service sectors (above). The term 'industrial/organizational' or 'industrial and organizational' is used in the United States of America, Australia, Canada and New Zealand, helpfully broadening the focus beyond merely 'industry'. More generally, 'organizational' is usually applied primarily at the level of groups or entire organizations, with an emphasis on social interaction, group norms and institutional structure. The label 'occupational' psychology is common in the United Kingdom, but is unfamiliar or unknown elsewhere. In many countries of continental Europe the reference is to 'work' psychology, but that suffers from the fact that 'work' has a wider reference than merely to paid employment. The limitation is sometimes overcome by broader reference to 'work and organizational' psychology. For example, the European Association of Work and Organizational Psychology exists to bring together psychologists from different countries working in the area of this book.

Although these labels vary, in each country the sub-discipline is clearly a form of 'applied' psychology. It is important to realize that this is not simply the application of 'pure' psychology. The distinction between pure and applied psychology is primarily in terms of the source of the issues to be studied. In 'pure' psychology, issues come from previous studies or theories, in effect from within psychology itself. On the other hand, 'applied' psychology draws topics for investigation from real-life settings, in our case from places of employment.

Applied investigators are thus by definition primarily concerned with issues arising in a particular setting of everyday life. However, applied psychologists may have theoretical as well as practical objectives. Some applied psychologists, typically those in academic departments (including the authors of this book), are primarily concerned to develop generalizable models and to test theoretical predictions against observed facts. Others work in organizations, using their psychological knowledge to solve immediate problems and to devise new procedures. Applied psychology, defined as having an external source for the issues to be addressed, can thus fall anywhere on a continuum from theory-development to problem-solution. Academic applied psychologists (located near the theory end of that continuum) have a concern for rigorous research designs and sound empirical evidence that is very similar to that of their counterparts in 'pure' aspects of the discipline.

These themes reflect the views of influential applied psychologists Frederic Bartlett and Donald Broadbent, to whom this book is dedicated. Bartlett (1886–1969) was Professor of Experimental Psychology at Cambridge University between 1931 and 1952 and an active Professor Emeritus until his death seventeen years later. Broadbent (1926–1993) took up employment in Bartlett's department soon after graduating with qualifications in engineering and psychology, and was active in Cambridge in a research and supervisory capacity until 1974. He then moved with a research team to the University of Oxford, where he worked until his death.

Bartlett argued that the fruitful development of psychology depended upon its involvement in day-to-day problems, stressing that the major theoretical advances were likely to come from those researchers whose prime concern was with genuinely practical problems. The juxtaposition of 'theoretical' and 'practical' here is most important. Bartlett's notion was that we certainly need theoretical structures, but that those have to be built on a foundation of practical importance rather than solely on the basis of what academics happen to find interesting. For example, he wrote: 'The history of psychology shows that if [a psychologist] shuts himself up narrowly in any particular small sphere of conduct inside or outside the laboratory (but specially inside), he will tend to get over-immersed in a terrific lot of detail about behaviour problems which he cleverly imagines for himself, and will approximate to a sort of puzzle solving which is often extremely interesting and, in a debating sense, intellectually attractive, but which leaves him revolving round and round his limited area' (Bartlett, 1949, p. 215).

Broadbent's approach (influenced by Bartlett) was similar. 'The test of intellectual excellence of a psychological theory, as well as its moral justification, lies in its application to concrete practical situations' (Broadbent, 1973, p. 7). 'Most great scientific advances have originated in practical problems . . . By looking at difficulties that arise in real life, one is forced to think more rigorously and to consider variables which it is easy to forget while in the fastnesses of theory' (Broadbent, 1973, pp. 124–5). He was concerned that academic research 'could slip over into excessive rationalism, where theories were devised for behaviour that human beings do not in fact show, or into a mandarin-like concern with small experimental paradigms' (Broadbent, 1980, p. 68).

In overview, applied psychology is that which examines issues of practical concern outside the discipline of psychology itself. Applied psychological projects can be located anywhere between studies of broad theoretical issues and the immediate solution of practical problems. Our focus here is on general themes and theoretical understanding, but the day-to-day importance of our subject matter will be clear.

CONTENTS OF THE BOOK

The chapters that follow have been specially prepared for this volume. They are directed primarily at students of psychology, business and management, but aim also to interest anyone who is curious about the role of psychology in work settings.

The first chapter introduces three principal objects of study: well-being, behaviour and attitudes. After that, topics have been arranged in a sequence that, roughly speaking, moves from an emphasis on the individual, through the study of groups, to the examination of organizations as a whole. This sequence is a straightforward one, but not necessarily the best for every reader. Course teachers may wish to emphasize certain features or recommend a particular sequence, and the general reader may prefer to dip into a selection of individual chapters.

The authors are all experienced and influential in their fields. They have provided substantial summaries, but have written in a style that makes clear their personal approach and preferred interpretations. Topics have been chosen because of their importance for the field and in order to reflect developments occurring within psychology and within society more broadly. Although the book explicitly seeks in part to reflect continuity and steady development, it specially aims to identify newly important areas and to anticipate future developments.

Several chapters thus present the latest research in well established fields, such as personnel selection, training, leadership, job-related stress, job design, corporate culture and how to implement change. Others introduce topics that are wholly new to the field, covering for instance the role of emotions at work, uses of the internet and the effects of human resource management practices. Other fresh themes include new types of working through virtual teams, health and safety from a psychological perspective, careers in a changed world, and the design and operation of computer-based systems. Specific computer applications are illustrated throughout the book, and relevant web-sites are presented in many chapters.

Aspects of psychology are also open to more general exploration through the world-wide web. Addresses of several national and international associations are given below. In most cases, links are provided to many other interesting sites.

- Australian Psychological Society: *www.psychsociety.com.au*
- British Psychological Society: *www.bps.org.uk*
- Canadian Psychological Association: *www.cpa.ca*
- European Association of Work and Organizational Psychology: *www.fss.uu.nl/eawop*
- International Association of Applied Psychology: *www.iaapsy.org*
- New Zealand Psychological Society: *www.psychology.org.nz*
- Society for Industrial and Organizational Psychology (a division of the American Psychological Association): *www.siop.org*

We hope that readers will come to share our enthusiasm. The topics addressed in this book impinge on the daily lives of millions of people. We are convinced that psychology can improve those lives in many ways, and would like more people to study and make use of its achievements.

REFERENCES

Anon (2001a). Usual main method and time taken to travel to work. *Labour Market Trends*, 109, 143.

Anon (2001b). Reasons for not wanting a full-time job. *Labour Market Trends*, 109, 144.

Bartlett, F. C. (1949). What is industrial psychology? *Occupational Psychology*, 23, 212–18.

Broadbent, D. E. (1973). *In Defence of Empirical Psychology*. London: Methuen.

Broadbent, D. E. (1980). Donald E. Broadbent. In G. Lindzey (ed.), *A History of Psychology in Autobiography*, volume 7, pp. 39–73. San Francisco: W. H. Freeman.

Delsen, L. (1995). *Atypical Employment: An International Perspective.* Amsterdam: Wolters-Noordhoff.

Department for Education and Employment (2000). *Labour Market and Skill Trends.* London: DfEE.

European Commission (2000). *Employment in Europe 1999.* Luxembourg: Office for Official Publications of the European Communities.

Myers, D. A. (1991). Work after cessation of a career job. *Journal of Gerontology,* 46, S93–S102.

	European Union (15 countries)			United Kingdom		
	Overall	*Men*	*Women*	*Overall*	*Men*	*Women*
Percentage of the working-age population in the labour market ('activity rate')	69	79	60	76	84	68
Percentage of the working-age population in employment	62	72	53	71	77	64
Percentage of the working-age population in full-time employment	57	68	42	60	76	45
Percentage of the employed population in self-employment	15	18	13	12	16	11
Percentage of the employed population in part-time employment	18	6	33	25	9	44
Percentage of the employed population on fixed-term contracts	13	12	14	7	6	8

Source: European Commission, 2000.

The Study of Well-being, Behaviour and Attitudes

Peter Warr

This chapter introduces the three principal outcomes that have been studied by psychologists in work settings: people's well-being, their behaviour and their attitudes. Different aspects of those three outcomes will be examined, and some interrelationships between well-being and behaviour will be explored: is more positive well-being accompanied by better work performance?

THE NATURE OF WELL-BEING

The concern in this book is mainly for 'psychological' rather than 'physical' well-being. The concept is sometimes called 'affective' well-being to emphasize the centrality of feelings. It may be studied with a restricted focus or through feelings about life that are more general. The more restricted concern here is for 'job-related' (or 'job-specific') well-being, people's feelings about themselves in relation to their job. 'Context-free' well-being has a broader focus, covering feelings about life in general without limitation to any particular setting (e.g., Warr, 1987, 1997).

Job Satisfaction

A traditional approach to job-related well-being has been in terms of people's satisfaction with their jobs. This may be examined at several levels of specificity. The most general construct is 'overall job satisfaction', the extent to which a person is satisfied with his or her job as a whole. More focused 'facet' satisfactions concern different aspects of a job, such as satisfaction with one's pay, colleagues, supervisors, working conditions, job security, promotion prospects, training opportunities, and the nature of the work undertaken. Different facet satisfactions tend to be positively intercorrelated, and satisfaction with one (the nature of the work undertaken) is particularly closely associated with overall job satisfaction.

Three Axes of Well-being

Measures of job satisfaction examine job-specific well-being along a single dimension, roughly from feeling bad to feeling good. Such a dimension can of course capture important feelings, but it is preferable to think in terms of a two-dimensional framework, as set out in Figure 1.1. Such a

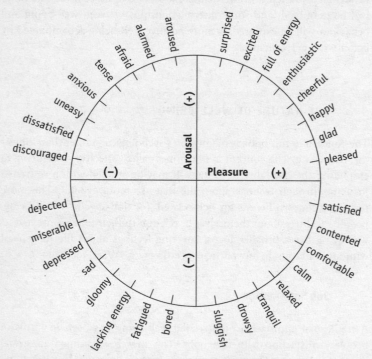

Fig. 1.1 *A two-dimensional view of psychological well-being*

framework has been substantiated in many investigations (e.g., Remington, Fabrigar and Visser, 2000; Watson, Clark and Tellegen, 1988), which have pointed to the importance of two independent dimensions of feeling, here labelled as 'pleasure' and 'arousal'.

We may describe a person's well-being in terms of its location relative to those two dimensions (representing the *content* of feelings) and its distance from the mid-point of the figure (such that a more distant location indicates a greater *intensity*). A particular degree of pleasure or displeasure (the horizontal dimension) may be accompanied by high or low levels of mental arousal (the vertical dimension); and a particular quantity of mental arousal (sometimes referred to as 'activation') may be either pleasurable or unpleasurable.

Within this framework, three principal axes of measurement are illustrated in Figure 1.2. In view of the central importance of feelings of low or high pleasure, the first axis is in terms of the horizontal dimension alone. In studies of job-related well-being, this axis is conventionally indexed as job satisfaction (above); in more general investigations, the focus may be on broader concepts such as life satisfaction. The other two axes take account of mental arousal as well as pleasure, by running diagonally between opposite quadrants through the mid-point of the figure. The arousal dimension on its own is not considered to reflect well-being, and its end-points are therefore left unlabelled.

In thinking about job-specific or context-free well-being, we may thus consider three main axes (Lucas, Diener and Suh, 1996). First is displeasure to pleasure, the positive pole of which is often examined as satisfaction or happiness. The second axis runs from anxiety to comfort. Feelings of anxiety combine low pleasure with high mental arousal, whereas comfort is illustrated as low-arousal pleasure. Third is the axis

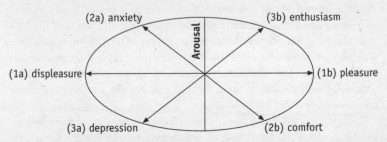

Fig. 1.2 Three axes for the measurement of well-being

from depression to enthusiasm. Feelings of enthusiasm and positive motivation are in the top-right quadrant, and depression and sadness (low pleasure and low mental arousal) are at the other end of the axis. A person may be characterized in terms of his or her location on each of the three axes, which are of course intercorrelated through heavy loadings on pleasure (the horizontal dimension).

Despite that general intercorrelation, different associations exist with certain other variables. For example, the level of a person's job is linked in opposite ways with job-specific anxiety and with depression. People in higher-level jobs report significantly *less* job-related depression than those in lower-level jobs, but also significantly *more* job-related anxiety (Birdi, Warr and Oswald, 1995; Warr, 1990b; Warr, 1992). That pattern of well-being seems likely also to be found among self-employed individuals relative to those employed in an organization. It may be interpreted in terms of the dimension of mental arousal; people in higher-level positions (and self-employment?) experience greater arousal, on both the diagonal axes in Figure 1.2.

The three axes of well-being have been measured through question-naires or interviews that ask about feelings of the kind illustrated in the relevant areas of Figure 1.1. It is of course possible to investigate other feelings, and the degree of detail examined depends upon a study's objectives. A fourth axis of particular importance in some occupational settings concerns feelings of fatigue or vigour, and scales to measure variations in that respect have been presented by Daniels (2000) and Warr (1990b, Appendix 2). In the terms of Figure 1.2, that fourth axis may be located through the mid-point from a position at the right of 3a to the left of 3b.

Associations between job-specific and context-free well-being

What is known about the association between a person's job-specific well-being and his or her more general well-being? In respect of the first axis, this has been examined through measures of overall job satisfaction and life satisfaction; the correlation between these is on average found to be about 0.35 (Tait, Padgett and Baldwin, 1989). Some overlap is of course logically necessary, since feelings about a job are themselves one component of wider life satisfaction.

Research has sought to identify the pattern of causality in this relation-ship: does job satisfaction cause life satisfaction, or vice versa? A longitudinal investigation by Judge and Watanabe (1993) indicated that the pattern was one of mutual influence, but that the effect from life satisfaction to job satisfaction was greater than in the other direction. A person's overall well-being has strong impact on his or her job-specific well-being, and job well-being also affects wider feelings.

It is likely that the relations between job-specific and context-free well-being vary between individuals and across situations, within the framework of an overall positive and reciprocal association. For example, Bamundo and Kopelman (1980) found that the association was stronger for high-income, more educated and self-employed individuals. Thompson, Kopelman and Schriesheim (1992) replicated this finding for self-versus organizational employment. Examining studies over a period of forty years, Tait *et al.* (1989) looked at differences between men and women. Prior to 1974, the correlation between job satisfaction and life satisfaction for women was quite low (0.16), but thereafter it increased to the level found for men (0.31). This increase may be due to a greater centrality of paid employment for women in more recent years.

Job strain

Some investigators have combined elements from more than one of the three axes in Figure 1.2 into overall measures of well-being. For example, much research has examined feelings of strain arising from certain job features (usually referred to as 'stressors'). Strain is often measured in terms of generalized distress (either job-specific or context-free), combining the two negative forms of well-being identified as 2a and 3a in Figure 1.2 (both anxiety and depression).

A specific form of strain is job-related 'burnout' (e.g., Maslach, 1999). This is typically viewed as an adverse reaction by workers in close interactions with clients in the helping professions, although it may also occur in other forms of work. Burn-out contains three job-related dimensions: emotional exhaustion, depersonalization (felt distance from others), and reduced personal accomplishment. The first of those is the aspect most often measured, covering feelings of job-related strain, being used up, fatigued and working too hard.

A minority of studies have examined psychosomatic symptoms of strain (in terms of reported sleeplessness, headaches and similar problems) or physiological variables such as heart rate, blood pressure and catecholamine levels. It is clear that negative well-being can have physiological as well as psychological aspects. Research into strain is reviewed in Chapter 8, and impacts on task performance are examined in Chapter 2.

Job characteristics and affective well-being

Many studies have investigated links between specific aspects of a person's work environment and his or her psychological well-being, usually that which is job-specific rather than context-free. Studies of particular job characteristics are illustrated in the chapters that follow. More broadly, the classification suggested by Warr (1987, 1994) seeks to embrace all the psychologically important attributes of work. Jobs differ in the amount they possess of each feature, and those variations give rise to differences in job-related well-being.

With the more recent addition of number 8 (Warr, 1999), the suggested key features are as follows. In each case below, a principal label is accompanied by other terms which are common in the employment-related literature.

1. *Opportunity for personal control*: employee discretion, decision latitude, autonomy, absence of close supervision, self-determination, participation in decision-making, freedom of choice.
2. *Opportunity for skill use*: skill utilization, utilization of valued abilities, required skills, multi-skilling.
3. *Externally generated goals*: job demands, task demands, quantitative or qualitative workload, work pressure, attentional demand, role responsibility, conflicting demands, role conflict, work–family conflict, normative requirements.
4. *Variety*: variation in job content and location, non-repetitive work, skill variety, task variety.
5. *Environmental clarity*: (a) information about the consequences of behaviour, task feedback; (b) information about the future, absence of job future ambiguity, absence of job insecurity; (c) information about required behaviour, role clarity, low role ambiguity.
6. *Availability of money*: income level, amount of pay, financial resources.
7. *Physical security*: absence of danger, good working conditions, ergonomically adequate equipment, safe levels of temperature and noise.
8. *Supportive supervision*: leader consideration, boss support, supportive management, effective leadership.
9. *Opportunity for interpersonal contact*: (a) quantity of interaction, con-

tact with others, social density, adequate privacy; (b) quality of inter-action, good relationships with others, social support, supportive colleagues, good communications.

10. *Valued social position*: (a) wider evaluations of a job's status in society, social rank, occupational prestige; (b) more localized evaluations of in-company status or job importance; (c) personal valuations of task significance, working in a valued role, contributions made to others, meaningfulness of job, self-respect from job.

There is considerable evidence for the importance of all those job features (e.g., Warr, 1999). Some of them are more predictive of one form of well-being than of others. For example, a very high level of job demands (3, above) is more strongly associated with low job well-being on axis two (anxiety to comfort) than on axis three (depression to enthusiasm); however, for very low opportunity for personal control (1, above) the opposite is the case (Warr, 1990a). Correlations of job demands and control opportunity also show this differentiated pattern with job-specific anxiety (well-being axis two) and overall job satisfaction (axis one); demands are more associated with anxiety, and control opportunity is more correlated with satisfaction (Spector and O'Connell, 1994).

Most investigators have examined only linear correlations between job features and well-being, although it might be expected that too much (as well as too little) of a feature is often undesirable (Warr, 1987). That is clear for externally generated goals (feature 3, above), where both underload and overload can yield lower well-being. In several other cases, extremely high levels of a feature are also expected to become unpleasantly coercive, rather than providing personal benefit as is the case at moderate levels. In addition to externally generated goals (above), these features are opportunity for personal control (feature 1, above), opportunity for skill use (2, above), variety (feature 4), environmental clarity (5), and opportunity for interpersonal contact (feature 9). All of those illustrate the possibility of 'having too much of a good thing'. Furthermore, extremely high levels of one feature are likely to be associated with other characteristics which are themselves undesirable; for example, unremit-tingly very high control opportunities (feature 1) tend also to result in relentless overload (feature 3).

There is some research evidence for non-linear associations of this kind between job features and well-being. Karasek (1979), Warr (1990a) and de Jonge and Schaufeli (1998) have demonstrated significant curvi-linearity for job demands: job-specific well-being scores were low with least demand, they increased (cross-sectionally) with moderate demand, and then declined again at particularly high levels of demand. The same pattern in respect of opportunity for personal control has been observed in laboratory situations by Burger (1989) and among employees by de Jonge and Schaufeli (1998). Other non-linear findings have been reported by Xie and Johns (1995), de Jonge, Reuvers, Houtman, Bongers and Kompier (2000) and Taris and Feij (2001).

What about the wider impact of jobs outside work; do job character-istics affect *context-free* well-being? The strong correlation reported earlier between job satisfaction (known to be affected by job content) and life satisfaction suggests that they do, and significant associations between specific job features and context-free well-being have been found in several studies (e.g., Martin and Wall, 1989; Roxburgh, 1996). However, context-free well-being is also influenced by a range of non-job features (state of health, social relationships, domestic difficulties, and so on), and these may collectively have more impact on context-free well-being for some people than do job features.

Personal characteristics and affective well-being

It is important to recognize that individual characteristics, as well as those in the environment, can affect well-being: people's feelings are influenced by their own continuing dispositions as well as by what occurs to them. These personal determinants of well-being have sometimes been viewed in terms of dispositions labelled as 'negative affectivity' (NA) and 'positive affectivity' (PA).

The personality trait of negative affectivity (NA) covers a broad range of unpleasant emotional states, such that people with high negative affectivity are more likely than others to experience distress and dissatis-faction in any circumstances (Watson and Clark, 1984). High-NA indi-viduals tend to focus on the negative side of themselves and the world in general; they scan the environment for impending trouble, and they experience anxiety about what they see. The characteristic is sometimes identified as 'neuroticism', which is consistently found to be associated with lower context-free well-being (DeNeve and Cooper, 1998).

The trait of positive affectivity (PA) is seen in high levels of energy, excitement and enthusiasm. High-PA individuals tend to lead more active lives than low-PA people and to view their environments in a more positive fashion. The characteristic is similar to extraversion, which is known to be accompanied by more positive well-being (DeNeve and Cooper, 1998).

In general, personality traits (extending across time) are liable to be reflected in a person's short-term state when he or she is in a trait-relevant situation. Well-being experienced at one point in time is a short-term state of that kind, and well-being axes two and three in Figure 1.2 are in practice 'state' measures of corresponding longer-term 'traits': negative affectivity and positive affectivity respectively. The content of the constructs remains the same between trait and state, but the time-frame is different. This means that persons with high trait negative affectivity (NA) are expected usually to be in a more anxious state than others when in work situations (that is, to exhibit lower job-specific well-being on axis two in Figure 1.2), and that individuals with high positive affectivity (PA) are likely to have raised job-related well-being on axis three.

These trait–state expectations have been supported by many research findings. For example, Elliott, Chartrand and Harkins (1994) examined correlations between trait negative affectivity (NA) and reports of recent anxiety at work, finding a median value of 0.45. Trait positive affectivity (PA) was shown by George (1989) to be significantly associated with the third axis of job-related well-being (from depression to enthusiasm). Other investigations have studied overall job satisfaction (axis one) as a function of these trait measures. In keeping with its intermediate position as the horizontal axis in Figure 1.2, this form of job-specific well-being is expected to be positively correlated with trait PA and negatively correlated with negative affectivity. Median values are in fact 0.33 from five studies of positive affectivity, and −0.26 from nine studies of negative affectivity (Warr, 1999).

Other continuing dispositions have been shown to predict current levels of job satisfaction. For example, Judge, Bono and Locke (2000) examined self-esteem and generalized feelings of self-efficacy. Employees with more positive self-evaluations of those dispositional kinds reported greater overall job satisfaction, over and above the impact of job characteristics. Furthermore, self-evaluative traits measured in childhood thirty years previously were found to predict job satisfaction, over and above current job influences.

The impact of these cross-situational dispositions on feelings of well-being suggests that job satisfaction and other indicators of well-being should be relatively stable across time. That is indeed the case (e.g., Steel and Rentsch, 1997). Arvey, Bouchard, Segal and Abraham (1989) asked whether between-individual variations in job satisfaction might in part be inherited. They reported data from pairs of identical twins (from the same fertilized egg) who had been reared apart, concluding that approximately 30 per cent of variance in overall job satisfaction is attributable to genetic factors. This conclusion was supported in a much larger investigation by Arvey, McCall, Bouchard, Taubman and Cavanaugh (1994). The precise magnitude of the effect of heredity is open to dispute for a range of methodological reasons, but some genetic influence on job satisfaction appears to occur. This genetic effect is presumably through inherited aspects of broader personality dispositions and ability levels, themselves affecting work preferences and the kinds of jobs that are undertaken.

Studies examining together the relative importance of job and personal factors have found that both sets of features contribute significantly to well-being (e.g., Agho, Mueller and Price, 1993; Judge *et al.*, 2000; Watson and Slack, 1993). In a comparison of independent contributions, Levin and Stokes (1989) showed that the impact of job characteristics on job satisfaction was stronger than that of trait negative affectivity.

SOME PRINCIPAL WORK BEHAVIOURS

The chapter has so far been concerned with the first of three broad outcome variables. Although it has been possible to identify in general terms some of the determinants of high or low psychological well-being, particular causal processes in specific work settings do of course require more detailed study. Recent approaches will be illustrated in the chapters that follow.

The second outcome variable of interest to psychologists, work behaviour, has also been investigated in numerous forms. Five aspects will be considered here: performance in a job, discretionary activities, specific skills, absence from work, and staff turnover. Different causal influences operate for each kind of behaviour, and overall accounts of the determinants of behaviour as suggested for well-being are not possible. However, one question can be reviewed in general terms: what is the association between employees' psychological well-being and their work behaviour of each of the five kinds?

Even if a significant association between well-being and behaviour were found, the direction of causality would remain unclear. It would not necessarily be the case that (say) high job satisfaction causes a particular form of behaviour, for example effective job performance. The opposite might be true: good performers might be more satisfied as a result of their effective performance. Alternatively, the causal pattern might be in both directions, or a third factor (or several of them) might bring about both high performance and high satisfaction. For instance, particular equipment characteristics or managerial styles might influence both behaviour and well-being. Note also that any work behaviour is determined by a wide range of different factors (organizational policies, management practices, group pressures, individual abilities, available options, etc.), so that the maximum possible correlation of behaviour with well-being alone is necessarily much less than 1.00.

Most studies in this area have examined the behaviour of individual employees. For instance, in studies of selection, training or computer use the unit of analysis is typically a single person. However, the behaviour of *groups* is investigated in some settings. For example, research might address the joint activities of members of a design team, with outcomes in terms of a new product attributable to the team as a whole rather than to any single individual. The behaviour of teams and entire organizations will be illustrated in Chapters 13 and 15 respectively; the main focus in this section is on individuals.

Job Performance

The term 'performance' is different from 'behaviour' in that it usually implies some evaluation of what is done. People behave in many different ways in the course of their work, but only a few behaviours (or 'actions' or 'activities') are evaluated as desirable aspects of performance. Nevertheless, the measurement of job performance is not easy. Although effectiveness in single tasks may be examined through specific activities (see Chapter 2), an overall measure of job performance in terms of the quantity of production or service is rarely available. Sometimes this is because a job has no accurately quantifiable output, but of particular importance is the fact that most jobs have multiple outputs: there is more to being a good worker than merely having a high output level.

For these reasons, it is usual for psychologists' studies of job performance to obtain ratings about a range of key behaviours. These are sometimes viewed as 'competencies', desirable behaviours in a particular job. For instance, managers' competencies might be assessed through their supervisors' ratings of the extent to which they exhibit behaviours that are innovative, demonstrate technical expertise, cope with pressure, control costs, define team objectives, and so on (see also Chapter 5). Job performance is thus usually studied in terms of several different dimensions, often as rated by a person's supervisor.

Supervisors' judgements are likely to be influenced by a range of extraneous factors, and agreement between judgements made by different raters is far from perfect (Viswesvaran, Ones and Schmidt, 1996; Warr and Bourne, 1999). However, supervisors' judgements underpin assessments of performance in day-to-day operations, in that it is a supervisor who decides about a person's future work allocations. On balance, the comprehensiveness and local relevance of supervisors' ratings of job performance may be thought to outweigh their potential unreliability.

Is greater well-being associated with better job performance? Iaffaldano and Muchinsky (1985) reviewed previous studies of job satisfaction (axis one in Figure 1.2), finding an average correlation with performance of 0.25. Petty, McGee and Cavender (1984) reported very similar findings (the average correlation was 0.23), and noted that the association of overall job satisfaction with rated performance was stronger for managerial and professional employees than for others (average correlations of 0.31 and 0.15 respectively). In a more recent examination of several hundred studies, Judge, Thoresen, Bono and Patton (2001) observed a mean correlation of 0.18, with a stronger association (0.27) when a person's work was of high complexity.

Ostroff (1992) examined satisfaction and performance at the level of entire organizations. In a study of schools, effectiveness was assessed in terms of academic performance, administrative efficiency and student behaviour. It was found that more effective schools had more satisfied employees (an average coefficient of 0.28). Manufacturing companies were investigated by Patterson and West (2001). The average of each company's employees' overall job satisfaction was found to predict later productivity (net sales per employee) and profitability (profit per employee); correlations were 0.44 and 0.36 respectively.

What about axis two, from feelings of job-specific anxiety to comfort? It seems likely that employees who report more job anxiety might be experiencing difficulty in coping with job demands and thus perform relatively less effectively; a negative association between job-related anxiety and job performance is thus probable. Very few investigations have examined this question, but Jamal (1984) found that higher levels of job-related tension were associated with lower supervisory ratings (a median correlation of −0.35).

The third axis of job-specific well-being in Figure 1.2 ranges from depression to enthusiasm. It appears likely that employees with positive job-related feelings of this active kind will be among the more productive, but few studies have been reported. Motowidlo, Packard and Manning (1986) examined the association between nurses' job-related depression and ratings of their effectiveness by supervisors and by co-workers, finding a significant negative association in both cases. A positive form of this third axis (job involvement) was linked to performance ($r = 0.23$) in Keller's (1997) study.

Discretionary Activities

Some work behaviours are discretionary, rather than being prescribed as requirements. It might be expected that employee well-being will be particularly associated with those voluntary behaviours, rather than with activities demanded by a role or by technological constraints. Three possibilities may be considered.

One form of discretionary behaviour is seen in *voluntary overtime*. Many jobs offer the possibility to undertake some unpaid work outside the required hours, and employees' job-specific well-being might be predictive of such behaviour. This was found to be the case in a study of school-teachers: overall job satisfaction was correlated 0.25 with the amount of additional (unpaid) time devoted to work-related activities (Gechman and Wiener, 1975).

A second kind of discretionary activity at work is sometimes referred to as *organizational citizenship behaviour*. Such activities include providing assistance to colleagues, volunteering to undertake needed tasks and making suggestions to improve effectiveness (e.g., Podsakoff, MacKenzie, Paine and Bachrach, 2000). Overall job satisfaction has frequently been shown to be significantly associated with this type of discretionary behaviour as rated by a boss or colleagues. In a review of previous research, Organ and Ryan (1995) reported an average correlation of 0.25 with ratings of citizenship behaviour.

Finally, forms of *adaptive behaviour* are increasingly valued in organizations that have to face intense market pressure or rapid technological change. Is employee well-being likely to be associated with this type of discretionary activity, seen in a willingness to take steps to acquire new skills and knowledge? Karasek and Theorell (1990) suggested that anxiety accumulated across time in a stressful job inhibits new learning for two reasons: employees under strain may become less able to handle a current situation, and they may be less likely to change their approach in the face of new requirements. A vicious cycle would thus be created, with mutual augmentation between anxiety and ineffectiveness. There is at present no direct evidence for this longitudinal pattern, but the idea appears plausible.

Related information has been provided by Parker and Sprigg (1999). They found that job-related anxiety was significantly associated with less proactive behaviour, measured in terms of self-reports of personal initiative and the tendency to persevere until success is attained. Birdi, Gardner and Warr (1998) asked whether overall job satisfaction is greater in employees who are more active in work-based development activities (undertaking personal projects, serving on project groups, etc.). A significant positive association was found. However, as in similar cases we cannot determine from this cross-sectional investigation alone whether greater well-being promoted learning, whether learning activities enhanced well-being, whether both effects occurred, or whether additional factors were responsible for the association recorded.

Specific Skills

Among behaviours of particular interest to psychologists are those that depend on prior learning. Such activities are sometimes referred to as 'skills', or viewed in terms of expertise, wisdom or habitual routines. They are found both in cognitive processing and in physical ('motor') activities (for instance, in skilled manual work).

Skilled performers usually have more substantial knowledge than others, but the difference is not merely one of quantity. Comparisons between the performance of novices and experts have distinguished between 'declarative' and 'procedural' knowledge (e.g., Anderson, 1995) (see Chapter 6). In the first case, a person acquires information about individual facts and their relationships. During subsequent learning, this declarative knowledge is gradually converted into a set of behavioural or cognitive routines through which it is applied in dealing with the environment. These routines gradually become collapsed into longer sequences of action or thought, which the person can execute as a whole.

Skilled behaviour thus involves 'automatization', as people move from controlled, effortful thinking to the execution of smooth routines. Those routines are often not under direct control once initiated, and they free mental resources and permit simultaneous processing of information. In addition, experts more easily perceive and recall meaningful patterns in their domain, and can more rapidly process new material within their established knowledge structures. Such processes are largely domain-specific, so that an expert in one area may be unskilled in others.

Psychologists have studied many forms of skilled behaviour in work situations, being interested in the processes of expertise acquisition (see Chapter 6) as well as in possible decrements as a function of job demands, environmental stressors and other factors (see Chapter 2). As summarized above, job performance and perceived opportunity for skill use are both significantly related to job-related affective well-being, so that some association of well-being with skilled behaviour also seems likely.

Absence from Work

Another index of employee behaviour is in terms of absenteeism (or its converse, attendance at work). In addition to sickness itself, social and family pressures can affect decisions to attend. Organizational influences include local policies to encourage attendance, support from a supervisor, and more broadly the 'absence culture' in which a person works – norms and sanctions (informal as well as formal) about reasonable levels of absence. Although employee well-being at work might be expected to be linked to absenteeism, other factors clearly also have an impact.

Absenteeism is conventionally measured in two different ways, through the Time-Lost Index and the Frequency Index. The Time-Lost Index is computed as the total duration of absence during a specified period, perhaps expressed as a proportion of the total time examined; and the Frequency Index is the number of separate incidents of absence in a specified period, regardless of their duration. The Time-Lost Index, which gives greater emphasis to long periods of absence, is considered primarily to represent *involuntary* responses to incapacitating sickness. On the other hand, the Frequency Index, in which a single day's absence is given the same weight as, say, a three-month absence, is widely thought to describe more *voluntary* choices to take time off work for brief periods of time.

How do the three axes of job-specific well-being correlate with these two indices of absenteeism? As with the behaviours examined above, the causes underlying any observed association would be complex and multiple.

In a review of previous studies, Farrell and Stamm (1988) found that overall job satisfaction (the first axis in Figure 1.2) was on average correlated only −0.10 with the Frequency Index and −0.13 with the Time-Lost Index. The average correlations of job-related anxiety (axis two) with the Frequency Index and the Time-Lost Index were found to be 0.11 and 0.18 respectively. (See also Hackett, 1989, and Jamal, 1984.) Examining subsequent absences by medical staff, Hardy, Woods and Wall (2001) found a correlation between the Time-Lost Index and overall job satisfaction of −0.29 and with job-related anxiety of 0.22.

The third axis of job-specific well-being ranges from feelings of depression to enthusiasm. George (1989) examined positive feelings of this kind, and observed a correlation of −0.28 with the number of single-day absences. In the study by Hardy *et al.* (2001) job-related depression (the negative pole of the axis) was correlated 0.33 with amount of subsequent absence. The review by Farrell and Stamm (1988) found that measures of job involvement (emphasizing active interest in one's role, as in positive forms of axis three) were on average correlated −0.28 with the Frequency Index. It appears that this third aspect of job-specific well-being is more associated with absenteeism than are the other two measurement axes.

Staff Turnover

A fifth behavioural measure which might be expected to be related to job-specific well-being is whether or not people remain with their current employer. There is a significant correlation between absence from work (above) and subsequent turnover (Griffeth, Hom and Gaertner, 2000), and precursors of the two forms of behaviour overlap in many ways. The average reported correlation between overall job satisfaction and employee turnover is −0.17 (Griffeth *et al.*, 2000). However, additional factors also influence turnover decisions, especially the availability or otherwise of suitable alternative employment; job satisfaction better predicts actual turnover when the local unemployment rate is lower (Hom, Caranikas-Walker, Prussia and Griffeth, 1992).

Some investigators have asked about people's future employment plans, finding that intentions to leave are predicted by low overall job satisfaction (axis one in Figure 1.2) (e.g., Hom *et al.*, 1992) and by job-specific anxiety (axis two) (e.g., Spector, Dwyer and Jex, 1988). Lee and Ashforth (1996) reported an average correlation between job-related emotional exhaustion (the main component of burnout) and turnover intention of 0.37. Intentions to leave are themselves correlated on average 0.35 with actual turnover (Griffeth *et al.*, 2000).

EMPLOYEE ATTITUDES

In addition to an interest in employee well-being and behaviour of the kinds illustrated above, psychologists' third main outcome variable is attitudinal. Many studies have examined the environmental and personal factors that influence the attitudes of people at work. Attitudes are usually viewed as evaluative tendencies (favourable or unfavourable) towards a person, group, thing, event or process. An attitude towards a particular object is thus a bias predisposing a person towards evaluative responses that are positive or negative (Eagly and Chaiken, 1993). Broad attitudes towards relatively abstract goals or end states (such as racial equality, environmental pollution or national identity) are usually referred to as 'values'.

These evaluative tendencies are conventionally viewed as having three aspects: cognitive, affective and behavioural. In the first case, an attitude contains positive or negative beliefs about its object. The second (affective) aspect consists of feelings, moods and emotions experienced in relation to the attitude object, and evaluative features of the behavioural kind are exhibited in actions in relation to that object. Research by social psychologists has tended to examine attitudes towards social policies, political ideologies or minority groups, but these evaluative tendencies are clearly important also in work settings.

For example, studies of 'organizational commitment' concern people's attitude to their employing organization. A principal component is a person's emotional attachment to that organization, and sources of employees' attachment have been identified both in their individual characteristics and in features of their employing organization (e.g., Meyer and Allen, 1997). Particular investigations of other attitudes might examine evaluative tendencies in relation to local safety procedures, communication systems, shift patterns, appraisal schemes, new equipment, or whatever is of interest in a given situation. Studies have focused on one or more of the cognitive, affective or behavioural aspects of an attitude.

Attitudes are also of interest in theories of motivation. For example, the theory of planned behaviour (Ajzen, 1991) seeks to predict people's actions from a range of factors including their attitude to an act (their overall assessment of the advantages and disadvantages of behaving in a certain way). Other general models of motivation have emphasized the 'valence' of possible outcomes from behaviour of different kinds, examining valence in terms of favourable or unfavourable feelings about those outcomes (in effect, as types of attitude).

Since both attitudes and well-being (examined earlier) reflect people's feelings, the two concepts do of course overlap. Psychological well-being is primarily the affective aspect of an attitude towards oneself. Some writers treat variables such as job satisfaction as an 'attitude', whereas it has here been included as an aspect of well-being. In view of the widely varying focus of attitudes, an overall account of their content and determinants is not possible; specific occupational examples are presented in almost all the following chapters. The general point being made at this stage is that it is useful to think of attitudes as a third outcome variable of interest to psychologists in work settings.

EXAMINING THE THREE OUTCOMES

As in all areas of psychology, research into principal outcomes at work may take four overlapping forms, investigating their nature, interrelationships, causes or consequences. In the first case, studies examine the characteristics and structure of, for example, psychological well-being, often also developing more effective procedures of measurement. A second set of investigations looks at the ways in which the three kinds of outcomes co-vary, for example exploring associations between well-being and behaviour.

Research into potential causes or consequences is often cross-sectional, recording intercorrelations between variables. For instance, a study might examine the associations between work behaviour and a certain job characteristic (assumed to be a possible cause). However, cross-sectional evidence about that relationship leaves uncertain the direction of causality: variable A might influence variable B, B might influence A, both may influence each other, or both may be influenced by one or more other variables. Nevertheless, cross-sectional studies are essential in order to identify patterns of association. We need to know whether or not certain between-variable associations exist, before seeking to explain the pattern in causal terms. Research often proceeds by first establishing patterns of intercorrelation at one point in time and then moving on to explore mechanisms of causation across time.

In some cases, causal information is gained from experimental studies in an organization. By manipulating one variable (for example, job content), it is possible to learn about its causal impact on another (for instance, job-related well-being); does well-being change as a result of changing the job? Causal evidence may also be obtained from longitudinal investigations that do not involve any experimental manipulation. In that research design, both the outcomes (well-being, behaviour or attitudes) and possible causal variables are measured at two or more points in time; are subsequent changes in the outcomes linked to earlier differences in the possible causal variables?

Most research into possible causes or consequences has dealt with a single type of outcome variable alone, either well-being, behaviour or attitudes. Many illustrative studies are described in the pages that follow.

Increasingly, however, attention is also being directed to outcomes in combination. For example, how do certain job features, management behaviours or organizational characteristics affect both well-being and behaviour? Single-outcome investigations can be scientifically exciting and organizationally valuable, but the simultaneous examination of multiple outcomes has particular promise in the field of this book.

SUMMARY

Psychology in work settings may be described in broad terms as the study of employees' well-being, behaviour and attitudes. It is important to distinguish between 'job-related' and 'context-free' well-being, and three principal axes of measurement may be identified in each case. Employee well-being is influenced by the characteristics of a job and an organization, and also by dispositional personal characteristics.

Work behaviours of interest include job performance, discretionary activities, specific skills, absence from work and staff turnover. Several of those are significantly associated with employee well-being, but the pattern of causality is complex. A third set of outcome variables is attitudinal, concerned with employees' evaluative tendencies towards occupational features. Attitudes underlie motives and values. Psychologists' research has typically examined each type of outcome variable on its own, but combinations of outcomes are increasingly being explored.

FURTHER READING

Many publications about the three outcomes examined here are illustrated in the chapters that follow. General treatments of aspects of well-being have been presented by Judge and Church (2000) and Danna and Griffin (1999). Work behaviours have been discussed by Borman (1991) and Roe (1999), and the nature of attitudes has been examined by Eagly and Chaiken (1993).

REFERENCES

Agho, A. O., Mueller, C. W. and Price, J. L. (1993). Determinants of employee job satisfaction: An empirical test of a causal model. *Human Relations*, 46, 1007–27.

Ajzen, I. (1991). The theory of planned behavior. *Organizational Behavior and Human Decision Processes*, 50, 179–211.

Anderson, J. R. (1995). *Learning and Memory: An Integrated Approach*, second edition. New York: Wiley.

Arvey, R. D., Bouchard, T. J., Segal, N. L. and Abraham, L. M. (1989). Job satisfaction: Environmental and genetic components. *Journal of Applied Psychology*, 74, 187–92.

Arvey, R. D., McCall, B. P., Bouchard, T. J., Taubman, P. and Cavanaugh, M. A. (1994). Genetic influences on job satisfaction and work values. *Personality and Individual Differences*, 17, 21–33.

Bamundo, P. J. and Kopelman, R. E. (1980). The moderating effects of occupation, age, and urbanization on the relationship between job satisfaction and life satisfaction. *Journal of Vocational Behavior*, 17, 106–23.

Birdi, K. S., Gardner, C. R. and Warr, P. B. (1998). Correlates and perceived outcomes of four types of employee development activity. *Journal of Applied Psychology*, 82, 845–57.

Birdi, K. S., Warr, P. B. and Oswald, A. (1995). Age differences in three components of employee well-being. *Applied Psychology*, 44, 345–73.

Borman, W. C. (1991). Job behavior, performance, and effectiveness. In M. D. Dunnette and L. M. Hough (eds.), *Handbook of Industrial and Organizational Psychology*, second edition, volume 2, pp. 271–326. Palo Alto CA: Consulting Psychologists Press.

Burger, J. M. (1989). Negative reactions to increases in perceived personal control. *Journal of Personality and Social Psychology*, 56, 246–56.

Danna, K. and Griffin, R. W. (1999). Health and well-being in the workplace: A review and synthesis of the literature. *Journal of Management*, 25, 357–84.

Daniels, K. (2000). Measures of five aspects of affective well-being at work. *Human Relations*, 53, 275–94.

de Jonge, J. and Schaufeli, W. B. (1998). Job characteristics and employee well-being: A test of Warr's Vitamin Model in health-care workers using structural equation modelling. *Journal of Organizational Behavior*, 19, 387–407.

de Jonge, J., Reuvers, M. M. E. N., Houtman, I. L. D., Bongers, P. M. and Kompier, M. A. J. (2000). Linear and non-linear relations between psychosocial job characteristics, subjective outcomes, and sickness absence. *Journal of Occupational Health Psychology*, 5, 256–68.

DeNeve, K. M. and Cooper, H. (1998). The happy personality: A meta-analysis of 137 personality traits and subjective well-being. *Psychological Bulletin*, *124*, 197–229.

Eagly, A. H. and Chaiken, S. (1993). *The Psychology of Attitudes*. Orlando, FL: Harcourt Brace Jovanovich.

Elliott, T. R., Chartrand, J. M. and Harkins, S. W. (1994). Negative affectivity, emotional distress, and the cognitive appraisal of occupational stress. *Journal of Vocational Behavior*, *45*, 185–201.

Farrell, D. and Stamm, C. L. (1988). Meta-analysis of the correlates of employee absence. *Human Relations*, *41*, 211–27.

Gechman, A. S. and Wiener, Y. (1975). Job involvement and satisfaction as related to mental health and personal time devoted to work. *Journal of Applied Psychology*, *60*, 521–3.

George, J. M. (1989). Mood and absence. *Journal of Applied Psychology*, *74*, 317–24.

Griffeth, R. W., Hom, P. W. and Gaertner, S. (2000). A meta-analysis of antecedents and correlates of employee turnover: Update, moderator tests, and research implications for the next millennium. *Journal of Management*, *26*, 463–88.

Hackett, R. D. (1989). Work attitudes and employee absenteeism: A synthesis of the literature. *Journal of Occupational Psychology*, *62*, 235–48.

Hardy, G. E., Woods, D. and Wall, T. D. (2001). The impact of psychological distress on absence from work. Submitted for publication.

Hom, P. W., Caranikas-Walker, F., Prussia, G. E. and Griffeth, R. W. (1992). A meta-analytical structural equations analysis of a model of employee turnover. *Journal of Applied Psychology*, *77*, 890–909.

Iaffaldano, M. T. and Muchinsky, P. M. (1985). Job satisfaction and job performance: A meta-analysis. *Psychological Bulletin*, *97*, 251–73.

Jamal, M. (1984). Job stress and job performance controversy: An empirical assessment. *Organizational Behavior and Human Performance*, *33*, 1–21.

Judge, T. A., Bono, J. E. and Locke, E. A. (2000). Personality and job satisfaction: The mediating role of job characteristics. *Journal of Applied Psychology*, *85*, 237–49.

Judge, T. A. and Church, A. H. (2000). Job satisfaction: Research and practice. In C. L. Cooper and E. A. Locke (eds.), *Industrial and Organizational Psychology: Linking Theory and Practice*, pp. 166–98. Oxford: Blackwell.

Judge, T. A., Thoresen, C. J., Bono, J. E. and Patton, G. K. (2001). The job satisfaction–job performance relationship: A qualitative and quantitative review. *Psychological Bulletin*, *127*, 376–407.

Judge, T. A. and Watanabe, S. (1993). Another look at the job satisfaction–life satisfaction relationship. *Journal of Applied Psychology*, *78*, 939–48.

Karasek, R. A. (1979). Job demands, job decision latitude, and mental strain: Implications for job design. *Administrative Science Quarterly*, *24*, 285–308.

Karasek, R. A. and Theorell, T. (1990). *Healthy Work*. New York: Basic Books.

Keller, R. T. (1997). Job involvement and organizational commitment as longitudinal predictors of job performance: A study of scientists and engineers. *Journal of Applied Psychology*, 82, 539–45.

Lee, R. T. and Ashforth, B. E. (1996). A meta-analytic examination of the correlates of the three dimensions of job burnout. *Journal of Applied Psychology*, 81, 123–33.

Levin, I. and Stokes, J. P. (1989). Dispositional approach to job satisfaction: Role of negative affectivity. *Journal of Applied Psychology*, 74, 752–8.

Lucas, R. E., Diener, E. and Suh, E. (1996). Discriminant validity of well-being measures. *Journal of Personality and Social Psychology*, 71, 616–28.

Martin, R. and Wall, T. D. (1989). Attentional demand and cost responsibility as stressors in shopfloor jobs. *Academy of Management Journal*, 32, 69–86.

Maslach, C. (1999). A multi-dimensional theory of burnout. In C. L. Cooper (ed.), *Theories of Organizational Stress*, pp. 68–85. Oxford: Oxford University Press.

Meyer, J. P. and Allen, N. J. (1997). *Commitment in the Workplace*. Thousand Oaks, CA: Sage.

Motowidlo, S. J., Packard, J. S. and Manning, J. S. (1986). Occupational stress: Its causes and consequences for job performance. *Journal of Applied Psychology*, 71, 618–29.

Organ, D. W. and Ryan, K. (1995). A meta-analytic review of attitudinal and dispositional predictors of organizational citizenship behavior. *Personnel Psychology*, 48, 775–802.

Ostroff, C. (1992). The relationship between satisfaction, attitudes, and performance: An organizational level analysis. *Journal of Applied Psychology*, 77, 963–74.

Parker, S. K. and Sprigg, C. (1999). Minimizing strain and maximizing learning: The role of job demands, job control, and proactive personality. *Journal of Applied Psychology*, 84, 925–39.

Patterson, M. G. and West, M. A. (2001). Employee attitudes and mental health as predictors of organizational productivity and profitability. Submitted for publication.

Petty, M. M., McGee, G. W. and Cavender, J. W. (1984). A meta-analysis of the relationship between individual job satisfaction and individual performance. *Academy of Management Review*, 9, 712–21.

Podsakoff, P. M., MacKenzie, S. B., Paine, J. B. and Bachrach, D. G. (2000). Organizational citizenship behaviors: A critical review of the theoretical and empirical literature and suggestions for future research. *Journal of Management*, 26, 513–63.

Remington, N. A., Fabrigar, L. R. and Visser, P. S. (2000). Re-examining the circumplex model of affect. *Journal of Personality and Social Psychology*, 79, 286–300.

Roe, R. A. (1999). Work performance: A multiple regulation perspective. In C. L.

Cooper and I. T. Robertson (eds.), *International Review of Industrial and Organizational Psychology*, pp. 231–335. London: Wiley.

Roxburgh, S. (1996). Gender differences in work and well-being: Effects of exposure and vulnerability. *Journal of Health and Social Behavior*, 37, 265–77.

Spector, P. E. and O'Connell, B. J. (1994). The contribution of personality traits, negative affectivity, locus of control and Type A to the subsequent reports of job stressors and job strains. *Journal of Occupational and Organizational Psychology*, 67, 1–11.

Spector, P. E., Dwyer, D. J. and Jex, S. M. (1988). Relation of job stressors to affective, health, and performance outcomes: A comparison of multiple data sources. *Journal of Applied Psychology*, 73, 11–19.

Steel, R. P. and Rentsch, J. R. (1997). The dispositional model of job attitudes revisited: Findings of a 10-year study. *Journal of Applied Psychology*, 82, 873–9.

Tait, M., Padgett, M. Y. and Baldwin, T. T. (1989). Job and life satisfaction: A re-evaluation of the strength of the relationship and gender effects as a function of the date of the study. *Journal of Applied Psychology*, 74, 502–7.

Taris, R. and Feij, J. A. (2001). Longitudinal examination of the relationship between supplies-values fit and work outcomes. *Applied Psychology*, 50, 52–80.

Thompson, C. A., Kopelman, R. E. and Schriesheim, C. A. (1992). Putting all one's eggs in the same basket: A comparison of commitment and satisfaction among self- and organizationally employed men. *Journal of Applied Psychology*, 77, 738–43.

Viswesvaran, C., Ones, D. S. and Schmidt, F. L. (1996). Comparative analysis of the reliability of job performance ratings. *Journal of Applied Psychology*, 81, 557–74.

Warr, P. B. (1987). *Work, Unemployment, and Mental Health*. Oxford: Oxford University Press.

Warr, P. B. (1990a). Decision latitude, job demands, and employee well-being. *Work and Stress*, 4, 285–94.

Warr, P. B. (1990b). The measurement of well-being and other aspects of mental health. *Journal of Occupational Psychology*, 63, 193–210.

Warr, P. B. (1992). Age and occupational well-being. *Psychology and Aging*, 7, 37–45.

Warr, P. B. (1994). A conceptual framework for the study of work and mental health. *Work and Stress*, 8, 84–97.

Warr, P. B. (1997). Age, work, and mental health. In K. W. Schaie and C. Schooler (eds.), *The Impact of Work on Older Individuals*, pp. 252–96. New York: Springer.

Warr, P. B. (1999). Well-being and the workplace. In D. Kahneman, E. Diener and N. Schwarz (eds.), *Well-being: The Foundations of Hedonic Psychology*, pp. 392–412. New York: Russell Sage Foundation.

Warr, P. B. and Bourne, A. (1999). Factors influencing two types of congruence in multirater judgments. *Human Performance*, 12, 183–210.

Watson, D. and Clark, L. A. (1984). Negative affectivity: The disposition to experience aversive emotional states. *Psychological Bulletin*, 96, 465–90.

Watson, D., Clark, L. A. and Tellegen, A. (1988). Development and validation of brief measures of positive and negative effect: The PANAS scales. *Journal of Personality and Social Psychology*, 54, 1063–70.

Watson, D. and Slack, A. K. (1993). General factors of affective temperament and their relation to job satisfaction over time. *Organizational Behavior and Human Decision Processes*, 54, 181–202.

Xie, J. L. and Johns, G. (1995). Job scope and stress: Can job scope be too high? *Academy of Management Journal*, 38, 1288–1309.

2

Human Performance in the Working Environment

Robert Hockey

This chapter reviews evidence concerning the maintenance of human performance under threats from the working environment. In many ways, the experience of work may be seen as a conflict between desired and undesired goals. Being effective means maintaining commitment to relatively onerous work goals in the face of competition from personal goals such as wanting to be relaxing at home, or seeing friends. An appreciation of this conflict appears to be central to the understanding of effects of workload and stress on performance. Recent interpretations of the performance literature suggest that individuals have to strive to maintain orientation towards primary task goals, and may suffer side-effects in terms of strain and impairments to other aspects of their job (Hockey, 1997; Wickens and Hollands, 1999). As a background to work performance, the chapter first considers the essential characteristics of skill and expertise, and the typical patterns of breakdown manifested as human error. It next reviews the maintenance of performance under heavy workload and environmental stress. These are major limiting features of the design of workplaces, though their effects on performance are not straightforward. Finally, it examines some of the ways in which work design may accommodate to the occurrence of error in skilled performance, by provision of appropriate support within the task structure.

FUNDAMENTALS OF PERFORMANCE

While there is considerable variation in the demands of work tasks, many of the broad conclusions presented in this chapter apply equally to skill in everyday activities and those relating to complex human–machine systems (e.g., air traffic control or chemical plants). Work tasks are made up of sequences of *actions*, carried out to achieve certain *goals*. Well-learned skills enable us to operate in a generally efficient manner with respect to work goals. However, environmental demands may sometimes cause problems for skilled performance, resulting in impaired quantity or quality of output, missed signals, mistakes in decision making, and so on. In some conditions, these failures will lead to accidents.

Figure 2.1 shows a generalized version of the many detailed attempts to model the structure of the mental processes that underlie human

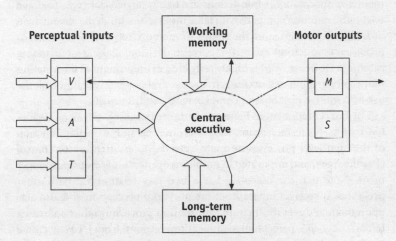

Fig. 2.1 Fundamental components of the human information processing system, showing visual (V), auditory (A) and tactile (T) perceptual processes, and manual (M) and speech (S) motor processes. Information inputs are shown by broad arrows and executive control processes by narrow arrows. In this case the central executive is set to attend to visual inputs and respond with manual outputs.

task-oriented behaviour. For the purposes of this chapter the linkages between sub-systems have been simplified: see, e.g., Matthews, Davies, Westerman and Stammers (2000), and Wickens and Hollands (1999) for more detailed models. Figure 2.1 illustrates the different information processing mechanisms underlying skilled action. Environmental inputs are processed through sensory and perceptual mechanisms, allowing them to be detected and recognized, and, if appropriate, acted upon through the execution of motor sequences involving movement and speech (outputs). Without storage and retrieval (memory) processes, however, these actions would be influenced *only* by changing inputs. The availability of long-term memory (LTM) and working memory (WM) means that we can make use of previous experience to moderate the effect of new events on actions.

Long-term memory represents the permanent store of information (knowledge) that we carry around with us, while WM may be conceived of as a kind of mental workspace (e.g., Baddeley, 1986). It can be used to maintain information while actions are being carried out (e.g., to dial a telephone number, compare with later inputs, or with items already held in LTM). It can also store the results of memory retrieval operations, or provide computation space for current decision making or planning activities. However, WM is highly restricted in the amount of information that can be maintained in this active state, and poses severe limits on the use of cognitive processes in complex work environments.

The final component in Figure 2.1 is the central executive (e.g., Baddeley, 1986). This term captures the co-ordinating and managing function of the high-level processes normally referred to as attention or control (Pashler, 1998) and implicated in problems of effort and resource management. Note that the executive has a two-way relationship with other processes. It receives inputs from memory and perception and also acts upon them to direct the focus of information processing effort according to current goals – perceptual identification, retrieval from LTM, accurate responding, and so on – and, where possible, to maintain these over the duration of the task.

Earlier research on skill focused on perceptual-motor tasks, such as those involved in visual monitoring and manual control (central and output processes in Figure 2.1), the dominant mode of industrial work during the post-war period. As modern work has increasingly placed demands on cognitive activities, the emphasis in research has switched to tasks involving attention, memory, planning, decision-making and problem-solving. Of course, differences between manual and cognitive work are a matter of degree rather than kind. Some overt actions are always necessary, even in highly cognitive work, and some internal information processing precedes actions in most manual activity – and central control is common in both.

Human Error and Expertise

When a major accident occurs (for example, the recent cases of capsized car ferries, train derailments or plane crashes), human error is commonly assumed to be at the root of the problem. It has been estimated that human error is the major contributory factor in between 50 and 80 per cent of all accidents (Spettell and Liebert, 1986). The analysis of error patterns has attracted much interest, both in accidents and in everyday life (e.g., Reason, 1990), and been shown to reveal important aspects of the cognitive basis of skilled actions.

A fundamental distinction (Reason, 1990) is that errors may occur because of failures of either intention (*mistakes*) or execution (*slips* and *lapses*). Mistakes may occur in situation appraisal, planning or goal selection, and refer to problems with executive control or knowledge. A car driver may incorrectly judge that he or she has enough space to overtake before a bend, or an officer on a ship's bridge may fail to give way (as required) when a vessel on the starboard bow is detected by the radar as being on a collision course. In Rasmussen's (1986) 'skill-rule-knowledge' framework mistakes are further separated into *knowledge-based* and *rule-based* types. Knowledge-based errors are assumed to occur because of a failure of the individual to understand the significance of situations and their requirements for effective action (e.g., novice motorway drivers fail to appreciate the effect of high speeds on the time available for taking corrective action). Errors are classified as rule-based when they derive from an inappropriate application of old solutions to new situations (e.g., misapplication of UK rules about roundabout use when driving in some other countries).

Slips and lapses are referred to in Rasmussen's model as *skill-based* errors. In terms of the processes referred to in Figure 2.1, slips may be considered as failures of output control and lapses as failures of perception or memory. In both cases, the intention is correct, but the action executed badly. Most errors in laboratory experiments are of the slip variety, particularly where speed is emphasized by the task. (Indeed, they are often immediately detected as errors, and corrected where possible.) Pressing the wrong number or letter on a telephone or computer keyboard are everyday examples of slips, where the consequences are usually trivial: pressing the accelerator instead of the (intended) brake in a driving emergency may be a more costly slip. Lapses occur when an operator misses an environmental event or forgets to do something. He or she may fail to notice a critical change in an indicator, or lose track of location in a sequence of actions.

In general, we expect that all kinds of errors are eliminated by extended practice or experience ('practice makes perfect'). It has been claimed that becoming an expert in any field requires at least ten years' experience, and the acquisition of many thousands of knowledge segments or 'production rules' (Anderson, 1999). These are sets of simple condition → action (IF ... THEN ...) rules serving a goal. For example, the first of a set of production rules for the goal of adding several numbers using standard column arithmetic might be: [IF (sum of digits in right hand column) > 9 THEN write number of units in right hand column and carry number of tens to next column]. Clearly, even moderate mathematical skills make use of hundreds or thousands of such bits of knowledge, combined in different ways to achieve specific goals. However, skill learning is not simply about what is known. By the end of a period of training, errors have normally been reduced to an acceptable minimum; though continued practice over an extended period will show further improvement in terms of timing, precision and economy of effort. While we take it for granted that experts 'know more' than novices, research on expertise has shown that there are qualitative as well as quantitative differences between the two groups.

Much of what we know about expertise comes from the study of skill in chess (see Charness and Schultetus, 1999). For example, expert players (masters) are known to access stored knowledge about previous games more effectively than club players, have a more abstract representation of problem situations, make more efficient use of working memory and are better at evaluating alternative search options. These advantages allow them to make better decisions: they respond more efficiently to new problems, and explore promising rather than unproductive solutions. In addition, research in other areas of expertise (e.g., computer programming, mathematical problem solving, medical diagnosis, decision-making) suggests that experts are also more efficient than novices in monitoring the environment for task-relevant information, and that they make more use of active hypothesis-generation in deciding upon appropriate actions (Charness and Schultetus, 1999). However, all this applies only when experts try to solve meaningful problems within the domain. Chess masters, for example, have no advantage when it comes to recalling random board positions.

From this, it may seem that experts are very unlikely to make errors, though that is, of course, not the case. Ironically, since responsibility tends to go with expertise, major accidents tend to involve human error at the highest level: the captain of an oil tanker; the pilot of an aircraft; the process engineer in a chemical plant. As Reason (1990) suggests, because of their extensive and flexible domain-specific knowledge, many of these errors are likely to be rule-based or skill-based (slips and lapses), rather than knowledge-based. However, the complexity of accident scenarios is such that experts may be working at the limits of even their highly developed competence. Mistakes may therefore arise from incomplete understanding or limited experience with the prevailing unfamiliar conditions.

Roth and Woods (1988) showed that more experienced operators in nuclear power plants preferred an 'open loop' mode of control (making infrequent use of feedback, and then only to carry out minor adjustments). This is in contrast to the 'closed-loop' behaviour of novices (where their behaviour is guided constantly by attention to feedback from their actions). While allowing more effective moment to moment management of the system, an open-loop strategy is more prone to error because of its high demands on working memory and planning. Such knowledge-based problem solving is the hallmark of expert skill, but it is also a vulnerable activity because it involves working at the limits. Controlling a production plant or captaining an oil tanker are tasks subject to perturbations from many external events. Open skills such as these may require emergency reactions to situations which not only have never occurred before, but which could not have been predicted.

THREATS TO PERFORMANCE IN THE WORK ENVIRONMENT

Threats to performance are found in many aspects of the work environment. It is not surprising, therefore, that prevention of skill breakdown is a major goal of the design of work and human–machine systems. In addition to inadequacies in knowledge and expertise, threats may result from excessive levels of *workload* or *environmental stress*. Rather surprisingly, serious effects of both workload and stress on task performance have been difficult to demonstrate (e.g., Hockey, 1997). However, this does not mean that the breakdown of performance under high demand and stress does not occur at all, or that job design should not be concerned with such problems. Rather, theoretical and methodological shortcomings have disguised the nature and extent of performance decrements.

Compensatory Control and Performance Regulation

As I suggested earlier, there is always a potential conflict in carrying out tasks. The individual has a choice of striving to maintain the goal of attending to task requirements, or reducing commitment to the task in order to deal with the stressor. The strategy of responding to external threat by increasing effort and concentrating even more on task goals is known as *performance protection*, and is the usual response in situations where the task is considered important. Within this framework of *compensatory control*, effects of threats to performance are considered as trade-offs between maintaining performance and neglecting other aspects of behaviour. The main benefit is to prevent decrement of *primary tasks* (those considered central to effective action). However, there is a cost of decrements in secondary features of tasks (see below) and a neglect of personal needs and other goals. Despite performance protection, primary task decrements may sometimes occur, when stress or work demands are extreme or prolonged. However, under normal circumstances, major impairment is highly unlikely. This framework is used throughout the rest of this chapter in reviewing the material on workload and stress effects below. For a more detailed discussion see Hockey (1997).

Mental Workload

Human performance theory has considered workload primarily in terms of competition for a limited mental resource (Kahneman, 1973). The most common cause of performance breakdown under high workload is the requirement to carry out two (or more) tasks simultaneously. The greater the overall processing demands of the two tasks the greater is the threat of performance decrement. However, the problem of high workload is not simply that of competition for a general supply of processing resources. A more specific source of impairment is *structural interference*, where tasks compete for the same kind of sensory or motor process. There may be little problem where the two tasks are to watch a screen and listen for alarms, and make speech responses to one and manual responses to the other. However, when two activities both demand access to visuo-spatial input and manual output, performance is likely to be impaired – as in the use of mobile phones while driving, particularly where manual rather than voice dialling is used (Goodman, Tijerina, Bents and Wierwille, 1999). In some cases errors may occur even at quite low levels of overall demand, as the result of 'cross-talk' between input or output channels (see Wickens and Hollands, 1999). The response for one task becomes attached to the input for the other (slips), or errors occur in the identification and selection of relevant inputs (lapses). This is not to say that overload cannot occur with a high level of general demand, but this may be a limiting condition rather than a requirement: see Matthews *et al.* (2000) and Wickens and Hollands (1999) for a full discussion of these issues.

Methods of Assessing Workload

In everyday conversations jobs are often referred to as if they themselves had a high workload. At a conceptual level this is misleading, however. Current theory rightly emphasizes the interactive or transactional nature of mental workload (e.g., Gopher and Donchin, 1986; Wickens and Hollands, 1999). This means that it is a product of the interplay between the (objective) demands of the task and the skill and ability of the individual, as well as the environmental and motivational context in which the work is carried out. Checking a set of accounts or monitoring a radar display may be perceived as demanding or not, depending on the employee's skill, effort capacity and motivational level, his or her level of training and familiarity with the work, tolerance of ambient environmental conditions (noise, heat, etc.), and so on.

In view of the multi-faceted nature of mental workload, it is not surprising that a number of different ways of measuring it have evolved. These include methods based on primary and secondary task performance level (referred to here as 'performance-based indicators'), and on psychophysiological and subjective assessments (referred to as 'indirect indicators'). While the use of different methods does not always lead to the same conclusions, there are clearly advantages for both the researcher and the practitioner in having a range of techniques at one's disposal. Different methods may be suitable for different work environments, as well as revealing potentially different features of the workload assessment problem.

The choice of which method to use is often dictated by criteria such as *sensitivity*, *diagnosticity* and *intrusiveness* (O'Donnell and Eggemeier, 1986). Sensitivity refers to the extent to which a method will detect any change in mental workload, irrespective of its source. In contrast, diagnosticity refers to the extent to which a measure can pinpoint the source of the problem in terms of specific information processing resources (e.g., having too much information to take in from displays, as opposed to having too many actions to carry out). On a practical level, any method may be unsuitable if it interferes with the work being measured. The intrusiveness of a technique refers to the extent to which it impinges directly on work, interfering with the task or job being assessed. Other desiderata, particularly for field studies, include *ease of use* and *acceptability*. Subjective response scales are easy to use, in that they can be administered reliably without extensive training or specialized equipment, in contrast to most secondary task and psychophysiological methods. Which techniques are acceptable will depend on many factors, though operators generally have less tolerance for methods that take longer, appear to interfere with work, or involve wires attached to the head or chest.

Performance-based indicators

Mental work may conveniently be separated into primary and secondary tasks, in terms of their relationship to task goals. This may be done informally or, for very complex jobs, following a task analysis. This is a formal way of defining the human requirements of a work system, typically by breaking down complex actions into a sequence of simpler actions or sub-goals. There are many versions of task analysis, designed for specific purposes: see Kirwan and Ainsworth (1992) for a detailed discussion. Traditionally, task analysis has assessed only overt actions, but recent developments, addressing the intensive cognitive nature of modern work (cognitive task analysis, or CTA), emphasize knowledge requirements and conceptual models of processes (Vicente, 1999; Roth and Woods, 1988). For example, in relation to the earlier reference to production rules, CTA tries to assess whether the conditions specified by the 'IF . . .' part of the operation actually exist, rather than simply being assumed by operators.

Task analysis may also be carried out at a more general level, to determine high and low priorities and which information-processing resources are involved. For example, in driving, speed regulation and steering/collision avoidance may be thought of as primary, and traffic monitoring and efficient use of controls as secondary. Furthermore, driving a car with automatic gear-change will make fewer demands on control than one with manual control, but make little difference to traffic monitoring. Assessment of *primary task* performance provides a direct measure of the effect of overall demands on the main work tasks of the individual, so should always be carried out in addition to any other measures. For example, we might expect to find increased manoeuvring errors while driving in heavy traffic or with fatigue from prolonged driving (e.g., Hicks and Wierwille, 1979). However, primary task measures are rarely sufficient as measures of mental workload. As we have seen earlier, people are often able to compensate for environmental problems by increased effort, so the problem may be underestimated by considering only primary tasks.

Secondary task performance provides an indirect measure of primary task load, in terms of spare capacity or 'spill-over' from primary task demand. In driving, this could mean reduced use of mirrors, non-optimal gear-selection, or failures to monitor events in side roads. In many practical investigations a standard *subsidiary task* is added to the primary task, with instructions to respond to it only when the primary task permits. Demands of different primary tasks may then be compared by examining performance on the fixed secondary task. A variant of this approach is the secondary task *probe*, in which operators, while performing a primary task, also respond to discrete events, such as tones presented over headphones, or light signals in driving mirrors, by making rapid manual or vocal responses. Differences in spare capacity can then be inferred from reaction times (RTs) to the probes or measures of how well they are detected. A third version of the dual-task method is the *loading task* procedure. In this case, operators are required to give priority to the secondary task itself, allowing differences in primary task load to be measured directly as resources are drawn away from it. Whatever the method adopted, there are work situations where the use of a secondary task is impracticable. Asking air traffic controllers or fighter pilots to carry out a second (to them, unnecessary) task may actually result in an impairment of performance of the primary task, compromising safety and reliability. In such cases, embedded secondary tasks may be preferred. These are natural but secondary features of primary tasks, such as the time taken by a pilot to acknowledge a communication from an air traffic controller, or the use of mirrors by car drivers (Wickens and Hollands, 1999). .

Indirect indicators

Measures of *subjective workload*, in the form of self-reports from operators, are probably the most widely used of the various workload assessment techniques. In field settings they are favoured because of their ease of use and low intrusiveness, but they are also generally sensitive to even small changes in perceived demand. Although the use of simple scales measuring undifferentiated workload levels are still common, it is more usual to use methods developed to assess the multi-dimensional features of the subjective response to work demands. The most widely used of these is the NASA-TLX (Task Load Index), developed within the aviation/space context (Hart and Staveland, 1988), and including six subscales (temporal demand, mental demand, physical demand, effort, frustration and performance). NASA-TLX has proved sensitive to a broad range of between-task manipulations of demand, particularly in aviation (Wierwille and Eggemeier, 1993), though the potential diagnosticity of the use of multiple scales has been demonstrated only rarely in applications to date.

The use of *psychophysiological* measures to estimate workload (Kramer, 1991) is often motivated by a desire to minimize intrusiveness. Measures of brain activity, particularly event-related potentials (ERPs), are usually assumed to reflect information-processing demands directly, in terms of the amplitude and timing of the brain response to a secondary task probe event, such as a tone or light signal. Such methods are moderately diagnostic (e.g., indicating whether the problem is one of visual or motor demands). The use of autonomic indices, such as suppression of heart rate variability (HRV) or increased pupil dilation, is based on the well-known shift towards sympathetic dominance in autonomic nervous system activity under conditions of mental challenge and involvement (Kahneman, 1973; Kramer, 1991). Such measures are relatively sensitive to increased attentional demands. Tattersall and Hockey (1995) found that HRV was suppressed in flight engineers for periods of a three-hour simulated flight where knowledge-based problem solving was required, but not for more routine (rule-based) activities. Measurements of the level of stress hormones (e.g., adrenaline and cortisol) are also sometimes used as markers of the costs of protecting performance under high workload. Although the need to collect blood or urine samples can make them intrusive and unacceptable, such techniques may have diagnostic value, for example, in differentiating between active and passive forms of engagement with task demands (Frankenhaeuser, 1986; Hockey, Payne and Rick, 1996).

Environmental Stressors

Traditionally, environmental conditions such as noise and heat have been considered major threats to both the effectiveness of work and the motivation and health of employees. The move away from heavy industry towards the typically office-type demands of the modern working environment has meant that such factors pose less of an obvious threat, at least in Western economies, though some problems still exist, notably from noise levels. While fewer people are required to work in noisy manufacturing industries, many more are subjected to noise from street traffic and airports, not just in work situations but in schools and homes. Other factors, such as sleep disturbances and fatigue (associated with increased travel time to work, increased workload, etc.) contribute a background of compromised resources against which work has to be carried out. The use of drugs such as sleeping tablets or caffeine to counteract such states may itself lead to performance disruption. Even incentives (in the form of bonuses or performance-related pay) may be considered as stressors, because of the increased demands made on employees.

In this chapter, environmental stressors are considered principally in terms of the general threat they pose to work goals, giving rise to compensatory changes in performance and internal state. However, stressors also appear to pose specific threats for different components of information processing tasks. An earlier analysis (Hockey and Hamilton, 1983) examined a wide range of stress effects, and found evidence of a number of distinctive patterns of decrement across a representative set of performance indicators. Only a brief summary is given here; see Hockey and Hamilton (1983) and Hockey (1986) for details.

The general conclusion from Hockey and Hamilton's analysis is that performance decrements depend both on the environmental condition and the task. For example, stressors that increase anxiety (loud noise, threat and uncertainty) reduce accuracy or working memory (WM), but may actually enhance speeded or highly selective responding. Incentives appear to enhance most aspects of performance, though they may reduce the capacity of individuals to respond to unexpected changes of goal priorities. By contrast, sleep deprivation and depressant drugs (e.g., sleeping tablets) have a widespread detrimental effect on performance – both speed and accuracy, as well as selective attention and most aspects of memory. Effects of fatigue from prolonged work have a moderating role – for example making performance more susceptible to impairment from noise and sleep deprivation at the end of long work periods. Very brief periods of work (up to ten or fifteen minutes), where fatigue is not normally experienced, rarely suffer performance decrements.

The set of indicators used in Hockey and Hamilton's analysis included general alertness, selectivity of attention, speed versus accuracy, and working memory. With changes in cognitive theory over the intervening period, and experience of effects in real work tasks, a more detailed analysis is now possible. However, as I have already indicated, there is also a need for a different level of analysis, which takes into account the trade-offs that result from compensatory regulation between primary task protection and the various associated costs. It is now clear that patterns of stressor effects cannot be interpreted without reference to an understanding of what the performer is trying to do when carrying out a task, and of what conflicts exist between different goals.

Latent Degradation in Performance

We have seen that compensatory effort may protect the primary task from serious disruption under stress or high workload. Maintaining selectivity of attention under high demand or environmental distraction has obvious adaptive value, in preserving high priority goals, but it may hide reduced effectiveness elsewhere in the task. In overcoming the imposed threat on primary task components, the level of available resources may become depleted, leaving the individual vulnerable to disruption from further or more extreme demands. Using appropriate performance measures, the impact of this *latent degradation* can be revealed as changes in secondary features of performance, or in the ways in which tasks are carried out: cutting corners in information processing, taking risks and so on. These changes can compromise safety and reliability by leaving no margin of error for unexpected demands or emergencies. Table 2.1 summarizes the various patterns of latent degradation in performance that may be observed under high levels of workload or environmental demand.

Table 2.1 Patterns of latent degradation in skilled performance under stress and high workload

Type of Latent Degradation	Nature of Effect
Secondary decrement	impaired performance on secondary task activities
Strategic adjustment	changes towards the use of less demanding modes of task management
Compensatory costs	increases in sympathetic activation and task-related effort
After effects	preference for low effort strategies on tests carried out following work period

Secondary decrement

This has already been discussed in connection with mental workload, as a more sensitive (and usually more diagnostic) marker of change in primary task load. Similar changes are also found as a consequence of factors such as noise, sleep deprivation and fatigue. In general, decrements in primary task performance under such conditions are rare and typically small (Hockey, 1993; 1997), while secondary task decrements are more common. As mentioned above, this may or may not have serious consequences for task performance, depending on the closeness of the relationship between primary and secondary task elements.

Strategic adjustment

One of the best-known forms of strategy shift under stress is an increase in selectivity (narrowing of attention), so that performance on central tasks is maintained (even enhanced) and that on peripheral tasks impaired. Such effects have been found under both laboratory and field conditions, for many situations that give rise to anxiety or perceived threat – loud noise, deep sea diving, social threat, etc. (Hockey, 1986). They may be seen as a strategic reduction in overall demands by focusing resources on what is really important.

In more complex cognitive activities, withdrawal from high-effort information-processing operations appears to involve a reduced dependency on the vulnerable working memory component of skill. A well-known, but still highly relevant, example is Sperandio's (1978) study of the strategies used by air traffic controllers to manage their workload in landing planes. When the number of aircraft was too great to handle comfortably, controllers switched from optimal routing of individual planes to a fixed procedure in which all contacts were given the same general instruction (by putting them into a holding pattern and requiring them to land in turn). This has the effect of reducing the load on planning and working memory, making the task manageable. It preserves the primary work goal of ensuring safety, while incurring time and other costs for secondary goals.

The same point is made by a series of studies carried out by Schönpflug and his colleagues (e.g., Schönpflug, 1983), using a simulated office environment. When participants had to work under time pressure or with loud noise they referred more often to externally available reference information before making decisions, rather than holding it in memory as usual. Again, reducing the load on working memory helped maintain accuracy goals, though at the expense of increased time costs. Finally, in a sleep deprivation study Chmiel, Folkard and Totterdell (1995) found that a night without sleep did not affect the accuracy of decision-making on an adaptive control task, although there was a marked reduction in the rate at which the task was carried out, particularly towards the end of a one-and-a-half hour work session.

Compensatory costs

These may be thought of as the unwanted side-effects of the compensatory behaviour that helps to maintain primary performance under stress and high workload. Two general kinds of cost can be distinguished – increased sympathetic activation, and increases in subjective effort and strain. For example, as part of a series of studies of effects of noise on mental work (Lundberg and Frankenhaeuser, 1978), noise was found to impair performance in one study but not in another. However, when perform-ance was maintained under noise, levels of adrenaline and subjective effort were increased, while no such costs were observed when noise impaired performance. A field study (Rissler and Jacobson, 1987) found little evidence of a disruption of performance during a busy period of reorganization, but levels of adrenaline and cognitive effort increased: employees were having to work harder to maintain the expected standard of work. Such effects illustrate the role of compensatory regulation in the protection of performance, and the trade-off between the protection of the primary performance goal and the threat to other body systems.

After effects

Finally, degradation associated with maintaining task goals under strain may appear only after the work period is over. Although after effects are not normally measured, they provide the most convincing evidence that the performance has been affected by a central fatigue state, rather than a more localized problem (such as distraction by noise), since impairment is observed even though the stressor is no longer present. Such effects are found with both high workload and environmental stress (Hockey, 1997). Because of its long-recognized importance, work fatigue has been studied extensively since the early days of psychology. However, the search for a sensitive test of the carry-over effect of sustained mental work to the performance of new tasks has proved elusive (Broadbent, 1979). Only recently has it become clear that fatigue encourages the adoption of strategies that make less demand on effort, particularly where there is a choice of alternative ways of carrying out a task (Holding, 1983; Hockey, 1997).

Illustrative study of latent degradation

A specific example illustrates the combination of several of these methods of assessing latent degradation. This comes from a study using a computer simulation of a cabin air pressure/life support system for a spacecraft (Hockey, Wastell and Sauer, 1998). Participants recruited as 'crew members' were highly trained on the task, then required to maintain critical parameters (oxygen, carbon dioxide, pressure) within target limits over a three-hour test period under various conditions. Perhaps surprisingly, operators were able to carry out this complex task equally well whether they had slept normally or been deprived of sleep. However, as predicted by the compensatory control theory (Hockey, 1997), this 'protection' of primary task performance also attracted various costs. First, performance on a secondary task of responding to false alarms was impaired under sleep deprivation. Second, crew members used simplified control strategies to manage the primary task when sleepy. They engaged less in monitoring system variables (which help in the anticipation of developing fault states), and relied more on correcting the system by all-or-none manual interventions, triggered by alarms whenever parameters went slightly out of range. There was also a marked increase in ratings of subjective effort and fatigue. Although subjective fatigue mainly reflects sleepiness in this situation, these ratings were higher for those who protected task performance more effectively (by working harder to prevent sleep deprivation from reducing their commitment to task goals).

PERFORMANCE MAINTENANCE IN COMPLEX SYSTEM

Issues concerned with skilled performance and its breakdown under demanding operational environments present major challenges to the design of work, and of complex human–machine systems in particular. From what has been discussed here, it is clear that work tasks need to be designed to avoid overloading the operator, particularly in terms of demands made on the more vulnerable parts of the information-processing apparatus, such as limited working memory and computational power.

An important consideration is the level of personal control that individuals experience in their work (see Chapter 8). The extensive literature on the role of personal control in moderating the effects of work stress (e.g., Ganster, 1989; Karasek and Theorell, 1990) suggests that high demands are more likely to be problematic when operators have only limited opportunities for planning the flow and timing of their work. A central tenet of human-centred design in automation (Billings, 1996) is that operators should be able to influence the shifts of control between human and computer elements of the system. In the above example of latent degradation in performance (Hockey et al., 1998), all the effects of sleep deprivation were markedly reduced when operators used a human-centred interface (in which they could interact freely with the computer to gain information and solve problems) rather than a machine-centred interface (where information was displayed only at pre-determined times). The increased level of personal control experienced in this kind of system allows operators flexibility for managing task demands and reducing the threat of stressors to performance goals.

Another desirable feature of complex work systems is that they should be 'error-tolerant' (e.g., Norman, 1988; Wickens and Hollands, 2000). Good design can assist in identifying and rectifying errors if the effects of the slips or mistakes are made clearly visible (e.g., by providing feedback on the effects of actions), and by building in 'reversibility'. In personal computer systems, for example, it is now routine for critical file management actions such as 'deleting' to require confirmation, and for all screen changes to be readily 'undone'. It has even been suggested that some errors are inevitable and should not be prevented entirely or 'trained out' (Norman, 1988). This would enable operators to explore the limits of possible actions to enhance learning – trying out strategies, testing hypotheses, etc. – and develop more robust conceptual models of the system. Exploration strategies of this kind would not incur serious costs if the system were designed to be error-tolerant, though they need to be adequately supported (by error-tolerant design) if operational problems are to be avoided. Hockey and Maule (1995) found that process operators sometimes experimented with the settings of system variables such as the end points of chemical processes (temperature, pH value, etc.), which not only speeded up production, but also enhanced their knowledge of cause–effect relationships. However, these 'unscheduled manual interventions' often compromised quality and safety goals. Such behaviour is also accepted as the root cause of the Chernobyl accident (Reason, 1990).

Supporting Performance in Automated Tasks

While systems may sometimes be designed to minimize general levels of workload, many complex work tasks have continually varying demands, with peak load changing from normal to some unmanageable amount within minutes. The limitations of working memory and attention in complex tasks has been recognized most clearly in the provision of decision aids. These are usually designed to be optional, so that a user may make use of them only if he or she requires assistance (for example, when demands become unmanageable). Generally, they may be seen as providing an 'external memory' for the human operator, to supplement one's own internal memory. For example, in modern Windows-driven programmes for PCs, the provision of menu displays for the most commonly-used functions helps us to navigate our way around quite complex tasks without having to remember what we need to do next. In troubleshooting, tasks, operators may be provided with alternative hypotheses about the meaning of a set of fault symptoms, summarized information about the history of the process, or updated information about effects of recent actions on process parameters.

In the case of automated tasks, humans and computers share control of the decision process. Tasks are allocated to one or the other in the design, usually after a task analysis, and based on considerations of relative capabilities of humans and machines. In traditional systems many sub-tasks are still carried out under direct human control, though an increasing number of complex systems (for example, in chemical and power plants, jet aeroplanes and modern manufacturing) make use of the highly-developed form of automation known as *supervisory* control (Sheridan, 1997; see Wickens and Hollands, 2000). This kind of system restricts the role of the human operator largely to that of monitor and troubleshooter for the automatic controller or computer; he or she only acts when something goes wrong. Many commentators have expressed concern that this effectively designs the operator 'out of the control loop'. The lack of regular contact with the process reduces the operator's understanding of what is going on in the process ('under the bonnet', as it were) and therefore their ability to intervene appropriately when something goes wrong (Wiener, 1984; see Wickens and Hollands, 2000). This is also sometimes referred to as a loss of situational awareness (Endsley and Kiris, 1995), particularly in highly complex systems such as aviation and process control that depend on maintaining an extensive active model of what is going on – past, present and future events, spatial constraints of actions, and so on.

On the other side of the equation, one of the main goals of increased automation is to reduce the threat of performance decrement from high workload. By removing the most demanding tasks, automation makes the operator's task more manageable. In practice, however, as Bainbridge (1987) has pointed out, one of the 'ironies of automation' is that this worthy goal can backfire when major problems occur. Because of reduced situational awareness the operator may have to manage a very high workload and sustain an extreme strain state in order to restore the system to normal functioning. Of course, advances in automation play a major role in enhancing both productivity and safety, and allow humans to carry out tasks that would not otherwise be possible. However, it is increasingly clear that the design of supervisory systems should consider more seriously the problem of supporting effective human intervention during times of difficulty.

Adaptive Automation

The problem of allocation of function is central to problems of automation. In addition to reducing the contribution of the operator to the overall control of the task, supervisory systems are usually designed in such a way that the functions available to the human are fixed. However, recent evidence suggests that some flexibility is possible in this allocation. Rouse and Morris (1987) describe a system that makes inferences about the current capabilities and performance of the operator, providing relevant feedback and information, monitoring actions and so on. Only if the operator transgresses acceptable boundaries does the computer system intervene by re-asserting control. A more recent development of this idea is the advent of adaptive automation (Scerbo and Mouloua, 1999). In this kind of design, the assignment of tasks is dynamically adjusted according to the changing workload or the operator's functional state under the demand of environmental stressors. In the adaptive automation solution, control is switched from human to computer when workload is detected as exceeding a threshold level. When workload falls again, control is switched back to the operator. This is, in part, a response to the natural conflict, referred to above, between the disadvantages of automation for situational awareness and out-of-the-loop problems and its benefits in reducing the threat of work overload. Current research has demonstrated a number of advantages of such a system, for both laboratory simulations and real-life tasks (see Wickens and Hollands, 1999).

This approach promises much for a genuine human-centred approach to complex tasks. However, as Wickens and Hollands (1999) point out, a number of major questions remain unanswered. In particular, it is at present unclear how the increase in workload should be inferred – from performance criteria, subjective reports, operator state measures, or even objectively-defined task factors. As we have seen, these often give different answers, and we still know relatively little about the reliability of measures which relate operator state changes to the likelihood of performance breakdown. Such a system could, in principle, take account of information about the operator's subjective and psychophysiological state, allowing the computation of performance–cost trade-off functions for the person. Thus, although performance meets task criteria, he or she may be showing relatively high levels of effort, or signs of cardiovascular strain. At present we have only a limited knowledge of how to combine these sources of information to provide reliable predictions of performance over long-duration tasks.

A second major issue is whether the switch of control should be mandatory or advisory. On detection of a problem, the computer could be programmed to signal this information to the operator, or resume control and maintain it until the operator state has stabilized once more. Which is better? It is likely that this will depend on judgements about the costs of human error. A strong case can be made out for allowing operators to decide for themselves if they need support. However, in the case of safety critical systems such as chemical plants and public transportation, we may prefer the choice to be taken out of the operator's hands. This is an exciting area of current research that promises much for the future design of complex systems, recognizing both the limitations and possibilities of human performance.

SUMMARY

A major goal of the application of psychological knowledge and methods to work is to maximize performance effectiveness in operational environments where maintenance of task goals is threatened by excessive workload and environmental conditions. Effects of workload are assessed by techniques based on performance, subjective reports, and psychophysiological indices of the response to demand. These methods can also be used to detect effects of threats to performance from outside the task, such as those associated with changes in operator state and environmental stressors. Compensatory effort typically ensures that primary goals are maintained under stress and high workload, so that performance may be only minimally affected, though various forms of latent degradation in skill may be observed. These include secondary task decrements, strategy changes, compensatory costs and after effects. It seems likely that the impact of workload and stress can be reduced by appropriate system design, based for example on error-tolerance and adaptive control. This may reduce the threats of workload and environmental demands to performance by providing greater opportunities for effective regulatory control.

FURTHER READING

The most generally useful companion volumes to this chapter are the excellent and informative third edition of *Engineering Psychology and Human Performance* by C. D. Wickens and J. G. Hollands (1999), and the highly readable text on *Human Performance* by G. Matthews, D. R. Davies, S. J. Westerman and R. B. Stammers (2000). Other major sources are three comprehensive texts relating to different aspects of the material. These are the second edition of G. Salvendy's (ed.) *The Handbook of Human Factors and Ergonomics* (1997), F. T. Durso's (ed.) *Handbook of Applied Cognition* (1999), and G. Fink's (ed.) *Encyclopedia of Stress* (2000).

REFERENCES

Anderson, J. R. (1999). *Learning and Memory: An Integrated Approach* (second edition). New York: Wiley.

Baddeley, A. D. (1986). *Working Memory.* Oxford: Oxford University Press.

Bainbridge, L. (1987). Ironies of automation. *Automatica, 19,* 775–9.

Billings, C. (1996). *Towards a Human-Centred Approach to Automation.* Englewood Cliffs, NJ: Erlbaum.

Broadbent, D. E. (1979). Is a fatigue test now possible? *Ergonomics, 22,* 1277–90.

Charness, N. and Schultetus, R. S. (1999). Knowledge and expertise. In F. T. Durso (ed.), *Handbook of Applied Cognition,* pp. 57–82. New York: Wiley.

Chmiel, N., Folkard, S. and Totterdell, P. (1995). On adaptive control, sleep loss and fatigue. *Applied Cognitive Psychology, 9,* S39–S53.

Durso, F. T. (ed.) (1999). *Handbook of Applied Cognition.* New York: Wiley.

Endsley, M. R. and Kiris, E. O. (1995). The out-of-the-loop performance problem and level of control in automation. *Human Factors, 37,* 381–94.

Fink, G. (ed.) (2000). *Encyclopedia of Stress.* New York: Academic Press.

Frankenhaeuser, M. (1986). A psychobiological framework for research on human stress and coping. In M. H. Appley and R. Trumbell (eds.), *Dynamics of Stress: Physiological, Psychological and Social Perspectives,* pp. 101–16. New York: Plenum.

Ganster, D. C. (1989). Worker control and well-being: a review of research in the workplace. In S. L. Sauter, J. J. Hurrell and C. C. Cooper (eds.), *Job Control and Worker Health,* pp. 3–24. New York: Wiley.

Goodman, M. J., Tijerina, L., Bents, F. D. and Wierwille, W. W. (1999). Using cellular telephones in vehicles: Safe or unsafe? *Transportation Human Factors, 1,* 3–42.

Gopher, D. and Donchin, E. (1986). Workload: An explanation of the concept. In K. Boff, L. Kaufman and J. P. Thomas (eds.), *Handbook of Perception and Performance* (vol. 2), pp. 41/1–49. New York: Wiley.

Hart, S. G. and Staveland, L. E. (1988). Development of NASA-TLX (Task Load Index): Results of empirical and theoretical research. In P. A. Hancock and N. Meshtaki (eds.), *Human Mental Workload,* pp. 139–83. Amsterdam: North Holland.

Hicks, T. G. and Wierwille, W. W. (1979). Comparison of five mental workload assessment procedures in a moving-base driving simulator. *Human Factors, 21,* 129–43.

Hockey, G. R. J. (1979). Stress and the cognitive components of skilled performance. In V. Hamilton and D. M. Warburton (eds.), *Human Stress and Cognition: An Information Processing Approach,* pp. 141–77. Chichester: Wiley.

Hockey, G. R. J. (1986). Changes in operator efficiency as a function of environmental stress, fatigue and circadian rhythms. In K. Boff, L. Kaufman and J. P. Thomas (eds.), *Handbook of Perception and Performance*, vol. 2, pp. 44/1–44. New York: Wiley.

Hockey, G. R. J. (1993). Cognitive-energetical control mechanisms in the management of work demands and psychological health. In A. D. Baddeley and L. Weiskrantz (eds.), *Attention, Selection, Awareness and Control: A Tribute to Donald Broadbent*, pp. 328–45. Oxford: Oxford University Press.

Hockey, G. R. J. (1997). Compensatory control in the regulation of human performance under stress and high workload: A cognitive energetical framework. *Biological Psychology*, 45, 73–93.

Hockey, G. R. J. and Hamilton, P. (1983). The cognitive patterning of stress states. In G. R. J. Hockey (ed.), *Stress and Fatigue in Human Performance*. Chichester: Wiley.

Hockey, G. R. J. and Maule, A. J. (1995). Unscheduled manual interventions in automated process control. *Ergonomics*, 38, 2504–24.

Hockey, G. R. J., Payne, R. L. and Rick, J. T. (1996). Intra-individual patterns of hormonal and affective adaptation to work demands: An n = 2 study of junior doctors. *Biological Psychology*, 42, 393–411.

Hockey, G. R. J., Wastell, D. G. and Sauer, J. (1998). Effects of sleep deprivation and user-interface on complex performance: A multilevel analysis of compensatory control. *Human Factors*, 40, 233–53.

Holding, D. H. (1983). Fatigue. In G. R. J. Hockey (ed.), *Stress and Fatigue in Human Performance*, pp. 146–67. Chichester: Wiley.

Kahneman, D. (1973). *Attention and Effort*. Englewood Cliffs, NJ: Prentice-Hall.

Karasek, R. A. and Theorell, T. (1990). *Healthy Work*. New York: Basic Books.

Kirwan, B. and Ainsworth, L. K. (1992). *A Guide to Task Analysis*. London: Taylor and Francis.

Kramer, A. F. (1991). Physiological metrics of mental workload: A review of recent progress. In D. L. Damos (ed.), *Multiple-Task Performance*, pp. 279–328. London: Taylor and Francis.

Lundberg, U. and Frankenhaeuser, M. (1978). Psychophysiological reactions to noise as modified by personal control over noise intensity. *Biological Psychology*, 6, 55–9.

Matthews, G., Davies, D. R., Westerman, S. J. and Stammers, R. B. (2000). *Human Performance: Cognition, Stress and Individual Differences*. Hove, UK: Psychology Press.

Norman, D. A. (1988). *The Design of Everyday Things*. New York: Basic Books.

O'Donnell, R. D. and Eggemeier, F. T. (1986). Workload assessment methodology. In K. Boff, L. Kaufman and J. P. Thomas (eds.), *Handbook of Perception and Performance*, vol. 2, pp. 42/1–49. New York: Wiley.

Pashler, H. (1998). *The Psychology of Attention*. Cambridge, MA: MIT Press.

Rasmussen, J. (1986). *Human Information Processing and Human Machine Interaction*. Amsterdam: North Holland.

Reason, J. T. (1990). *Human Error*. Cambridge: Cambridge University Press.

Rissler, A. and Jacobson, L. (1987). Cognitive efficiency during high workload in final system testing of a large computer system. In H. J. Bullinger and B. Shackel (eds.), *Human Computer Interaction (Interact '87)*. Amsterdam: Elsevier-North Holland.

Roth, E. M. and Woods, D. D. (1988). Aiding human performance, I: Cognitive analysis. *Le Travail Humain*, 51, 39–64.

Rouse, W. B. and Morris, N. M. (1987). Conceptual design of a human error-tolerant interface for complex engineering systems. *Automatica*, 23, 231–5.

Salvendy, G. (ed.) (1997). *The Handbook of Human Factors and Ergonomics* (second edition). New York: Wiley.

Scerbo, M. and Mouloua, M. (1999). *Automation Technology and Human Performance*. Mahwah, NJ: Erlbaum.

Schönpflug, W. (1983). Coping efficiency and situational demands. In G. R. J. Hockey (ed.), *Stress and Fatigue in Human Performance*, pp. 299–330. Chichester: Wiley.

Sheridan, T. B. (1997). Supervisory control. In G. Salvendy (ed.), *Handbook of Human Factors and Ergonomics* (second edition), pp. 1295–1327. New York: Wiley.

Sperandio, A. (1978). The regulation of working methods as a function of workload among air traffic controllers. *Ergonomics*, 21, 367–90.

Spettell, C. M. and Liebert, R. M. (1986). Training for safety in automated person–machine systems. *American Psychologist*, 41, 545–50.

Tattersall, A. J. and Hockey, G. R. J. (1995). Level of operator control and changes in heart rate variability during simulated flight maintenance. *Human Factors*, 37, 682–98.

Vicente, K. (1999). *Cognitive Work Analysis*. Mahwah, NJ: Erlbaum.

Wickens, C. D. and Hollands, J. G. (1999). *Engineering Psychology and Human Performance* (third edition). Upper Saddle River, NJ: Prentice-Hall.

Wiener, L. (1984). Beyond the sterile cockpit. *Human Factors*, 27, 75–90.

Wierwille, W. W. and Eggemeier, F. T. (1993). Recommendations for mental workload measurement in a test and evaluation environment. *Human Factors*, 35, 263–81.

3

Shiftwork: Body Rhythm and Social Factors

Simon Folkard and Joanne Hill

Humankind has evolved as a diurnal species, one that is habitually active during daylight hours and sleeps at night. Since the Industrial Revolution, however, an increasing proportion of our workforce has attempted to overcome this natural bias, and to work at night. This colonization of the night can result in a number of problems both for the individuals concerned and for the organizations employing them. This chapter summarizes these problems and the manner in which researchers from many disciplines, including psychologists, have attempted to solve them. Following an introduction to the concept of an underlying 'body clock', the characteristics of this clock are then considered in some detail to provide a framework within which the major problems associated with shiftwork are discussed.

THE BODY CLOCK

Evolution in a Rhythmic World

Life on earth has evolved in an environment subject to regular and pronounced changes produced by planetary movements. The rotation of the earth on its own axis results in the twenty-four hour light/dark cycle, while its rotation around the sun gives rise to seasonal changes in light and temperature. The combined influence of the moon and sun leads to variations in gravitational pull on the earth's surface that are reflected in complex but predictable tidal movements of the sea approximately ($\sim$)

every 12.4 and 24.8 hours. These resultant tides themselves vary in magnitude every ~14.7 and ~29.5 days according to the phase of the moon.

During the process of evolution, these periodic changes have become internalized and it is now widely accepted that living organisms possess a 'body clock', such that environmental changes are not merely responded to by organisms, but may be actually anticipated by them. Such an anticipatory ability clearly has an adaptive value for most species, and has presumably been strengthened through natural selection.

Circadian Rhythms and the Internal Body Clock

The anticipation of environmental events is mediated by regular cyclic changes in body processes. In humans, the most pronounced of these are the ~24 hour 'circadian' ('around a day') rhythms that occur in almost all physiological measures. The most important characteristics of these rhythms are (a) their *period*, which is the time taken for one complete cycle of the rhythm (normally twenty-four hours), (b) their *phase*, which is a measure of their timing with respect to some external criterion such as clock time, and (c) their *amplitude*, which is usually measured as the difference between the maximum value and the average value over a complete cycle.

The best evidence that human circadian rhythms are at least partially controlled by an internal, or 'endogenous', body clock comes from studies in which people have been isolated from their normal environmental time cues, or 'zeitgebers' (from the German for 'time givers'). In their pioneering studies, Aschoff and Wever (1962) removed individuals from all environmental time cues in a temporal isolation unit for up to nineteen days, while Siffre (1964) lived in an underground cave for two months. In both studies, people continued to wake up and go to sleep on a regular basis, but instead of doing so every twenty-four hours, they did so every ~25 hours. The circadian rhythms in other physiological measures, including body temperature and urinary electrolytes, typically showed an identical period to that of their sleep/wake cycle.

However, about a third of the people who have subsequently been studied in this way have shown a rather different pattern of results that has important theoretical and practical implications. In these cases, the sleep/wake cycle and body temperature rhythms have become 'spontaneously internally desynchronized', meaning that the temperature rhythm continues to run with an average period of ~25 hours, while the sleep/wake cycle shows either a much shorter or a much longer period than either ~25 hours or 24 hours (Wever, 1979). Interestingly, this phenomenon has been shown to occur more frequently in older people, and in those with higher neuroticism scores. As discussed later in the chapter, these individual differences may relate to the dimension of 'morningness' and have important implications for the adjustment to shiftwork.

Endogenous and Exogenous Components

At a more theoretical level, the fact that the temperature rhythm and sleep/wake cycle can run with distinctly different periods from one another has been taken to suggest that the human 'circadian system' comprises two, or perhaps more, underlying processes. The first of these is a relatively strong endogenous (internal) body clock that is dominant in controlling the circadian rhythm in body temperature (and in other measures such as urinary potassium, and plasma cortisol) and is relatively unaffected by external factors. The second is a weaker process that is more exogenous in nature, i.e., it is more prone to external influences, and is dominant in controlling the sleep/wake cycle (and other circadian rhythms such as those in plasma growth hormone and urinary calcium). There is some debate as to whether this second process is truly clock-like in nature, but there seems to be general agreement that some circadian rhythms are dominantly controlled by the endogenous body clock, while others are more influenced by external factors.

The important points to bear in mind are (1) that circadian rhythms in different measures are not all controlled by a single system, so that different rhythms may adjust at very different rates from one another when people work at unusual times of day, and (2) that sleep is likely to be disrupted unless the temperature rhythm has adjusted to such a change. Some rhythms, such as those in urinary noradrenaline and pulse rate, appear to be almost entirely due to variations in activity level, i.e., they are exogenous in origin, while others, such as those in body temperature, urinary adrenaline and potassium, and subjectively rated alertness are at least partially controlled by the endogenous body clock.

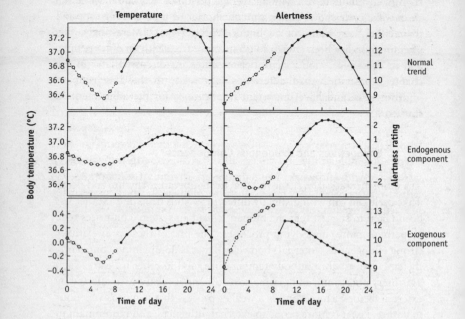

Fig. 3.1 *The normal trends in temperature and alertness over the twenty-four-hour day (top panels) broken down into their endogenous (middle panels) and exogenous (lower panels) components. The dotted lines (open points) indicate readings taken or estimated during sleep. The discontinuity in the normal trend in alertness, and in its exogenous component, on awakening reflects a 'sleep inertia' effect. (Derived from Folkard, 1988, and Folkard and Akerstedt, 1992.)*

In these latter cases the size and shape of the endogenous and exogenous components can be estimated from various types of temporal isolation studies. This is illustrated in Figure 3.1 for the circadian rhythms in temperature (after Folkard, 1988) and alertness (after Folkard and Akerstedt, 1992).

Two important points emerge from inspection of Figure 3.1. First, the normal or 'overt' rhythms in both these variables reflect both endogenous and exogenous components that are of similar magnitude to one another. Secondly, however, for temperature these two components are approximately 'in phase' with one another, such that the exogenous component (bottom panel) enhances the amplitude of the endogenous component (middle panel) in 'producing' the normal rhythm (top panel). In contrast, the two components of the normal rhythm in alertness show somewhat different phases, such that the normal rhythm in alertness is of approximately the same amplitude as its endogenous component.

This difference in the phase relationship between the endogenous and exogenous components of these overt rhythms will result in them responding rather differently to the abrupt changes in the timing of sleep associated with shiftwork. The temperature rhythm of shiftworkers will tend to flatten when they move on to the night shift, since the normally phased endogenous and the shifted exogenous components will tend to cancel each other out. However the alertness rhythm, which can normally only be measured when people are awake, is less prone to this cancelling out effect because the two underlying components differ in their normal phase. It would appear that this is why these two rhythms have been shown to behave rather differently in abnormal day length studies (Folkard and Monk, 1985a) and why temperature cannot be used as a 'marker' for alertness (Owens, Macdonald, Tucker, Sytnik, Totterdell, Minors, Waterhouse and Folkard, 2000).

Even without this complication it is clear that some rhythms will be virtually entirely dependent on the timing of sleep and wakefulness, and the concomitant timing of activity and meals. Others will be relatively uninfluenced by these factors and will depend more on the strong endogenous oscillator that, as we have seen, is likely to adjust rather slowly, if at all, to the shifts of the sleep/wake cycle associated with night work.

Adjustment to Shiftwork

Under normal circumstances both the endogenous body clock and the weaker exogenous process will be entrained to a twenty-four hour period by strong natural zeitgebers, including the light/dark cycle. As a result, all our circadian rhythms normally show a fixed phase relationship to one another. For example, our urinary adrenaline level reaches a maximum around midday, while our body temperature peaks at about 8.00 p.m. Similarly, all other circadian rhythms will reach their maxima at their appointed time, allowing us to fall asleep at night and waking us up in the morning. The occasional late night may affect those rhythms controlled by the weaker process, but is less likely to upset the strong oscillator and hence our body temperature rhythm and the time at which we spontaneously wake up.

However, this inherent stability in the human circadian system can pose problems if a mismatch arises between our internal timing system and our external time cues. The simplest example of this occurs when people fly across time zones since all the zeitgebers change. A flight from Europe to the USA involves crossing several time zones, so that on arrival our timing system is five to nine hours too early for the local zeitgebers. Although people seldom experience problems falling asleep after their arrival, their body temperature rhythms usually take over a week to delay their timing by the appropriate amount (Wegmann and Klein, 1985). For the first few nights, this often results in people waking up in the early hours of the morning and being unable to get back to sleep. The rhythms in other processes adjust at different rates, depending on the degree to which they are controlled by the endogenous clock or the weaker exogenous process. As a result, the normal phase relationship between rhythms breaks down and is only slowly re-established as the various rhythms adjust to the new time zone. This internal dissociation between rhythms is thought to be responsible for the disorientation and general malaise typical of 'jet-lag'.

These feelings of jet-lag are normally worse following an eastward flight that requires an advancing of the body's timing system, than following a westward one requiring a delay. This 'directional asymmetry' effect is thought to be related to the fact that the endogenous period of our circadian system is somewhat greater than twenty-four hours. Thus, in the absence of any zeitgebers our rhythms will tend to delay rather than to advance, assisting adjustment to westward flights but inhibiting it to eastward ones.

This difference has implications for the design of shift systems. When shiftworkers go on to the night shift, most environmental zeitgebers remain constant and discourage adjustment of the circadian system. The natural light/dark cycle, the clock time, and most social cues do not change, while the timing of shiftworkers' work can be delayed by up to sixteen hours and that of their sleep by up to twelve hours. From what we have learnt so far, it is clear that the adjustment of a shiftworker's body clock to these changes is likely to be very slow, if indeed it occurs at all. We shall return to this and associated problems after we have considered the influence of the body clock on performance capabilities.

The Body Clock and Performance

Psychologists have long recognized that people's efficiency at performing mental tasks is not constant, but varies over the course of the day. Interestingly, early theorists ascribed these variations either to a build-up of 'mental fatigue' with increased time awake (Thorndike, 1900) or to an underlying 'sleepiness rhythm', which was independent of whether people had actually slept (Michelson, 1897). Recent evidence suggests that, as in the case for physiological rhythms, both exogenous (the length of time since waking) and endogenous (body clock) factors contribute to variations in 'alertness' or 'fatigue' over the day.

Many of the early studies on time of day and performance were concerned with the optimization of work schedules in industrial and educational contexts. These, and subsequent studies, indicate that at least for some types of task there are fairly consistent trends in efficiency over the day, but that the nature of the trend varies according to task demands. There is some evidence that the short-term memory load involved in the performance of a task may be critical in determining the precise trend over the day. Simple serial search speed such as that involved in proof reading involves little, if any, memory component and reaches a maximum in the evening. On more complex, working memory tasks, such as logical reasoning, performance tends to improve to about midday and then declines. These tasks require the use of a working memory system involving a number of different cognitive sub-systems (e.g., short-term storage, information processing, throughput, etc.) and it is likely that the pattern observed is the outcome of a combination of different trends associated with the different cognitive mechanisms involved. When the task is one of immediate retention which emphasizes memory mechanisms and requires people to memorize digit strings or passages of text, then immediate recall tends to be best early in the day and to decline steadily over the rest of the day (see Folkard and Monk, 1980). However, although immediate retention is better in the morning, the available evidence indicates that delayed (seven days or more) retention is generally better following afternoon or evening presentation (see Folkard and Monk, 1985a).

These differences in the performance trend over the day associated with task demands complicate any recommendations for the scheduling of work over the normal day. Indeed, to some extent this complexity was recognized by early educational researchers in this area, who, on the basis of the different trends found in immediate memory and simple performance measures, suggested that more 'mentally taxing' school subjects should be taught in the morning (e.g., Gates, 1916). This recommendation is clearly questionable in the light of the superior delayed retention following afternoon presentation (see Folkard and Monk, 1985a) and the finding of superior examination results by students who attend classes in the afternoon or evening rather than in the morning (Skinner, 1985).

SHIFTWORK

There is no doubt that shiftwork can result in a variety of problems for the individual worker. These range from difficulties with sleep that depend, at least in part, on a disturbed circadian timing system, through impaired subjective (and sometimes objective) measures of health, to an impoverished social life. These problems are often reflected in general feelings of malaise and may result in various consequences for both the individual and the employer (Waterhouse, Folkard and Minors, 1992). However, not all shift systems result in equal problems for (some of) the individuals employed on them. As we shall see below, there is a great diversity of shift systems, and it appears to be primarily those that necessitate a change in the timing of sleep that are most problematic.

Nature and Prevalence

The prevalence of shiftwork has increased considerably over the past fifty years in most industrialized countries, and is currently rapidly increasing in the developing countries. There appear to be three main reasons for this that can be broadly classified as social, technological and economic. There is an increased demand for the provision of twenty-four-hour services such as medical care and transportation, while technological advances have resulted in the use of continuous processes in, for example, the steel and chemical industries. However, the major reason for this increased prevalence appears to be economic, in that shiftwork can improve the return on capital investment.

In view of this, it is not surprising that the prevalence of shiftwork varies dramatically with both the size and nature of the organization concerned. European statistics indicate that the incidence of night work is twice as high in larger organizations (those employing more than fifty individuals) and that the involvement in night work varies from about 5 per cent in building and civil engineering to about 40 per cent in transport and communication (Wedderburn, 1996). Interestingly, over 10 per cent of those employed in banking and finance work at night for at least 25 per cent of the time. Similar statistics for developing countries are not normally available, but the incidence of shiftwork in these countries appears to be increasing for primarily economic reasons (Ong and Kogi, 1990). Economic factors also appear to be resulting in the spread of shiftwork out of traditional shiftworking industries into white-collar jobs, such as computer operating, although there are few statistics on the prevalence of shiftwork in these jobs.

This sizeable minority of the workforce is engaged on a wide variety of shift systems. These can be classified according to their key features (see Kogi, 1985), the most important of which is whether the system involves a displacement of normal sleep time. Other features include whether an individual always works on the same shift (e.g., evening or night) or rotates from one shift to another, and, if so, the speed and direction of rotation. However, even most so-called 'permanent' night workers typically rotate from a nocturnal routine on their workdays to a diurnal (i.e. day-oriented) one on their days off. Thus, in terms of their endogenous circadian timing systems, the label of a 'permanent' shift system is somewhat misleading.

Disturbed Rhythms and Sleep

Studies of the effects of shiftwork on circadian rhythms in physiological functions have been largely confined to the body temperature rhythm. This is mainly due to the ease with which temperature rhythms can be measured, and is perhaps unfortunate in view of the fact that the endogenous and exogenous components enhance one another in producing the overt rhythm (see Figure 3.1). Nevertheless, there is considerable agreement that, whereas the body temperature rhythm is often disturbed by working at night, it rarely adjusts completely over a normal span of night duty and rapidly reverts to its normal state when the individual has a rest day or changes to a different shift. Indeed, any adjustment to night work that is observed could simply reflect a shifted exogenous component and an unaltered endogenous one. Thus, the temperature rhythm typically shows a 'flattening' or reduction in amplitude but little evidence of a real phase shift.

Studies of other physiological rhythms for which there is evidence of an endogenous component (e.g., urinary potassium and plasma cortisol) typically show a similar pattern of results to body temperature. In contrast, some rhythms, such as pulse rate and urinary noradrenaline, may show relatively good adjustment to night work, but this probably simply reflects their largely exogenous origin (Akerstedt, 1985).

One of the major complaints of shiftworkers is that their day sleeps between successive night shifts are disturbed. Although they often attribute this to increased environmental noise, it seems probable that the major cause of disturbed day sleeps is that they take place at an inappropriate phase of the endogenous timing system (see above). Thus, unless this system has adjusted to night work, day sleeps will be of reduced duration compared to night sleeps. This has been confirmed using both objective sleep measures and large-scale survey measures.

Figure 3.2 (lower line) shows the reported sleep duration of shiftworkers as a function of the time of day at which they fell asleep (Kogi, 1985). It is clear from this figure that normal length sleeps (i.e., of eight hours) were only obtained when the shiftworkers went to sleep between about 21:00 and 01:00. Later sleep onsets resulted in a progressive shortening of sleep duration to a minimum of about two hours for sleeps started between 13:00 and 17:00. It is noteworthy that a very similar trend in

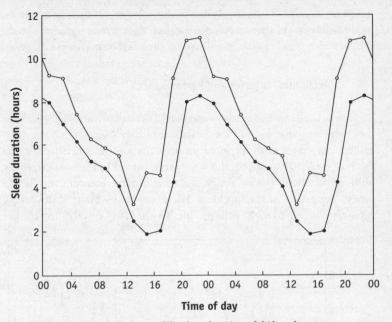

Fig. 3.2 *The dependence of the sleep duration of shiftworkers on the time of day at which they went to sleep (lower line) and the influence of the endogenous body clock on the sleep duration of internally desynchronized people (upper line). Both curves are 'double-plotted' to emphasize their rhythmic nature. (Adapted from Folkard, 1988.)*

sleep duration has been observed in people removed from all external influences (upper line), suggesting that the sleep duration of shiftworkers is largely determined by their endogenous body clocks (Folkard, 1988). Further, the generally longer sleeps of the 'temporally isolated' people simply reflects the fact that, on average, they only went to sleep once every thirty-three hours.

The day sleeps of shiftworkers taken between night shifts are typically between one to four hours shorter than normal night sleeps, and this is largely due to a reduction in Stage 2 and rapid eye movement (REM) sleep, rather than in the deeper slow wave sleep (SWS). Loss of SWS, but not that of REM or Stage 2 sleep, is typically recovered on night sleeps taken on days off. Thus, largely due to the influence of their body clocks, night workers will show a cumulative sleep deficit over successive night shifts, which is only partially restored on their rest days (Akerstedt, 1985).

Accidents, Injuries and Performance

In view of the disturbed rhythms and partial sleep deprivation, it is perhaps not surprising that most of the available evidence suggests that the night shift is associated with impaired productivity and safety. However, the body of evidence to support this is not large, since it has proved extremely difficult to obtain the necessary, uncontaminated, measures needed to assess the extent of this problem. For example, in many shiftworking situations impaired night-time productivity or safety could reflect the use

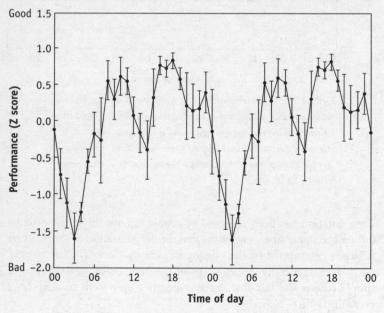

Fig. 3.3 The mean trend (and standard errors) in job performance measures based on a Z transformation of the results from six published field studies of shiftworkers' performance. The curve is 'double-plotted' to emphasize its rhythmic nature. (See Folkard and Monk, 1979, for details of the studies concerned.)

of less efficient or more dangerous machines, since their maintenance is often confined to the day shift. Nevertheless a number of studies have managed to obtain relatively continuous measures of performance speed or accuracy over the twenty-four hour period and these are summarized in Figure 3.3. It is clear from this figure that job performance is low during much of the night shift, reaching its minimum at about 03:00.

With regard to safety, a number of authors have pointed out that many major catastrophes, such as those at Three Mile Island and Chernobyl, have occurred at night (Mitler, Carskadon, Czeisler, Dement, Dinges and Graeber, 1988), but there appear to be only a few studies that have managed to examine accident (injury) frequencies across shifts in situations where the *a priori* risk appeared to be constant (see Folkard and Hill, 2000 for further details). By expressing the risk on the afternoon and night shifts in each study relative to that on the morning shift it is

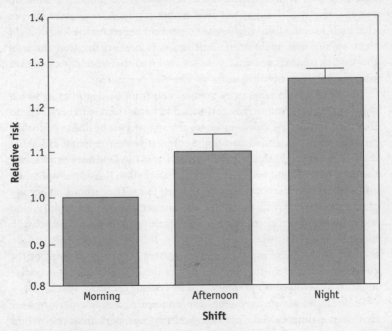

Fig. 3.4 *The mean relative risk (and standard errors) of accidents/injuries across the three shifts. (See Folkard and Hill, 2000, for details of the studies concerned.)*

possible to calculate the average risk on each shift, and this is shown in Figure 3.4. It is clear from this figure that, on average, accident risk increased in an approximately linear fashion across the three shifts, showing an increased risk of about 10 per cent on the afternoon shift, and of just over 25 per cent on the night shift, relative to that on the morning shift. Further, the small standard errors of the means (SEMs) shown in Figure 3.4 indicate that this rise was fairly consistent across the four studies.

Another reasonably consistent trend in accident risk is that over successive night shifts. The authors are aware of a total of six studies that have reported accident and/or injury data separately for each night of a span of at least four successive night shifts (see Folkard and Hill, 2000). As before, in order to compare across these studies the risk on each night was expressed relative to that on the first night shift and the results were then averaged. Figure 3.5 shows the resultant trend. It is clear that, on average, risk was about 15 per cent higher on the second night, 30 per cent higher on the third night, and 50 per cent higher on the fourth night than on the first night shift. Further, it is noteworthy that three of the studies summarized in Figure 3.5 reported that accident rates over successive day or morning shifts were relatively constant.

The results from laboratory studies, and from field studies in which shiftworkers have voluntarily performed tasks for the researchers, suggest that these trends in accident or injury risk may in part be due to disturbed circadian rhythms, and in part to the cumulative sleep deficit that accrues over successive night shifts. Some researchers in this field have emphasized the parallelism found between the circadian rhythm in body temperature and that in performance efficiency on some tasks. They argue that permanent shift systems will maximize the adjustment of temperature, and hence performance, rhythms as well as resulting in longer sleeps between night shifts (Wilkinson, 1992). However, this perspective fails to take account of either the rapid readjustment that occurs on days off or the cumulative sleep debt that builds up over the longer spans of successive night shifts involved on permanent shift systems (Folkard, 1992).

In addition, as we have seen, the concept of a single performance rhythm is erroneous. Like physiological rhythms, performance rhythms differ not only in their normal phase but also in the degree to which they are endogenously controlled. Indeed, there is evidence that memory-loaded cognitive tasks, which are becoming increasingly common in paid

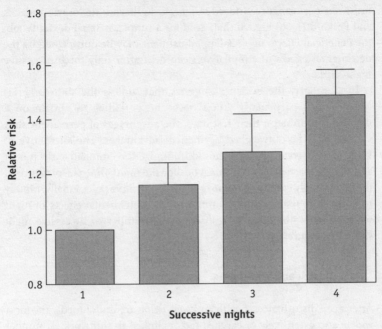

Fig. 3.5 *The mean relative risk (and standard errors) of accidents/injuries across four successive night shifts. (See Folkard and Hill, 2000, for details of the studies concerned.)*

employment, may be performed particularly well at night (Folkard and Monk, 1980, 1985a). Further, the adjustment to night work of this type of circadian rhythm, which normally peaks at night, has been found to occur relatively rapidly (e.g., Hughes and Folkard, 1976). This rapid adjustment will result in a progressive impairment of night-shift performance, and so suggests that, for cognitive, memory-loaded performance tasks, shift systems that minimize adjustment (i.e., rapidly rotating shift systems) may be preferable (see Monk and Folkard, 1985).

In the light of this, it is noteworthy that the only field study to have found superior performance on the night shift concerned the data-logging errors of computer operators (a task with a high memory load) on a rapidly rotating shift system (Monk and Embrey, 1981). In terms of work performance such rapidly rotating systems also have the advantage of minimizing the cumulative sleep debt, which may itself result in impaired performance. Indeed, Vidacek, Kaliterna, Radosevic-Vidacek and Folkard (1986) argued that, even for a simple, manual dexterity job, the beneficial effects of circadian adjustment may be outweighed by the detrimental effects of cumulative sleep debt after only three successive night shifts.

In summary, the evidence suggests that, unless the shiftworker is engaged in a particularly crucial task and is willing to remain on a nocturnal routine on their rest days, the advantages of permanent shift systems may be outweighed by their disadvantages. The alternative of using rapidly rotating shifts should minimize the cumulative sleep debt and may be particularly advantageous for the night-time performance of the increasingly common memory-loaded, cognitive tasks. Finally, rapidly rotating shift systems should minimize the detrimental effects of night work on safety by severely restricting the number of successive night shifts (see Figure 3.5).

Health and Well-being

After sleep disturbances, health and well-being are undoubtedly the most widely and extensively researched factors linked to shiftwork. A number of studies have reported an increased morbidity for affective disorders (such as depression), gastrointestinal disorders, especially ulcers (sometimes attributed to the concomitant disturbance of eating patterns), and cardiovascular risk in shiftworkers (Waterhouse, Folkard and Minors, 1992). Recent reports have also linked shiftwork with impaired immune function and reproductive health problems in females (ranging from disturbed menstrual cycles to an increased risk of miscarriage and premature birth). However, caution should be taken in interpreting the results since, as yet, there is no clear evidence that such complaints are a direct consequence of the disturbed circadian rhythms associated with shiftwork.

When discussing the health outcomes of shiftwork it is also important to recognize that they may take many years before manifesting themselves. Recent evidence suggests that it is the severity, rather than the number, of health complaints that changes with increasing shiftwork exposure. The situation is further complicated by the 'healthy shiftworker effect', the natural selection of ill-adapted workers out of shiftwork such that the remaining population comprises a self-selected group of individuals better able to cope with working shifts. This is supported in a number of studies, which have found a higher incidence of health complaints in former, compared with current, shiftworkers (Koller, 1983).

Social Factors

In addition to the circadian disruption discussed so far, it is important to bear in mind that the impact of shiftwork is likely to depend on a large number of situational variables, such as housing conditions, work conditions, availability of public transport, commuting time, and the availability of canteen facilities, all of which may in turn be influenced by the type of shift worked. In the same way the quality of the shiftworker's social and domestic life may be compromised, since a shift system determines not only the amount of time off work, but also the opportunity the worker has to spend this time as desired. 'Time budget' studies have shown that there is a distinct pattern in the perceived value of time off work. Weekends are more highly valued than weekdays and evenings more valuable than days (Wedderburn, 1981). This is sometimes recognized in the form of shift premiums that attempt to compensate financially for the inconvenience of working outside the nine-to-five schedule.

In general, shiftwork tends to facilitate so-called 'time flexible' activities (i.e., those which are not organized and fit into whatever time is available, such as shopping and household chores) and hinders inflexible ones. Although more socially unacceptable, night work has the advantage of regular time off and allows the nightworker to pursue solitary hobbies (e.g., gardening and fishing) during daylight hours. Rotating shiftworkers typically complain of insufficient time for friends, missing out on being active members of organizations (e.g., political parties and parent–teacher associations) and participating in institutionalized activities. Many also complain that they have had to give up some form of hobby or leisure activity and have fewer friends than day workers (Colligan and Rosa, 1990), a situation which may lead to a sense of social isolation. This is made worse by the fact that even contact with members of their own family tends to occur at unusual and often inconvenient times.

On this latter point there is some suggestive evidence that the partners and children of shiftworkers may also be susceptible to similar problems, since, in order to maximize the quantity and quality of family time, they too have to rearrange their routines around the shift schedule. For partners this may include interference with household chores, having to keep children quiet to protect the sleep of night workers, being alone during the night and evenings and having to prepare and eat meals at odd times. Moreover, both lower school achievement (see Volger, Ernst, Nachreiner and Hanecke, 1988) and a higher incidence of emotional problems (Barton, Aldridge and Smith, 1998) have been reported in the children of shiftworkers compared with those of dayworkers.

Individual Differences

The problems of shiftwork do not arise equally in all individuals. Indeed, it has been estimated that about 10 per cent of shiftworkers may positively enjoy their pattern of working, while about 60 per cent are able to tolerate it reasonably well. It is only a minority (20–30 per cent) who positively dislike working shifts (Harrington, 1978). The role of individual differences in the ability to adjust to shiftwork has important implications for the selection of individuals better suited to specific types of working patterns (see below), and as such has received much attention in the literature.

The dimension of morningness–eveningness (Smith, Rilley and Midkiff, 1989) is the most widely studied chronobiological factor in this respect, and one that has been consistently linked with various other individual difference variables. Morning types ('larks') are characterized by an early circadian phase and tend to wake up early and quickly, while evening types ('owls') are characterized by a late phase and prefer to get up and stay up later. The performance of extreme morning types deteriorates over much of the day, while that of evening types improves. Further, evening types are better able to adjust their core temperature rhythms to 'permanent' night work, while morning types show little adjustment to night work even after twenty-one successive night shifts.

Folkard, Monk and Lobban (1979) suggested that better adjustment to shiftwork would be shown by individuals who could sleep at unusual times of the day ('flexibility' as opposed to 'rigidity') and who could overcome drowsiness ('vigorousness' as opposed to 'languidity'). Support for this was found by Ognianova, Dalbokova and Stanchez (1998), who showed languidity to be associated with digestive, psychosomatic and mental health problems, in addition to distractibility, irritability and reduced alertness during the night shift, while flexibility was negatively correlated with sleep disturbances and chronic fatigue.

In terms of demographic factors, age has also been linked to shiftwork tolerance. Thus older individuals may encounter more problems as a result of working shifts, especially on rotating systems that require a constant readjustment in routine. Although some people presume that older shiftworkers will be better able to tolerate shiftwork as a result of their greater experience of shift-related problems, Koller (1983) found a sharp increase in sleep disturbances, gastrointestinal and cardiovascular disorders and absence from work in shiftworkers after the age of forty to fifty-five years, suggesting exactly the opposite.

In terms of gender, there is evidence showing that female shiftworkers have higher absenteeism rates and more frequently report chronic fatigue and psychoneurotic, digestive, and circulatory complaints (e.g., Oginska, Pokorski and Oginski, 1993). One explanation for such findings comes from the known differences in the body clocks of men and women. Women typically show a shortening of their sleep/wake cycle when they spontaneously desynchronize (indicative of morningness) while men are more likely to show a lengthening (indicative of eveningness). Further, although women have a greater habitual sleep need, requiring around ninety minutes more than males (Oginska and Oginski, 1990), the sleep they do gain is typically characterized by frequent and premature awakenings and difficulties in sleep onset.

An alternative explanation lies in the so-called 'double burden' of females that results in them being exposed to greater work/non-work conflict. For example, Beerman and Nachreiner (1995) found off-the-job workload to be the most important discriminating factor in the levels of stress in men and women performing the same job under comparable conditions. It is also the case that many female shiftworkers give family-oriented activities priority over their day sleep.

Finally, both locus of control and hardiness have been shown to moderate shiftwork-related problems. Both dimensions have been used when discussing individuals who employ active strategies in dealing with problems, and thus experience less stress-related illness such as digestive problems as a consequence.

Possible Interventions

There are a number of possible interventions that may help to alleviate the problems associated with shiftwork. First, and foremost, the shift system can be optimized. The earlier bias towards permanent systems, that assumed complete adjustment of circadian rhythms, has now been virtually reversed in Europe to a bias in favour of rapidly rotating systems that should minimize the disruption of such rhythms. Theorists have argued both that slowly rotating shift systems are probably undesirable, and that shift systems that delay (i.e. in the order: morning–evening–night) result in fewer problems for the individuals concerned than those that advance (night–evening–morning), although the evidence on this latter point is far from conclusive (see Tucker, Smith, Macdonald and Folkard, 2000).

Ideally, this choice between rapidly rotating and permanent systems needs to be considered not only in relation to performance efficiency (see above), but also in relation to medical and social criteria, but there are insufficient medical data available for any valid comparison to be made. However, it is arguable that the reduced sleep deprivation and undisrupted circadian rhythms associated with rapidly rotating systems may make them the lesser of two evils. Further, when social criteria are considered a widespread resistance to change results in most shiftworkers favouring their current system. Nevertheless, when rapidly rotating shift systems have been introduced, they have usually proved highly acceptable, since they allow at least some normal social activity every week.

Other important features of shift systems include the timing and duration of shifts, the duration of the rest period between shifts, and the accumulated hours worked before a rest day. While many researchers in this area agree that there is probably no single 'best' shift system for all situations, most would support the move towards placing specific limitations on various features of shift systems such as those contained in the European Union's 'Working Time Directive'.

In the future, a second form of intervention may well be to try to maximize the adjustment of an individual's circadian rhythms to their work schedule by the use of appropriately timed administrations of bright light or melatonin. Advances in the last decade suggest that this is certainly a possibility and there have been a few experimental trials on real shiftworkers showing that these manipulations may improve circadian adjustment and reduce sleep problems. However, the long-term consequences of adjusting individuals' circadian rhythms to their shifts and then re-adjusting them back to normal for their rest days have yet to be determined.

Indeed, a plausible explanation for many of the health problems associated with shiftwork is that they stem from exactly the continual adjustment and re-adjustment of individuals' rhythms that manipulations such as bright light and feeding melatonin are designed to maximize, suggesting that these manipulations may actually exacerbate longer-term health problems. While there is some recent, but indirect, evidence to support this point, there is clearly a strong need for more direct research on the potential long-term effects of the use of these manipulations before they can be recommended for widespread use.

Two final forms of intervention are more concerned with the individual, and are based on individual differences in tolerance to shiftwork, and on the development of appropriate coping strategies. It is obvious that individuals differ substantially from one another in their ability to tolerate shiftwork, and individual difference measures have met with some success in predicting these differences in a longitudinal research programme (e.g., Kaliterna, Vidacek, Radosevic-Vidacek and Prizmic, 1993). However, they could not readily be used for personnel selection purposes because it would be very easy for candidates to fake desirable scores on them. Nevertheless, they might prove useful in counselling individuals as to whether they would be likely to tolerate shiftwork and, if so, how best to develop adequate coping strategies.

A number of authors have argued that the adoption of appropriate coping strategies should reduce the problems that an individual encounters as a result of shiftwork. These coping strategies are primarily concerned with the scheduling of various activities, such as sleep and meals, which are under voluntary control. However, there is only very limited evidence for the efficacy of coping strategies, and even this may have been confounded by differences between individuals in whether they had chosen to work on their particular schedule (Barton, 1994).

Nevertheless, it is clear that sleeps taken at a regular time are likely to stabilize circadian rhythms, while an irregular sleeping pattern may disrupt them. Indeed, there is evidence that four hours' sleep taken during the night, in combination with an additional four hours taken at an irregular time of day, is sufficient to prevent the disruption of most rhythms. In practice, many night workers do take a night-time nap (often unofficially) although this is seldom of four hours' duration.

Finally, in addition to sleep, the timing of meals, the scheduling of social contacts and leisure activities, and improving physical fitness have all been suggested as ways in which an individual may improve their tolerance to shiftwork (Wedderburn, 1991). While these suggestions would seem sensible, there is a strong need for further research in this area to identify the most effective way(s) for people to cope with their shift system.

SUMMARY

A substantial proportion of our workforce is employed on some form of shift system. This can result in a variety of problems for both the individuals concerned and the organizations employing them. Central to these problems is the fact that we have evolved as a diurnal species with an internal body clock that sends us to sleep at night. This internal body clock is disrupted when people work at abnormal times, and this disruption is thought to mediate many of the shiftworkers' problems. Consideration of the nature of our body clocks allows a better understanding of these problems as well as suggesting ways in which they may best be alleviated.

FURTHER READING

Most of the topics covered in this chapter are considered in greater detail in Folkard and Monk (1985b) *Hours of Work: Temporal Factors in Work Scheduling*, Colquhoun, Costa, Folkard and Knauth, P. (1996) *Shiftwork: Problems and Solutions*, and Hornberger, Knauth, Costa and Folkard (2000) *Shiftwork in the 21st Century*. These also have extensive bibliographies for those wishing to examine this area in greater detail. A more popular account is by Monk and Folkard (1992), *Making Shiftwork Tolerable*, while the health problems associated with shiftwork are reviewed by Costa, Folkard and Harrington (2000). A general introduction to human circadian rhythms and their practical implications is Lamberg's (1994) *Bodyrhythms: Chronobiology and Peak Performance*.

REFERENCES

Akerstedt, T. (1985). Adjustment of physiological circadian rhythms and the sleep–wake cycle to shiftwork. In S. Folkard and T. H. Monk (eds.), *Hours of Work: Temporal Factors in Work Scheduling*, pp. 185–97. Chichester: Wiley.

Aschoff, J. and Wever, R. A. (1962). Spontanperiodik des Menschen bei Ausschluss aller Zeitgeber. *Naturwissenschaften*, 49, 337–42.

Barton, J. (1994). Choosing to work at night: A moderating influence on individual tolerance to shiftwork. *Journal of Applied Psychology*, 79, 449–54.

Barton, J., Aldridge, J. and Smith, P. (1998). The emotional impact of shiftwork on the children of shiftworkers. *Scandinavian Journal of Work Environment and Health*, 24, 146–50.

Beerman, B. and Nachreiner, F. (1995). Working shifts – different effects for women and men? *Work and Stress*, 9, 289–97.

Colligan, M. J. and Rosa, R. R. (1990). Shiftwork effects on social and family life. *Occupational Medicine: State of the Art Reviews*, 5, 315–22.

Colquhoun, W. P., Costa, G., Folkard, S. and Knauth, P. (eds.) (1996). *Shiftwork: Problems and Solutions*. Frankfurt am Main: Peter Lang.

Costa, G., Folkard, S. and Harrington, J. M. (2000). Shift work and extended hours of work. In P. J. Baxter, P. H. Adams, T-C. Caw, A. Cockroft and J. M. Harrington (eds.), *Hunter's Diseases of Occupation, 9th edition*, pp. 581–9. London: Arnold.

Folkard, S. (1988). Circadian rhythms and shiftwork: adjustment or masking? In W. Th. J. M. Hekkens, G. A. Kerkhof and W. J. Rietveld (eds.), *Trends in Chronobiology*, pp. 173–82. Oxford: Pergamon Press.

Folkard, S. and Monk, T. H. (1979). Shiftwork and performance. *Human Factors*, 21, 483–92.

Folkard, S. (1992). Is there a 'best compromise' shift system? *Ergonomics*, 35, 1453–63.

Folkard, S. and Akerstedt, T. (1992). A 3-process model of the regulation of alertness–sleepiness. In R. J. Broughton and B. D. Ogilvie (eds.), *Sleep, Arousal and Performance*, pp. 11–26. Boston: Birkhauser.

Folkard, S. and Hill, J. (2000). Shiftwork and accidents. In T. Marek, H. Oginska, J. Pokorski, G. Costa and S. Folkard (eds.), *Shiftwork 2000 – Implications for Science, Practice and Business*, pp. 11–28. Kraków: Institute of Management, Jagiellonian University.

Folkard, S. and Monk, T. H. (1980). Circadian rhythms in human memory. *British Journal of Psychology*, 71, 295–307.

Folkard, S. and Monk, T. H. (1985a). Circadian performance rhythms. In S. Folkard and T. H. Monk (eds.), *Hours of Work: Temporal Factors in Work Scheduling*, pp. 37–52. Chichester: Wiley.

Folkard, S. and Monk, T. H. (eds.) (1985b). *Hours of Work: Temporal Factors in Work Scheduling*. Chichester: Wiley.

Folkard, S., Monk, T. H. and Lobban, M. C. (1979). Towards a predictive test of adjustment to shiftwork. *Ergonomics*, 22, 79–91.

Gates, A. I. (1916). Variations in efficiency during the day, together with practice effects, sex differences, and correlations. *University of California Publications in Psychology*, 2, 1–156.

Harrington, J. M. (1978). *Shiftwork and Health: A Critical Review of the Literature*. London: HMSO.

Hornberger, S., Knauth, P., Costa, G. and Folkard, S. (2000). *Shiftwork in the 21st Century*. Frankfurt am Main, Berlin, Bern, New York, Paris, and Vienna: Peter Lang.

Hughes, D. G. and Folkard, S. (1976). Adaptation to an 8-hour shift in living routine by members of a socially isolated community. *Nature*, 264, 232–4.

Kaliterna, Lj., Vidacek, S., Radosevic-Vidacek, B. and Prizmic, Z. (1993). The reliability and stability of various individual difference and tolerance to shift-work measures. *Ergonomics*, 36, 183–90.

Kogi, K. (1985). Introduction to the problems of shift-work. In S. Folkard and T. H. Monk (eds.), *Hours of Work: Temporal Factors in Work Scheduling*, pp. 165–84. Chichester: Wiley.

Koller, M. (1983). Health risks related to shift work. *International Archives of Occupational and Environmental Health*, 53, 59–75.

Lamberg, L. (1994). *Bodyrhythms: Chronobiology and Peak Performance*. New York: William Morrow and Company.

Michelson, M. (1897). Ueber die Tiefe des Schlafes. *Psychol. Arbeiten.*, 2, 84–117.

Mitler, M. M., Carskadon, M. A., Czeisler, C. A., Dement, W. C., Dinges, D. F. and Graeber, R. C. (1988). Catastrophes, sleep, and public policy: consensus report. *Sleep*, 11, 100–109.

Monk, T. H. and Embrey, D. E. (1981). A field study of circadian rhythms in actual and interpolated task performance. In A. Reinberg, N. Vieux and P. Andlauer (eds.), *Night and Shift Work: Biological and Social Aspects*. Oxford: Pergamon Press.

Monk, T. H. and Folkard, S. (1985). Shiftwork and performance. In S. Folkard and T. H. Monk (eds.), *Hours of Work: Temporal Factors in Work Scheduling*, pp. 239–52. Chichester: Wiley.

Monk, T. H. and Folkard, S. (1992). *Making Shiftwork Tolerable*. London: Taylor and Francis.

Oginska, H. and Oginski, A. (1990). Sex differences in sleep behavior of shiftwork-ers. In G. Costa, G. Cesana, K. Kogi and A. Wedderburn (eds.), *Shiftwork, Health, Sleep and Performance*, pp. 589–94. Frankfurt am Main: Peter Lang.

Oginska, H., Pokorski, J. and Oginski, A. (1993). Gender, ageing and shiftwork tolerance. *Ergonomics, 36*, 161–8.

Ognianova, V. M., Dalbokova, D. L. and Stanchez, V. (1998). Stress states, alertness and individual differences under 12-hour shiftwork. *International Journal of Industrial Ergonomics, 21*, 283–91.

Ong, C. N. and Kogi, K. (1990). Shiftwork in developing countries: current issues and trends. *Occupational Medicine: State of the Art Reviews, 5*, 417–28.

Owens, D. S., Macdonald, I., Tucker, P., Sytnik, N., Totterdell, P., Minors, D., Waterhouse, J. and Folkard, S. (2000). Diurnal variations in the mood and performance of highly practised young women living under strictly controlled conditions. *British Journal of Psychology, 91*, 41–60.

Siffre, M. (1964). *Beyond Time* (edited and translated by H. Briffault). New York: McGraw Hill.

Skinner, N. F. (1985). University grades and time of day of instruction. *Bulletin of the Psychonomic Society, 23*, 67.

Smith, C. S., Rilley, C. and Midkiff, K. (1989). Evaluation of three circadian rhythm questionnaires with suggestions for an improved measure of morningness. *Journal of Applied Psychology, 74*, 728–38.

Thorndike, E. (1900). Mental fatigue. *Psychological Review, 7*, 466–82.

Tucker, P., Smith, L., Macdonald, I. and Folkard, S. (2000). Effects of direction of rotation in continuous and discontinuous 8-hour shift systems. *Occupational and Environmental Medicine, 57*, 678–84.

Vidacek, S., Kaliterna, Lj., Radosevic-Vidacek, B. and Folkard, S. (1986). Pro-ductivity on a weekly rotating shift system: circadian adjustment and sleep deprivation effects? *Ergonomics, 29*, 1583–90.

Volger, A., Ernst, G., Nachreiner, F. and Hanecke, K. (1988). Common free time of family members under different shift systems. *Applied Ergonomics, 19*, 213–18.

Waterhouse, J. M., Folkard, S. and Minors, D. S. (1992). *Shiftwork, Health and Safety: An Overview of the Scientific Literature 1978–1990*. London: HMSO.

Wedderburn, A. A. I. (1981). How important are the social effects of shiftwork? In L. C. Johnson, D. I. Tepas, W. P. Colquhoun and M. J. Colligan (eds.), *Biological Rhythms, Sleep and Shiftwork*, pp. 257–69. New York: Spectrum Publications.

Wedderburn, A. A. I. (1991). *Guidelines for Shiftworkers. Bulletin of European Studies on Time No 3*. Shankhill: European Foundation for the Improvement of Living and Working Conditions.

Wedderburn, A. A. I. (ed.) (1996). *Statistics and News. Bulletin of European Studies on Time No 9*. Shankhill: European Foundation for the Improvement of Living and Working Conditions.

Wegmann, H-M. and Klein, K. E. (1985). Jet-lag and aircrew scheduling. In S. Folkard and T. H. Monk (eds.), *Hours of Work: Temporal Factors in Work Scheduling*, pp. 263–76. Chichester: Wiley.

Wever, R. A. (1979). *The Circadian System of Man: Results of Experiments under Temporal Isolation*. New York: Springer.

Wilkinson, R. T. (1992). How fast should the night shift rotate? *Ergonomics*, 35, 1425–46.

4 | People and Computers: Emerging Work Practice in the Information Age

Ken Eason

The world of work is undergoing rapid transformation. Explosive growth in the use of computers and telecommunications is creating an information revolution which Toffler (1980) called the 'third wave', a revolution similar in scale of impact to the earlier agricultural and industrial revolutions. The changes affect many aspects of the psychological relation between people and work, and this chapter explores the new forms of work practice that are emerging and their implications for people at work.

In the last century, the work that people undertook within organizations typically involved direct, hands-on experience of the objects of work, whether it was digging potatoes on a farm, assembling a product in a factory or selling garments to a customer in a shop. The process of work involved face-to-face engagement with other human beings as colleagues, customers or suppliers. It also meant that people became employees of organizations, went daily to the premises of the organization and quite possibly devoted a forty-year career to one employer.

For many people these are now characteristics of work in the past. The work they now undertake is increasingly 'virtual', characterized not by direct interaction with the objects of work but by indirect contact mediated by computers and forms of telecommunication. The operator in an e-commerce company does not, for example, meet the customer face-to-face and may never see the products that are being sold. The person who works from home may never meet colleagues working in the same organization. The pattern of working life is increasingly varied, not forty years with one firm but perhaps several different careers with many employers.

These changes mean that experiences of work, and the relations it creates between people, are in transition. For some commentators this is a time of great optimism, a time when people will be empowered by technology to achieve personal fulfilment in the work they do (Weisbord, 1990). Others are much more pessimistic, seeing the technology as presaging tight organizational control of the pace and structure of work and the exclusion of people from meaningful human relationships at work (Downing, 1980).

Before exploring the effects that are now being observed and assessing whether the optimism or the pessimism is justified, five short scenarios are offered to illustrate the new work practices that are emerging.

FIVE ILLUSTRATIONS OF EMERGING WORK PRACTICE

The nomadic worker

Jeff Smith left the company he had just visited with an order for a range of the products he sold. He returned to his car and opened his laptop computer. He had used the computer to demonstrate the products to the customer, and now he used it to send confirmation of the orders to the processing centre that would fulfil the order and bill the customer. He then checked his e-mails and voice mails and switched on his traffic management system to assess the best way of making his next visit. He did all of his office work from the car and rarely had occasion to go to head office. When he did he was allocated a 'hot desk', a workplace with full computing and telecommunications facilities, so that he could access all his electronic files. He had the same facilities at home. He could truly 'work from anywhere'.

The teleworker

Neil Saunders left the kitchen in his home and went through to his office. He checked his fax, e-mails and voice mails, and got up-to-date with the business his colleagues in a global company had been doing during the night. He was a technical advisor on international tax law and there were several urgent queries. He checked some electronic databases to confirm his understanding of tax law in several countries, and e-mailed colleagues in Spain and Argentina sending them the specific legal clauses and advice they needed. He then settled down to further electronic research, to enable him to complete the taxation advice he was preparing for a customer who was assessing whether to manufacture products in one of three countries. He had been working from home for five years now and only worked part-time, on a contract basis, for his original employer. He now used a website to advertise his services and had a list of clients from around the world who sought his expertise. He subscribed to all the professional websites he needed and found very little need to leave his home to serve his customers.

The call centre operator

Jean Fellows logged into her console at 6 p.m. on Saturday. Ahead of her was an eight hour shift with one thirty minute break. The computer put her first customer through. She went through the mandatory script to check the authenticity of the customer and then entered the details of the changes the customer wanted to make to a standing order on her bank account. The customer wanted to explain the reasons for the change, which involved a rather stressful family row, but Jean moved the conversation forward because she was already behind the average time per call. As she hung up, the computer put through the next customer, who was irate and wanted to complain about being left to listen to music for twenty minutes. Jean went through the script for dealing with irate customers and got to the purpose of the call as quickly as possible. The console in front of her showed how many calls she had handled in the past five shifts and the total elapsed time. She knew her supervisor also had a display of this information and would be listening to some of her calls today. She was well behind the target rate, and yesterday her supervisor had warned her that she would lose her job if she did not improve. She had been told that the frequency with which calls would be monitored would be doubled following this warning.

The expert medical assistant

Dr Alison Hill entered the list of symptoms of her patient from the long list provided by the medical diagnosis expert system. After a few seconds it came back with another three questions. Alison was a General Practitioner working in a local community hospital. She turned to another screen which was her telemedicine system. On the screen she could see a live picture of her patient, who was in the surgery of a colleague who was a General Practitioner in a remote village. She asked her colleague the questions the computer had raised, and her colleague examined the patient and reported the conclusions. Alison entered the new information, and was surprised when the computer came back with a high probability that the patient had a very common complaint that could be easily treated by the General Practitioner. She and her colleague felt sure the patient's condition was more serious and they knew the patient would not believe the diagnosis. She asked her colleague to take a blood sample and make another appointment for the patient. Later she contacted her colleague by telephone to discuss the case. The Health Service had introduced the expert system to cut down the number of referrals to hospital specialists. To encourage its use, the Health Service had made it much more expensive for the practice to refer patients to specialists. Nevertheless, Alison and her colleague felt they needed to get a specialist opinion, and Alison called the general hospital to make arrangements for that.

The virtual group

Vera Matthews got to the local work centre, where she had an office, at 5.30 a.m. The conference call was scheduled for 6 a.m. because that was the most convenient time for the other six members of the team who were scattered around the world in different time zones. Vera logged into the meeting scheduler and was pleased when the pictures of colleagues in Spain and South Africa appeared on the screen. They were working together on a marketing plan for a new product their company was going to launch globally in a month's time. She just had time to voice some doubts about the views of their team leader in the USA when the rest of the team appeared on the screen. They had all filed their latest reports the previous day, and they now reviewed each report using a separate display screen. The team leader followed the agenda he had put into the system, and the computer automatically provided the team members with relevant documents as each of the agenda items was discussed. Vera had never met any of the other team members personally and felt the plan being discussed would not be effective in the British market. She had tried to make this point in her report but the other members of the team did not seem to understand, and Vera found herself struggling to explain her position. The international connection was timed out before the matter was settled.

There are many issues raised by these forms of work practice which psychologists have been investigating. Some issues concern the interaction of people with information and telecommunications technology and with the performance of complex tasks mediated by technology. There are also issues about the maintenance of relations with other people, when they are not at the same location and when technology is the only means of communication. Beyond these questions are issues about the future nature of organizations and the kind of employment practices and careers which will become commonplace. Some of these issues arise directly from the use of the technology, but some are broader, arising from the new patterns of work that technology is making possible. In the section below, the direct issues of interacting with the technology are examined. Subsequently, implications for the nature of jobs and interaction with other people will be explored. Since the treatment of these issues depends on the design and application process by which new systems are created and implemented, the final section considers human-centred approaches to design.

HUMAN–COMPUTER INTERACTION

Work in the information age requires that people interact with computer systems in sophisticated ways. The computer is a complex 'black box', and specialist knowledge is necessary to understand how it works. In the five illustrations above none of the computer users were specialists in computing, yet they were all required to be competent in the use of a wide range of technology to communicate with others, search for information, send information, etc. Many people are now 'knowledge workers', earning their livings through skills acquired in particular knowledge domains but needing to be computer literate to operate effectively. Fortunately, this does not mean they have to learn the arcane workings of the innards of the black box, because major research and development efforts have been devoted to the construction of forms of human–computer interaction which are natural and easy for people to use. The aim of this research is to make the computer work in ways suitable for human use and reduce the need for people to fit the way the computer works.

It is convenient to divide human–computer interaction into two parts: the processes by which the computer can communicate with people, and the processes which enable people to communicate with the computer. As technology has advanced, many new forms of interaction have become possible, and considerable research effort has been devoted to finding ways of mapping the technology to the natural input and output characteristics of human beings (Norman, 1988).

Early computers could only communicate with people through printed outputs using numbers and codes. For example, ERR24 might mean an input error because of an unrecognized character. The arrival of the visual display screen led to the Graphical User Interface (GUI), which now includes a range of multimedia opportunities – text, diagrams, movies, animations, sound, speech etc. These alternatives mean the computer should be able to present information in a form ideal for the human to assimilate. For example, graphs might show trends, animations show dynamic relations, text be presented in large fonts for the visually impaired, and so on. In practice, much of what we see on screens employs the range of media in a chaotic fashion, producing screens that are garish, cluttered and confusing. Designers try to attract the user's attention by using colour, highlighting, movement, sound, etc. The result, unfortunately, is often a bewildering array of confusing messages, which can be difficult to understand and to navigate. These are very common characteristics of internet web sites, which are often difficult to use. Nielsen (2000) is one source of guidance for web site designers emphasizing the need for simplicity and clear organization if a site is to be user-oriented.

Many different ways of presenting information have been tested for ease of use and comprehension, and the results of this research are influencing the development of the technologies. One research area is the design of menu structures to enable the user to navigate complex materials. Card (1982), for example, has studied the menu structures by which the commands for operating the computer can be presented to the user.

Card organized eighteen items in three ways: randomly, by alphabetic group (e.g., all the terms from A to F), and by function (e.g., all commands to edit text – delete, replace etc.). Users were presented with a list of commands to find and select with a mouse. It was found that the average time was 0.8 seconds for the alphabetic list, 1.3 seconds for the function categories and 3.2 seconds for the random structure. The expectation had been that the functional structure would perform well, because users were looking for ways of performing functions. The reason it did not was that the users did not share with the designer a common view of what items would be found under which heading. For instance, was 'cut and paste' under 'edit' or 'insert'? As a consequence they often started by looking under the wrong heading. By contrast, they did share with the designers a common understanding or 'mental model' of the alphabet. People are able to interact well with a computer when both the designers and the users are working with a common set of mental models. However, the designers' model is often more technical than that of the average user, and if that model becomes manifest on the screen the users may struggle.

The processes by which people can input to computers have also gone through a revolution. The keyboard remains the most common input device and, although many alternatives have been proposed, the QWERTY layout of keys has survived the entire computer revolution (Noyes, 1998). This layout was originally introduced to reduce the risk of clashes of the mechanical arms of the typewriter. This is no longer necessary, and the survival of the layout demonstrates the value of consistency in the design of equipment. A large number of people have learned their keyboard skills using this layout, and they would require very considerable retraining to use an alternative. They expect every keyboard they meet to have a standard layout, and QWERTY is what they know. As a result all major manufacturers now follow this unofficial standard.

Many users are not skilled typists, and the designers of systems have sought to reduce the amount of keying by creating the WIMP interface (Windows, Icons, Menus and Pointing Devices). In the 1970s, designers at the Xerox PARC Laboratories in California (Canfield-Smith, Irby, Kimball and Verplank, 1992) developed a form of computer interaction by which people could act directly on the screen rather than typing lengthy instructions. They created a pointing device (the mouse) which by drag and click can locate any part of the screen and select an action to be taken. The addition of icons (symbols to represent common functions) and pull-down menus of available facilities means that a few mouse clicks can command the computer to undertake a wide range of complex activities. These features provide what Shneiderman (1992) calls 'direct manipulation', which enables a user to evoke the action required without having to remember complex codes and instructions.

The design of specific input devices to support direct manipulation has been influenced by experimental research in which subjects perform identical tasks with prototype forms of different devices. An example is the study undertaken by Zhai, Smith and Selker (1997) to test the mouse, the joystick and the track wheel as input devices for scrolling and pointing. When searching information systems, users need to point at and select items of interest, and if they open a complex document they have to scroll through it to find relevant sections. The investigators found that the mouse was a good device for pointing and clicking, but a clumsy way to scroll through a document. They found that the joystick was the best device for scrolling, and furthermore that the users could switch easily from mouse to joystick to get the best from each device.

Although the mouse and the keyboard dominate computer input, devices which use other human skills are also being developed. An approach which has been seen as the ultimate easy-to-use input is speech recognition. It has been a dream of many developers to create a system that a person could speak into, which would understand the instructions being given, prepare the text, record the data, etc. This has proved a major development task. Not only do individual sounds need to be recognized, but the ways in which they group into words and sentences in different languages and dialects have to be understood. Recognizers are now effective with individual words from a known lexicon spoken by a voice the system has been trained to recognize. However, continuous speech by a voice the system has not previously encountered usually leads to many recognition errors (Roe and Wilpon, 1994).

In addition to research on forms of human–computer interaction, there has been increasing recognition of the human issues associated with the workplaces at which people use this equipment. Many people spend most of their working day using computer equipment, and this may mean long periods in sedentary and fixed postures. There is growing evidence that this can be stressful and can lead to health complications. A particular set of problems which have concerned physical ergonomists are work-related upper limb disorders ('wrulds'): pains in the wrists, arms, shoulders, neck and back caused by sitting in fixed positions at a workstation and perhaps engaging in repetitive actions such as keying (Hagberg, 1996). In the scenarios presented at the beginning of the chapter, Jean Fellows in the call centre is particularly vulnerable to health problems of this kind because of the repetitive nature of her work, undertaken for many hours with few breaks.

Research on these issues has identified a number of strategies for the avoidance of health complications. One approach is the design of furniture and equipment so that it can be adjusted to fit the particular postural needs of the individual worker. Another is the design of the physical environment, lighting, heating, noise etc. to support the needs of the worker. Finally, there are job design solutions to avoid the requirement for long periods of repetitive work, such as short breaks every hour, the provision of varied work, discretion in the performance of the tasks, etc. (see also Chapter 11). The results of this research are being incorporated in health and safety legislation enacted in many countries, which requires employers to develop appropriate workplaces for staff using computers.

The stereotypical image of using computers at work is of people in offices sitting at visual display units. And yet, as the examples at the beginning of the chapter show, this is increasingly not the case. Jeff Smith the nomadic worker operates his computer anywhere and most often from his car, whilst Neil Saunders works from home. An increasing amount of communication and computer use is undertaken whilst travelling, using mobile phones, laptops, palmtops, etc. This further spread of the technology has raised more concerns. Do the new forms of technology, for example, introduce additional health hazards such as through the use of mobile phones when driving? Second, how can the good practice for workplace design developed for the office at work be applied in the office at home?

THE CONTEXT OF USE: SUPPORTING THE USER AND THE TASK

Computing and communications technology has become more sophisticated and easier to use in recent years. And yet there are countless reports of users having problems with their systems. A major reason is that people are very varied in their needs and characteristics and no one form of interaction can suit them all.

The need to match computer facilities to specific characteristics of users, tasks and contexts has led to the development of usability engineering. This is a form of design which begins by analyzing the users of the planned system, the setting in which they will use the system, and the tasks they will be undertaking. Prototype systems are then developed and usability tests undertaken in which users perform realistic tasks with the prototype. An improved system can then be created which is usable by the relevant people for the specified tasks (Galer, Harker and Ziegler, 1992; Preece, Rogers, Sharp, Benyon, Holland and Carey, 1994). For some developments the designers have to meet the requirements of a wide range of users, but in others the user population might be quite specific. The users of an automatic teller machine for withdrawing cash, for example, may come from any background. They are typically infrequent users and will be using the machine in an outdoor environment. Given these circumstances, designers have created forms of interaction suitable for the least experienced user: simple menu structures with completely structured form-filling to guide the novice through every transaction. By contrast, another design task might be to create a computer-aided design package for an architect. In this case, designers have recognized the expert knowledge of the architects and have provided a computer package that is more like a toolset, allowing users to select the functions they wish to undertake as they proceed with their work.

One area in which usability research has a special significance is in the design of computer support for people with special needs. The computer has great potential for enabling people with severe disabilities to engage in human affairs in ways previously not possible (Newell, 1993). Usability research which tests prototype systems for use by people who are disabled is a necessary precursor to the design of effective systems. An example of such a study is the development of a navigational aid for blind travellers (Petrie, Johnson, Strothotte, Michel, Raab and Reichert, 1997). This device provides auditory information to the blind traveller at all points of a journey. The device uses satellite-tracking systems which can pinpoint the exact location of the traveller. Before travelling, a pre-journey system is used to plan the journey and create a database of detailed information about every stage, including for example the number of steps in flights of stairs, the location of traffic lights, etc. The traveller can request different types of information from the system during the journey by using a small keyboard.

Such a system has great potential, but is it usable by these travellers in the context of their journey? The investigators faced a problem common in usability research; they had to answer this question before a working version of the system was available. To do so they used the 'Wizard of Oz' technique. In this, a human being plays the role of the system. The designers did the pre-journey planning with a blind traveller, all the instructions were recorded on cassette, and a human assistant played the relevant section of the tape whilst walking the route with the blind traveller. Eighteen blind users took part in this trial, which yielded positive results about the general concept of the tool. More importantly, detailed information was obtained about specific features of the system, such as what information was needed, how long messages could be and what kind of earpiece would be acceptable.

JOB DESIGN AND THE ROLE OF COMPUTER SYSTEMS IN THE WORK PROCESS

As computer systems become the dominant work tool of 'knowledge workers', they also have a pervasive influence on the nature of the job and sources of worker well-being. Two quite different theories have been advanced about the impact of computer systems on jobs. One may be called the 'empowerment' hypothesis: the belief that providing people with computer systems that can process information quickly, facilitate access to vast stores of knowledge and enable communications with other people, will greatly increase their work ability and the satisfaction they derive from it. The alternative is the 'replacement and control' hypothesis, which predicts the loss of jobs (replacing people by computers) and the control of those that remain by the computer system. Blackler and Brown (1980), for example, demonstrate how the computer can be used as an instrument of management control, specifying the procedures and timing of task performance.

Many studies have demonstrated that both kinds of outcome are possible and common. In the example earlier in the chapter, for instance, Neil Saunders, the teleworker, has a range of computer tools at his disposal which he can use as he considers appropriate to process information, search databases and communicate with others. By contrast, Jean Fellows, in the call centre, is controlled by the computer in the timing, procedures and even verbal scripts she uses with customers, and her performance is continuously monitored by the system. In reviewing predictions about the effect of computers on jobs, it seems that both the optimists and the pessimists are right.

The impact of a computer system is often very sensitive to the way it is used in relation to specific jobs. Buchanan and Boddy (1983), for example, report a case study of the changes in the jobs of the doughman and the ovenman in a biscuit-making factory when it was computerized. The doughman had previously held a skilled and varied job, in which he knew the recipes to prepare sixty biscuit mixes. The new computer system contained a tape with a mix for each type of biscuit; this tape now controlled the mixing process. After implementation, the doughman's job became a simple, repetitive machine-minding task, in which he changed the computer tapes as necessary and kept the hoppers full of ingredients. The ovenman was responsible for the processing of the biscuits as they passed along the baking line through the oven, and had responsibility for their weight, texture, evenness of cooking, etc. The new computer system weighed the biscuits as they emerged from the oven and gave continuous feedback to the ovenman. This constituted much richer information than had previously been available and enabled the ovenman to refine his control of the oven. In the doughman's case the job had been deskilled, but in the ovenman's case it had been enriched.

The conclusion from these studies is that computer systems can be used to improve the well-being of people at work, but they can equally have the opposite effect. If job enrichment is the target, it is necessary in the development and application of technical systems to create forms of interaction which enhance user discretion, control, feedback, etc. This requirement has led to what are termed 'socio-technical systems' approaches to the design and implementation of computer systems from a user-centred perspective. These approaches will be considered at the end of the chapter.

As technology advances it can play an even greater role, to such an extent that the function of people in the work process may be called into question. The pilot of an airliner may rely on its autopilot to land the aircraft, and the control room operator of a chemical process may spend most of the time watching automated control systems run the plant. On the road, a car's speed may be controlled by an intelligent cruise control system and adjusted automatically to the speed of the vehicle in front. At a less dramatic level, a word processing system may correct spelling and grammar or format the text for its user. These are examples of machine intelligence or 'expert systems', and they are appearing in many specific task domains. There are, for example, banking systems which hold and apply the rules by which applications for loans are assessed. A bank employee can refer a customer's application for a loan to the computer system which may accept or reject the application. Dr Alison Hill in the telemedicine example makes use of a modern form of a system called MYCIN, pioneered by Buchanan and Shortliffe (1984), which stores the symptoms of a wide variety of diseases and can offer medical diagnosis when the patient's symptoms are entered.

When computers control work processes and make decisions, the role of the human in the work system can be problematic. The increasing use of computers is raising new issues about 'allocation of function', which duties in a work system should be given to human beings and which to technology. What happens in human–computer partnerships when the human has little to do, when the decisions taken by the machine prove to be wrong, or when the computer system breaks down? Can the human override the 'expert'? Such an issue was worrying Dr Alison Hill and her colleague. They did not know how the computer used the information they had provided to make its diagnosis and how far they could trust the conclusion it had reached.

The use of machine intelligence has made greatest progress in process control, and Bainbridge (1987) has identified a number of 'ironies' of the automation that has been introduced. These systems are employed to replace unreliable human operators, but one irony is that people are asked to monitor the systems and intercede if there are problems. Under these conditions controllers are not actively involved in the work process for long periods, and another irony is that they tend to lose their skill and their awareness of the situation. As a result, as was shown in the investigation of the accident at the Three Mile Island Nuclear Power Station in the USA, operators may be unable to diagnose problems quickly and take effective action.

Weizenbaum (1976) points out that, when a person works closely with a machine, it is the human who is held responsible for errors and disasters rather than his or her machine even when the machine is regarded as the 'expert' part of the relationship. Since humans remain responsible, we need forms of human–machine partnerships which put the human in a supervisory role and have procedures to sustain and develop the skill, knowledge and situational awareness of the human. This can be done, for example, by 'dynamic allocation of function' or 'adaptive automation' (Parasuraman, 2000), so that the human can transfer control to and from the machine quickly and easily (see also Chapter 2). The human being in this situation has to be able to judge the knowledge and competence of the machine partner, and it can be very difficult to know the assumptions on which the machine is operating. An approach being used in the design of expert systems is to provide interrogation facilities, so that the human operator can ask the machine for the rationale behind any recommendation. This is an attempt to reproduce the conversation we might have with another human being who is offering us advice. An interrogation facility of this kind might have helped Dr Alison Hill in the scenario presented earlier.

COMPUTER-SUPPORTED CO-OPERATIVE WORK

As human–computer interaction has advanced, there has been greater recognition that people undertake many tasks by working together and that they need computer systems which support co-operative activities. This field of study has become known as Computer Supported Co-operative Work (CSCW) (Baecker, 1993; Olson, Card, Landauer, Olson, Malone and Leggett, 1993). A major concern in CSCW is the design of systems which enable people to communicate with one another.

A basic distinction is between synchronous and asynchronous communications. Synchronous communications occur when two or more people exchange information in 'real time' as in a meeting or a telephone conversation. Asynchronous communication occurs when there is a delay between sending a message, it being received, and a response being sent. Traditionally letter writing has been a very familiar form of asynchronous communication. The new technologies have provided novel forms of both kinds of communication. The explosive growth of e-mail shows the enormous potential for many business and personal purposes of a form of communication which is asynchronous but which can be very fast, easy to use and potentially global in its reach. By contrast, synchronous communications mediated by the technology have developed less quickly. For example, the growth in use of real-time teleconferencing, such as that used by Vera Matthews and her colleagues in the virtual group scenario, has not been so dramatic.

To understand what forms of communication are required by people who need to co-operate, CSCW researchers have undertaken studies of group behaviour at work. Although much is already known about working in teams (see Chapter 13), CSCW researchers have in particular focused on the use of information amongst group members. In their studies many CSCW researchers have used 'ethnographic' methods (Suchman, 1987), which are based on the approach of social anthropologists and entail intensive and lengthy observation of the group at work. Ethnographers then construct explanations of group behaviour by reference to the shared cultural norms, values, procedures and language of the community in question.

An illustration of this kind of study is Hutchins's (1995) investigation of the way the pilot and crew on board ship and the port staff on shore worked together to bring ships through difficult and busy shipping channels. No individual has all the knowledge and information necessary to accomplish the task, and Hutchins describes it as an example of 'distributed cognition', in which success depends on timely and accurate exchange of information. When the team members are physically dispersed, the computer and telecommunication systems have to permit the exchange of appropriate information and to represent that information conveniently and explicitly in order to provide 'external memories' for those engaged in the task.

People in different locations are increasingly working together as a team. The nomadic worker, Jeff Smith, and the virtual group member, Vera Matthews, in the example scenarios are both engaged in work at a distance from their colleagues and are dependent upon the technology to enable them to communicate effectively. A major research goal has been to construct systems that enable group members to relate to 'virtual' colleagues as effectively as they can to people in a 'face-to-face' group. One approach has been to use video-conferencing to enable team members to see one another and sustain a sense of 'tele-presence'. This might, for example, permit non-verbal communications, through facial expressions, head positions and so on. This is important in interpersonal or intergroup co-operation, because it may indicate people's emotional states and provide a context for understanding spoken or written communications. However, despite many attempts, it remains difficult to achieve good rapport with colleagues when using video-telephony. Furthermore, research studies show that people working together spend little time looking at one another and more time jointly considering 'work objects', such as documents, drawings, charts, etc., which they need to complete their collective task. As a result, systems are being developed to assist collaborative working through the co-authoring of documents and joint design work, in which participants can take it in turn to work on the shared work objects (Kaufer, Neuwirth, Chandhok and Morris, 1995).

The development of CSCW systems involves many technical challenges, but it is also becoming evident that these systems need to be carefully mapped onto the social processes in an organization if they are to be acceptable and useful. The new system may, for example, shift the balance of power and influence in a working group. Eason (1996) described a working group in the electricity industry for which a new system had been developed. Calls for domestic electricity services such as cooker repairs were received by a telephone operator, who passed them to a depot foreman who allocated them to a team of electricians. In order to speed up the process, a computer system was introduced which enabled the operator to send details of the job directly to an electrician's van. In consequence, the telephone operators became the job allocators, the foremen did not know what work staff were doing, and electricians returning to their van from a job found they had been allocated new work. This process robbed the electricians and the foremen of any control over their work schedules and did not allow them to use their local knowledge to plan work. After a trial period, the system was removed.

VIRTUAL ORGANIZATIONS

A common theme in the emerging forms of work practice described at the beginning of this chapter is that work is becoming more 'virtual'; people increasingly engage with work objects and with one another through their computer systems. Jeff works from his car, Alison deals with patients through a computer screen, Vera works with colleagues around the world by using a video-conferencing system, and Jean in the call centre serves customers on the telephone by dealing with their requests through her computer system. These developments have led some commentators to conclude that we are in the process of a major revolution, which will produce virtual organizations and indeed a virtual society. It would, for example, be a paperless society with virtual libraries, because all communications and books would be electronic. Organizations would not need large premises, because they would become 'virtual' as staff work from home or on the move.

Studies are being made of these movements towards a virtual world and are beginning to show what happens. Many teaching programmes are now, for example, offered as distance learning. This is very convenient for students who want to study at home, but research shows people often miss the contact with tutors and with fellow students that is available in face-to-face teaching (Crook, 1994). Teleworking has grown in popularity, but people who work from home can feel isolated and can lose the informal, social contact with colleagues which enables them to share in the life of the work community (Felstead, 1999). Typically, staff who work from home become detached from the organization and become sub-contractors rather than employees. Organizations are also using technology to 'outsource' much of their work. This can include, for example, 'off-shore working'. Companies in developed countries which undertake large quantities of routine data-processing, for example insurance companies, find they can send bulk files to a developing country where the work can be done much more cheaply. Software development can also be undertaken in this way. India, for example, has a thriving community of information technology professionals undertaking software development for companies in the developed nations.

There are many human consequences of these forms of working. Companies who encourage staff to work from home or to be nomadic can find it difficult to sustain a sense of corporate identity and staff loyalty. Studies of groups that have the facilities to be virtual show that face-to-face meetings remain common. Turner (1999), for example, found that design teams working at different sites still travelled long distances to meetings, although they had access to video-conferencing facilities. These technologies appear most effective when group members have already met one another face-to-face, and have developed a degree of shared understanding that can sustain rapport when they are limited to telecommunication channels of interaction.

The general finding that technology cannot meet all the psychological and organizational needs of people at work means that progress towards the virtual society is rather piecemeal. An example is the development of electronic journals. If virtual libraries are to replace physical libraries, the scientific writing and scholarship which is currently available in scientific and professional journals will have to be offered electronically. There are now many services which offer electronic full text versions of journal articles. Eason, Yu and Harker (2000) report an evaluation of the use of an electronic service by 3000 users. They found that users valued the service because it enabled them to locate and display articles on their own computers. However, when they wanted to study an article in detail the common response was to print it. As Dillon (1994) has reported, it is difficult to study extensive text on a screen. Paper is a much more flexible and usable medium for this purpose.

Evidence of this kind suggests that we are not actually in the middle of a revolution in which virtual forms of working are replacing traditional forms. We are seeing instead a process in which virtual forms are beginning to complement traditional forms of work (Woolgar, 1998). As experience of virtual work grows, we are finding ways of blending traditional and virtual forms of work practice to make effective use of the different contributions they can make.

HUMAN-CENTRED DESIGN PROCESSES

The new information and communication technologies are very powerful, but they do not have inevitable and specific effects on the people that use them. The same technology can be used in many different ways, so that its impact on work practice can take several forms. As this chapter has illustrated, the technology can support the automation of work processes, the control of worker productivity, the co-operation of people who are widely dispersed, people working from home, and so on. From the perspective of the person at work, these developments may be enriching and empowering. In some cases, however, the outcome from use of the same technology may be tightly controlled environments with negative implications for long-term health and well-being.

The flexibility of this technology means that there are many decisions to be made when a new system is designed and implemented in an organization. Studies of the design process have found that these decisions are usually dominated by economic and technical considerations. The typical aim is to create a technical system which will help the organization be more cost effective. Relatively little attention is paid to the human and organizational issues associated with new forms of work practice (Docherty and King, 1998; Clegg, Older-Gray and Waterson, 2000). As a consequence, opportunities to design jobs and work organizations for effective human performance and well-being may be missed.

There have been many initiatives to render the design process more human-centred. These approaches focus on the people who will use the new technology and seek to develop work practices which match their needs, characteristics and tasks in the organizational setting. Three different forms of user-centred design exist:

● Usability Engineering – This approach focuses on the creation of technical systems which offer effective support for tasks and are usable by the kind of staff who undertake these tasks. In this approach, for example, prototype systems are tested by the relevant users, be they secretaries, architects, salesmen or doctors, to check that they are suitable, safe and usable in their context of use. The user-centred design processes necessary for these purposes are now being enshrined in international standards (Harker, 1995).

● Participative Design – The dominant consideration in this approach is that the people who will be affected by the new system should have an effective role in the decision-making process. Greenbaum and Kyng (1991), for example, provide case studies in which groups of users identified the technical systems they needed and were involved in the creation of the new work practices within which they work.

● Socio-technical Systems Design – This approach recognizes that it is not just a technical system that is being developed but a new social structure. The agenda for the design process is therefore the creation of a socio-technical system capable of integrating human and technical resources in the fulfilment of human and organizational objectives (Mumford, 1987; Eason, 1988; Weisbord, 1990) (see also Chapter 11).

The emergence of human-centred design approaches offers a route by which the research results discussed in this chapter can be applied. The dominant approach to design is still based upon economic and technical criteria, and the likelihood is that systems will continue to be implemented which do not meet the needs of people at work. However, as human-centred approaches are more widely employed, the implementation of systems which support effective human performance and well-being should also become more widespread.

SUMMARY

The adoption of information and communication technologies has wide implications for work practice. Sophisticated and usable forms of these technologies are now widely available and they have become the major work tools of many workers. New forms of work practice are emerging in which the technologies enable people to work in more virtual ways. Research has shown how these technologies can be used to enhance human effectiveness and well-being at work and to facilitate co-operation between people engaged in collaborative activities. It has also shown that the opposite effects are quite common. The application of these technologies in organizations is dominated by economic and technical criteria, and the result is often a system that is difficult to use, which de-skills the person at work and makes co-operative work more difficult. The development of human-centred approaches to design, however, provides an opportunity to create systems and procedures which better meet the psychological needs of people at work.

FURTHER READING

A good text for human–computer interaction is by Preece, Rogers, Sharp, Benyon, Holland and Carey (1994), and a source book by leading researchers and practitioners is the *Handbook of Human–Computer Interaction* edited by Helander, Landauer and Prabhu (1997). Issues of human–computer interaction on the internet are discussed by Nielsen (2000) (*http://www.useit.com*). The physical ergonomics of computer technology and related health hazard issues are examined by Grandjean (1986). Job design and organizational behaviour issues are covered in *Organizational Behaviour* by Buchanan and Huczynski (1985), and a good introduction to computer supported co-operative work is by Baecker (1993). Human-centred approaches to the development and implementation of new systems are described by Winograd and Flores (1986) and Eason (1988).

REFERENCES

Baecker, R. M. (1993). *Readings in Groupware and Computer-Supported Co-operative Work*. San Mateo CA: Morgan Kaufman.

Bainbridge, L. (1987). The ironies of automation. In J. Rasmussen, K. Duncan and J. Leplat (eds.), *New Technology and Human Error*, pp. 276–83. Chichester: Wiley.

Blackler, F. H. M. and Brown, C. A. (1980). Job design and social change: Case studies at Volvo. In K. D. Duncan, M. M. Gruneberg and D. Wallis (eds.), *Changes in Working Life*, pp. 311–28. Chichester: Wiley.

Buchanan, B. G. and Shortliffe, E. H. (1984). *Rule-Based Expert Systems*. Reading, Mass.: Addison-Wesley.

Buchanan, D. A. and Boddy, D. (1983). Advanced technology and the quality of working life: The effects of computerised controls on biscuit-making operators. *Journal of Occupational Psychology*, 56, 109–19.

Buchanan, D. A. and Huczynski, A. A. (1985). *Organizational Behaviour*. London: Prentice-Hall.

Canfield-Smith, D., Irby, C., Kimball, R. and Verplank, B. (1992). Designing the STAR user interface. *Byte Magazine*, April, 210–23.

Card, S. K. (1982). User perceptual mechanisms in the search of computer command menus. *Proceedings of Human Factors in Computer Systems*, pp. 190–96. Gaithersburg, SIGCHI.

Clegg, C. S., Older-Gray, M. T. and Waterson, P. E. (2000). The charge of the 'Byte Brigade' and a socio-technical response. *International Journal of Human Computer Systems*, 52, 235–51.

Crook, C. K. (1994). *Computers and the Collaborative Experience of Learning*. London: Routledge.

Dillon, A. (1994). *Designing Usable Electronic Text*. London: Taylor and Francis.

Docherty, N. F. and King, M. (1998). The consideration of organizational issues during the systems development process: An empirical analysis. *Behaviour and Information Technology*, 17, 41–51.

Downing, H. (1980). Word processors and the oppression of women. In T. Forester (ed.), *The Microelectronics Revolution*. Oxford: Blackwell.

Eason, K. D. (1988). *Information Technology and Organizational Change*. London: Taylor and Francis.

Eason, K. D. (1996). Division of labour and design of systems for computer support for co-operative work. *Journal of Information Technology*, 11, 39–50.

Eason, K. D., Yu, L. and Harker, S. D. P. (2000). The use and usefulness of functions in electronic journals. The experience of the SuperJournal Project. *Program*, 34, 1–28.

Felstead, A. (1999). *In Work, at Home: Towards an Understanding of Homeworking*. London: Routledge.

Galer, M. D., Harker, S. D. P. and Ziegler, J. (1992). *Methods and Tools in User-Centred Design for Information Technology*. Amsterdam: North Holland.

Grandjean, E. (1986). *Ergonomics in Computerised Offices*. London: Taylor and Francis.

Greenbaum, J. and Kyng, M. (eds.) (1991). *Design of Work: Co-operative Design of Computer Systems*. Hillsdale, NJ: Erlbaum.

Hagberg, M. (1996). Neck and arm disorders. *British Medical Journal*, 313, 419–22.

Harker, S. D. P. (1995). The development of ergonomics standards for software. *Applied Ergonomics*, 26, 275–9.

Helander, M. G., Landauer, T. K. and Prabhu, P. V. (eds.) (1997). *Handbook of Human Computer Interaction*. Amsterdam: Elsevier.

Hutchins, E. (1995). *Cognition in the Wild*. Cambridge, Mass.: MIT Press.

Kaufer, D. S., Neuwirth, C. M., Chandhok, R. and Morris, J. (1995). Accommodating mixed sensory modal preferences in collaborative writing systems. *Computer Supported Collaborative Work*, 3, 271–95.

Mumford, E. (1987). Socio-technical systems design: Evolving theory and practice. In G. Bjerknes, P. Ehn and M. Kyng (eds.), *Computers and Democracy*, 1, pp. 59–77. Aldershot: Avebury.

Newell, A. F. (1993). Interfaces for the ordinary and beyond. *IEEE Software*, 10 (5), 76–8.

Nielsen, J. (2000). *Designing Web Usability: The Practice of Simplicity*. Indianapolis New Riders: (*http://www.useit.com/*).

Norman, D. A. (1988). *The Psychology of Everyday Things*. New York: Basic Books.

Noyes, J. M. (1998). QWERTY – the immortal keyboard. *Computing and Control Engineering Journal*, 9, 117–22.

Olson, J. S., Card, S., Landauer, T., Olson, G. M., Malone, T. and Leggett, J. (1993). Computer-supported co-operative work: Research issues for the 90s. *Behaviour and Information Technology*, 12, 115–29.

Parasuraman, R. (2000). Designing automation for human use: Empirical studies and quantitative models. *Ergonomics*, 43, 931–51.

Petrie, H., Johnson, V., Strothotte, T., Michel, R., Raab, A. and Reichert, L. (1997). User-centred design in the development of a navigational aid for blind travellers. In *INTERACT '97*, pp. 220–27. London: Chapman and Hall.

Preece, J., Rogers, Y., Sharp, H., Benyon, D., Holland, S. and Carey, T. (1994). *Human Computer Interaction*. Wokingham: Addison Wesley.

Roe, D. and Wilpon, J. (eds.) (1994). *Voice Communications between Humans and Machines*. Washington, DC: National Academy Press.

Shneiderman, B. (1992). *Designing the User Interface: Strategies for Effective Human–Computer Interaction*. Reading, Mass.: Addison-Wesley.

Suchman, L. (1987). *Plans and Situated Actions: The Problem of Human–Machine Communication*. Cambridge: Cambridge University Press.

Toffler, A. (1980). *The Third Wave*. London: Collins.

Turner, S. (1999). *Towards Computer Supported Co-operative Design*. PhD thesis, Open University.

Weisbord, M. R. (1990). *Productive Workplaces: Organising and Managing for Dignity, Meaning and Community*. Oxford: Jossey-Bass.

Weizenbaum, J. (1976). *Computer Power and Human Reason*. San Francisco, CA: W. H. Freeman.

Winograd, T. and Flores, F. (1986). *Understanding Computers and Cognition: A New Foundation for Design*. Norwood, NJ: Ablex.

Woolgar, S. (1998). A new theory of innovation. *Prometheus, 16*, 441–53, (*http:// www.virtualsociety.sbs.ox.ac.uk*).

Zhai, S., Smith, B. A. and Selker, T. (1997). Improving browsing performance: A study of four input devices for scrolling and pointing tasks. In S. Howard, J. Hammond and G. Lindgaard (eds.), *Human–Computer Interaction: INTERACT '97*, pp. 286–93. London: Chapman and Hall.

5 | Personnel Selection and Assessment

*Ivan Robertson, Dave Bartram and
Militza Callinan*

This chapter is concerned with the process of choosing between people based on their potential to successfully perform a particular job role in a particular organization. Making good personnel selection decisions is important for employing organizations, because good decisions of that kind can provide significant improvements in productivity and minimize the direct costs of training and replacements due to unwanted staff turnover.

In fact the monetary value of one standard deviation in performance of workers has been estimated to be at least 40 per cent of the mean salary for the job. So, if the average salary for a job is £30,000, an improvement of one standard deviation in performance obtained by selecting more effective people will benefit the organization by at least £12,000 per person per year. Direct benefits have also been demonstrated at the organizational level. In a longitudinal study of British manufacturing firms, human resource practices (central to which are selection and assessment) accounted for 19 per cent of the variation in profitability between the companies (Patterson, West, Lawthom and Nickell, 1997) (see Chapter 14 for further details).

There are also less direct costs to poor selection. In a commercial situation, an organization may risk losing customers to its competitors by allowing them to build a workforce of more able employees who collectively provide a superior product or service. Organizations that are concerned with their longer-term flexibility and ability to adapt to future market conditions may use selection in a proactive, strategic way by thinking beyond current job roles. They might predict the kinds of skills and characteristics that employees will need to possess to meet future demands as well as those currently required, and select employees on that basis. The cost of not doing this may be an inability to respond to the market and, at the extreme, the decline of the organization. In brief, the role of personnel selection in an organization needs to be developed in relation to the strategy and goals of that organization.

Personnel selection is not driven by financial goals alone. In some situations the effectiveness of the organization also depends on additional criteria of at least equal importance to financial efficiency. Public service organizations like the police force and the civil service need to ensure that their workforce is representative of the population at large. In these cases, a further goal of personnel selection will be to ensure that qualified candidates are attracted and hired from all social and ethnic groups in the population. Finally, good personnel selection decisions are also very important for individual recruits. Work is a central part of many people's lives, and a lack of fit between a person's abilities and interests and the requirements of the job can be upsetting and stressful.

Almost everyone has experience of being a candidate for a job. Although some form of assessment procedure is always used when people join organizations, it is also quite common for procedures such as interviews or psychological tests to be used to evaluate existing members of staff for promotion or placement in a different role. Many large organizations also use assessment procedures in a more developmental fashion, to provide feedback and guidance to assist individuals in their career development. This chapter is concerned particularly with the use of assessment methods for selection or placement purposes, rather than for personal development.

Personnel selection and assessment involve a number of stages. Attracting an adequate number of suitable job applicants is the first step and will ultimately affect the quality of hiring decisions. Potential applicants must be made aware of the job and encouraged to apply for it. This means providing information about the vacancy in the right places and in the right manner to reach the kinds of potential applicants that the organization wants to see. Recruiting applicants is a substantial area of research in itself, and the interested reader is directed to the comprehensive review of the topic conducted by Breaugh and Starke (2000).

Once a pool of applicants has been gathered, assuming there are many more applicants than jobs, a sifting procedure may be used to 'select out' those people who fail to meet the basic requirements. Traditionally, this second-stage sifting has been required in order to reduce the numbers of applicants to a practical size for the next, more formal and more resource-intensive stage, managed assessment. This third stage is referred to here as 'managed' because there is much tighter control over the assessment processes used. Tests are supervised and applicants' credentials are closely inspected and checked. Procedures such as interviews, psychometric tests and assessment centres are used to 'select in' those applicants with the best potential for success in the job.

These are the stages of selection that involve candidates and so are probably familiar to anyone who has applied for a job. But before attracting and assessing potential candidates, there is some fundamental decision-making to be done that underlies and guides the selection process. Equally, once hiring decisions have been made and the new recruits have joined the organization, some evaluation of those decisions must be made to ensure that they are accurate, that the people who are being chosen are in fact being successful. Well-established procedures exist for the effective design and evaluation of personnel selection procedures. The process of selection, from planning to assessing applicants to making and validating hiring decisions, is displayed in Figure 5.1. Each of the major components of the process will be covered in this chapter, beginning with the recruiter's first task, job analysis. We will work through the traditional selection process, later discussing the impact that the internet has had on personnel selection and finally looking at some current research issues in the field.

JOB ANALYSIS

The conventional design process begins with a detailed examination of the job for which selection decisions are to be taken. Algera and Greuter (1998) describe job analysis as the 'glue' of the selection process. It serves as a guide for the activities that follow, by specifying the nature of the job that is to be done and the characteristics for which applicants are to be assessed. The job analysis also forms the basis of the job description which will be used by the organization internally and externally, as a guide for communication between the organization and potential applicants.

It is worth noting an important assumption underlying most job analysis. Very simply, the demands of the job are identified in order that

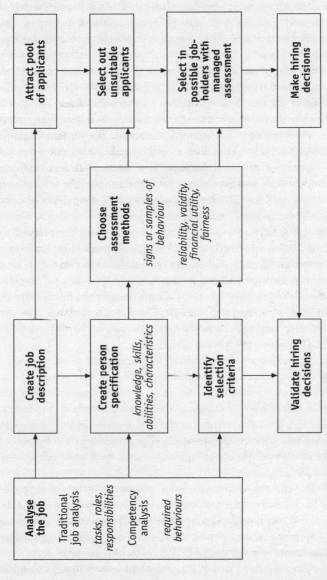

Fig. 5.1 *The personnel selection and assessment process*

individuals can be assessed for their potential to meet those demands. This process presumes, at least implicitly, that a largely unchanging set of job demands exists and is stable across a reasonable period of time. But in many practical settings a job may not yet exist, or may be expected to change over time.

It is possible to make allowances for the dynamic nature of some jobs by including current and anticipated future tasks in the initial description of the job. For instance, an organization may feel that to stay ahead of its competitors in the future it will need to be more proactive in communicating with its customers. For example, although the current customer service employees only respond to incoming queries, in future they will be asked to call customers 'cold' as well, which may demand different and additional skills and approaches. Such projections can be accommodated, but the need for fixed points of reference is nevertheless a potential limitation to the conventional job analysis process.

Smith and Robertson (1993) identify nine different methods of job analysis, including structured questionnaires and checklists, interviews, diaries, observation, participation and critical incidents (Flanagan, 1954). The common feature of all the methods is that they seek to provide a clear view of the principal job components, usually the tasks, roles and responsibilities associated with the role. This job description is then used as a basis for identifying the characteristics that successful job incumbents will need to display – the 'person specification'.

The step from job analysis to person specification is an integral part of the traditional approach to personnel selection, but there is no foolproof way of translating knowledge of the job into knowledge of the attributes that lead to success in the job. Some job analysis methods produce an indication of the personal attributes that are suggested by the job analysis, but linking job features with personal requirements in a job-holder is conducted with a mixture of scientifically established knowledge, theory and personal judgement.

There is an alternative approach to identifying and using job characteristics as the basis for selection that has become popular within many organizations. This approach can reduce some of the problems of translating job requirements into person characteristics. 'Competency analysis' focuses on identifying the desirable and essential behaviours required to perform a job, compared to the tasks, roles and responsibilities identified by traditional job analysis. The two approaches are essentially ways of looking at the same thing and can complement each other, as they have different areas of strength and weakness (Shippmann, Ash, Battista, Carr, Eyde, Hesketh, Kehoe, Pearlman, Prien and Sanchez, 2000).

Competencies can be described as sets of behaviours that are instrumental in the delivery of desired results and outcomes (Bartram, Robertson and Callinan, 2002). For example, 'accepting new ideas' is a competency that involves supporting change initiatives, changing one's own views appropriately when presented with new ideas, etc. These are aspects of competency that are assessable through observation of behaviour. Competencies are not the underlying personal attributes (such as 'flexibility' or 'adaptability') that allow a person to exhibit the behaviours, and neither are they the results or outcomes. This focus on observable behaviour is seen by many as a major benefit of using the competency approach because, defined in this way, what organizations want and expect from applicants and employees can be more easily and clearly communicated and assessed.

Although popular, Shippmann *et al.* (2000) show that there is considerable confusion about what competencies are considered to be and how they should be measured. Competency-based assessment has suffered in the past from being used and developed by a wide range of practitioners, many of whom have no training in psychological measurement. But there is also evidence of increasing rigour in the competency approach. The work of Tett, Guterman, Bleir and Murphy (2000) and Kurz and Bartram (2002) has shown that it is possible to provide a comprehensive and well-articulated description of what competencies are and the domain they cover.

Furthermore, this description can usefully be provided either in broad terms as organizational core competencies or in more detail as job-specific competencies, depending on the nature of the application. Traditional work-oriented job analysis has focused narrowly on job characteristics: activities, tasks, duties and responsibilities. While this approach has been useful for defining the skills needed to perform many blue-collar jobs, it has been less successful in defining what is required for someone to be successful as a manager. Task-based job analyses tend to provide only part of the picture for higher-level jobs and also tend to miss the person-characteristics that enable us to generalize about the transfer of competence from one job or position to another. Person-oriented approaches to job analysis, however, target differences between individuals. These approaches, which complement the work-oriented analyses, have evolved into the competency-based approaches that are in widespread use today. The competency approach has been very successful in building models that lay the foundations for organization-wide integrated human resources applications. In providing a common language that can be used at the individual, team and organizational levels, competencies make it easier for organizations to link their strategic business requirements to the behaviour of individual employees.

Consideration of the links between personnel selection and the nature of the organization itself generates a number of very important areas for examination, such as the strategic goals of the organization, its stage of development and the extent to which labour market conditions should be integrated with human resource management practice (see Snow and Snell, 1993).

Whichever method or combination of methods is used, the output of this analysis stage will be some description of the job and a related person specification. Now that the candidate characteristics thought to be desirable have been identified, attention may be given to the methods that might be used to assess candidates. But first it is important to identify the criteria by which the success or otherwise of the applicants hired, and consequently the whole selection and assessment process, will be evaluated. The criteria chosen may lead to greater emphasis being placed on some aspects of the job and person description than on others.

JOB SUCCESS CRITERIA

The capacity to conduct the tasks of a job to a high standard is not the only ingredient in overall job success. A consistent person who performs to a modest standard and is rarely absent from work may sometimes be more useful to an organization than a person who is capable of out-standing performance but is given to frequent bouts of unexplained and unpredictably poor performance. Such contrasting types of be-haviour may be considered acceptable for sporting personalities and entertainers. But in a telephone call centre struggling with high staff turnover, the priority of personnel selection is likely to be hiring workers who are reliable and consistent. This is because answering promptly all the customers who call may be more important in the short term than providing an excellent service to some and leaving others with no assistance at all.

This example illustrates how different circumstances will often lead to emphasis being placed on different aspects of an employee's overall performance. In the call centre example, once staff turnover is no longer at damaging levels, managers may begin to concentrate on improving the quality of employees' interactions with customers, and new recruits will be assessed against that current priority. So the emphasis of selection will move from seeking very reliable people to those who also have excellent social skills. There are several different performance criteria that might be important in any particular setting, and it is not always clear which one should receive primary attention.

The position is further complicated by the existence of different and interrelated criteria of job performance. The need for one criterion may not be compatible with the need for another. A small company with modest growth potential may find it difficult to recruit high-performing graduate trainees and hold on to them for much longer than two to three years, indicating a tension between the two different criteria of proficiency and tenure.

Some of the major types of criteria that might need to be considered are outlined in Figure 5.2. Criterion variables might be actual data about production, such as quantity and quality of work, judgemental data such as managers' ratings of job performance, or personnel data such as attendance records. Criteria can also represent different levels of functioning, from the individual to the organization. Success can be measured in relation to people's day-to-day behaviour, their results and those of a work group, and ultimately in terms of contribution to the goals of the organization. In general, the more removed from an individual's behaviour is the job success criterion, the more consideration must be given to factors outside the person's control that may have influenced the outcome.

Regardless of the type or level of criteria chosen, the extent to which those factors can be measured accurately is of primary importance. This is because personnel selection is essentially an attempt to predict job success. Any checking on how successful this attempt has been (a process of 'validation') requires that job success is measured accurately. A criterion variable that is not measured accurately is impossible to predict

Fig. 5.2 *Criteria of job success*

Performance/proficiency: *effectiveness in conducting work tasks.*
This might be examined by obtaining performance ratings from supervisors, by observing work outputs, or by a variety of other means.

Attendance: *reliable attendance at normal work times.*
This may be particularly important in settings where absence is a problem for the organization.

Tenure: *length of stay in the job.*
Long tenure is not always a target when personnel selection schemes are developed. There are many positions where some staff turnover is expected, or even desirable.

Progression: *progress through relevant grades in the organization's hierarchy.*
Some personnel selection or assessment schemes are specifically designed to identify 'high fliers'.

Training Performance: *effectiveness in assimilating and benefiting from training provided by the organization.*
New recruits in many jobs require training. Progress in training gives an early indication of suitability.

---

accurately. For example, it would be impossible to work out how to predict language skills from factors such as number of years' residence in a country if no accurate measure of language proficiency was available.

The choice of criteria will determine the conclusions drawn about the job holder's success and so about the quality of the hiring decisions. Sometimes very different judgements would be made if different criteria were in use. Take the example of a bus driver who drives his or her bus recklessly in order to arrive at bus stops exactly on time. If time-keeping is the only criterion used by the organization to assess the driver's performance, he or she will be considered an excellent performer. However, the reckless driver has had a number of accidents, and many customers, worried by the driver's behaviour, now use another bus company. If passenger numbers and accidents were also used as criteria for job success, the driver's performance and the decision to hire him or her would be seen somewhat differently.

Importantly, in relation to the job and person descriptions that form the basis of the selection procedure, the criteria used to evaluate job-holders' success will help to determine the qualities that are to be looked for in candidates. Reliability and agreeableness may be important if long-term tenure is the dominant criterion, whereas creativity and high analytical ability may be important if outstanding job performance is the dominant criterion.

How far have we got in the process of personnel selection and assessment? Job analysis has identified the components of the job on offer and formed the basis for the creation of a person specification outlining the main skills and characteristics to look for in candidates. The selection criteria, by which job holders and hiring decisions will be evaluated, have been identified. It is therefore known how job success will be measured, and some estimate can be made about which of the characteristics that we are looking for are of greater priority. These measures of job success will also be used later to validate the hiring decisions made. The next stage is to choose which methods will be used to assess candidates' potential. Different assessment methods measure different underlying attributes. The following section describes the kinds of attributes and qualities that can be measured which are useful in choosing between people for a particular job.

INDIVIDUAL DIFFERENCES AND PERSONNEL SELECTION PROCEDURES

It is clear from what has been covered so far that it is crucial to have a good understanding of the job and organizational setting within which the person will work. Despite this, the principal focus of attention at the personnel selection stage is on the person and his or her attributes. Everyday experience suggests that all people are not equally suited to all jobs.

The cornerstone of personnel selection and assessment is the demonstrated existence of measurable psychological differences between people that are of importance in determining job success. It is known from research into the psychology of individual differences that people differ from each other in stable and noticeable ways. Some differences and their links with job performance criteria are easy to identify, at a fairly general level. For example, basic numerical skills are needed for shop assistants, and manual dexterity is important for a plastic surgeon. Other features are less straightforward: is it important for a salesperson to be outgoing? What role does emotional stability play in the creative arts?

For most jobs and people it is quite difficult to be certain about the precise mix of psychological characteristics that are important for success. Ideally, psychologists would be able to establish a definitive blueprint of an 'ideal type' of person who will be successful in a particular job. But several factors mean that selection decision-making is not that easy. Sometimes people with quite different characteristics can perform equally well. Also, for many jobs, there are several factors that combine to produce effective performance. Therefore, personnel selection seeks to identify the common characteristics of those people who perform well, even though those individuals may be very different in other ways. Successful personnel selection achieves results by isolating the key components of effective performance and ensuring that these are assessed at the selection stage.

The goal of much personnel selection research has been to establish specific links between individual difference variables and job success. For instance, studies have explored relationships between intelligence and success in a wide range of occupational areas. Research has also investigated the links between personality variables and job success and between the biographical history of candidates and job-related criteria.

In broad terms, the most important individual difference characteristics for personnel selection are cognitive ability (Carroll, 1993) and personality (Costa and McCrae, 1992, Digman, 1990). Understanding cognitive ability has been one of the central concerns of psychologists since early last century, and the immense attention devoted to the issue by researchers has produced a reasonable consensus concerning the structure and measurement of cognitive abilities. The statistical technique of factor analysis is a procedure for identifying underlying factors that help to explain the inter-correlations observed between different variables. In studies conducted over a number of years, factor analyses have revealed that the pattern of correlations between people's scores on different ability tests is consistent with underlying factors of both general ability and specific abilities, ordered in a hierarchical pattern.

The hierarchical pattern shown in Figure 5.3 for the structure and components of cognitive ability is accepted in some form or other by the vast majority of individual difference psychologists. Nevertheless, particular researchers may disagree about the relative status of the components in the hierarchy, affording more or less generality to one or other of the factors. A full account of alternative theories about the structure of intelligence can be found in Sternberg (2000). The model discussed here is the three-stratum theory of Carroll (1993).

The most general factor, at the top of the hierarchy, is general intelligence, 'g'. General intelligence, or general mental ability, indicates a person's capacity for the processing, storage and retrieval of information. It is statistically related to all of the lower-order factors. The next level in the hierarchy consists of eight facets, including the major facets of 'g': fluid and crystallized intelligence. Fluid intelligence relates to abstract reasoning abilities such as the ability to perceive relations amongst stimuli; it is not experience-based and peaks in early adulthood after which time it declines. Crystallized intelligence relates to the skills and knowledge acquired through learning and experience, such as in vocabulary and general knowledge. This ability is maintained throughout the life span, only showing decline in very old age. The lowest stratum in the hierarchy includes a larger number of more specific aspects of intelligence, such as mathematical reasoning and lexical knowledge.

The subject of human 'intelligence' has stimulated some interesting developments in individual difference research in recent years. Hands-on experience and observation have led some researchers and managers to the conclusion that in work situations, the most successful individuals have some basic abilities, not picked up by traditional measures, that nonetheless represent fundamental aspects of human intelligence.

'Practical intelligence' is one of these hypothesized abilities (Wagner, 2000). There is more than one definition of practical intelligence. The central point, however, is that it relates to problem-solving ability in the real world, rather than in abstract contexts. Unlike the kinds of problems posed in traditional intelligence tests, real world problems are characterized as: ambiguous rather than well defined; lacking all the information required for a solution; having more than one correct answer; having more than one method for reaching a correct answer; and requiring the use of prior experience.

Sternberg (1997) has investigated one aspect of practical intelligence, referred to as tacit knowledge. Tacit knowledge is procedural, about knowing what to do and when to do it in order to succeed in a particular endeavour. A person may have tacit knowledge about organizing and motivating himself or herself, about how to get along with others, and about getting a particular task done. Such knowledge is not formally

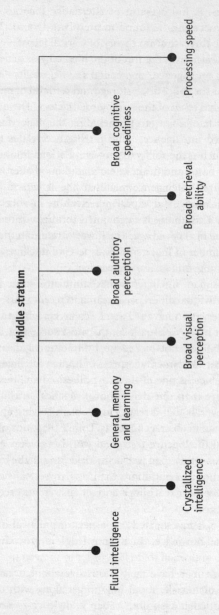

Fig. 5.3 *Carroll's (1993) three-stratum structure of cognitive ability*

taught and is often not even verbalized. Research using questionnaire measures of tacit knowledge for different jobs has shown them to be correlated between .3 and .4 with job performance, but show only very small positive correlations with traditional measures of intelligence (Sternberg, 1997). The findings suggest that tacit knowledge is both an important factor in job success and distinct from general cognitive ability.

Possibly the most well-known example of the intelligence concepts receiving attention has been termed 'emotional intelligence' (Mayer, Salovey and Caruso, 2000). A very general description of emotional intelligence would be that it refers to the set of mental abilities underlying accuracy in the perception, understanding and management of emotion (see also Chapter 9). It has been claimed that people with high levels of emotional intelligence are more socially effective because they are more able to achieve their goals through managing emotions in themselves and others (Goleman, 1995). This concept has struck a chord with managers in organizations, and emotional intelligence has become a popular term of reference. Much scientific research has been stimulated on the topic, although the knowledge base is not yet established enough to support some of the claims that have been made about the relationship of emotional intelligence to job success. Current research is focused on the distinct but related tasks of establishing some consensus about what emotional intelligence consists of and developing a valid and reliable measure of the construct (Ciarrochi, Chan and Caputi, 2000; Fox and Spector, 2000; Mayer et al., 2000). As noted earlier, accurate measurement of any construct is essential before it can be included in any personnel selection procedure.

Personality is the second individual difference characteristic important for selection purposes. The trait factor-analytic approach (Kline, 1993), has dominated research and practice in the field of personality as well as of mental ability. In both areas, the approach is used to explore underlying interrelationships. In the personality domain, factor analysis is applied to correlations that are found between people's responses to questions about their typical behaviour, usually derived from questionnaires that ask them to agree or disagree with statements relevant to the construct under examination.

In a long programme of research, Eysenck isolated three major underlying factors: extroversion, neuroticism and psychoticism (e.g., Eysenck and Eysenck, 1985). Using similar research methods, Cattell (1965) produced a model incorporating 16 factors. In fact, differences between these models were more to do with preferences for different levels of analysis than with fundamentally different results. A large number of more recent factor-analytic studies have rationalized the position and produced a hierarchical model of personality structure, in which the highest level of generality is described by the five major factors shown in Figure 5.4. This is the so-called 'big five' framework (e.g., Matthews and Deary, 1998).

There is a reasonable degree of consensus amongst personality researchers that the big five factors are adequately comprehensive for describing the major portion of human personality. But when it comes to making specific predictions about how people will behave, research has found that it is often necessary to look below the level of the big five in the hierarchy at the more specific facets of personality of which each broad factor is composed. Consequently, a range of personality inventories exist that allow measurement at both the big five and facet levels (e.g., Costa and McCrae, 1992).

The individual differences discussed so far are stable underlying abilities and predispositions that will be related in some way to a person's behaviour in most, if not all, situations he or she encounters. When ability and personality measures are used in personnel selection as predictors of job success criteria, the prediction is based on 'signs' or indicators of likely behaviour (Wernimont and Campbell, 1968). This is in contrast to the approach of basing predictions on actual 'samples' of that behaviour. In some circumstances, where the job requirements are well defined,

Fig. 5.4 *The big five factors of personality*

Extroversion: the extent to which a person is sociable and outgoing. Extroverts also tend to enjoy excitement and may be aggressive and impulsive.

Neuroticism: the extent to which a person is emotionally unstable. Neurotics are generally tense and anxious with a tendency to worry.

Openness to experience: the extent to which a person is imaginative and flexible, with a positive, open-minded response to new experiences.

Conscientiousness: the extent to which a person is well-organized, planful and concerned about achieveing goals and deadlines.

Agreeableness: the extent to which a person is good-natured, warm and compassionate with others.

---

measures of more specific job or role-related skills, knowledge, abilities and behaviour may be used as the basis of personnel selection decisions.

For instance, the competency approach described earlier seeks to identify and measure individual differences in specific work-related behavioural constructs that can be seen as samples not signs of behaviour. If 'leadership' is identified in the analysis phase as an important behavioural competency for job success, an assessment procedure such as a group exercise might be used to assess candidates on the degree to which they display leadership behaviours. The extreme of the sample approach to prediction is to choose between candidates on the basis of their performance on an actual task or tasks from the job in question. Sometimes, depending on the particular situation, it may be preferable to assess what people actually do rather than what they could or might do. However, there can be practical difficulties with this kind of assessment, and understanding a person's potential to perform may be of more interest to the organization than knowing what he or she can do right now.

Good predictions can be made about a candidate's likely success in a job based on measures of the person characteristics described above. Although generally personnel selection and assessment is focused on evaluating aspects of the person, it is important to understand that a substantial amount of psychological research makes it clear that behaviour is not determined solely by the person. The situation (e.g., a particular work setting) (see Pervin, 1989) will also influence how a person will behave. Situational factors such as the physical environment, the characteristics of the task, the social environment and the culture of the organization will all have some impact on how people act and react (Schneider and Hough, 1995) (see also Chapter 15). Consequently, a person's tendencies to behave in certain ways much of the time can be predicted, but specific aspects of work behaviour will be impossible to predict without adequate knowledge of the situation in which he or she will work.

CHOOSING SELECTION METHODS

Organizations and professional recruiters do have preferences for certain types of selection methods. Interviews are by far the most widely used personnel selection procedure (Newell and Tansley, 2001), but many other methods, including cognitive ability tests and personality inventories, are also widely used. For a personnel selection method to be of any value it needs to provide a basis for distinguishing between candidates and identifying those who are likely to be more successful in the job. The methods need to be chosen with reference also to the characteristics that are to be assessed, and they should satisfy a number of other evaluative criteria. In general the following standards should be applied.

● The information provided should be as accurate as possible.
● Selection methods should provide information about the qualities that have been identified as important for the job.
● Assessments based on the method should be indicative of candidates' likely job success.
● The information about candidates produced by a method (for instance, their test scores) should not be unfairly influenced by characteristics that are not relevant to job success (e.g., their gender or ethnic origin).
● The method should be acceptable to candidates and consistent with the organization's norms and culture.
● The method should be cost-effective.

Each of these standards will be dealt with in the next two sections. The first three items in the list above concern the reliability and validity of the method. These features of personnel selection methods are the evaluative criteria that most personnel psychologists consider to be of prime importance.

VALIDITY AND RELIABILITY

'Reliability' refers to the extent to which a measurement procedure is free from unsystematic error. Various methods are available for assessing the reliability of a measure, including estimates of stability across time (e.g., test–retest reliability) and estimates of internal consistency (e.g., Cronbach's coefficient alpha). For more information see Moser and Schuler (1989). The reliability of a measure is quantified by a reliability coefficient, which gives a direct indication of the proportion of variance in the measure that is free from unsystematic error. Essentially, the reliability of a measure refers to the consistency of the scores given by the measure.

An unreliable measure is like a ruler that changes length in a random fashion: the same object would be measured as of different lengths on different occasions. It is obviously crucial for psychological measurements to be as reliable as possible.

Although a measurement procedure cannot give accurate results if it is unreliable, it is perfectly possible for a measurement procedure to be reliable (i.e., free from random error) but still inadequate as an assessment instrument. The length of a person's hair could be measured with great accuracy, but it would be worthless as an indication of intelligence! On a more realistic level, a test involving answers to questions about behaviour at parties could also be reliable but may not give a good indication of someone's level of extroversion. The extent to which a measurement procedure gives appropriate information about the quality under investigation is referred to as the 'validity' of the measure. Validity may be looked at in a number of ways (see Smith and Robertson, 1993), as illustrated in Figure 5.5.

Both construct validity and criterion-related validity are of major importance for personnel selection. Construct validity concerns the extent to which a test, or other assessment process (such as interview), measures a specific construct (e.g., intelligence or extroversion) accurately. This information can assist in understanding the psychological construct(s) assessed by the instrument. Criterion-related validity is measured in terms of the relationship between performance on a selection procedure and performance on some key criterion variable, such as overall job proficiency.

Fig. 5.5 Types of validity

Face validity: the extent to which a measuring procedure seems 'at face value' to assess the qualities in question. This is to do with the acceptability of the test and is not a form of statistical validity.

Content validity: the extent to which the items or procedures in a measuring instrument sample the domain of interest.

Construct validity: the extent to which the measure gives accurate information about the psychological construct that it is designed to measure.

Criterion-related validity: the extent to which the measure produces scores related on a measure of some relevant criterion. In the case of personnel selection, the relevant criteria are usually indicators of job success, such as supervisors' ratings of job performance.

For many personnel psychologists, criterion-related validity is the major yardstick by which any selection method should be judged. Like reliability, criterion-related validity is usually quantified by a coefficient: the validity coefficient. Criterion-related validity coefficients may be derived by two principal methods: predictive and concurrent data-gathering. In both cases the validity coefficient is calculated by computing the correlation between scores on the selection method and scores on a relevant criterion, such as work performance, absenteeism, salary increase or job tenure. The concurrent method involves collecting selection scores for a sample of people who are already in the organization, that is, existing job incumbents. For that sample of people, criterion scores, such as ratings by supervisors of work performance, are also collected. The validity coefficient may then be derived by correlating the two sets of scores.

Although the concurrent approach provides a speedier way of obtaining a validity coefficient than the predictive approach, there are some draw-backs. The first and most obvious problem is that there is a restriction in the range of people who are likely to be examined. Anyone who is already in the organization is likely to have achieved at least a minimum level of job competence. Otherwise, he or she would probably have been moved to other employment or have left the organization. A second concern is about the motivation and behaviour of individuals when the selection method scores are gathered. In a concurrent validation study members of the sample already have jobs in the organization. Their motivational state and need to do well on the selection method are likely to be somewhat different from those of real job candidates.

In the predictive approach to validation, selection method scores are collected on a sample of actual job candidates. Their scores are then stored for a suitable period of time. After the time period has elapsed, scores on a relevant criterion are collected for those selected applicants who are still employed in the company. The time period involved will depend on the complexity of the job and the length of time it might take for any successful candidate to be able to develop proficiency in the job.

There are several requirements that make conducting a predictive validity study much more difficult than a concurrent study. For example, it is desirable that the selection method scores are not used to make actual selection decisions. This is to ensure that a full range of scores on the selection method is available when the validity coefficient is calculated. Another requirement is that the scores obtained for candidates are not made available to anyone in the organization who is expected to provide follow-up information on job performance or any other criterion measure. This requirement is designed to ensure that later criterion scores are not contaminated by the expectations that individuals may have, based on their knowledge of selection method scores.

Until the late 1970s, results published from studies into the criterion-related validity of various personnel selection methods were not particularly encouraging. When the studies were reviewed (e.g., Ghiselli, 1973) the validity evidence for each personnel selection method appeared to be erratic, in that different studies tended to show different levels of validity for the same method. Another problem was that, in general, the validity coefficients obtained were quite modest. This led personnel selection researchers to a number of conclusions.

For example, it was decided that the validity of most methods was not particularly good, and that for any particular application of a method a new local validation study was needed to check that the method was producing sufficiently good validity. This requirement seemed sensible in view of the considerable variation in the validity of methods from one study to another. However, with the benefit of hindsight it is now clear that these conclusions were not appropriate. Researchers at the time failed to pay sufficient attention to some features of the validation studies that had been published. The most important point that was underemphasized was the fact that the validation studies were almost always conducted with rather small samples (often less than 100 people).

Since the early 1980s a significant shift has occurred in the research base concerning the criterion-related validity of most personnel selection methods. Two American psychologists, Jack Hunter and Frank Schmidt, paid careful attention to the influence that sampling error and other artefactual features might have on a resulting validity coefficient. Most importantly, they developed statistical procedures that enabled researchers to combine the results from various individual, small-sample studies which had looked at the validity of any particular selection method (Hunter, Schmidt and Jackson, 1982; Hunter and Schmidt, 1990). This technique, known as meta-analysis, enabled researchers to use the results from the many validation studies done on specific selection methods to derive overall estimates for the validity of each method.

Meta-analysis also allows investigators to control statistically for the effects of two further flaws that often arise in validation studies. One of these is range restriction. This occurs when the spread of scores on one of the measures (the selection method or the criterion) does not span the full spread that occurs in the population. As noted earlier, this is frequently the case for criterion scores when concurrent validation methods are used. For example, it may be that selection decisions have been based upon data from the selection method. If candidates with selection scores only above a specific cut-off have been chosen, criterion scores for candidates with low selection scores will not be available. The net effect of range restriction is to reduce the maximum possible magnitude of any correlation coefficient that is calculated. In other words, when a restricted range of scores is available, the magnitude of the maximum correlation coefficient (i.e., the validity coefficient) that might be obtained is reduced artificially.

Another factor that influences the possible magnitude of a correlation coefficient is the reliability of measurement. As reliability decreases, the amount of randomness in the scores for any particular variable (the selection predictor or the job criterion) will increase. The existence of this random error will necessarily reduce the probability that high correlations between the variables can be observed.

It is important to recognize that sampling error, range restriction and unreliability of measurement are all aspects of study design that can create misleading impressions of the underlying relationship between two variables (e.g., scores from a selection method and a criterion of work performance). If a study uses a small sample with a restricted range of scores derived from unreliable measuring instruments, the observed correlation between the selection method and the criterion is likely to be smaller than the true correlation between those two variables. What this means is that many validation studies are likely to give misleadingly low impressions of the validity of personnel selection methods.

Meta-analytic procedures have been used to cumulate and correct validity data for most of the major selection methods. When this was done, the results led to different conclusions from those of the late 1970s. The results of this work are discussed in a later section of this chapter.

This section has covered the first three items in the list of evaluative criteria for choosing selection methods. The next section is concerned with the last three items that must be considered, which relate to cost effectiveness, fairness, and acceptability to candidates.

BEYOND VALIDITY: FINANCIAL UTILITY AND FAIRNESS

The use of meta-analytic procedures to derive better estimates of the criterion-related validity of personnel selection methods is one of two significant methodological developments for personnel selection research since the mid-1970s. The second important development concerned the use of 'utility formulae' to estimate the financial gain to be derived from personnel selection procedures (see Boudreau, 1989; Schmidt, Mack and Hunter, 1984). In some settings, improved selection procedures may be of little benefit. For example, when there are as many jobs as there are candidates and if the jobs need to be filled, selection is pointless, although placement (i.e., matching applicants to the available jobs) could be extremely important. At the other extreme, when there is a large field of candidates, the benefits from improved selection may be considerable. The selection ratio (i.e., the ratio of jobs to candidates) is thus an important determinant of the gain that can be realized from better selection.

For any organization the financial impact of personnel selection will depend on the gains and losses that flow from differences in the performance of more and less successful recruits. Obviously the financial gain from an improvement in performance will vary from job to job. An improvement of just five or six goals in a whole season in the goal-scoring performance of a Premier League footballer could make the difference between winning major honours or not, resulting in a difference of several million pounds for the football club. For other jobs the differences may be less substantial. In any work setting, assuming that performance can be measured, the likely range of differences in performance across different workers will determine how much can be gained by personnel selection.

To grasp the financial benefits to organizations of improved selection it is useful to identify the factors that influence these benefits. The key elements in the model of financial utility are:

● the selection ratio
● the accuracy of selection (i.e., the validity of the method(s) used)
● the financial gain obtained from improved job performance.

Using this approach it is possible to apply a simple formula to enable financial gain to be estimated for any combination of the relevant variables. A more detailed discussion of the estimation of the financial utility of personnel selection, including the relevant formulae, may be found in various sources, including Boudreau (1989) and Cooper and Robertson (1995).

But there is another consideration in the use of selection methods in addition to their validity, reliability and financial utility. Acceptable selection methods must be fair to all sub-groups of the population for which they are likely to be used. The purpose of selection is, of course, to discriminate between candidates, but this discrimination must not be based on attributes of candidates that are irrelevant to the job, such as age, gender or ethnic origin. Nevertheless, it is important to recognize that a selection method is not necessarily unfair if members of a specific sub-group do less well on the test. Men are less likely than women to sing soprano well, and women are less good at singing bass notes than men. This does not mean that a test for one role or another that produces different numbers of successful males or females is unfair.

A selection method is unfair only if it rejects or accepts members of a sub-group disproportionately, compared with their ability to do the job. This definition of unfairness was developed in the late 1960s (Cleary, 1968). It is the classical definition of fairness and is accepted as a reasonable view of fairness by both psychologists and employment lawyers. The definition may be expressed more technically: 'A test is biased for members of a sub-group of the population if, in the prediction of a criterion for which it was designed, consistent nonzero errors of prediction are made for members of the subgroup' (Cleary, 1968, p. 1/5).

When a method is biased against a sub-group, whatever the cause of that bias, the effect on the disadvantaged group is termed 'adverse impact'. Bias can arise in two main ways. First, the test may not be as accurate for members of the sub-group as it is for the remainder of the population; that is, the validity of the test is different for different groups. When this arises it is referred to as 'differential' validity. Any selection method showing differential validity can result in unfair disadvantage to one sub-group of the population. Second, bias can arise when the validity of the test is the same for all sub-groups, but the average scores obtained by the sub-groups differ. If people are selected on the basis of reaching some particular minimum score on a test, this will result in proportionately more people being selected from the sub-group with the higher average score than from the sub-group with the lower one. The research evidence suggests that the main cause of adverse impact is the second of these two types of bias.

This approach to fairness may seem unnecessarily complex but it is important to recognize that adverse impact, as evidenced in the disproportionately low selection of members of a particular sub-group, is unfair only if it is based on *errors* of prediction.

There has been an increased focus on eliminating adverse impact in personnel selection and the subject has generated a great deal of research. Although adverse impact does not imply unfairness in the technical sense, the consequence is that disproportionately small numbers of qualified candidates may be hired from minority groups. Many organizations are now more concerned with having employees from a wide range of backgrounds and some take proactive steps to ensure this happens. Managing diversity in the workplace, as it has been termed, has been demonstrated to have business benefits (Kandola and Fullerton, 1994) but a sense of social responsibility still underlies much work in this area.

Almost all selection procedures will show some degree of difference in average scores between groups and hence result in differential selection rates. Schmitt, Clause and Pulakos (1996) calculated the average level of group differences associated with particular selection methods. As is discussed later in the chapter, cognitive ability tests consistently show the greatest differences, with white test-takers scoring higher, on average, than black test-takers. The pattern for other ethnic groups is less clear, with some non-white groups (e.g., Asians and Orientals) sometimes having higher average scores than whites and sometimes lower. But, compared to other selection procedures, cognitive ability tests also have the highest predictive validity.

Because the highest validity method also has the greatest potential adverse impact, maximizing the accuracy of selection and eliminating adverse impact are often seen as conflicting goals in personnel selection. The financial utility model outlined above clearly indicates that the highest validity method will bring the greatest financial gains. Sometimes, though, an organization may seek to balance more than one critical goal in designing their personnel selection process. Maximizing financial utility may be disastrous for the organization if the consequences are high adverse impact against a protected minority group. A workforce that is not representative of the wider population in a public service organization, or in a profession with stringent standards of entry such as law and medicine, could lead to government scrutiny, bad publicity and expensive legal challenges. Hoffman and Thornton (1997) describe a case where it was crucial for the organization to avoid adverse impact as well as have an efficient selection process. Taking into account the level of adverse impact associated with each method, as well as the standard components of the utility model, the researchers found that running an assessment centre would have higher utility than cognitive ability testing despite being more costly in the short term.

This discussion of financial utility and fairness highlights an important point about personnel selection. The overall effectiveness of personnel selection procedures can only be determined in relation to the context in which they are used. When assessments are used in an organization to make important decisions between people, they become the subject of broader and more diverse evaluations than the technical, scientific evaluations made by those who design them.

People's perceptions of the fairness and acceptability of selection procedures do not always correspond exactly with technical definitions of fairness. In fact, the reaction of candidates to selection procedures is increasingly seen as an important issue in personnel selection research, because of the possible impact that those reactions may have on the attitude of candidates to the organization and their subsequent behaviour. Applicants' reactions may be important before, during and after the actual assessment process. Organizations face a double pressure relating to their ability to attract well-qualified applicants in the first place. Competition to recruit the best applicants and concerns about fairness and workplace diversity are both growing. This has led recruiters to think about how the perception of their procedures may contribute to their ability to attract applicants from different population groups.

During assessment itself, it has been suggested that the performance differences between population groups seen in some procedures may be influenced by the initial perceptions of the process by candidates. When assessment is over, the applicants' reactions to their experience can influence their likelihood of accepting a job offer, as well as their recommendations to others about the organization. So far research has established that the reactions of applicants help to determine their satisfaction with the selection procedure, their job acceptance decisions and self-perceptions (e.g., Bauer, Maertz, Dolen and Campion, 1998). Ryan and Ployhart (2000) provide a comprehensive review of the research on applicants' perceptions of selection procedures.

We have now covered the identification of person characteristics through job analysis, choosing job success criteria, understanding the nature of the person characteristics in question in order to adopt an appropriate assessment approach, and the standards that should be applied when evaluating particular selection methods. The next section reviews the main selection methods, concentrating especially on the research evidence for their validity.

PERSONNEL SELECTION METHODS AND THEIR EFFECTIVENESS

The main focus of attention here will be on criterion-related validity, although other forms of validity are discussed when appropriate. This emphasis reflects the relative prominence of criterion validation in personnel selection research to date. It is difficult to give absolute guidance, but validity coefficients of less than 0.2 are unlikely to be of much significance, except in special circumstances. Most personnel specialists would be content with coefficients of 0.3 and above. Validity coefficients above 0.5 are rare for single methods.

Assessment Centres

An assessment centre is not a place, it is an assessment process involving multiple assessors evaluating groups of candidates on a variety of tasks. Interviews, work-sample tests, group discussions and psychometric tests are often the components of such a centre. Assessment centres have a long history of use for personnel assessment, stretching back to pre-Second World War procedures used to assess military officers in Germany (Vernon and Parry, 1949). Subsequently, similar techniques were developed and used by the British War Office Selection Board (WOSB; see Vernon and Parry, 1949) and later the British Civil Service Selection Board (CSSB; see Vernon, 1950). The American Office of Strategic

Services (OSS) developed procedures derived from WOSB (Mackinnon, 1977; Wiggins, 1973). Feltham (1989) provides a review of these developments.

Modern assessment centres are descendants of the CSSB method and a process devised for managerial assessment in the American Telephone and Telegraph (AT&T) company (Bray and Grant, 1966). The AT&T procedures have a special place in the development of assessment centres, partly because of the systematic follow-up work that was done to assess the predictive validity of the assessments made (Bray and Grant, 1966). The validity evidence for the AT&T procedures was favourable and attracted the attention of assessment specialists in other organizations, who then developed assessment centres, modelled on the AT&T approach, for use in their own organizations. The British CSSBs are still in use today for the selection of new entrants to the British Civil Service and have also had a substantial impact on the design of other assessment centres.

Assessment centres take place over a period of time varying between half a day and three days. A typical centre might involve twelve candidates, working in groups of six. Candidates are evaluated by trained assessors, probably line managers in the organization. A ratio of two candidates per assessor is likely. Sometimes specialist chartered occupational psychologists might also be part of the assessment team, and psychologists are often involved in the design of centres. All centres make use of job-related work-sample exercises, such as in-trays, leaderless group tasks and individual presentations. Work-sample tests are designed to include the major tasks of the job (see Robertson and Kandola, 1982, for a review). For example, a typical in-tray exercise contains the kind of letters, memoranda, messages, reports, etc. that might normally appear in a job-holder's in-tray. The items will have been developed after a detailed analysis of the job and consideration of the components that are critical for successful performance. More detailed information on the several components and assessment processes of assessment centres may be found in Woodruffe (1992) and Spychalski, Quiñones, Gaugler and Pohley (1997).

The performance of candidates is assessed on a set of dimensions which should also have been derived from job analysis. 'Dimension' is the traditional term used to describe what would now often be called 'competency', one of the underlying psychological constructs that are thought to determine performance on the assessment tasks. Various generic competency frameworks exist (e.g., Dulewicz, 1989; Tett *et al.*, 2000), and assessment centres tend to use competencies that are drawn from those identified as 'core' for the organization. These general competencies (e.g., leadership, communication, creativity, etc.) will be defined in terms of the specific relevant behaviours associated with the job(s) in question.

These competencies or dimensions are the building blocks for assessment centres. They are used to determine which exercises will be most appropriate, and exercises are chosen on the basis of their likely ability to provide information about candidates on the relevant dimensions. Promotion, selection and placement decisions are taken after consideration of the candidates' profiles on these dimensions, and results are typically fed back to candidates in terms of each dimension.

The criterion-related validity of assessment centres could, in principle, be looked at in two different ways: by examining the validity of the component parts of the centre (e.g., the in-tray, psychometric tests or group exercises), or by assessing the validity of the overall scores derived from the centre. With some notable exceptions (e.g., Wollowick and McNamara, 1969; Schippman, Prien and Katz, 1990), most validation studies have concentrated on the validity of centres as a whole. This makes sense, since it is results from the centre as a whole that are typically used for decision-making. Meta-analytic reviews of the criterion-related validity of assessment centres (Schmitt, Gooding, Noe and Kirsch, 1984; Gaugler, Rosenthal, Thornton and Bentson, 1987) have revealed favourable results, with uncorrected mean, sample-size-weighted validity coefficients of about 0.30. The clear conclusion from both individual validation studies and meta-analytic reviews is that assessment centres show good levels of criterion-related validity.

Unfortunately, evidence of *construct* validity (in terms of the extent to which assessment centres produce accurate assessments of the dimensions on which they are built) is less convincing. Beginning with a study reported by Sackett and Dreher (1982), a series of investigations in both the UK and USA (see Robertson, Gratton and Sharpley, 1987; Reilly, Henry and Smither, 1990) has revealed problems with this aspect of assessment centres. If assessment centres are in fact measuring specific, stable differences between candidates, the cross-exercise correlations of the same dimension should be large.

In other words, the correlation for a particular competency (dimension), such as analytical ability, should be quite high when scores of individual candidates on two different exercises are compared. Of course the correlation would not be perfect, since each specific exercise will have some influence on how each candidate performs. However, the correlations for the same dimension across different exercises should certainly be higher than correlations of different dimensions within the same exercise. For example, the correlation for ratings of analytical ability for a sample of candidates across two different exercises should be greater than the correlation between, say, analytical ability and persuasiveness within the same exercise.

In fact, results show that correlations of different dimensions on *the same* exercise are generally larger than correlations of the same dimension across different exercises! Such results cast doubt on the construct validity of assessment centre scores and mean that, although there is confidence about the *criterion-related* validity of the overall assessment rating from assessment centres, the source of this validity (i.e., what exactly it is that assessment centres measure) is uncertain. Although it is not necessarily an indication of poor construct validity, the lack of a strong relationship between assessor ratings and candidates' self ratings (Clapham, 1998) is not an encouraging signal. Further research is needed to clarify the extent to which assessment centres are able to provide meaningful and independent scores on specific dimensions.

Selection Interviews

When evaluating the role of interviews in personnel selection, it is important to be clear that there are many different types of interview, and that criterion-related validity is not the same for each type. There is consistent evidence that structured interview formats produce better criterion-related validity than unstructured interviews (Weisner and Cronshaw, 1988; Wright, Lichenfels and Pursell, 1989; Huffcut and Arthur, 1994). A meta-analytic investigation of the criterion-related validity of interviews was conducted by McDaniel, Whetzel, Schmidt and Maurer (1994). Although they found that the overall mean validity for all types of interview was 0.20 (uncorrected for range restriction or unreliability), they showed that the validity for structured interviews (0.24) was better than the validity for unstructured interviews (0.18). After statistical corrections for range restriction and unreliability were applied to the data, the criterion-related validity coefficients for structured and unstructured interviews were 0.44 and 0.33 respectively.

Structure may be imposed on an interview in a variety of ways. One of the most popular and sensible options is to use job analysis results and information about the competencies that are thought to be important in the job to provide the main components for the interview structure. Questions in the interview can then be focused on the key elements of the job and the competencies needed.

The development and use of 'situational interviews' provided a good example of this general approach. A situational interview can be designed in the stages given below.

- Conduct a systematic job analysis.
- Use the results of the job analysis to identify key tasks that are important for overall job success. An integral part of the job analysis, when situational interviews are being developed, is the identification of specific examples of challenging situations that might confront a job holder. The critical incident technique (Flanagan, 1954) is often useful for this and involves asking job holders to recall incidents of particularly good or poor performance.
- Use the results of job analysis to identify the key competencies for job success.
- Develop a set of questions about hypothetical behaviour in the position, based on the challenging situations identified at the job analysis stage. These questions involve asking candidates how they *would* behave in the specific work situation in question.
- Develop a scoring key so that the replies of candidates can be assessed on each of the relevant dimensions. The scoring key needs to be as objective as possible and may be derived by obtaining sample replies from existing job incumbents who are known to be at different levels of overall job competence.

The questions in this form of situational interview are often written on cards and read to candidates in a predetermined sequence. The situational interview approach was developed by Latham and colleagues (Latham, Saari, Pursell and Campion, 1980). Successful validation studies using situational interviews have also been reported by other investigators (Weekley and Gier, 1987; Robertson, Gratton and Rout, 1990).

The success of the structured interview compared with other forms of interview has not been explained in any definitive way, and there is still uncertainty about the reasons for its relatively good validity. It seems likely that one important function of structure is to focus the interviewer's attention on particularly salient features, so that candidate attributes that are irrelevant to job success do not intrude and influence decision-making.

Huffcutt and Woehr (1999) looked at a large sample of 120 different studies of interview validity, with a total sample size of over 18,158. Their results provided further reinforcement of the importance of interview structure for validity and also showed that validity is better when interviewers are provided with training. This is also true when the interview itself is not structured. In addition, they found that using the same interviewer across all candidates (or the same panel of interviewers) is linked with better validity. A further finding was that the use of a panel of interviewers is not associated with better validity, although this result has been contradicted by other research (Weisner and Cronshaw, 1988) and the superiority or otherwise of panel interviews needs to be clarified. Campion, Palmer and Campion (1997) have offered a model of interview structure and fifteen different ways to improve interviews.

Cognitive Ability Tests

Meta-analytic evidence offers good support for the criterion-related validity of cognitive ability tests in many employment settings. Several studies based on very large samples have indicated that general cognitive ability is significantly associated with successful performance in most jobs. For example, the average correlation with overall performance (after correction for low criterion reliability and restriction of range in predictor scores) was 0.51 in the meta-analysis by Schmidt and Hunter (1998). These findings completely overturn the earlier cautious conclusion (Ghiselli, 1973) that selection methods need to be checked by a local validation study prior to use in any specific setting.

Schmidt and Hunter (1998) also showed that, as job complexity increases, the criterion-related validity of cognitive tests also increases. The corrected validity estimates for unskilled and professional and managerial jobs were 0.23 and 0.58 respectively. These positive results might be taken to suggest that cognitive tests are useful for selection in almost any setting and that they are particularly good for higher-level jobs. Unfortunately things are not as simple as this!

Two important complications are apparent when the practical use of such tests is concerned. First, when senior jobs are studied the pool of candidates tends to contain people all of whom have high levels of cognitive ability, not differing greatly in terms of their intellectual capabilities. In other words, there is often a restriction in the range of scores for the candidate group. Because of this 'bunching' of scores, it may be difficult to make meaningful comparisons between candidates. Even the best cognitive tests are subject to measurement error, and small differences in scores may not be large enough for this to be discounted as the source of the difference between rival candidates.

The second complication with cognitive ability testing is related to the differences in scores that are found amongst different sub-groups. There is clear evidence that members of different ethnic groups in the United States of America produce different scores on tests of general cognitive ability, with black people and Hispanics showing lower average scores (see Gottfredson and Sharf, 1988) than white groups. When cognitive ability tests are used to select people for jobs, members of some ethnic groups are likely to score less well and hence are less likely to be selected. As noted earlier, this imbalance in success rates does not necessarily mean that the tests are unfair (Cleary, 1968), although it will cause adverse impact on a particular sub-group. The available research indicates that the differences in average scores between groups are reflected in comparable differences in average scores on relevant job criteria (e.g., Payne, 1995). To the extent that this is true, the tests are technically 'fair' even though they may give rise to adverse impact. In other words, there is little evidence of differential validity. On the other hand, the consequences of adverse impact caused by the use of cognitive testing are likely to be socially divisive and damaging.

So, the position for cognitive ability tests is that: the criterion-related validity of the tests is good; the scores of some ethnic groups on the tests are consistently low; there is no evidence of differential validity. When selection decisions are being made with applicants from several ethnic groups, should such tests be included in the selection battery? There is no unequivocal answer to this question. An overriding concern for social justice leads many to recommend caution in the use of such tests when mixed applicant groups are involved.

Several schemes exist to allow cognitive tests to be used with minimum adverse impact. For example, it is possible to group candidates into bands based on their test scores and then select from each band, in accordance with sub-group proportions in the applicant pool. This procedure produces no adverse impact, though it does require the selection of candidates from lower-scoring bands and hence the efficiency of selection is compromised. It is also deemed illegal in many countries, as most employment legislation requires selection to be based on individual merit. Positive action to counter the effect of adverse impact on selection rates for sub-groups can only legally be taken in terms of encouraging applications from minority groups or, after selection, in terms of training.

There is no dispute concerning the importance of cognitive ability to performance in a wide range of jobs, and in many settings such tests may well be the most cost-effective and accurate single component in the selection procedure. However, the complications noted above should warn against the unquestioned use of such tests in all settings, particularly in situations where mixed groups of applicants and/or higher level jobs are involved.

Personality Scales

Some researchers have used meta-analytic methods to examine the links between personality constructs and overall job proficiency (e.g., Barrick and Mount, 1991, Salgado, 1997). These studies have shown significant correlations between personality constructs (especially conscientiousness) and overall job performance.

Stronger validity coefficients have emerged from meta-analytic research when the personality constructs used in the original studies have been based on clear hypotheses about what characteristics are needed for overall job success (Tett, Jackson and Rothstein, 1991). The clearest links with personality variables and criterion measures are likely to emerge when specific personality constructs are linked to specific competencies, rather than overall job proficiency. Robertson and Kinder (1993) showed that specific personality constructs were indeed associated with specific job competencies, with levels of criterion-related validity from 0.09 up to about 0.30. In that study hypotheses were generated by asking people who were familiar with the personality scales in question to indicate which scales they believed would be associated with specific job competencies. For those aspects of personality expected to be linked to specific competencies, criterion-related validity reached moderate levels; for unrelated personality–competence pairs, validity was much lower.

It is clear from the results of meta-analytic studies that a number of the big five personality constructs are predictive of subsequent work performance. Conscientiousness, extroversion, emotional stability and agreeableness have all produced results in meta-analytic studies. The best validities have been found for conscientiousness and integrity (a construct closely related to conscientiousness which also includes aspects of agreeableness and emotional stability). Conscientiousness is perhaps the most important of the big five personality factors in determining success at work. Although it is clearly important for work success, personality is complex and it is unlikely that performance in all occupational areas is determined mainly by the job-holder's level of conscientiousness. In fact, Robertson, Baron, Gibbons, MacIver and Nyfield (2000) have produced results for a large sample of managers showing that conscientiousness is not strongly related to current job success but is actually negatively related to promotion prospects!

Another reason to be wary about the importance of conscientiousness (or any other big five personality factor) in determining work performance is that all of the big five personality constructs are rather broad personality variables. Earlier in this chapter we drew attention to the hierarchical structure of human personality and indicated that working at the facet level rather than the broad factor level may sometimes be more appropriate. One reason for this is that the broad factors are not always defined and measured in exactly the same way between different studies. Conscientiousness, for example, includes facets of personality related to both dependability and the will to achieve. But not all studies using this construct include both of these facets (see Barrick and Mount, 1991 and Robertson et al., 2000). Several researchers believe that work performance is better predicted by more specific personality factors (Paunonen, Rothstein and Jackson, 1999) than by the big five. For a review of research evidence on the links between personality and aspects of work behaviour see Robertson and Callinan (1998).

Other Methods

In addition to interviews, assessment centres and psychological tests, a variety of other personnel selection methods are in common use.

References about job applicants tend to be used a great deal in some countries. In general they are not utilized for the main decision-making process. Instead, they are typically used at a fairly late stage in the process to confirm candidates' claims and to check that there are no major barriers to making an appointment. The restricted role of references is probably just as well, since evidence about their criterion-related validity is not particularly good. The available evidence (e.g., Hunter and Hunter, 1984) shows references to have poor levels of criterion-related validity (less than 0.2). As well as poor levels of criterion-related validity, the opportunities for bias in reference reports are obviously quite substantial. Unfortunately, there are few recent, systematic studies to support or refute the possibility of bias of references (see Dobson, 1989).

In contrast to references, work-sample tests have a very good track record for both validity and fairness. The validity evidence for such tests is strong and there is good support for their fairness and acceptability to candidates (Robertson and Kandola, 1982; Hunter and Hunter, 1984). Work-sample tests have been developed and used for a wide range of occupations, although usage is more widespread in jobs involving practical skills. They have been used in management selection (e.g., in-tray exercises in assessment centres), in studies of clerical work, and for practical skills in such diverse areas as dentistry, sewing machine operating and bricklaying.

Some of these work-sample tests are in 'trainability test' format. In a trainability test the candidate is given a period of learning and then tested on how well this has been assimilated by asking him or her to conduct the tasks involved in the work sample. Validity evidence for this type of work sample is good; the approach is also well received by candidates (Robertson and Downs, 1989). One reservation concerning the use of work-samples is that they are very closely linked to the job in question and may lose validity if and when the demands of the job change. There is some evidence that the validity of work-sample tests does decline over time (Robertson and Downs, 1989), although the reduction may be no greater than that of other selection methods. See Callinan and Robertson (2000) for a recent review of work-sample testing.

Biodata questionnaires ask about a person's activities and experience. They may be developed by empirical, logical or mixed procedures. In the empirical approach, correlations between job success criteria and items of biographical data are established by carrying out concurrent validation studies. When purely empirical methods are adopted, there is a risk that the items in the biodata questionnaire that are found to be correlated with job success may have no logical link with the job. For example, in one study conducted several years ago, a history of holidays in Spain was a contra-indication of job success! In another study, living in a certain part of a city with a high percentage of people from a particular ethnic group was associated with a lack of job success. Modern procedures for developing biodata systems require the use of both empirical and logical procedures to identify appropriate items. Any item used for actual selection decisions needs to have a clear empirical link (i.e., it needs to show criterion-related validity) and a clear logical link with the job success criteria. In settings where large numbers of candidates are available, the use of biodata can be an efficient selection procedure. Criterion-related validity for well-developed biodata systems is generally good (Drakeley, 1989; Stokes and Reddy, 1992).

One difficulty with biodata has been the need for a specific set of questions to be validated for each organization. This places biodata at a disadvantage when compared with other assessment procedures, such as psychometric tests of ability or personality. More recently, researchers have been looking at ways of extending the degree to which biodata can be generalized across different organizations. Wilkinson (1997), for example, developed a biodata instrument which predicted vocational interests, regardless of job or organization. Carlson, Scullen, Schmidt, Rothstein and Erwin (1999) developed a biodata instrument in one organization for predicting general managerial performance, and found that it worked in other, different organizations. Their article provides guidance on the factors that influence the extent to which a biodata questionnaire will generalize across different settings.

The Use of Technology in Selection

There is a growing use of computers in personnel selection in place of paper-and-pencil for the administration, scoring and interpretation of ability and personality tests (see Bartram, 1994). While computers have been with us for a long time, their use in testing has not been great. They have been used more for the automated generation of reports based on test performance than for the actual administration of tests. The reason for this is logistical: testing for selection tends to involve the administration of tests to groups of people, rather than single individuals. It has been impractical until recently to provide the quantity of hardware necessary for computer delivery of group testing sessions.

The main exceptions have been large organizations with a regular stream of people coming in for testing. The military, in particular, have pioneered the use of computer-based testing both for the delivery of traditional ability and self-report measures and for the administration of new types of tests. Among the new types of tests are task-based simulations (a little like computer games) and adaptive tests. The latter adapt to the person who is taking the test, so that if he or she is performing well the test will get harder, and if performance is poor the test will get easier.

When one considers the administration of a paper-and-pencil test by computer, the question of equivalence arises. Would you get the same score if you undertook the test on computer as you would if you did it on paper? A great deal of research has been carried out to see whether 'computerizing' tests changes their nature. The results of this research tend to show that this can be a problem for some tests but not for others (for a summary see Bartram, 1994). Equivalence depends on whether computerization changes the ergonomics of the test in a significant way. In practice, this tends to mean that tests that are highly speeded (e.g., clerical checking tasks) will not transfer well, whereas self-report inventories will transfer without any difficulty.

While the impact of the personal computer on testing for selection has been relatively small outside the area of large-scale military testing programmes, we are now beginning to see a very significant change. The internet is rapidly modifying the way in which selection and recruitment are carried out. The following section focuses on the impact of the internet. While the main use of computers in the past was during the managed assessment stage of personnel selection, the internet's impact has been mainly in the first two stages of the process: attraction and recruitment.

INFORMATION TECHNOLOGY AND THE
WORLDWIDE WEB IN PERSONNEL SELECTION

In order to evaluate the potential impact of the internet on computer-based assessment in general and on assessment for recruitment and selection in particular, it is important to gain a realistic view of just how widespread the internet is, and how rapidly accessibility is likely to increase. Current estimates (reviewed in Bartram, 2000) indicate that by 2005 over 10 per cent of the world's population will be internet users. For the top twenty-five user countries, that level of penetration has already been achieved. The main areas where the internet is widely used are North America, Europe and Asia-Pacific.

The dates given in the following sections are important because the situation is changing so rapidly. If you are reading this book in 2005, it will be interesting to consider whether the changes predicted here have come about or whether the impact of the internet has been either over- or under-estimated.

Attraction and Recruitment on the Internet

A major consequence of the rapid growth of the internet and its increasing accessibility is that more and more organizations are recruiting and selecting applicants for jobs online. In addition, applicants for jobs and job-seekers are increasingly expecting to find work through the internet rather than more traditional means. The following figures (Lawrence, 1999) provide some idea of the volume of traffic handled by the top sites. In mid 1999, Monster.com had 3 million registered users all of whom were receiving customized e-mail updates about relevant jobs offered by 60,000 employers. There were 215,000 job vacancies listed and 1.5 million resumés/CVs on the site with about 4,000 new resumés/CVs coming in each day.

Within the United Kingdom, the number of organizations using the internet for recruitment has risen from 14 per cent in 1997, through 19 per cent in 1998, to 32 per cent in 1999 (IPD, 1999). More recently, the Association of Graduate Recruiters in the UK (AGR, 2000) reported the results of a survey showing that the proportion of recruiters recruiting online has doubled since 1999 from one-third to two-thirds. Nearly 90 per cent of university graduates are now seeking their first jobs on the internet and nearly 50 per cent are applying online. What is more interesting is that employers report that the quality of applicants who apply online is higher than that of those who apply by traditional methods. Interestingly, the major change envisaged by the survey respondents as a consequence of growing use of the internet was the demise of the handwritten application form. This reflects a growing trend away from the posting of CVs and resumés, to the use of structured application forms systematically covering biographical data, experience, skills, etc. Many recruitment systems now employ adaptive, branching questionnaires, often referred to as online interviews, whereby the questions asked are tailored to each individual's particular circumstances and previous answers.

There is a widespread assumption that the internet is only used to recruit people into technical positions (primarily jobs in IT). This is no longer the case. Sites that recruit for non-technical and management positions have become the major growth area (Hoffman, 1999). The top two categories of job on the internet in 1999 were management and sales – not information technology.

The Importance of the Corporate Website

In larger organizations we are seeing the emergence of a new position in the human resources department: that of internet recruiter. It is being realized that the company's website is a key component in creating the image of the organization. The most frequent use of the website is by job seekers who use it to move on to the organization's careers site (the area of a corporate website that contains information about current vacancies and through which people can apply for jobs in the organization). As the number of general job boards on the internet increases, so job seekers will increasingly need to target their searches effectively. Going direct to the careers site of preferred organizations is one way of doing this.

A recent report (Creative Good, cited in CyberAtlas, 1999) suggested that US corporations could be losing $30 million per day because their recruiting sites are too difficult for many job seekers to use. The survey looked at the problems encountered in applying for jobs on six corporate sites. Three-quarters of all job seekers reported having some technical problems applying for the job online. Nearly half of them reported that tests they took online had not been completed for some technical reason or other. This is a failure rate that would be quite unacceptable for any other medium.

On the more positive side, a survey (Wroe, 2000) of over 45,000 candidates who completed an online selection process at two corporate websites showed that most were either positive or very positive about the process and found it easy or very easy to complete, with only 1 per cent finding it difficult or very difficult. Even more interesting is that they were fairly evenly split between those who viewed the company they were applying to more positively after completing the process, and those who reported no change; only 1 per cent viewed the company less positively. Wroe concludes that 'the results may indicate that companies who provide an online application and true selection process on the internet are viewed as more interactive, accessible and cutting-edge than companies who don't offer these services'.

Access to Technology and the 'Digital Divide'

There has been much concern expressed about the internet creating a 'digital divide' between those with access and those without (Keller, 1996). Such a divide currently exists on a geographical basis, with nearly all of the infrastructure and development of internet business taking place in North America, Europe and Asia-Pacific. This pattern will change over the coming decade, but for some time it will be impossible to use the internet as the sole source of recruitment and selection in countries outside these three main areas.

However, if we consider just those areas where the infrastructure is well developed, does everyone have equal access to it? In considering any selection and recruitment process we need to consider its potential for adversely impacting on one or more particular groups within the population. From the point of view of litigation, the main 'protected' groups are ethnic minorities, women, and people with disabilities. More generally, we should be concerned about equality of access in terms of geographical dispersion (rural versus urban), age, educational background, and any other factors that may not be directly job-relevant but have an effect on access to the recruitment process.

The Georgia Institute of Technology has tracked changing demographic patterns in use of the web in a series of surveys carried out every six months, starting in January 1994 (e.g., Kehoe, Pitkow, Sutton, Aggarwal and Rogers, 1999). These show very interesting patterns of change in the demographics of web users, as well as an increase in the total numbers (see Bartram, 2000, for details). Results suggest that we can define two generations of web users. The first generation users are those who were there in the early days, who made the transition from the pre-www internet to the www in the mid 90s, and who are predominantly computer-skilled, young, white, male users. The second generation users are those who have come to employ the www as it has become a part of the fabric of their work and home life (typically, since late 1997 to early 1998 in the USA and about a year later in Europe). The latter users are roughly equally divided between males and females and reasonably balanced in terms of ethnic mix, are older than first generation users, and do not aspire to the higher levels of technical user-skill of the earlier generation.

In relation to recruitment and selection, it will be important to ascertain that there is equality of access amongst the relevant applicant populations. The data suggest that inequality of access may be a greater issue for lower paid jobs than, say, for graduate level ones, and more of an issue when the only available means of application would be a home-based personal computer.

In taking such effects into account it will be important for recruiters to seek up-to-date information on relevant local demographics. As has been noted, patterns of access and use are changing very rapidly, and differ from country to country. As with other methods of recruitment (telephone, mail, fax, etc.), the test should not be whether everyone has access, but whether they could reasonably be expected to obtain access.

Future Job-seeking Scenario

In the light of the above, consider a possible way to look for a new job in the near future. As a job seeker, you will access a job-seeker website and complete a number of inventories to provide a general competency profile of yourself. You will have an online 'intelligent agent' that knows about your interests and preferences. This personal web agent will e-mail your profile to relevant job boards, with your multi-media structured 'CV' attached (providing standard biographical information, qualifications, experience, etc.). It will also search the net for you for information on companies that you might be interested in working for. You will be able to read the company reports, track back their performance on the stock market, and see who their key clients are. You may decide to view some realistic job previews and may try out some work sample exercises. If you like what you see, you will submit an initial application directly for a job.

Having declared an active interest in certain types of position, recruitment search processes will bring you to the attention of relevant companies, and you will receive invitations from some of these to make an application. The companies you decide to apply to will sift your application and, if you are successful, contact you through your mobile internet portal and ask you to provide additional information about yourself, complete some questionnaires and schedule an interview appointment. All this could be done within the space of a couple of hours, interactively through your digital mobile phone or TV internet browser, without you leaving your armchair. Even the initial interview could be carried out using a TV-based videophone.

Having passed the initial interview, you will be invited to take some tests and complete some assessment exercises. As they have to be supervised, you will be given the online booking form to book a convenient time at your local assessment centre, where your identity will be checked, and the centre's administrator will authenticate and supervise your assessments (which will, of course, all be computer-administered).

Of course, you may not be sure what sort of job to apply for. The net will provide you with the opportunity to explore your profile of skills and competencies, work on personal development plans and help you consider your potential fit to various employers.

Impact of the Internet on the Managed Assessment Stage

To date, the main impact of the internet has been on attraction and recruitment (the first two of the three stages identified earlier) rather than the final managed assessment stage. However, the future impact is likely to be increasingly seen on this final stage as well. We can expect to see a number of selection processes moving partly or wholly online:

- Interviews – the internet will provide the means of using video-conferencing techniques for conducting 'face-to-face' interviews at a distance. Already, video-conferencing is used to reduce the cost of bringing candidates to one location for an interview, especially when the applicants are spread around the world.

- Reference checks – many of the checks that need to be carried out to verify an applicant's claims will become more automated. Referees can be e-mailed with easy-to-complete structured forms both for their evaluation of your competencies and for checking qualification and experience claims.

- Assessment centre exercises – there is tremendous potential for the development of internet-based multi-user interactive exercises, and for virtual assessment centres. There is already a range of computer-based in-tray exercises available. Multi-user workplace simulations are being developed, in which you interact with other people in problem-solving exercises. The other people may be other candidates, assessors or computer-simulated role-players.

- Objective assessments (psychometric tests of personality, ability and so on) – these are already beginning to appear on the internet. There are many instances of personality inventories that are available for delivery in either supervised or unsupervised assessment settings. The technology needed to administer timed ability tests is more complex, but this is also now sufficiently well advanced for some publishers to offer to deliver verbal and numerical reasoning tests over the internet.

MORE EFFECTIVE PERSONNEL SELECTION

Although research into personnel selection has made significant progress since the mid-1980s, there are clear limitations to the traditional approach. Personnel selection researchers have tended to focus their attention on investigating the criterion-related validity of their methods. This is undeniably a useful endeavour but needs to be supplemented by an interest in the nature of the constructs that are measured. An illustrative example of this point, discussed above, is that of assessment centres. Although assessment centre scores show clear relationships with criterion measures of job success, the construct validity of the competencies (dimensions) that are assessed in assessment centres is uncertain (see above).

In terms of data analysis and conceptual models, the conventional reliance on linear correlation between variables as the main indicator of criterion-related validity sets a limit on the complexity of the models that can be evaluated. Many relationships between selection measures and job success criteria are likely to be curvilinear. Consider, for example, the relationship between extroversion and customer-relations skills. Very low levels of extroversion are not likely to be linked to successful customer relations, because the level of interaction initiated by the job holder would be too low. On the other hand, extremely high levels of extroversion might, for other reasons, be unlikely to bring empathy with customers in many settings.

Similarly, most validity studies examine the validity of just one single selection method, whereas most real selection decisions are made with the aid of multiple methods. The combination of meta-analysis, for deriving accurate estimates of the validity of personnel selection procedures, with utility analysis, for deriving estimates of the likely financial benefit, provides a powerful way of demonstrating how important good personnel selection is for the success of an organization. The results of meta-analysis and utility analysis can also be used to explore the potential benefits of different selection methods used in combination. Schmidt and Hunter (1998) provide a wide-ranging overview of the validity and utility of all the main selection procedures and concentrate specifically on the combination of general mental ability with each of the other possible methods.

They adopted this approach because, as explained earlier in this chapter, the results of meta-analysis have consistently shown general mental ability to be the best predictor of work performance across different organizations and jobs. Their results showed that the best combination of methods was a test of general mental ability and a work-sample test, with a mean criterion-related validity of 0.63. Other researchers have also recently turned their attention to evaluating the role of selection methods in combination. Results have revealed that personality traits (Judge, Higgins, Thoresen and Barrick, 1999), biodata (Mount, Witt and Barrick,

2000) and interviews (Cortina, Goldstein, Payne, Davison and Gilliland, 2000) all provide incremental validity beyond general mental ability alone.

When multiple methods are used to assess candidates, the results from the different methods need to be combined in some way. One of the strongest findings from personnel selection research is that the statistical combination of scores is always superior to combination processes that involve using the skills and judgement of assessors, although the combination of both approaches may produce the best results of all (Ganzach, Kluger and Klayman, 2000).

There is a growing awareness amongst some selection researchers that the assumptions made in research investigating the validity of individual methods may not hold in practice. For example, it is assumed that candidates with the highest marks on a psychological test will be hired, and the benefits of using the test are conventionally calculated on that basis. In reality, recruiters must weigh up a number of factors to reach a decision. Individuals with the highest score on one test will not necessarily be hired. This and other differences between the scenario assumed in research and the practical reality of personnel selection may serve to reduce the possible gains that will be experienced from those reported in academic literature (Murphy and Bartram, 2002). Future personnel selection research will need to focus more on the process of selection, how methods and procedures are used in practice, instead of their technical properties.

Another limitation of the traditional approach is that job success criteria are almost inevitably conceptualized and measured at the individual level, whereas in many settings the co-ordinated efforts of several people are inextricably linked to job success. A major difficulty confronted by personnel selection researchers here is that measures of team effectiveness and commensurate measures of individual effectiveness are not available, nor is there any recognized procedure for developing them. It is clear from everyday experience that the addition of a new person to a previously efficient or inefficient group can make a considerable difference. Surprisingly little scientific work has been done to explore this kind of effect, and there is no substantial body of personnel selection research involving the use of criterion measures that are not measured exclusively at the individual level.

It is important to recognize that personnel selection decisions are not taken in a vacuum; they occur within an organizational setting and they involve real people. It is now clear that truly comprehensive models of the selection process need to go beyond merely the examination of single jobs to review their place within broader organizational units and strategic needs. This requires a deeper understanding of the social-psychological context of personnel selection.

The traditional approach could be enhanced by giving more attention to personnel selection as a complex social process. For example, Herriot (1989b) has shown how the personnel selection process can be seen as a series of episodes involving the applicant and the organization. Viewing the personnel selection process in this way concentrates attention on the actors involved, a perspective that is neglected in the traditional paradigm. It is this perspective that has brought into focus issues such as the impact of the assessment process on candidates (Robertson, Iles, Gratton and Sharpley, 1991).

SUMMARY

Personnel selection occupies a central role within work psychology. The process of personnel selection begins with an analysis of the job. Job analysis is used to identify the key components of the job, and forms the basis for creating a person specification which indicates the main skills and characteristics to look for in candidates. Candidates for any post will be different from each other. Understanding and assessing those differences between candidates is at the heart of personnel selection.

A variety of personnel selection methods can be used to assess candidates for jobs. Whichever methods are used, they need to satisfy certain criteria. Key criteria include validity and reliability. Criterion-related validity coefficients of less than 0.2 are unlikely to be of much assistance within the personnel selection process except in special circumstances. A number of personnel selection methods, including assessment centres, interviews and psychometric tests, have been shown to have worthwhile validities. The use of information technology within personnel selection has had some impact, and a variety of procedures that were previously administered by paper and pencil are now available in a computer-based version. The growth and development of the internet has also had a significant impact on the way in which personnel selection is conducted, and an increasing number of organizations are recruiting and selecting applicants for jobs through this medium. The growth of the internet also has implications for the organizations, who need to ensure that they have a strong presence on the internet, and for candidates, who will find their job search procedures changing significantly in years to come.

FURTHER READING

The central issues in personnel selection are best followed up by reference to general texts devoted to the topic (e.g., Cooper and Robertson, 1995; Schmitt and Chan, 1998). Good examples of meta-analytic articles focusing on the criterion-related validity of specific methods include those on personality (Barrick and Mount, 1991) and interviews (McDaniel *et al.*, 1994). An up-to-date and detailed review of the validity of all personnel selection methods is provided by Salgado (1999).

REFERENCES

AGR (2000). Going to work on the Web: Web-based graduate recruitment. *AGR Briefing* #11, 2000. Warwick: Association of Graduate Recruiters.

Algera, J. A. and Greuter, M. A. M. (1998). Job analysis. In P. Drenth, H. Thierry and C. J. de Wolf (eds.), Volume 3, *Handbook of Work and Organizational Psychology*, Second Edition. Hove: Psychology Press.

Barrick, M. R. and Mount, M. K. (1991). The big five personality dimensions and job performance: A meta-analysis. *Personnel Psychology*, 44, 1–26.

Bartram, D. (1994). Computer based assessment. *International Review of Industrial and Organizational Psychology*, 9, 31–69.

Bartram, D. (2000). Internet recruitment and selection: Kissing frogs to find princes. *International Journal of Selection and Assessment*, 9, 261–74.

Bartram, D., Robertson, I. and Callinan, M. (2002). Introduction: A framework for examining organizational effectiveness. In I. Robertson, M. Callinan and D. Bartram (eds.), *Organizational Effectiveness: The Role of Psychology*. Chichester: Wiley.

Bauer, T. N., Maertz, C. P. Jr., Dolen, M. R. and Campion, M. A. (1998). Longitudinal assessment of applicant reactions to employment testing and test outcome feedback. *Journal of Applied Psychology*, *83*, 892–903.

Boudreau, J. W. (1989). Selection utility analysis: A review and agenda for future research. In M. Smith and I. T. Robertson (eds.), *Advances in Selection and Assessment*, pp. 227–57. Chichester: Wiley.

Bray, D. W. and Grant, D. L. (1966). The assessment center in the measurement of potential for business management. *Psychological Monographs*. General and Applied Whole, pp. 625–7.

Breaugh J. A. and Starke, M. (2000). Research on employee recruitment: So many studies, so many remaining questions. *Journal of Management*, *26*, 405–34.

Callinan, M. and Robertson, I. T. (2000). Work sample testing. *International Journal of Selection and Assessment*, *8*, 248–60.

Campion, M. A., Palmer, D. K. and Campion, J. E. (1997). A review of structure in the selection interview. *Personnel Psychology*, *50*, 655–702.

Carlson, K. D., Scullen, S. E., Schmidt, F. L., Rothstein, H. and Erwin, F. (1999). Generalizable biographical data validity can be achieved without multi-organizational development and keying. *Personnel Psychology*, *52*, 731–55.

Carroll, J. B. (1993). *Human Cognitive Abilities: A Survey of Factor-analytic Studies*. Cambridge: Cambridge University Press.

Cattell, R. B. (1965). *The Scientific Analysis of Personality*. Baltimore: Penguin.

Ciarrochi, J. V., Chan, A. Y. C. and Caputi, P. (2000). A critical evaluation of the emotional intelligence construct. *Personality and Individual Differences*, *28*, 539–61.

Clapham, M. M. (1998). A comparison of assessor and self dimension ratings in an advanced management assessment centre. *Journal of Occupational and Organizational Psychology*, *71*, 193–203.

Cleary, T. A. (1968). Test bias: Prediction of grades of negro and white students in integrated colleges. *Journal of Educational Measurement*, *5*, 115–24.

Cooper, D. and Robertson, I. T. (1995). *The Psychology of Personnel Selection*. London: Routledge.

Cortina, J. M., Goldstein, N. B., Payne, S. C., Davison, H. K. and Gilliland, S. W. (2000). The incremental validity of interview scores over and above cognitive ability and conscientiousness scores. *Personnel Psychology*, *53*, 325–51.

Costa, P. T. and McCrae, R. R. (1992). *Manual for the NEO Personality Inventory*. Odessa, Fla: Psychological Assessment Resources Inc.

CyberAtlas (1999). Corporate recruiting sites need help. *http://Cyberatlas.Internet.com/big_picture/demographics/article/0.1323.5971_197811.00.html*

Digman, J. M. (1990). Personality structure: Emergence of the five-factor model. *Annual Review of Psychology*, *41*, 417–40.

Dobson, P. (1989). Reference reports. In P. Herriot (ed.), *Assessment and Selection in Organizations*, pp. 455–68. Chichester: Wiley.

Drakeley, R. J. (1989). Biographical data. In P. Herriot (ed.), *Assessment and Selection in Organizations*, pp. 437–53. Chichester: Wiley.

Dulewicz, V. (1989). Assessment centres as the route to competence. *Personnel Management*, November, 56–9.

Eysenck, H. J. and Eysenck, M. J. (1985). *Personality and Individual Differences: A Natural Science Approach*. New York: Plenum Press.

Feltham, R. (1989). Assessment Centres. In P. Herriot (ed.), *Assessment and Selection in Organizations*, pp. 401–19. Chichester: Wiley.

Flanagan, J. C. (1954). The critical incident technique. *Psychological Bulletin*, *51*, 327–58.

Fox, S. and Spector, P. E. (2000). Relations of emotional intelligence, practical intelligence, general intelligence, and trait affectivity with interview outcomes: It's not all just 'G'. *Journal of Organizational Behavior*, *21*, 203–20.

Ganzach, Y., Kluger, A. N. and Klayman, N. (2000). Making decisions from an interview: Expert measurement and mechanical combination. *Personnel Psychology*, *53*, 1–20.

Gaugler, B., Rosenthal, D. B., Thornton, G. C. and Bentson, C. (1987). Meta-analysis of assessment center validity. *Journal of Applied Psychology*, *72*, 493–511.

Ghiselli, E. E. (1973). The validity of aptitude tests in personnel selection. *Personnel Psychology*, *26*, 461–77.

Goleman, D. (1995). *Emotional Intelligence: Why it can matter more than IQ*. New York: Bantam Books.

Gottfredson, L. S. and Sharf, J. C. (1988). Fairness in employment testing. *Journal of Vocational Behavior Whole*, *33*, 225–447.

Herriot, P. (1989b). Selection as a social process. In M. Smith and I. T. Robertson (eds.), *Advances in Selection and Assessment*, pp. 171–87. Chichester: Wiley.

Hoffman, C. C. and Thornton, G. C. (1997). Examining selection utility where competing predictors differ in adverse impact. *Personnel Psychology*, *50*, 455–70.

Hoffman, K. E. (1999). Recruitment sites changing their focus. Internet Careers, *http://www.iw.com/print/1999/03/15/intcareers/19990315-recruitment.html*

Huffcutt, A. I. and Arthur, W. Jr. (1994). Hunter and Hunter (1984) revisited: Interview validity for entry-level jobs. *Journal of Applied Psychology*, *79*, 184–90.

Huffcutt, A. I. and Woehr, D. J. (1999). Further analysis of employment interview validity: A quantitative evaluation of interviewer-related structuring methods. *Journal of Organizational Behavior*, *20*, 549–60.

Hunter, J. E. and Hunter, R. F. (1984). Validity and utility of alternative predictors of job performance. *Psychological Bulletin*, *96*, 72–98.

Hunter, J. E. and Schmidt, F. L. (1990). *Methods of Meta-Analysis*. Newbury Park, CA: Sage.

Hunter, J. E., Schmidt, F. L. and Jackson, G. B. (1982). *Meta-analysis: Cumulating Research Findings across Studies*. Beverly Hills, CA: Sage.

IPD (1999). *IPD Survey Report 5: Recruitment*. London: Institute of Personnel and Development.

Judge, T. A., Higgins, C. A., Thoresen, C. J. and Barrick, M. R. (1999). The big five personality traits, general mental ability, and career success across life span. *Personnel Psychology*, 52, 621–52.

Kandola, R. and Fullerton, J. (1994). *Managing the Mosaic: Diversity in Action*. London: IPD.

Kehoe, C., Pitkow, J., Sutton, K., Aggarwal, G. and Rogers, J. D. (1999). *Results of GVU's Tenth World Wide Web User Survey*. http://www.gvu.gatech.edu/user_surveys

Keller, J. (1996). Public access issues: An introduction. In B. Kahin and J. Keller (eds.), *Public Access to the Internet*. Boston, Mass.: The MIT Press.

Kline, P. (1993). *Personality: The Psychometric View*. London: Routledge.

Kurz, R. and Bartram, D. (2002). Competency and individual performance: Modelling the world of work. In I. Robertson, M. Callinan and D. Bartram (eds.), *Organizational Effectiveness: The Role of Psychology*. Chichester: Wiley.

Latham, G. P., Saari, L. M., Pursell, E. D. and Campion, M. A. (1980). The situational interview. *Journal of Applied Psychology*, 65, 422–7.

Lawrence, S. (1999). Employment Sites. *Iconocast*, 10 June 1999. http://www.iconocast.com

Mackinnon, D. W. (1977). From selecting spies to selecting managers. In J. L. Moses and W. C. Byham (eds.), *Applying the Assessment Centre Method*, pp. 13–30. New York: Pergamon Press.

McDaniel, M. A., Whetzel, D. L., Schmidt, F. L. and Maurer, S. D. (1994). The validity of employment interviews: A comprehensive review and meta-analysis. *Journal of Applied Psychology*, 79, 599–616.

Matthews, G. and Deary, I. J. (1998). *Personality Traits*. Cambridge: Cambridge University Press.

Mayer, J. D., Salovey, P. and Caruso, D. (2000). Models of emotional intelligence. In R. J. Sternberg (ed.), *Handbook of Intelligence*. Cambridge: Cambridge University Press.

Moser, K. and Schuler, H. (1989). The nature of psychological measurement. In P. Herriot (ed.), *Assessment and Selection in Organizations*, pp. 281–305. Chichester: Wiley.

Mount, M. K., Witt, L. A. and Barrick, M. R. (2000). Incremental validity of empirically keyed biodata scales over GMA and the five factor personality constructs. *Personnel Psychology*, 53, 299–323.

Murphy, K. and Bartram, D. (2002). Recruitment, personnel selection and organizational effectiveness. In I. Robertson, M. Callinan and D. Bartram (eds.), *Organizational Effectiveness: The Role of Psychology*. Chichester: Wiley.

Newell, S. and Tansley, C. (2001). International uses of selection methods. In C. L.

Cooper and I. T. Robertson (eds.), *International Review of Industrial and Organizational Psychology*, pp. 195–213. Chichester: Wiley.

Patterson, M., West, M. A., Lawthom, R. and Nickell, S. (1997). *Impact of People Management Practices on Business Performance*. Issues in People Management Report No. 22. London: Institute of Personnel and Development.

Paunonen, S. V., Rothstein, M. G. and Jackson, N. J. (1999). Narrow reasoning about the use of broad personality measures for personnel selection. *Journal of Organizational Behavior*, 20, 389–405.

Payne, T. (1995). Evaluating test fairness. *International Journal of Selection and Assessment*, 3, 47–51.

Pervin, L. A. (1989). Persons, situations, interactions: The history of a controversy and a discussion of situational models. *The Academy of Management Review*, 14, 350–60.

Reilly, R. R., Henry, S. and Smither, J. W. (1990). An examination of the effects of using behavior checklists on the construct validity of assessment center dimensions. *Personnel Psychology*, 43, 71–84.

Robertson, I. T., Baron, H., Gibbons, P., MacIver, R. and Nyfield, G. (2000). Conscientiousness and managerial performance. *Journal of Occupational and Organizational Psychology*, 73, 171–80.

Robertson, I. T. and Callinan, M. (1998). Personality and work behaviour. *European Journal of Work and Organizational Psychology*, 7, 321–40.

Robertson, I. T. and Downs, S. (1989). Work sample tests of trainability: A meta-analysis. *Journal of Applied Psychology*, 74, 402–10.

Robertson, I. T., Gratton, L. and Rout, U. (1990). The validity of situational interviews for administrative jobs. *Journal of Organizational Behavior Management*, 11, 69–76.

Robertson, I. T., Gratton, L. and Sharpley, D. A. (1987). The psychometric properties and design of assessment centres: Dimensions into exercises won't go. *Journal of Occupational Psychology*, 60, 187–95.

Robertson, I. T., Iles, P. A., Gratton, L. and Sharpley, D. A. (1991). The impact of personnel selection methods on candidates. *Human Relations*, 44, 963–82.

Robertson, I. T. and Kandola, R. S. (1982). Work sample tests: Validity, adverse impact and applicant reaction. *Journal of Occupational Psychology*, 55, 171–83.

Robertson, I. T. and Kinder, A. (1993). Personality and job competences: The criterion-related validity of some personality variables. *Journal of Occupational and Organizational Psychology*, 66, 225–44.

Ryan, A. M. and Ployhart, R. E. (2000). Applicants' perceptions of selection procedures and decisions: A critical review and agenda for the future. *Journal of Management*, 26, 565–606.

Sackett, P. R. and Dreher, G. F. (1982). Constructs and assessment center dimensions: Some troubling empirical findings. *Journal of Applied Psychology*, 67, 401–10.

Salgado, J. F. (1997). The five factor model of personality and job performance in the European community. *Journal of Applied Psychology*, 82, 30–43.

Salgado, J. F. (1999). Personnel selection methods. In C. L. Cooper and I. T. Robertson (eds.), *International Review of Industrial and Organizational Psychology*, pp. 1–54. Chichester: Wiley.

Schmidt, F. L. and Hunter, J. E. (1998). The validity and utility of selection methods in personnel psychology: Practical and theoretical implications of 85 years of research findings. *Psychological Bulletin*, 124, 262–74.

Schmidt, F. L., Mack, M. J. and Hunter, J. E. (1984). Selection utility in the occupation of US park ranger for three modes of test use. *Journal of Applied Psychology*, 69, 490–97.

Schmitt, N., Clause, C. S. and Pulakos, E. D. (1996). Subgroup differences associated with different measure of some common job-relevant constructs. In C. L. Cooper and I. T. Robertson (eds.), *International Review of Industrial and Organizational Psychology*, vol. 11. Chichester: Wiley.

Schmitt, N., Gooding, R. Z., Noe, R. A. and Kirsch, M. (1984). Meta-analysis of validity studies published between 1964 and 1982 and the investigation of study characteristics. *Personnel Psychology*, 37, 407–22.

Schmitt, N. and Chan, D. (1998). *Personnel Selection: A Theoretical Approach*. London: Sage.

Schneider, R. J. and Hough, L. M. (1995). Personality and industrial/organizational psychology. In C. L. Cooper and I. T. Robertson (eds.), *International Review of Work and Organizational Psychology*. Chichester: Wiley.

Shippmann, J. S., Ash, R. A., Battista, M., Carr, L., Eyde, L. D., Hesketh, B., Kehoe, J., Pearlman, K., Prien, E. P. and Sanchez, J. I. (2000). The practice of competency modelling. *Personnel Psychology*, 53, 703–40.

Shippmann, J. S., Prien, E. P. and Katz, J. A. (1990). Reliability and validity of in basket performance measures. *Personnel Psychology*, 43, 837–59.

Smith, M. and Robertson, I. T. (1993). *Systematic Personnel Selection*. London: Macmillan.

Snow, C. C. and Snell, S. A. (1993). Staffing as strategy. In N. Schmitt and W. Borman (eds.), *Personnel Selection in Organizations*, pp. 448–78. San Francisco: Jossey-Bass.

Spychalski, A. C., Quiñones, M. A., Gaugler, B. B. and Pohley, K. (1997). A survey of assessment center practices in organizations in the United States. *Personnel Psychology*, 50, 71–90.

Sternberg, R. J. (1997). Tacit knowledge and job success. In N. Anderson and P. Herriot (eds.), *International Handbook of Selection and Assessment*. Chichester: Wiley.

Sternberg, R. J. (ed.) (2000). *Handbook of Intelligence*. Cambridge University Press.

Stokes, G. S. and Reddy, S. (1992). The use of background data in organizational decisions. In C. L. Cooper and I. T. Robertson (eds.), *International Review of Industrial and Organizational Psychology*, pp. 285–321. Chichester: Wiley.

Tett, R. P., Guterman, H. A., Bleir, A. and Murphy, P. J. (2000). Development and content validation of a hyper-dimensional taxonomy of managerial competence. *Human Performance*, 13, 205–51.

Tett, R. P., Jackson, D. N. and Rothstein, M. (1991). Personality measures as predictors of job performance: A meta-analytic review. *Personnel Psychology*, 44, 703–42.

Vernon, P. E. (1950). The validation of civil service selection board procedures. *Occupational Psychology*, 24, 75–95.

Vernon, P. E. and Parry, J. B. (1949). *Personnel Selection in the British Forces*. London: University of London Press.

Wagner, R. A. (2000). Practical intelligence. In R. J. Sternberg (ed.), *Handbook of Intelligence*. Cambridge University Press.

Weekley, J. A. and Gier, J. A. (1987). Reliability and validity of the situational interview for a sales position. *Journal of Applied Psychology*, 72, 484–7.

Weisner, W. H. and Cronshaw, S. F. (1988). A meta-analytic investigation of the impact of interview format and degree of structure on the validity of the employment interview. *Journal of Occupational Psychology*, 61, 275–90.

Wernimont, P. F. and Campbell, J. P. (1968). Signs, samples and criteria. *Journal of Applied Psychology*, 52, 372–6.

Wiggins, J. S. (1973). *Personality and Prediction: Principles of Personality Assessment*. Reading, Mass.: Addison-Wesley.

Wilkinson, L. J. (1997). Generalizable biodata? An application to the vocational interests of managers. *Journal of Occupational and Organizational Psychology*, 70, 49–60.

Wollowick, H. B. and McNamara, W. J. (1969). Relationship of the components of an assessment center to management success. *Journal of Applied Psychology*, 53, 348–52.

Woodruffe, C. (1992). *Assessment Centers*. London: IPM.

Wright, P. M., Lichenfels, P. A. and Pursell, E. D. (1989). The structured interview: Additional studies and a meta-analysis. *Journal of Occupational Psychology*, 62, 191–9.

Wroe, N. (2000). SHL survey suggests online selection process increases positive perception of companies. *SHL News Release*, February 1, 2000. Boulder, Colorado: SHL USA Inc.

6

Learning and Training

Peter Warr

This chapter will review some of the processes by which people acquire and apply new knowledge, skills and attitudes. Factors in the environment and in the individual that can influence those processes will be examined, and frameworks for evaluating training programmes will be outlined. General themes applicable to learning in many situations will be explored in their particular applications to paid work.

Several factors emphasize the importance of learning by members of the work-force: the rapid pace of change in organizations, increased international pressure for greater competitiveness and for more effective ways of working, expanded use of computer-based systems, and a tendency toward more frequent transitions between jobs. These factors have given rise to the advocacy of 'lifelong learning' and the creation of 'learning organizations', and processes of learning underlie most of the issues considered in this book.

LIFE IS A LEARNING PROCESS

Learning is fundamental to life. In its absence a person is unlikely to survive, and at a societal level the existence of a culture depends on people acquiring common knowledge and norms. This pervasiveness presents difficulties for researchers, inside work organizations or elsewhere. If behaviour and social interactions are based on a steady stream of learning, usually in very small increments, how can we chop up this stream into discrete elements for study? Most often in the area of this book, the answer has been to focus primarily on processes of *formal* learning, those which have been planned and structured, for example within a training programme.

In broad terms, learning may be viewed as cognitive and physical activity giving rise to a relatively permanent change in knowledge, skill or attitude. 'Training' involves organized efforts to assist learning through instruction and practice. Two main kinds are 'job-specific' training, and procedures to promote 'development'. Job-specific training seeks to improve effectiveness in a current role, whereas development activities take a longer-term perspective and may extend into career planning and reviews of personal progress (Noe, Wilk, Mullen and Wanek, 1997). Training and development activities may be described as either 'off the job' (occurring away from the work-place, for example in a training centre) or 'on the job' (involving work tasks which can contribute to learning).

The Outcomes of Learning

Learning brings about changes in knowledge, skills or attitude. In addition, the outcomes of learning can include increased employability, a greater income, or several less tangible changes. These results can benefit an employer, an employee, or both of those.

Knowledge (the first outcome mentioned above) can be viewed as either 'declarative' or 'procedural'. Declarative knowledge comprises factual information about what is the case, whereas procedural knowledge is made up of routines specifying how to do something. Those may be either physical or mental, so that the effective handling of a cricket bat or the conduct of mental calculations are both instances of procedural knowledge. Declarative knowledge is usually explicit, in that a person can report it; but procedural knowledge is often implicit, revealed in outcomes rather than in conscious awareness of the routines themselves.

Most learning involves the acquisition of knowledge of both kinds, but some declarative knowledge must be acquired before proceduralization is possible (Anderson, 1982, 1995). Initially (in what is often termed the 'cognitive' phase) a learner gains information about individual facts and their inter-relationships in different situations. Some of this declarative knowledge is converted through additional processing into cognitive or behavioural procedures, through which it is applied in dealing with the environment. These procedures can become joined within increasingly long strings of actions, which (in the 'autonomous' stage) the person can execute as a whole, often with only limited conscious attention. Learners thus shift from cognitive effort and responses to single stimuli towards pre-structured, automated sequences of co-ordinated thought or action; once started, the latter can be difficult to interrupt.

Procedural knowledge is very similar to what is sometimes referred to as 'skill'. Skilled behaviour involves effective handling of particular situations, and the term 'skill' usually implies that a person's performance is a result of learning. 'Knowledge' and 'skill' contain similar elements, but 'knowledge' is more declarative and 'skill' is more procedural. Among the procedures that are built up within a skill are 'cognitive strategies', providing higher-order guidelines about appropriate priorities and sequencing of activities (e.g., Kraiger, Ford and Salas, 1993).

A related concept is 'expertise'. As described in Chapter 2, studies have contrasted experts in a particular domain against novices in that domain. Experts have been shown to have a superior and more organized knowledge-base, they perceive and recall larger meaningful patterns in their domain, search for and locate information more effectively, are better at anticipating future developments and potential faults, make more sophisticated plans, and can more quickly process new information within their established knowledge structure. They are able to execute fast strings of actions, that are not always under direct control once initiated (being 'autonomous' as described above) but which free mental resources and permit simultaneous processing of information (e.g., Sonnentag, 2000).

The outcomes from learning introduced above as knowledge and skill may thus also be viewed in terms of increased expertise. In addition, learning may give rise to shifts in a person's attitudes, values or preferences. For example, training programmes may be intended to modify employees' opinions and feelings about a working procedure, a piece of equipment, customers, a style of management behaviour, or the employing organization itself. These potential outcomes of training are more affective (based on feelings) than are the cognitive and behavioural components of knowledge, skill or expertise. As outlined in Chapter 1, attitudes are usually viewed as evaluative tendencies (favourable or unfavourable) towards an object.

Another potential outcome has been described in terms of greater 'employability', drawing attention to the fact that individuals need to continue updating their expertise in order to maintain the potential to move into different jobs with the same or another employer. The enhancement of employability can be an important objective for individuals considering future learning activities.

A related benefit is in terms of increased income. It is well established that members of the workforce with more training are likely to receive higher incomes than others (e.g., Blundell, Dearden, Meghir and Sianesi, 1999). The reasons for this pattern are multiple, in that high-income people may differ from others in respects apart from the training they have received (in terms of ability or previous education, for instance), but the differential in training-related income remains significant after statistical control for additional factors.

Other potential outcomes are less tangible. For instance, Nordhaug (1989) asked employees about the consequences of their most recent training course, and found that many reported an increased interest in learning in general (51 per cent of respondents), greater feelings of self-actualization (65 per cent) and increased self-confidence (42 per cent). In some settings training may have those outcomes as explicit goals. For instance, in seeking to encourage traditional non-learners to become more active in training and development (Birdi, Allan and Warr, 1997), it may be necessary first to enhance self-confidence and learning motivation, before more substantial skill acquisition becomes possible.

Some Training Methods and Their Effectiveness

In both off-the-job and on-the-job training, information is obtained in part by listening to and watching other people. Those activities may be formal, for instance through structured programmes of lectures, or they may be informal, through observation of colleagues' work behaviour. A third activity in most learning is practice of the behaviours to be improved, providing feedback (sometimes termed 'knowledge of results') about the effectiveness of specific responses or routines.

These three activities (listening, observing and practising) have been brought together systematically in 'behaviour modelling' training. Based in part on theorizing by Bandura (1977), this identifies 'learning points' (specific issues to be studied) and presents those first verbally and then visually. The verbal account usually takes the form of a brief description or longer lecture, and this is followed by a visual presentation to demonstrate key behaviours. (These may involve a practical demonstration by one or more trainers, or the material might be shown on video-tape.) Learners are then required to 'model' those behaviours by practising the activities that have been presented. Feedback about each person's performance (guidance about strengths, limitations and possible improvements) is provided by trainers or fellow-learners. Different learning points are presented separately, before being combined into more extended activities.

Behaviour modelling has been shown to be effective, for example in managerial and computer training (Burke and Day, 1986; Gist, Schwoerer and Rosen, 1989). In a study of instruction to use a software package, Simon and Werner (1996) compared behaviour modelling against two other training procedures: lectures with visual aids, and self-directed exploration of teaching material. A control condition (no teaching) was also examined, and trainees were randomly allocated to different conditions. In addition, variations in learners' general cognitive ability were statistically controlled. Measures were taken of post-training comprehension, practical success, and attitudes toward the system in question. Behaviour modelling was found to be the most successful training procedure in all respects.

A refinement of the general approach is in terms of 'active interlocked modelling', which promotes learning through observation of another student. In this procedure trainees work in pairs, taking it in turn to carry out part of the task to be learned, and for the rest of the time observing and providing feedback to a partner. Dyadic learning of this kind has been compared by Arthur, Day, Bennett, McNelly and Jordan (1997) against individual training activities. Despite having half the amount of hands-on practice, participants in the dyadic condition achieved the same level of performance. In effect, this represents a 100 per cent increase in effective use of time, since twice the number of trainees attained the desired outcome in the same amount of time.

It is of course also important that learned material is retained subsequent to its acquisition, and some studies have examined retention after different training procedures. For example, the two experimental comparisons summarized above (by Simon and Werner, 1996, and Arthur *et al.*, 1997) both demonstrated that patterns at the end of training were replicated several weeks later: retention was better for the procedure that had been more effective during learning.

Skill loss or forgetting (the opposite of retention) occurs if learned material is not applied or further practised. The usual forgetting pattern across time is one of an initial sharp decrement followed by a levelling-off, and the strongest predictor of how much will be retained is the degree of overlearning (Arthur, Bennett, Stanush and McNelly, 1998). This means that subsequent retention can be increased by additional learning, either during an initial programme (for example, continuing well beyond merely adequate performance) or in later activities (for instance in 'relapse prevention' or remedial practice linked to the original training pro-visions). Retention is also better when different elements of the material are somewhat interdependent, so that they may better support each other by providing mutual associations, and when cognitive interference between different elements is not great.

Off-the-job learning activities have traditionally been undertaken in a training centre, school or college, but there is a growing interest in 'open' forms of learning. In these cases, individuals work on their own to learn material presented in books, computer files or audio- or video-tapes. A key feature is that open learners have more autonomy to decide what is studied, as well as how, when, where, and at what pace they will proceed.

Although open learning may be undertaken at home or elsewhere away from a place of employment, some organizations have computer-based learning facilities that can be used during the working day. These are sometimes located in an 'employee development centre', a company site in which written, audio-taped, video-taped or computer-based material can be studied or borrowed for use elsewhere. In a minority of cases, material is presented through an intranet, a computer network accessible only from within the company. Computer-based training is becoming increasingly common, and it has clear advantages when large numbers of employees are to be trained, especially if they are geographically dispersed. Individualized sequencing of instruction is possible, immediate feedback can be provided, students may undertake self-assessment tests, and their progress may be recorded and analyzed. In some cases, multi-media computer presentations can permit the powerful integration of written, diagrammatic and auditory information.

There appear to have been few experimental evaluations of computer-based systems, but there are frequent suggestions that training time is reduced and that employees find the procedures attractive. Some systems make it possible for dispersed members of the organization to add fresh material, thus combining information from different sources. Conversely, some computer-based systems are inflexible, being difficult to change and with a content that becomes irrelevant or out of date.

The training methods examined so far in this section have tended to be off-the-job, as employees undertake learning away from their daily work. In addition, much learning occurs in actual job settings, either through formal training programmes or through informal activities. Formal on-the-job training is most common early in a person's career. That may involve scheduled periods of observation and practice under the guidance of a colleague or a trainer, and is sometimes interspersed with linked off-the-job instruction. However, most on-the-job learning is informal, gained through experience of one's own and others' activities in the absence of planned training inputs. Given that experience is acquired idiosyncratically, and that learning may accumulate slowly across long periods, this process is obviously difficult to study.

On-the-job learning is most likely when individuals are required to undertake activities that provide difficult challenges (McCauley, Ruderman, Ohlott and Morrow, 1994). Particularly important are unfamiliar and increased responsibilities, having to prove oneself in a new role, undertaking transitions to different positions, coping with job overload, and having to take risks. These activities can be stressful, pointing to the fact that lowered well-being is sometimes inevitable as part of an overall satisfying career.

There is a trend towards work-based learning through membership of temporary problem-solving groups, undertaking specific projects, shadowing other employees, job rotation, or secondment to other parts of the organization. For example, Campion, Cheraskin and Stevens (1994) studied the consequences of job rotation (for periods of several months) in managers and executives. They found four sets of benefits: positive well-being in terms of greater job satisfaction and career involvement, organizational integration benefits through wider networks and greater transfer of knowledge, work content benefits such as greater stimulation through task demands and work variety, and personal development benefits in the form of better coping skills and greater insights into personal strengths and limitations.

As outlined earlier, specific learning activities may be viewed more broadly, as part of a person's overall development. Many large organizations link career development to training through a process of annual reviews. In discussion with a supervisor, an employee examines his or her work progress each year, identifying areas and activities in which additional learning could be valuable and planning that learning for the following year. In some organizations, employees are encouraged to prepare and update a 'personal development plan', summarizing short-term and longer-term career goals and progress toward those.

Other Environmental Features Affecting Learning

As with most variables examined by psychologists, learning behaviour is a function of both environmental and personal factors. Among relevant environmental features (exerting their influence from outside the person) are the different methods of training illustrated in the previous section. A more general aspect of the environment is the amount of support provided by an employee's supervisor or organization as a whole.

Support of this kind might influence either participation in learning or success in learning. We thus need to examine two issues: the relationship between supervisors' support for learning and employees' participation in learning activities, and the association between that support and the amount learned. In both cases, correlations have been found to be significantly positive.

For example, Birdi et al. (1997) examined how often in the past twelve months workers had taken part in five types of activity: required training courses in work time, work-based development activities in work time (in project groups, personal projects, etc.), voluntary job-related learning in one's own time (e.g., taking a job-relevant college course), career planning activities in work or own time (for instance, updating a career development plan), and voluntary non-job learning in one's own time (e.g., learning a foreign language). Employees' participation was significantly predicted by the amount of perceived supervisory support in all cases except for voluntary non-job learning.

In respect of the second issue (concerning the amount of learning), Colquitt, LePine and Noe (2000) reviewed previous studies, finding that both declarative knowledge and skill acquisition were significantly greater when more support was received from supervisors. The causal influence is unlikely to be only from supervisors' support to participation or to learning success (for example, it might be in both directions), but some supervisory impact of that kind appears probable. For example, Colquitt *et al.* (2000) reported a significant positive association between support from supervisors and the probable mediator of raised motivation for training. Receiving encouragement from one's supervisor is thus likely to enhance both participation and learning success.

Some Individual Characteristics Affecting Learning

As well as being influenced by the environment, participation in learning is affected by a person's own characteristics. Studies have repeatedly shown that different kinds of people undertake different amounts of development activity. For example, employees with longer tenure in a job receive significantly less training than others, as do those in lower-level jobs, those with fewer educational qualifications, older workers, and those in smaller establishments (e.g., Department for Education and Employment, 1999; Osterman, 1995; Warr, 1994).

In terms of learning achievement, differential success has been shown to occur as a function of several individual characteristics. Particularly important are cognitive ability, learning motivation, aspects of personality, learning strategies, age and relevant previous knowledge.

Many studies have reported a significant positive correlation between scores on tests of general intelligence (sometimes referred to as 'g' or 'general mental ability') and learning achievement (Schmidt and Hunter, 1998; Colquitt *et al.*, 2000). The association with intelligence is particularly strong when tasks are novel or demanding, for example early in a training programme. Kanfer and Ackerman (1989) showed that the correlation between intelligence and learning performance was greatest in early trials and declined with increasing practice; this difference reflects a shift from the 'cognitive' to the 'autonomous' stage (see above). Conversely, the association with intelligence is lower when ability differences are outweighed by variations in knowledge. Prior knowledge then assists learning, irrespective of cognitive ability level.

Intelligence is also less predictive of learning in structured rather than unstructured tasks. In more structured learning, a teacher or teaching system controls content, timing and feedback, for instance ensuring that tasks are undertaken in a pre-defined sequence. This structure particularly helps lower-intelligence learners, so that the correlation between learning success and cognitive ability is reduced in structured settings. In contrast, high-ability individuals gain from low-structure opportunities, and the ability–learning correlation is then greater. There is thus an 'aptitude–treatment interaction' (Snow, 1989), in which learner intelligence and task structure jointly determine learning success.

A second individual characteristic is affective rather than cognitive. Learning motivation has been studied in two ways, through scales with self-descriptive statements (e.g., 'I am enthusiastic about learning new things') or through measures of the perceived benefits and costs (the 'valence') of learning activity. In both cases, learning motivation has been shown to predict learning success (Colquitt et al., 2000).

The factors underlying variations in learning motivation are both individual and environmental. For example, this motivation is greater among younger employees, those in higher job grades, people with higher educational qualifications and those with stronger organizational commitment. Support from supervisors and co-workers is also linked to greater motivation to learn (Warr and Birdi, 1998; Colquitt et al., 2000).

Learning motivation may be viewed within a broader personality trait of conscientiousness (see also Chapter 5). Employees with higher conscientiousness scores have been found to be more successful in learning (Colquitt and Simmering, 1998), and this personality attribute predicts learning success over and above general cognitive ability (Schmidt and Hunter, 1998). A second personality trait associated with learning attainment is openness to experience. This broad notion includes a preference for complex thinking, new ideas, artistic developments, abstract concepts, and so on. Its focus on new ideas also suggests that a high-scoring person has a stronger motivation for learning. It is thus not surprising that this aspect of personality significantly predicts training performance (Barrick and Mount, 1991).

Other studies of individual characteristics have examined differences in the use of learning strategies. Those have been defined as 'overt and covert information-processing activities used by learners at the time of encoding to facilitate the acquisition, storage, and subsequent retrieval of information to be learned' (Kardash and Amlund, 1991, p. 119). Measurement is usually through self-completion questionnaires, in which individuals report how much they used each strategy in a previous learning activity.

Principal learning strategies may be viewed as cognitive, behavioural or self-regulatory activities (Warr and Allan, 1998). Among cognitive strategies are rehearsal (repeating to oneself the material to be learned) and elaboration (examining implications and connections between material). Behavioural learning strategies include trying things out in practice and seeking help from other people. Self-regulation may be in terms of emotion control (procedures to ward off anxiety) or motivation control (procedures to maintain motivation and attention despite limited interest in the task).

There is evidence from research in schools and colleges that students reporting greater use of specific strategies tend to learn more than others (Warr and Allan, 1998). Findings about occupational learning are less consistent, possibly because of wider differences between learning tasks in employment settings. For example, cognitive elaboration is sometimes associated with better learning (Warr and Bunce, 1995) but not always (Warr, Allan and Birdi, 1999). However, learning through practical application has been found generally helpful in occupational training.

An important question about learning strategies concerns their overlap with other concepts. For example, it may be that individuals who report greater use of certain strategies are also more motivated to learn. Observed associations between strategies and learning performance could in that case reflect differences in motivation. In other cases, learners may seek help from other people (a behavioural strategy) because they are particularly anxious about the difficulty facing them; in this case, learning anxiety might have more effect on learning outcomes than does the strategy (Warr and Downing, 2000). The place of learning strategies among the other concepts examined in this section is not yet clear.

What about age differences in learning? Kubeck, Delp, Haslett and McDaniel (1996) examined previous research into training, deriving the overall conclusion that older individuals, relative to younger ones, showed less mastery (in post-tests) of training material and took longer to complete the training. The average correlation between employees' training attainment and age was found to be −0.21; for time to complete training, the correlation was 0.40.

In general, older people are less likely to achieve equivalent learning outcomes in a given period of time. It follows that, if maximum training time is restricted to that appropriate for younger ones, learning will on average be poorer at older ages. This can occur even in relatively young samples, if training time is short and the task is difficult. For example, age and post-test knowledge score were correlated −0.27 in a study of two-day intensive training for vehicle technicians, despite the fact that their average age was only thirty-one years (Warr *et al.*, 1999). In other cases, for example in open learning where individuals can adjust the time allocated to different elements, age may not be linked to poorer outcomes but older learners may report greater learning difficulty, having to adapt to a perceived greater workload by investing greater effort (Warr and Bunce, 1995; Warr, 2001).

That compensatory activity by older learners reminds us that the several factors outlined here should be viewed in combination rather than singly. For example, learning motivation and cognitive ability have a joint influence in any situation (e.g., high motivation can outweigh low ability), and their impact can also depend on the nature of the learning task (for example, its degree of structure).

Finally in this consideration of individual factors related to learning success it is important to include relevant previous knowledge. People who are more knowledgeable at the outset are likely to perform better on post-training tests. For example, the correlation between pre-test and post-test scores was 0.22 across nine months of training in Warr and Downing's (2000) study.

It is thus desirable in studies of learning to control for prior scores. However, that is rarely done. Most investigations record only post-test scores, although those may reflect previous knowledge as well as learning during the programme. It is nevertheless preferable to measure changes in knowledge from beginning to end of a learning episode (sometimes termed 'learning gain'), rather than merely attainment at the end (Warr *et al.*, 1999).

The Transfer of Learning

It is clear from everyday experience that material learned in one setting is not always applied in others. For instance, employees attending a course in a company training centre may make little use of the course content when back at work. Ford, Quiñones, Sego and Sorra (1992) found that employees performed only half of trained tasks in the subsequent four months. Training transfer has two components: the retention of the learned material over time, and its generalization to new settings. In reviewing the factors affecting transfer, both those aspects need to be examined.

As indicated above, the principal determinant of retention is the degree of consolidation achieved in initial learning or through subsequent remedial activities; continued learning protects against forgetting. As well as merely the quantity of learning, greater cognitive elaboration also aids recall. Elaboration is a matter of reviewing personal meanings, implications, associations and so on, and memory for material is usually improved by its elaborate processing (Anderson, 1995). In addition, since items held in memory store can interfere with each other, retention is likely to be better if elements do not conflict with others (for instance, in linking one component with a range of inconsistent others).

The second aspect of transfer, generalizing to other settings, has been shown to be associated with five kinds of variable: appropriateness of the training content, opportunities available for use of the learned material, organizational support for its application, an employee's commitment to the organization, and his or her level of confidence.

The appropriateness of training content is partly a question of the similarity of elements between the training and application situations; greater overlap will naturally assist transfer. (In studies of training in simulators, for example by airline pilots, this overlap is referred to as the 'fidelity' of a simulation.) Instruction in general principles which might be applied across situations (rather than merely in training) is also helpful. Transfer of training is thus more likely for content that is relevant to a job and has emphasized general themes and their applicability in varied settings.

Second, does an employee have opportunities to apply what he or she has learned? Application opportunities derive in part from the similarity in content between training and job (above), but such similarity does not itself guarantee transfer of learning. If work pressure is continuous, an employee may have no opportunity to try out and develop new behaviour. In addition, task-allocation decisions taken by a supervisor are important. For example, Ford et al. (1992) found that employees who were perceived by a supervisor to be more competent and likeable were more often asked to undertake tasks which provided a greater breadth of experience and were more complex.

Another influence on transfer is general organizational support. When supervisors and colleagues encourage and reward the application of taught material (providing a positive 'transfer climate'), motivation to transfer is greater and training is more likely to yield positive outcomes in the work setting (Tracey, Tannenbaum and Kavanagh, 1995; Colquitt *et al.*, 2000).

A fourth factor associated with transfer of learning is an individual's commitment to his or her organization. Transfer has been shown to be greater for employees reporting stronger attachment to their organization (Colquitt *et al.*, 2000). Another relevant individual feature is a person's confidence, reflected in assertiveness in seeking out opportunities and undertaking new behaviours. This characteristic combines with other factors to affect the extent to which training is applied. For example, Ford *et al.* (1992) found that employees previously describing themselves as confident in performing the trained tasks were more likely to report later having had opportunities actually to perform them. In the study by Warr *et al.* (1999), trainees' learning confidence not only predicted later transfer but did this in combination with organizational support; both learning confidence and a positive transfer climate contributed to the extent of later changes.

THE EVALUATION OF TRAINING

An important aspect of training is the provision of feedback. This is needed by trainers as well as trainees. In order to improve their effectiveness, trainers have to obtain feedback about their performance. How can the quality of training be measured?

A first issue is that of perspective. From whose standpoint is effectiveness to be determined: an individual, his or her employer, or society more widely? In seeking learning outcomes such as increased income or employability, the goals of an employee are likely to be primary, but from an organization's perspective training initiatives are intended to improve productivity, profitability, flexibility and so on. Training evaluation is typically undertaken from an employer's rather than employees' viewpoint.

Two primary goals of training evaluation are to 'prove' or to 'improve' a training programme. In the first case, the aim is to learn about the value of the programme: has it been worthwhile? That can be of major importance to an organization seeking to spend wisely its limited resources or to a training department that needs to justify its funding. However, it is not easy to define unambiguously the worth of a training programme (see below), and in many settings the principal goal of evaluation is different: to improve presentations of a repeated programme. Material obtained after one application of the course is fed back to improve the next application (or a continuation of the first one), and information is gathered then to improve the following one.

The two forms of evaluation are conventionally termed 'summative' and 'formative'. Summative evaluation involves observation without any intervention (since it is the programme that is being evaluated, not the programme plus the intervention), but formative evaluation uses the information gathered to modify current and later activities. Thus summative evaluation gathers information to appraise a programme, whereas formative evaluation is more concerned with revision and improvement. Studies of training evaluation in many organizations start with a summative goal, but often become formative as improvements are suggested by early findings. (Given that the information gathered can improve current training, it seems sensible to use it; but that frustrates the original summative objective.)

Levels of Evaluation

Two frameworks for training evaluation will be reviewed here. The first was proposed by Kirkpatrick in the 1950s (e.g., Kirkpatrick, 1959), and identifies four principal 'levels' for examination. These are referred to as reaction, learning, behaviour and results.

Reaction
The easiest form of evaluation is through measurement of participants' subsequent opinions. Kirkpatrick advocated the assessment of how well trainees like a programme, describing this response as similar to an index of customer satisfaction.

Reactions can be measured through rating scales completed after a particular training session or after the course as a whole. That procedure is widespread in organizations (including universities), but the data are rarely analyzed in depth. Although the focus is primarily on participants' feelings ('I found this programme to be enjoyable' is a typical item), reactions of this kind are known to be uncorrelated with learning or behaviour (Alliger, Tannenbaum, Bennett, Traver and Shotland, 1997). Thus, although enjoyment ratings may be of interest within organizations, they provide no indication of a programme's value in terms of likely changes in a work setting. Furthermore, these reactions reflect in part characteristics of a trainee rather than merely the nature of the training. Warr *et al.* (1999) measured participants' training motivation before a course and their reactions after it, finding a significant positive correlation: trainees who entered the course feeling positive about it gave more positive reactions afterwards.

Different reactions (other than enjoyment) may better predict learning or behaviour. For example, Warr and Bunce (1995) studied three aspects that were found to be factorially distinct: enjoyment of the training, its perceived job usefulness and its perceived difficulty. The review by Alliger *et al.* (1997) indicated that perceived usefulness was more likely than the reaction of enjoyment to predict behavioural outcomes. Judgements of usefulness concern both training content and the demands of the work-place, and this dual perspective may enhance their predictive value. The reaction of perceived difficulty has rarely been measured, but it can be associated with lower learning attainment (Warr *et al.*, 1999).

Learning

The second level of evaluation in Kirkpatrick's framework concerns the knowledge, skills, expertise, attitudes, etc. acquired as a result of training. This learning may be measured by tests administered immediately after training, but is preferably indexed as a gain score from prior levels (see earlier).

Behaviour

At the third evaluation level, measures are taken of criterion behaviours in a job (those identified as the targets of training). Criteria may sometimes be objective indicators (sales, time taken, errors, and so on), but such summary objective information is not available for most jobs. Instead, measures of job behaviour are usually obtained through ratings made by a supervisor or colleagues. In order to record progress attributable to training, change scores from before to afterwards are preferable, rather than ratings of subsequent work behaviour alone.

Results

Finally, Kirkpatrick argues for evaluation in terms of changes at the level of a group or organization. For example, has the training brought about improvements in the performance of a work-team (rather than only in individuals' training-related behaviour, identified as level three) or in company profitability, market share, customer loyalty, and so on?

Any changes observed at this fourth level may arise from a combination of factors, and it is unlikely that a particular training programme can be identified as their single cause. Level-four evaluation is thus difficult in logical as well as practical terms, and it is attempted only infrequently. Similar problems occur in respect of level-three evaluation (job behaviour), since transfer of training is in part determined by features unconnected with that training (see above). Very few organizations attempt level-three evaluation in terms of job behaviour (asking instead about reactions or learning), although changes in job settings are essential if training is to be successful.

How closely are indicators intercorrelated between levels two, three and four? (Level one has been considered above.) For example, does learning at the end of a course predict later job behaviour? The review by Alliger *et al.* (1997) found only non-significant associations of that kind, presumably because transfer depends also on the favourability of a job setting and the characteristics of an employee (see earlier).

This general independence between evaluation scores at different levels presents practical difficulties. Different outcomes are likely at each level, and correlations between levels are likely to be non-significant. (However, reactions in terms of perceived usefulness and difficulty, rather than enjoyment, are more likely to be predictive; see above.) In this circumstance, on which set of data should evaluation decisions be based: reactions, learning or behaviour? Coupled with the general difficulty of placing a value on specific findings (how high a mean score at each of those levels is needed to conclude that the course has been successful?) and the high cost and complexity of administration, this inconsistency between levels can lead many organizations to bypass evaluation or to rely simply on a level-one questionnaire.

A second evaluation framework builds on Kirkpatrick's thinking, but examines some features not present in his account. Originally developed by Warr, Bird and Rackham (1970), this framework has been expanded with the abbreviation 'CIROOOP'. Those initials refer to context, input, reactions, three levels of outcomes, and process, as follows.

Context evaluation examines what action is desirable in a current setting. In the particular context in question, what is needed to advance toward strategic goals for the organization and behavioural goals for the employees? Performance must be examined relative to those two kinds of goals (broad targets for the organization as well as specific outcomes for trainees), recognizing that future requirements often need investigation as well as those that are more immediate. Procedures can involve observation, work samples, interviews, questionnaires, group discussions or examination of company records. Context evaluation recognizes that in some settings the analysis may not point towards training; instead, goals might be better attained by modifying working procedures or selecting new staff.

Context evaluation thus asks: is there a *training* problem? Organizations often commence training without adequate confirmation that training is the best solution. In cases when training is in fact inappropriate, evaluation levels one or two in the Kirkpatrick framework are irrelevant; reactions and immediate learning are of no concern if the activity was misplaced.

Input evaluation: assuming that some training is desirable, it is important to check that the best learning procedure has been selected. Many organizations continue with previous modes of delivery (for example, conventional lectures), rather than review all possible types of input. The objective of input evaluation is to ascertain and examine all possible options and to assess their likely benefits and costs.

Reaction evaluation: is level one in Kirkpatrick's framework (above).

Outcome evaluation: 'OOO' in the 'CIROOOP' abbreviation refers to immediate outcomes, intermediate outcomes and longer-term outcomes. Those are levels two, three and four in Kirkpatrick's framework.

Process evaluation: it is important to examine aspects of the training process that are not included in other enquiries. For example, how suitable were the training rooms and facilities, how did trainee–trainer relationships develop, how effective was the sequencing of material, the provision of feedback, the availability of time, and so on? These process features are assessed through observation, interviews or questionnaires, perhaps from trainers as well as trainees.

The CIROOOP framework can be viewed from the perspective of

'systems approaches' to training. Those specify and operationalize the components of an overall 'system', such as 'define objectives', 'develop criterion measures' and 'design training materials'. Systems approaches usually include 'evaluate the training' as one of the components. However, treating evaluation merely as a single part of the system is inappropriate. Instead, evaluation should be viewed as a superordinate or over-arching process. We need to evaluate the whole system, not merely the single component of instruction alone. The CIROOOP approach seeks to recognize this fact by assessing a wider range of system components than does the Kirkpatrick framework.

It is clear that comprehensive evaluation is time-consuming, difficult and expensive. Many organizations lack skills and resources for statistical analyses of quantitative material, and it is often felt that trainers' limited time should instead be applied to instructional work. Furthermore, evaluation results can be ambiguous. For example, there may be differences between levels (such that reactions to a course are favourable but no change in job behaviour occurs, for instance). An *overall* conclusion (combining all the different information) can be difficult. Full-scale evaluation of training programmes is thus rarely undertaken.

Given these problems, what form of training evaluation should be encouraged? An essential minimum should focus on reaction evaluation, personal action plans and context evaluation. First, the study of reactions should be expanded to examine opinions about specific features of the training that might be modified in future. For instance, measures should cover perceived usefulness and difficulty, instead of merely enjoyment; views about the instructors, practice time, facilities and so on should be obtained; and trainees should be asked about possible obstacles to application of the training content.

Second, this focus on job behaviour should be linked to the creation of personal action plans, drawn up by each trainee and subsequently reviewed with his or her supervisor. It is helpful if trainers can be included in that process, for instance by creating 'transfer partnerships' between trainees, supervisors and trainers. A major problem preventing effective transfer of learning is that no one is explicitly responsible for that process; it falls between trainers and supervisors. Joint examination of the barriers to transfer is likely to modify the work-place (making the climate more supportive of transfer) as well as the content of training provisions (making training more applicable) (Broad and Newstrom, 1992), and such an examination serves as a valuable component of formative evaluation.

A third minimum form of evaluation examines the context. Much training is at least partly irrelevant to trainees' needs. A greater emphasis is now needed on whether any training at all is needed. Better context evaluation could considerably reduce wasted expense as well as improving transfer from what is provided, because that training would by definition be more relevant to job needs.

LEARNING AND ORGANIZATIONS

This chapter has emphasized that employees' participation in learning and their application of that learning depend greatly on characteristics of an employing organization. Two additional strands of research have explicitly focused on organizational features.

The Learning Organization

First are studies giving rise to the argument that managers should turn their company into a 'learning organization' (Burgoyne, Pedler and Boydell, 1994; Marquardt, 1996). This term has been defined in many ways, but the general prescription is that more employees should learn about more issues. Recommendations are thus made to increase participation in learning, the effectiveness of learning procedures and the transfer of learning; themes are similar to those addressed above. Associated terms are a 'continuous learning culture' and a 'positive learning climate'.

A positive learning climate has characteristics of the following kind: a persistent emphasis on the acquisition of new skills and knowledge, the provision of many different kinds of learning opportunities, support and encouragement from bosses and colleagues, an openness to change, regular reviews of learning processes and their possible improvement, an acceptance of mistakes during learning and early application, and a continuous concern to identify individuals' learning needs and to meet those in an effective manner (e.g., Tracey *et al.*, 1995). In practice, short-term work pressures, coupled with some staff absenteeism (which makes it difficult to free employees for training) can prevent those developments.

There is no doubt that a positive learning climate can only be sustained with strong encouragement from senior members of management.

Organizational Learning

A second line of thinking is based on the need to encourage learning in groups and larger organizations as well as merely by individuals. Studies have examined the characteristics of organizational learning, seeking to differentiate those from individual processes. It seems clear that the acquisition of knowledge, skills and attitudes by individual members of staff is central to learning at the organizational level, but that supra-individual features are also present.

To say that an organization (rather than a person) has learned is to indicate that the changes are to some degree independent of individual members of that organization; even if the current staff were replaced, the knowledge would remain. That can be achieved by a process of institutionalization, whereby new material becomes spread across the organization. In part, this may be through formal records and policy documents, but more often the change is in norms, rules, procedures, strategies, technologies and collective frames of reference applied widely in the organization (Huysman, 2000). For example, the development of shared mental models in teams is illustrated in Chapter 13.

Organizational learning thus involves the distribution and storage of knowledge as well as its acquisition. There has to be some sharing of new learning between members of an organization. In part, this may be through meetings or project groups, but one difficulty is that the outcomes of learning cannot always be expressed to oneself, let alone to other people. Another form of sharing is through application, ensuring that new ideas are spread by practical activities. The future research agenda in the area of this chapter thus extends to the management of knowledge across an organization, as well as covering individual-level themes of the kind reviewed above.

SUMMARY

The outcomes from learning include changed knowledge, skills, attitudes, employability and self-perceptions. Several training methods have been shown to be effective in terms of their immediate outcomes and later retention of material. Retention itself depends on the degree of initial learning and the interdependence between elements learned.

Processes of learning are influenced by environmental and individual features. For instance, support from supervisors (an environmental feature) promotes both participation and effective learning. In evaluating training it is important to examine all components of the process (including the identification of training needs) rather than merely reactions or immediate learning. However, comprehensive evaluation is difficult in practice.

FURTHER READING

Many issues in this chapter are examined in *Improving Training Effectiveness in Work Organizations* (Ford, Kozlowski, Kraiger, Salas and Teachout, 1997). Other general texts are by Anderson (1995) (reviewing laboratory research and theoretical approaches to learning), Buckley and Caple (2000) (setting practical issues in a research context) and Goldstein and Ford (2002) (emphasizing the assessment of training needs). Approaches to the evaluation of learning activities are discussed by Patrick (1992), Kraiger *et al.* (1993) and Bramley (1996). Skills-related aspects of the British labour market are included in the website of the Department for Education and Skills (*www.dfee.gov.uk/datasphere*).

REFERENCES

Alliger, G. M., Tannenbaum, S. I., Bennett, W., Traver, H. and Shotland, A. (1997). A meta-analysis of the relations among training criteria. *Personnel Psychology*, *50*, 341–58.

Anderson, J. R. (1982). Acquisition of cognitive skill. *Psychological Review, 89,* 369–406.

Anderson, J. R. (1995). *Learning and Memory: An Integrated Approach,* second edition. New York: Wiley.

Arthur, W., Bennett, W., Stanush, P. L. and McNelly, T. L. (1998). Factors that influence skill decay and retention: A quantitative review and analysis. *Human Performance, 11,* 57–101.

Arthur, W., Day, E. A., Bennett, W., McNelly, T. L. and Jordan, J. A. (1997). Dyadic versus individual training protocols: Loss and reacquisition of a complex skill. *Journal of Applied Psychology, 82,* 783–91.

Bandura, A. (1977). *Social Learning Theory.* Englewood Cliffs, NJ: Prentice Hall.

Barrick, M. R. and Mount, M. K. (1991). The big five personality dimensions and job performance: A meta-analysis. *Personnel Psychology, 44,* 1–26.

Birdi, K., Allan, C. and Warr, P. B. (1997). Correlates and perceived outcomes of four types of employee development activity. *Journal of Applied Psychology, 82,* 845–57.

Blundell, R., Dearden, L., Meghir, C. and Sianesi, B. (1999). Human capital investment: The returns from education and training to the individual, the firm and the economy. *Fiscal Studies, 20,* 1–23.

Bramley, P. (1996). *Evaluating Training Effectiveness,* second edition. London: McGraw-Hill.

Broad, M. L. and Newstrom, J. W. (1992). *Transfer of Training.* Reading MA: Addison-Wesley.

Buckley, R. and Caple, J. (2000). *The Theory and Practice of Training,* fourth edition. London: Kogan Page.

Burgoyne, J., Pedler, M. and Boydell, T. (1994). *Towards the Learning Company.* London: McGraw-Hill.

Burke, M. J. and Day, R. R. (1986). A cumulative study of the effectiveness of managerial training. *Journal of Applied Psychology, 71,* 232–45.

Campion, M. A., Cheraskin, L. and Stevens, M. J. (1994). Career-related antecedents and outcomes of job rotation. *Academy of Management Journal, 37,* 1518–42.

Colquitt, J. A., LePine, J. A. and Noe, R. A. (2000). Toward an integrative theory of training motivation: A meta-analytic path analysis of 20 years of research. *Journal of Applied Psychology, 85,* 678–707.

Colquitt, J. A. and Simmering, M. J. (1998). Conscientiousness, goal orientation, and motivation to learn during the learning process: A longitudinal study. *Journal of Applied Psychology, 83,* 654–65.

Department for Education and Employment (1999). *Education and Training Statistics for the United Kingdom.* London: The Stationery Office.

Ford, J. K., Kozlowski, S., Kraiger, K., Salas, E. and Teachout, M. (eds.) (1997). *Improving Training Effectiveness in Work Organizations.* Hillsdale, NJ: Erlbaum.

Ford, J. K., Quiñones, M. A., Sego, D. J. and Sorra, J. S. (1992). Factors affecting the opportunity to perform trained tasks on the job. *Personnel Psychology*, 45, 511–27.

Gist, M. E., Schwoerer, C. and Rosen, B. (1989). Effects of training methods on self-efficacy and performance in computer software training. *Journal of Applied Psychology*, 74, 884–91.

Goldstein, I. L. and Ford, J. K. (2002). *Training in Organizations: Needs Assessment, Development, and Evaluation*, fourth edition. Belmont, CA: Wadsworth.

Huysman, M. (2000). An organizational learning approach to the learning organization. *European Journal of Work and Organizational Psychology*, 9, 133–45.

Kanfer, R. and Ackerman, P. L. (1989). Motivation and cognitive abilities: An integrative aptitude–treatment interaction approach to skill acquisition. *Journal of Applied Psychology*, 74, 657–90.

Kardash, C. M. and Amlund, J. T. (1991). Self-reported learning strategies and learning from expository text. *Contemporary Educational Psychology*, 16, 117–38.

Kirkpatrick, D. L. (1959). Techniques for evaluating training programs. *Journal of the American Society of Training Directors*, 13, 3–9.

Kraiger, K., Ford, J. K. and Salas, E. (1993). Application of cognitive, skill-based, and affective theories of learning outcomes to new methods of training evaluation. *Journal of Applied Psychology*, 78, 311–28.

Kubeck, J. E., Delp, N. D., Haslett, T. K. and McDaniel, M. A. (1996). Does job-related training performance decline with age? *Psychology and Aging*, 11, 92–107.

Marquardt, M. (1996). *Building the Learning Organization*. New York: McGraw-Hill.

McCauley, C. D, Ruderman, M. N., Ohlott, P. J. and Morrow, J. E. (1994). Assessing the developmental components of managerial jobs. *Journal of Applied Psychology*, 79, 544–60.

Noe, R. A., Wilk, S. L., Mullen, E. J. and Wanek, J. E. (1997). Employee development: Issues in construct definition and investigation of antecedents. In J. K. Ford, S. Kozlowski, K. Kraiger, E. Salas and M. Teachout (eds.), *Improving Training Effectiveness in Work Organizations*, pp. 153–88. Hillsdale, NJ: Erlbaum.

Nordhaug, O. (1989). Reward functions of personnel training. *Human Relations*, 42, 373–88.

Osterman, P. (1995). Skill, training, and work organization in American establishments. *Industrial Relations*, 34, 125–46.

Patrick, J. (1992). *Training Research and Practice*. London: Academic Press.

Schmidt, F. L. and Hunter, J. E. (1998). The validity and utility of selection methods in personnel psychology: Practical and theoretical implications of 85 years of research findings. *Psychological Bulletin*, 124, 262–74.

Simon, S. J. and Werner, J. M. (1996). Computer training through behavior modeling, self-paced and instructional approaches: A field experiment. *Journal of Applied Psychology*, *81*, 648–59.

Snow, R. E. (1989). Aptitude–treatment interaction as a framework for research on individual differences in learning. In P. E. Ackerman, R. J. Sternberg and R. Glaser (eds.), *Learning and Individual Differences*, pp. 13–59. New York: Freeman.

Sonnentag, S. (2000). Expertise at work: Experience and excellent performance. In C. L. Cooper and I. T. Robertson (eds.), *International Review of Industrial and Organizational Psychology*, pp. 223–64. Chichester: Wiley.

Tracey, J. B., Tannenbaum, S. I. and Kavanagh, M. J. (1995). Applying trained skills on the job: The importance of the work environment. *Journal of Applied Psychology*, *80*, 239–52.

Warr, P. B. (1994). Training for older managers. *Human Resource Management Journal*, *4*, 22–38.

Warr, P. B. (2001). Age and work behaviour: Physical attributes, cognitive abilities, knowledge, personality traits and motives. In C. L. Cooper and I. T. Robertson (eds.), *International Review of Industrial and Organizational Psychology*, pp. 1–36. Chichester: Wiley.

Warr, P. B. and Allan, C. (1998). Learning strategies and occupational training. In C. L. Cooper and I. T. Robertson (eds.), *International Review of Industrial and Organizational Psychology*, pp. 83–121. Chichester: Wiley.

Warr, P. B., Allan, C. and Birdi, K. (1999). Predicting three levels of training outcome. *Journal of Occupational and Organizational Psychology*, *72*, 351–75.

Warr, P. B., Bird, M. W. and Rackham, N. (1970). *Evaluation of Management Training*. London: Gower Press.

Warr, P. B. and Birdi, K. (1998). Employee age and voluntary development activity. *International Journal of Training and Development*, *2*, 190–204.

Warr, P. B. and Bunce, D. (1995). Trainee characteristics and the outcomes of open learning. *Personnel Psychology*, *48*, 347–75.

Warr, P. B. and Downing, J. (2000). Learning strategies, learning anxiety and knowledge acquisition. *British Journal of Psychology*, *91*, 311–33.

7

Careers and Career Management

Jennifer M. Kidd

This chapter explores careers from a psychological perspective. First it examines the psychological processes involved in career experiences, particularly career choices and transitions. Then the focus turns to the attempts by organizations and career practitioners to help individuals manage their careers.

Seen from the outside, many people's careers seem to lack coherence, with frequent moves in and out of the workforce and apparently random job changes. Using the word 'career' to describe their working lives may therefore seem inappropriate. But the power of the word lies in its potential to help individuals link apparently unconnected work experiences to form a personally meaningful pattern and in turn to use this to plan future career development. So, as well as analyzing objective job moves, psychologists interested in careers attempt to understand how people experience and make sense of changes in work roles and of transitions into and out of the workforce.

The definition of career that will be used in this chapter is that suggested by Arnold (1997, p. 16): 'the sequence of employment-related positions, roles, activities and experiences encountered by a person'. As Arnold argues, using this definition has several implications. First, and most importantly, it refers to a *sequence* of positions. The study of careers emphasizes the ways in which experiences unfold over time, and how experiences at one stage affect what happens later in one's career. Arnold's definition also implies that some aspects of career are *objective*, and others are more *subjective*, being best understood in terms of specific personal experiences. It is possible to study careers in terms of sequences of generally-understood job titles or occupations, and it is also possible to study individuals' needs, values, aspirations and attitudes towards these positions and towards work generally and how these attributes change over the life span. Another important feature of this definition of career is the deliberate omission of any reference to specific professions and types of occupation, or to increasing status over time. No one who spends any time in employment or seeking employment is excluded from having a career. Furthermore, the use of the term 'employment-related' implies a wide range of positions, for example, self-employment, or being a student on an educational course.

CURRENT CAREER PATTERNS

The context of careers has been somewhat neglected by work psychologists, yet many writers agree that recent changes in career patterns are largely due to external factors. These include: globalization; rapid technological changes; labour market deregulation; shifts in employment patterns; changes in organizational structures. Globalization, or the internationalization of markets, has been viewed as providing the impetus for organizational restructuring, as companies experience an increased need for cost competitiveness and high innovation and quality. The process of globalization has been hastened by advances in information and communications technology which enables rapid transmission of information across the world. Other technological advances have led to the automation of previously labour-intensive processes which has displaced skilled workers, particularly in manufacturing (Jackson, Arnold, Nicholson and Watts, 1996).

In the UK and the USA, rationalization resulting from global competition in the private sector has been facilitated by deregulation of the labour market. For example, in the United Kingdom the qualifying period for many basic employment rights has been extended, wages councils have been abolished, and restrictions have been imposed on trades unions. Within the public sector, many organizations have been privatized, while others have been required to contract out parts of their operations. Deregulation is likely to reduce job security and increase the need to adapt to more flexible forms of working. It is also seen as contributing to the intensification of individuals' need to maintain employability (regularly updating their skills and knowledge) in the context of fewer opportunities for life-long employment (Storey, 2000). In other countries, deregulation is less evident. In Germany, France and Scandinavia, for example, corporate partnerships between the state, employers and unions aim to enhance employment stability (Watts, 2000).

As a consequence of these various developments, changes in organizational structures have occurred. Downsizing and delayering are commonplace, as are rapid changes in skill requirements. Many employees have to make do with lateral rather than vertical movement within their organization, and when promotions do occur there tend to be greater jumps in responsibility. British labour market statistics show that more flexible forms of employment are becoming more common. Forty per cent of the 1,706 managers from a nationally representative sample of different employers questioned in the 1998 Workplace Employee Relations Survey reported that they had increased their recruitment of part-time workers over the last five years; 20 per cent said they had increased the number of employees on fixed-term contracts; and 17 per cent said they had more temporary agency employees. Also, in about 25 per cent of organizations, most workers in the largest occupational group are trained to be functionally flexible: they are expected to do jobs other than their own (Cully, O'Reilly, Millward, Forth, Woodland, Dix and Bryson, 1998).

Arthur (1994) introduced the notion of the 'boundaryless' career to describe this increasing mobility and flexibility. He suggests that careers need to be seen in the context of the breaking down of a range of traditional boundaries, for example, employer boundaries, job boundaries of specialist functions and skills, and the social boundaries separating paid employment and family roles. However, we need to be careful about accepting uncritically the current rhetoric about dramatic changes in careers. Job mobility is still fairly low in the United Kingdom. Between 1985 and 1993 58 per cent of men and 44 per cent of women had been with the same employer for more than five years (Burgess and Rees, 1998). It has also remained quite stable since 1975 (Gregg and Wadsworth, 1999). There is also very little evidence that there has been any decline in individuals' perceptions of job security over the last ten to twelve years. Sixty per cent of the 27,500 employee respondents in the Workplace Employee Relations Survey (Cully et al., 1998) felt that their job was secure.

CAREER THEORY

There are two distinct areas of literature devoted to the study of career development and career management. The first stems from the field of vocational psychology and has been largely concerned with occupational choice, early career decision-making and career counselling (see Brown, Brooks and Associates (1996) for an overview). The second area of literature focuses on organizational careers, and has been influenced primarily by organizational psychology, sociology, and management studies (see, for example, Arthur, Hall and Lawrence, 1989). Unfortunately the field is fragmented and there has been very little interaction between researchers and writers in the two areas.

Person–Environment Fit

Vocational psychologists have been particularly concerned with the impact of individual attributes such as abilities, interests and values on early decisions about careers, especially occupational choice. The predominant focus on occupation in initial decision-making is a little puzzling, however, since there are many types of choices that need to be made at the beginning of a working life, for example, decisions about educational opportunities, choice of employer, and type of organization.

The notion of person–environment fit (the degree of 'congruence' or 'correspondence' between workers and their environments) has been the main construct for understanding career decision-making since the beginning of the twentieth century. One of the earliest models in this vein was that of Parsons (1909), who established one of the first vocational guidance agencies in Boston, USA. The theory which guided his work was simple and it consisted of three propositions: people are different from each other; so are jobs; and it should be possible, by a study of both and a process of 'true reasoning', to achieve a match between person and job.

From that time, thinking about occupational choice was increasingly dominated by the assumed need to generate valid and reliable data about individuals and jobs. Psychometric tests were developed, first to assess aptitudes (basic components of cognitive functioning) and later occupational interests (preferences for particular work activities). Parsons' model may seem simplistic, but his matching approach has been substantially accepted and elaborated upon by later writers.

Tinsley (2000) has reviewed work published on person–environment fit over the last fifty years. He concludes that the general model is to a large extent valid, in that fit is positively related to employee well-being and negatively related to employee discontent. There exists a wide range of person–environment fit models, but all feature two broad groups of individual attributes: rewards sought from work and employee abilities. Thus fit is measured in terms of congruence between rewards sought and satisfactions offered, and individual abilities and the demands of the work. Much of the research into fit has examined the relationship between degree of congruence and job outcomes, and generally findings indicate that fit is related to a variety of these, including job satisfaction, productivity, low absenteeism and low turnover (Tinsley, 2000).

A wide range of theories is subsumed under the umbrella title person–environment fit. These include the Minnesota Theory of Work Adjustment (Dawis and Lofquist, 1984) which focuses on rewards sought and abilities used, and Schneider's Attraction–Selection–Attrition model (Schneider, Goldstein and Smith, 1995), which proposes that fit is a result of individual recruitment and selection of limited kinds of people and their subsequent adjustment to the organization. One of the most influential and widely researched matching theories, however, is that of Holland (1997), who proposed that people seek occupational environments that are congruent with their occupational interests. Holland's theory states that: people fall into six interest types (realistic, investigative, artistic, social, enterprising and conventional); occupational environments can be classified in the same terms; and individuals seek to achieve congruence between interests and environment.

Realistic individuals enjoy practical activities and are not very interested in social interaction. Those with *investigative* interests are logical and critical, and are interested in concepts. *Artistic* individuals like to use their creativity. *Social* types enjoy working with others and tend to be warm and caring. People described as *enterprising* are keen on managing and persuading others and often seek leadership roles. *Conventional* people are happiest in structured environments and value security and clarity at work.

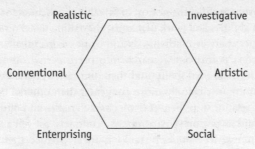

Fig. 7.1 Holland's model of occupational interests (from Holland, 1997)

Holland set out a hexagonal model of occupational interests where some of the six types are closely related, while others are more distant. This model is described in Figure 7.1, with types at adjacent angles more closely related than those at opposite angles.

Several instruments have been developed to identify Holland's interest types. These typically ask respondents to indicate their interests, and sometimes their skills, in specific activities related to each of the six types. Examples are the Self-Directed Search (SDS) (Holland, 1985) and the Strong Interest Inventory (Harmon, Hansen, Borgen and Hammer, 1994). One of Holland's key predictions is that individuals who experience 'congruence' between their interests and their work environments will be more satisfied and successful than those with less congruence.

Several researchers have carried out meta-analyses of studies testing aspects of Holland's theory. (Meta-analyses pool the results of large numbers of studies to draw conclusions that are more reliable than those from individual pieces of research.) Examples are work by Assouline and Meir (1987) and Tranberg, Slane and Ekeberg (1993). These studies suggest that the relationship between congruence and job outcomes is rather weak (in the case of job satisfaction, for example, correlations are in the order of 0.21), and complicated by the range of measures used. Other work has suggested that Holland's theory may be more valid for some interest types than others. Meir (1995), for example, found that the correlation between congruence and satisfaction was higher for social types than for others (0.33 as compared with 0.05–0.15). So, while person–environment fit theories generally have found some support, evidence for the validity of Holland's theory is weaker. This may be because the

Holland model oversimplifies the notion of fit, taking inadequate account of the fit between abilities and work demands, and failing to acknowledge reciprocal influences between individuals and work environments.

As Tinsley (2000) points out, research into person–environment fit has tended to ignore the probability that there are certain types of work environment that are intrinsically more congenial than others. 'Present status' models of relationships between job characteristics and outcomes may be just as valid as person–environment fit models, as well as more parsimonious. In essence, present status models predict that work environments affect workers in a uniform way, regardless of individuals' desires and abilities. Chapter 1 of this book suggests that desirable characteristics of work environments include environmental clarity and feedback, variety, level of pay, physical security, externally generated goals, interpersonal contact, opportunity for skill use, opportunity for control, and valued social position.

Considerable attention has recently been given to the validity of Holland's hexagonal structure of interests and occupational environments. Prediger (2000), for example, prefers to describe individuals according to their relative interests in people as opposed to things, and data as opposed to ideas, and he argues that these two dimensions should be incorporated into the model. Others have raised broader issues about the constructs used to describe work and their value in career counselling. Hirsh, Kidd and Watts (1998), for example, question the currency of traditional classifications like Holland's hexagon, and the extent to which any one framework can be equally valid in describing individuals' work-related attributes (e.g., interests, skills or values), on the one hand, and work environments on the other. Also, arguably, frameworks based upon differences between occupations have been over-emphasized, given that choice of occupation is only one aspect of career decision making. Many mid-life career decisions, for example, will be concerned with progression within the current organization or with moves to a new employer.

Until recently, person–environment fit research has tended to ignore the contribution of personality in fit. There is now some agreement that personality can reliably be described in terms of five broad dimensions (often called the 'Big Five'): extroversion, agreeableness, conscientiousness, neuroticism and openness to experience (see also Chapter 5). Tokar, Fischer and Subich (1998) report that the most consistent links between interests and personality are positive associations between openness (being responsive to new experiences and ideas) and investigative and artistic interests, and between extroversion (outgoing, and enjoying the company of others) and enterprising and social interests. Personality is likely to make an independent contribution to work outcomes, irrespective of fit. Hesketh (2000), for example, argues that because social and enterprising Holland types tend to be extroverts, and extroverts are generally happier than introverts, these individuals are likely to be more satisfied in any work environment. This may be because extroverts are more prepared to take steps to improve their jobs to suit themselves, or because they have higher levels of positive affect (see also Chapter 1).

As Tinsley (2000) argues, further development of fit models is needed to take account of conceptual links between interests, values and personality. Work by Ackerman and Heggestad (1997) supports this view but also suggests that models of fit should include abilities as well. From a wide-ranging review of studies assessing relationships between abilities, interests and personality, they provide evidence for the existence of four clusters of traits across the three domains of individual attributes. These clusters are: social; clerical/conventional; science/maths; and intellectual/cultural. Apart from the social cluster, which comprises interests and personality traits only, all include traits across all three domains. The authors propose that: 'Abilities, interests and personality develop in tandem, such that ability levels and personal dispositions determine the probability of success in a particular task domain and interests determine the motivation to attempt the task' (Ackerman and Heggestad, 1997, p. 239). This suggests that explanations of career development should use frameworks of fit which integrate the traditionally separate domains of abilities, personality and interests.

A Developmental Theory

Proponents of person—environment fit theories of career choice and behaviour have been criticized for not taking enough account of the processes leading up to the making of an occupational choice or later adjustment to employment. Other writers have taken a developmental view of careers. Donald Super is perhaps the most well-known proponent of this type of theory. Drawing on developmental psychology, Super's original theory (Super, 1957) proposed that career development proceeds through five stages. These were described as follows:

Growth (0-14 years)
The self concept develops through identification with members of the immediate family and key figures at school.

Exploration (15-24 years)
The self concept crystallizes through the process of experimentation and reality testing.

Establishment (25-44 years)
Having found an appropriate field, the individual makes efforts to establish a permanent place in it.

Maintenance (45-64 years)
The individual is concerned to hold onto the place that has been established in the world of work.

Decline (65+)
Mental and physical powers decline, and the pace of work eases off and finally ceases.

Later work detailed sub-stages within each stage and substituted the term 'disengagement' for 'decline' (Super, Thompson and Lindeman, 1985). Super also developed a more general theory of career development: his 'life-span, life-space' model (Super, 1980). This uses the image of a rainbow to describe the individual's 'life space' and the various roles within it. The bands in the rainbow represent the different roles a person assumes during the course of his or her life. Initially, the life space contains only one role, that of the child, but during adulthood many people experience seven or eight roles, as when a person is employed in an occupation, studying part-time, being a parent, being a spouse, maintaining a home, supporting ageing parents and pursuing hobbies. Clearly other roles could be identified, and not all roles apply to all individuals. In addition, the sequencing of roles may vary.

Super's rainbow also shows the impact of both internal and external forces upon life roles (though, with respect to external forces, he fails to specify in any detail how these factors affect development). His list of 'personal determinants' is intended to summarize the most important components of individuals' biological and social make-up which affect the way roles are experienced and how they are performed. These include the abilities, interests and values discussed in more detail by person–environment fit theorists.

Super's models have stimulated a vast amount of research into the exploration stage of development, particularly into the role of self concepts in the entry into work (e.g., Kidd, 1984). Much less research effort has been directed to issues within the establishment and maintenance stages, however. One reason for this is that the processes set out as being characteristic of the later stages are discussed by Super in only a very general descriptive way. Unlike his exposition of the earlier stages, there is little attempt at explanation and it is difficult to formulate testable hypotheses beyond general statements. The model also fails to deal with the question of how organizations foster or inhibit growth and development.

Interactive Models of Careers

Rather than a single set of career stages, several writers (mostly those with an interest in organizational processes, rather than vocational psychologists) have suggested that career development is better viewed as a series of work-role transitions or mini-stages across roles, functions, organizations and other work boundaries. Nicholson (1987) has set out a model of the 'transition cycle' which focuses on the career-related tasks which need to be carried out at each stage. During *preparation*, some anticipatory socialization takes place in advance of the transition, but expectations may not be realistic. At the next stage, *encounter*, a process of sense-making takes place, and this stage is marked by a change from previous roles. During *adjustment*, personal and role development take place, which tend to increase the fit between the individual and the job. Lastly, at the *stabilization* stage, increased commitment to the organization ensues based on successful coping. Development of role may take place, together with more influence on the organization, and preparation for further change begins.

The model emphasizes the cyclical nature of career stages. In addition, experiences at one stage are considered to influence what happens at later stages. Inappropriate preparation, for example, is thought to increase the challenge of encounter and adjustment. It is noteworthy that many employees in the armed forces and in the Civil Service are deliberately moved every two or three years to prepare them as 'generalists'. Offering them new challenges is thought to keep them fresh.

Research is lacking as to whether these stages exist in precisely this form. Instead, researchers have focused on individuals' experiences within each stage and on the organizational processes that facilitate achievement of particular tasks within each. For example, Premack and Wanous (1985) concluded that realistic job previews, which attempt to give job applicants (those in the *preparation* stage) an accurate view of jobs and organizations, are effective in helping individuals develop more realistic expectations, and can increase job survival.

Viewing careers as sequences of transitions overcomes some of the problems of age-related descriptions of career development. This and other more recent models emphasize that career development can best be understood in interactive terms, taking account of the relationship between the individual and the social and organizational context. Each job experience can be viewed in terms of processes of social exchange – with the organization, with managers and with co-workers. For instance, the ways individuals perform work tasks are influenced by other workers' demands and expectations, which in turn are affected by individuals' past performance.

Also, over the longer term, individuals' careers have an impact on organizations, and on the broader social context. Arthur, Inkson and Pringle (1999), drawing on earlier ideas from the Chicago School of Sociology, have proposed a cyclical model of how these reciprocal processes operate. The model uses case studies of the careers of seventy-five New Zealanders to show how careers interface with four social institutions: companies and other employment organizations, occupations, industries and societies. A boat-builder's career, for example, produced a new institution – his own company – and it also influenced commercial developments in his own occupation. And at a broader level collaboration among workers in the field led to developments in the boat-building industry as a whole, by attracting business from overseas. The model also describes how institutional forms give rise to 'career scripts', which in turn influence the actions individuals take. For example, the boat-builder reports how he has been constrained by obligations to his company in the way he carries out his work.

The psychological contract

The importance of social exchange processes in career development has led to suggestions that at the interpersonal level of analysis the notion of the 'psychological contract' is central in understanding how careers are experienced in organizations. Definitions vary, but we will define the psychological contract as 'an individual's belief regarding the terms and conditions of a reciprocal exchange agreement between that focal person and another party' (Robinson and Rousseau, 1994, p. 246).

The psychological contract is a useful concept in thinking about careers and career management for two main reasons. First, it can help us understand the ways in which the employment relationship has changed in recent years. Herriot and Pemberton (1995) have strong views on this: they argue that employers have destroyed the old psychological contract and failed to negotiate its replacement. The *content* of the psychological contract has changed, particularly perhaps in that employee loyalty is less likely to be reciprocated by employment security. Secondly, taking a psychological contract perspective provides a frame for understanding careers in an interactive way, emphasizing communication and negotiation between the parties. Indeed, Herriot and Pemberton (1996, p. 762) define organizational careers as simply 'the repeated renegotiation of the psychological contract'.

Herriot and Pemberton's model does more than simply *describe* the way careers in organizations are experienced. In a sense, it also contains *prescriptions* about ways to manage careers. For example, both parties should regularly exchange information about their needs and requirements, and employers should recognize that individuals may have different needs at different life stages. When enough care is put into their implementation, specific career management interventions – processes which aim to influence individuals' career development – are likely to contribute to the maintenance of psychological contracts. Indeed, provision of career management interventions could be viewed as a manifestation of an equitable psychological contract (Kidd, 1996a). We turn now to examine the practice of career management in more detail, both within and independent from organizations.

CAREER MANAGEMENT

In the context of less predictable labour markets, career management is coming to be seen as the responsibility of individual employees as well as organizations. Some commentators argue that the promise of a job for life has disappeared. 'Employability' has become the buzz word: organizations are thought more likely to see their role as helping individuals to develop portable skills than as facilitating development through ready-made career paths. First in this section we discuss the role of public policy in relation to the provision of career management interventions generally. Then we turn to the provision of career interventions, focusing particularly on organizational settings. In the third part we discuss the practice of career counselling.

Public Policy

Some individuals live out their working lives with the same employer. In the late 1990s, around 40 per cent of men and 20 per cent of women in the UK were in the same jobs as they had twenty years before (Burgess and Rees, 1998). Others will experience more diverse career forms. It is still unfortunately the case that very few adults have access to career counselling. Career guidance and counselling services by and large deal with young people entering the world of work for the first time, and very little public money has been invested in providing career guidance or career management services to adults, despite the rhetoric of 'life-long learning'.

Career guidance and counselling need ideally to be available at all career decision points, not just at the point of leaving full-time education. They also need to be available at other times, not just when individuals are contemplating a job move. As Watts (1999) argues, this raises questions of public policy, since career guidance is not only a 'private good' but also a 'public good'. It also has the potential to reduce mismatches in the labour market and increase social equity in access to educational and occupational opportunities. Watts suggests five alternative forms of delivery for the future. Guidance could be provided: through the formal education system; by employers; within intermediary structures, for example trades unions and professional associations; as a separate public service; or as a stand-alone fee-paying service.

All have drawbacks, and one important question underlying the different options is whether a commercial market in career guidance and counselling is likely to develop. Can career counselling be 'commodified'? The problem with marketing career counselling is that it is a process, helping people clarify long-term goals. It is not a product which satisfies immediate desires. Also, much depends on individuals' willingness to work on their own behalf. (All this, though, has not prevented therapeutic counselling becoming established as a stand-alone profession.)

Career Management within Organizations

An increasing number of organizations are offering a wider range of career management interventions to their employees than hitherto. There has been a shift away from processes managed by the employer (for example, promotion boards) towards new types of activities managed more by individual employees (for instance, personal development planning). However, it is not the case that employers have simply handed over responsibility for career management to their employees. A survey conducted in 1996 of human resource managers in over 500 British companies showed that only 8 per cent saw individual employees as having prime responsibility for their development. Most respondents took the view that their organizations and employees had joint responsibility for careers (Thomson, Mabey, Storey, Gray and Iles, 2000).

Hirsh and Jackson (1996) have observed that there are now several pressures driving some large employers back towards once more accepting responsibility for careers. As 'downsizing' levels off, these pressures include: the recognition of the need for a flexible workforce; the demands of 'total quality' and business which is 'customer focused'; the fear of demotivating or losing key staff, who are still concerned about a career with the company; and worries about succession. Hirsh and Jackson reported a series of case studies of the career management practices of fifteen large organizations. Three distinct groups of employees were identified, each of whom were treated rather differently. Senior managers were the group most likely to have a 'career deal', which offered planned development along organizational career pathways. Organizations with a high proportion of graduates and professional employees often favoured the 'negotiated career' model, where the responsibility for development was shared by employer and employee. The position of the wider workforce was more difficult to generalize about. However, organizations which were more uncertain about their business futures often offered most of their workforce merely a 'job for now', with little support for development.

So career management strategies are likely to vary across different groups of employees. Some of the assumptions about increased personal responsibility for careers in the context of new 'boundaryless' careers are too simplistic. As long as companies have to groom their high fliers, the careers of valuable employees are likely to be supported.

The variety of career interventions currently offered by organizations is considerable. Arnold (1997) discusses these in some depth, distinguishing between those that are and are not bound up with the employee's day-to-day work. Interventions in the former category include developmental work assignments, performance appraisal, personal development plans and mentoring. Those in the latter include succession planning, development centres, career development workshops and outplacement. Lack of space precludes a discussion of each, so we will focus on two commonly used techniques: mentoring and development centres.

Mentoring

Mentors are usually seen as individuals with considerable expertise and knowledge who provide support and mobility to mentees' careers. Kram's (1985, p. 2) definition is still pertinent: 'a relationship between a younger adult and an older, more experienced adult that helps the (less experienced) individual learn to navigate in the world of work', though these days there is not always a large age difference between mentors and mentees.

The support provided by mentors has been conceptualized as having two components: support for career development which facilitates the mentee's advancement in the organization; and psychosocial support, which contributes to the mentee's personal and professional growth and development. A series of studies has shown that mentoring is associated with a range of positive outcomes. For example, mentees have higher incomes (Chao, 1997) and they experience more career mobility

(Scandura, 1992) and job satisfaction (Seibert, 1999) than those without mentors. Evidence also suggests that mentees in informal mentoring relationships, which develop spontaneously, receive greater benefits than those in formal relationships set up by the organization (Ragins and Cotton, 1999). It should be noted, however, that it is not always possible to establish cause and effect in research on mentoring because often mentors are only assigned to high fliers in the first place.

Development centres

Development centres tend to use assessment centre techniques (see Chapter 5) to assess participants on key competencies using a range of exercises, tests and interviews. The focus is on observable behaviour, and criteria are often specified in terms of competency frameworks. In contrast to assessment centres, they feed back information to participants themselves: encouraging participants to develop particular competencies; encouraging discussions between participants and their supervisors and providing feedback to HR about development needs; reviewing the range of competencies available to the organization; and identifying high potential staff who may be 'fast-tracked' (Arnold, 1997).

In contrast to evaluations of assessment centres, research on the effectiveness of development centres is scarce. Jones and Whitmore (1995) followed up 113 development centre participants who were employed in an insurance company in the United States. The career progress of participants was followed up over several years and findings showed that those participants who took part in the development activities recommended by the assessors were more likely to achieve managerial positions than those who did not. Either taking part in development improved work performance, which in turn led to promotion, or doing these activities was seen by managers as an indication of commitment and motivation which deserved promotion.

Career management as an emotional and political activity

Much of the literature on career interventions ignores the potential problems with introducing and implementing these initiatives. Career development and career management are highly emotional and political processes (Kidd, 1998) and messages about opportunities for development can appear to promise more than can be delivered. This may lead to disappointment, frustration and cynicism (Hirsh and Jackson, 1996). Strategies for developing a career management initiative need to anticipate and work with emotionally-loaded resistance within the organization, arising from, for example, lack of trust in the person proposing it or fear of the unknown. A related issue is that encouraging individuals to be responsible for their own careers may mean that an organization's collective problems with development may come to be portrayed as individual difficulties, preventing the organization from recognizing the need for change in human resource practices.

Career Counselling

As noted previously, early approaches to career counselling originated in the work of Parsons (1909). In Parsons' view, the aim of career counselling was to facilitate this 'true reasoning' to relate personal and occupational information. But career counselling involves much more than helping people choose an occupation. Many need help in dealing with the frustrations and disappointments of redundancy and unemployment, with decisions about *whether* to return to study or to paid employment, or with finding ways to balance different life roles.

A range of approaches to career counselling has emerged since Parsons' work, including person–environment fit, developmental, person-centred and goal-directed approaches (Kidd, 1996b). A recent development is the emergence of a narrative approach (e.g. Cochran, 1997), where the career counsellor helps clients identify themes within their 'life-story', encourages them to link these within a meaningful narrative, and helps them understand how they can take charge of their future. Despite this range of theoretical approaches, the work of many career counselling prac-

Table 7.1 Stages and associated tasks of career counselling (from Kidd, 1996c)

Stages	Tasks
Building the relationship	Establishing the working alliance
Enabling clients' self-understanding	Assessment
Exploring new perspectives	Challenging Information giving
Forming strategies and plans	Reviewing progress Goal setting

titioners can be described in terms of four stages and associated tasks (Kidd, 1996c) (see Table 7.1).

Building the relationship

At an early stage it is important to seek to clarify the client's individual needs and agree how best to proceed. This early 'working alliance' (Bordin, 1979) is likely to include making several issues explicit, including goals, roles and tasks. This process is usually seen as running throughout the counselling relationship, and is designed to minimize discrepancies between the views of both parties.

Enabling clients' self-understanding

Many clients will gain important insights through the vehicle of the counselling process itself, and this will be sufficient for progress to be made. Frequently, however, career counsellors use structured assessment tools and techniques. Psychometric tests and inventories are commonly used to assess occupational interests, work values, aptitudes and personality as well as career decision-making style and career maturity. For example, the Strong Interest Inventory (Harmon *et al.*, 1994) is commonly used to assess interests. More informal self-report tools and exercises may also be used.

Exploring new perspectives

It will often be important to help clients develop and explore new perspectives on their problems, by sensitively helping them to confront ways in which they may be preventing themselves from moving on. Challenging and confronting clients' beliefs may be important at this stage. This is also the point at which career information may be most relevant. The vast range of information about jobs, much of which is constantly being updated, means that it is virtually impossible for career counsellors to keep up to date with information about opportunities, even in one specific area. Accordingly, and as Nathan and Hill (1992) suggest, it is more appropriate for career counsellors to view themselves as 'general practitioners' with respect to knowledge of occupational and educational opportunities. This is more in line with the counsellor's facilitative role, too. Nevertheless, it is important for career counsellors to possess: knowledge of sources of information about specific opportunities, and how to access them; knowledge of labour market information (the structure and working of labour markets); and knowledge of the constructs and frameworks used to describe work, so as to help clients to relate themselves to opportunities.

Computers are potentially a powerful resource in career counselling. However, there is a danger that they mechanize the human interaction that is considered by many to lie at the heart of career interventions. As Watts (1996) argues, the challenge for career counselling is to use information and communications technology in ways that extend the potential of the career counselling process, rather than restrict or replace it. A vast range of software to help with career decision-making is now available, from the internet or on CD-ROM, which can be employed on a stand-alone basis or with the support of a career practitioner. One example is PROSPECT (HE) which is used (either on a stand-alone basis or supported) in nearly all higher education institutions in the United Kingdom. This enables users to assess their skills, values and interests, and to match profiles of these with occupations. It also offers help with job applications and CVs.

Forming strategies and plans

Reviewing progress is likely to be an integral part of the career counselling process at several of its stages. Also, a key activity in preparing for the end of the counselling relationship is helping clients set goals and decide on the steps they need to take to achieve them. Goal-setting theory has been applied to the action-planning stage of career counselling, and Miller, Crute and Hargie (1992) set out what this theory suggests as the central features of effective goal setting: clear and behaviourally specific; measurable; achievable, owned by the goal setter; congruent with his or her values; and appropriately time scaled.

Evaluation of the effectiveness of career counselling

The principal outcome criteria in evaluation studies of career counselling are 'learning outcomes', defined as 'the skills, knowledge and attitudes which facilitate rational occupational and educational decision making and the effective implementation of occupational and educational decisions' (Kidd and Killeen, 1992, p. 221). These include self awareness, knowledge of opportunities, and decision-making skills and attitudes. One recent study, for example, assessed the impact of a multi-faceted career guidance intervention on career indecision (how decided individuals were about their career choice or choice of college subject) (Jurgens, 2000). One group of students participated in a decision-making workshop, a computer-aided guidance exercise and individual counselling and listened to speakers on certain professions. The other group participated only in the computer-aided guidance and individual counselling. Both groups showed decreased levels of career indecision after the interventions. Meta-analyses of studies using learning outcome criteria are unanimous that career counselling and guidance produces statistically significant but modest gains. Oliver and Spokane (1988), for example, assessed the average standardized mean differences between respondents receiving career guidance and control groups across 58 US studies. The resulting effect size of 0.82 was equivalent to an improvement in the average respondent receiving guidance of 29 percentile points.

As Killeen, White and Watts (1992) point out, however, evaluators of career counselling tend to work almost entirely at the individual level rather than the system level. From an organizational and public policy perspective, outcomes like increased productivity, reduced staff turnover, lower unemployment and even increased GDP growth rate should be considered. Here the evidence for effectiveness is less clear-cut because of methodological deficiencies and differences in the practices evaluated. For example, in relation to staff turnover, Killeen's review of the evidence concludes that career counselling and guidance 'may have a small positive effect on job retention, but the evidence for a positive impact on the *quality* of job movement is too limited even for a preliminary conclusion to be drawn' (Killeen, 1996, p. 86).

SUMMARY

Recent changes in labour markets have meant that careers are becoming less predictable and traditional career boundaries more permeable. There is some evidence that individuals are required to be more flexible in the skills they develop. However, the dramatic changes in careers described by some commentators are overstated.

The literature on careers originates from two rather discrete areas of enquiry. Vocational psychologists have been more interested in early career decisions, while organizational psychologists are more concerned with career development within employing organizations. Recent work has identified the need to develop more comprehensive models of person–environment fit and has proposed models of careers which are more dynamic and interactive than previously.

Employees are increasingly expected to take responsibility for managing their own careers. Those who are more valued by their employers, however, may still receive a considerable amount of support for development. Career counselling practitioners use a range of approaches and techniques. Their work covers broader career management issues as well as career decision-making. Research into the effectiveness of career management and counselling is patchy, though evidence for the benefits of some interventions is fairly clear-cut.

FURTHER READING

Two volumes mentioned earlier provide good overviews of the literature on career development: Brown, Brooks and Associates (1996) *Career Choice and Development* (3rd edition), and Arthur, Hall and Lawrence (1989) *Handbook of Career Theory*. However, Arnold's (1997) text, *Managing Careers into the 21st Century*, is perhaps the best introduction to the field in the UK context. It focuses mainly on career management, but it also provides a valuable review of the literature on career decision-making and transitions.

Rethinking Careers Education and Guidance by Watts and colleagues (1996) aims to help careers practitioners, particularly those working in educational settings, develop an intellectual base for their work. A good introduction to career counselling for those in the early stages of training is Nathan and Hill's (1992) *Career Counselling*, which is a practical guide to the skills and techniques of career counselling with adults. An aid to exploration of the internet as a careers resource is Offer's (2000) *Careers Professionals' Guide to the Internet*, which provides frameworks for assessing websites.

Individuals looking for self-help guides to career planning have a wide choice of materials. One book which sets out a clear model of career planning is Hirsh and Jackson's (1998) *Planning Your Own Career in a Week*. In addition, there is a rapidly developing range of self-help material on the internet.

REFERENCES

Ackerman, P. L. and Heggestad, E. D. (1997). Intelligence, personality and interests: Evidence for overlapping traits. *Psychological Bulletin, 121,* 219–45.

Arnold, J. (1997). *Managing Careers into the 21st Century.* London: Chapman.

Arthur, M. B. (1994). The boundaryless career: A new perspective for organizational inquiry. *Journal of Organizational Behavior, 15,* 295–306.

Arthur, M. B., Hall, D. T. and Lawrence, B. S. (eds.) (1989). *Handbook of Career Theory.* Cambridge: Cambridge University Press.

Arthur, M. B., Inkson, K. and Pringle, J. K. (1999). *The New Careers: Individual Action and Economic Change.* London: Sage.

Assouline, M. and Meir, E. (1987). Meta-analysis of the relationship between congruence and well-being measures. *Journal of Vocational Behavior, 31,* 319–32.

Bordin, E. (1979). The generalizability of the psychoanalytic concept of the working alliance. *Psychotherapy: Theory, Research and Practice, 16,* 252–60.

Brown, D., Brooks, L. and Associates. (1996). *Career Choice and Development* (3rd edition). San Francisco: Jossey-Bass.

Burgess, S. and Rees, H. (1998). A disaggregate analysis of the evolution of job tenure in Britain, 1975–1993. *British Journal of Industrial Relations, 36,* 629–55.

Chao, G. T. (1997). Mentoring phases and outcomes. *Journal of Vocational Behavior, 51,* 15–28.

Cochran, L. (1997). *Career Counseling: A Narrative Approach.* Thousand Oaks, CA: Sage.

Cully, M., O'Reilly, A., Millward, N., Forth, J., Woodland, S., Dix, G. and Bryson, A. (1998). *The 1998 Workplace Employee Relations Survey: First Findings* (*www.dti.gov.uk/er/emar/*).

Dawis, R. V. and Lofquist, L. H. (1984). *A Psychological Theory of Work Adjustment: An Individual Differences Model and its Applications.* Minneapolis: University of Minnesota Press.

Gregg, P. and Wadsworth, J. (1999). Job tenure, 1975–98. In P. Gregg and J. Wadsworth (eds.), *The State of Working Britain,* pp. 109–26. Manchester: Manchester University Press.

Harmon, L. W., Hansen, J. C., Borgen, F. H. and Hammer, A. L. (1994). *Strong Interest Inventory: Applications and Technical Guide.* Palo Alto, CA: Consulting Psychologists Press.

Herriot, P. and Pemberton, C. (1995). *New Deals.* Chichester: Wiley.

Herriot, P. and Pemberton, C. (1996). Contracting careers. *Human Relations, 49,* 757–90.

Hesketh, B. (2000). The next millennium of 'fit' research: Comments on 'The congruence myth: An analysis of the efficacy of the person–environment fit model' by H. E. A. Tinsley. *Journal of Vocational Behavior*, 56, 190–96.

Hirsh, W. and Jackson, C. (1996). *Strategies for Career Development: Promise, Practice and Pretence*. Brighton: Institute for Employment Studies.

Hirsh, W. and Jackson, C. (1998). *Planning Your Own Career in a Week*. London: Hodder and Stoughton.

Hirsh, W., Kidd, J. M. and Watts, A. G. (1998). *Constructs of Work Used in Career Guidance*. Cambridge: National Institute for Careers Education and Counselling.

Holland, J. L. (1985). *The Self-Directed Search: Professional Manual*. Odessa, Florida: Psychological Assessment Resources.

Holland, J. L. (1997). *Making Vocational Choices* (3rd edition). Odessa, FL: Psychological Assessment Resources.

Jackson, C., Arnold, J., Nicholson, N. and Watts, A. G. (1996). *Managing Careers in 2000 and Beyond*. Brighton: IES/CRAC.

Jones, R. G. and Whitmore, M. D. (1995). Evaluating developmental assessment centres as interventions. *Personnel Psychology*, 48, 377–88.

Jurgens, J. C. (2000). The undecided student: Effects of combining levels of treatment parameters on career certainty, career indecision and client satisfaction. *Career Development Quarterly*, 48, 237–50.

Kidd, J. M. (1984). The relationship of self and occupational concepts to the occupational preferences of adolescents. *Journal of Vocational Behavior*, 24, 48–65.

Kidd, J. M. (1996a). Career planning within work organisations. In A. G. Watts, B. Law, J. Killeen, J. M. Kidd and R. Hawthorn, *Rethinking Careers Education and Guidance: Theory, Policy and Practice*, pp. 142–54. London: Routledge.

Kidd, J. M. (1996b). The career counselling interview. In A. G. Watts, B. Law, J. Killeen, J. M. Kidd and R. Hawthorn, *Rethinking Careers Education and Guidance: Theory, Policy and Practice*, pp. 189–209. London: Routledge.

Kidd, J. M. (1996c). Career development work with individuals. In R. Woolfe and W. Dryden (eds.), *Handbook of Counselling Psychology*, pp. 460–84. London: Sage.

Kidd, J. M. (1998). Emotion: An absent presence in career theory. *Journal of Vocational Behavior*, 52, 275–88.

Kidd, J. M. and Killeen, J. (1992). Are the effects of careers guidance worth having? Changes in practice and outcomes. *Journal of Occupational and Organizational Psychology*, 65, 219–34.

Killeen, J. (1996). The learning and economic outcomes of guidance. In A. G. Watts, B. Law, J. Killeen, J. M. Kidd and R. Hawthorn, *Rethinking Careers Education and Guidance: Theory, Policy and Practice*, pp. 72–91. London: Routledge.

Killeen, J., White, M. and Watts, A. G. (1992). *The Economic Value of Careers Guidance*. London: Policy Studies Institute/NICEC.

Kram, K. E. (1985). *Mentoring at Work: Developmental Relationships in Organizational Life.* Glenview, IL: Scott, Foresman.

Meir, E. I. (1995). Elaboration of the relation between interest congruence and satisfaction. *Journal of Career Assessment, 3,* 341–6.

Miller, R., Crute, V. and Hargie, O. (1992). *Professional Interviewing.* London: Routledge.

Nathan, R. and Hill, L. (1992). *Career Counselling.* London: Sage.

Nicholson, N. (1987). Work role transitions. In P. B. Warr (ed.), *Psychology at Work* (3rd edition), pp. 160–77. Harmondsworth: Penguin.

Offer, M. (2000). *Careers Professionals' Guide to the Internet.* Richmond: Trotman.

Oliver, L. W. and Spokane, A. R. (1988). Career intervention outcome: What contributes to client gain? *Journal of Counseling Psychology, 35,* 447–62.

Parsons, F. (1909). *Choosing a Vocation.* Boston, Mass.: Houghton Mifflin.

Prediger, D. J. (2000). Holland's hexagon is alive and well – though somewhat out of shape: Response to Tinsley. *Journal of Vocational Behavior, 56,* 197–204.

Premack, S. L. and Wanous, J. P. (1985). A meta-analysis of realistic job preview experiments. *Journal of Applied Psychology, 70,* 111–28.

Ragins, B. R. and Cotton, J. L. (1999). Mentor functions and outcomes: A comparison of men and women in formal and informal mentoring relationships. *Journal of Applied Psychology, 84,* 529–50.

Robinson, S. L. and Rousseau, D. M. (1994). Violating the psychological contract: Not the exception but the norm. *Journal of Organizational Behavior, 15,* 245–59.

Scandura, T. A. (1992). Mentorship and career mobility: An empirical investigation. *Journal of Organizational Behavior, 13,* 169–74.

Schneider, B., Goldstein, H. W. and Smith, D. B. (1995). The ASA framework: An update. *Personnel Psychology, 48,* 747–73.

Seibert, S. (1999). The effectiveness of facilitated mentoring: A longitudinal quasi-experiment. *Journal of Vocational Behavior, 54,* 483–502.

Storey, J. A. (2000). 'Fracture lines' in the career environment. In A. Collin and R. A. Young (eds.), *The Future of Career,* pp. 21–36. Cambridge: Cambridge University Press.

Super, D. E. (1957). *The Psychology of Careers.* New York: Harper & Row.

Super, D. E. (1980). A life-span, life-space approach to career development. *Journal of Vocational Behavior, 16,* 282–98.

Super, D. E., Thompson, A. S. and Lindeman, R. H. (1985). *The Adult Career Concerns Inventory.* Palo Alto, CA: Consulting Psychologists Press.

Thomson, A., Mabey, C., Storey, J., Gray, C. and Iles, P. A. (2000). *Management Development in Theory and Practice.* Oxford: Blackwell.

Tinsley, H. E. A. (2000). The congruence myth: An analysis of the efficacy of the person–environment fit model. *Journal of Vocational Behavior, 56,* 147–79.

Tokar, D. M., Fischer, A. R. and Subich, L. M. (1998). Personality and vocational behavior: A selective review of the literature. *Journal of Vocational Behavior*, 53, 115–53.

Tranberg, M., Slane, S. and Ekeberg, S. E. (1993). The relation between interest congruence and satisfaction: A meta-analysis. *Journal of Vocational Behavior*, 42, 253–64.

Watts, A. G. (1996). Careers guidance and public policy. In A. G. Watts, B. Law, J. Killeen, J. M. Kidd and R. Hawthorn, *Rethinking Careers Education and Guidance: Theory, Policy and Practice*, pp. 380–91. London: Routledge.

Watts, A. G. (1999). *Reshaping Career Development for the 21st Century* (*www.derby.ac.uk/cegs/*).

Watts, A. G. (2000). The new career and public policy. In A. Collin and R. A. Young (eds.), *The Future of Career*, pp. 259–75. Cambridge: Cambridge University Press.

Watts, A. G., Law, B., Killeen, J., Kidd, J. M. and Hawthorn, R. (1996). *Rethinking Careers Education and Guidance: Theory, Policy and Practice*. London: Routledge.

8

Job-related Stress and Burnout

Michael P. O'Driscoll and Cary L. Cooper

Occupational stress is a topic of substantial interest to organizational researchers and managers, as well as society at large. Stress arising from work conditions can be pervasive and significant in its impact on individuals, their families and organizations. There is also a widespread belief that management of job stress is a key factor for enhancing individual performance on the job, hence increasing organizational effectiveness. Sethi and Schuler (1984) outlined four major reasons why job stress and coping have become prominent issues: (a) concern for individual employee health and well-being; (b) the financial impact on organizations (including days lost due to stress-related illness); (c) organizational effectiveness; and (d) legal obligations on employers to provide safe and healthy working environments.

The costs of occupational stress to business and industry are well documented. According to recent research conducted by the International Labour Organization (cited by Olson, 2000), one in ten workers globally suffer from stress, anxiety and depression on the job, and job-related stress costs employers in Europe and the US more than $120 billion annually. In the European Union, up to 4 per cent of gross national product is spent on work-related mental health problems, and in the US job stress accounts for 200 million lost working days each year. Similarly, in the UK the Confederation of British Industry's sickness absence survey for 2000 revealed that workplace stress was the second most frequent cause of sickness absence, costing roughly about £4 billion per annum. While some degree of stress is probably desirable, since it may stimulate people to perform at higher levels, excessive stress can lead to a variety of psychological and physical health problems (Fletcher, 1988), as well as impeding work productivity, causing accidents, and increasing absentee-ism and turnover (Ganster and Schaubroeck, 1991).

In this chapter we overview some key issues concerning the develop-ment and management of job stress and burnout. We begin by defining concepts used to describe stress and burnout. We then present a theoreti-cal model of the stress process, and overview some methods of assessing work-related stress and burnout. This leads to a discussion of both the sources and outcomes of stress and burnout, and some factors which may 'buffer' the effects of occupational stress. Finally, we examine procedures which organizations might utilize to alleviate stress and burnout among their employees.

WHAT IS STRESS?

In one of the earliest systematic attempts to define stress, Selye (1936) characterized it as a non-specific outcome (either physical or psychologi-cal) of any demand made upon the organism. He also described the response an organism makes as the *General Adaptation Syndrome* or stress response. Unfortunately, despite the wealth of research conducted to understand stress phenomena, there is still considerable confusion over the actual meaning of 'stress', which is reflected in the various ways in which it has been defined. Figure 8.1 presents a working definition of relevant concepts.

Beehr and Franz (1987) commented that stress 'has commonly been defined in one of three ways: as an environmental stimulus often described as a force applied to the individual, as an individual's psychological or physical response to such an environmental force, or as the interaction between these two events' (p. 6). Researchers agree that the term 'stressor' refers to the environmental stimulus or event, and that the term 'strain' refers to the person's response to the stimulus or event. Stressors, there-fore, are the antecedents and strain is the consequence of a stressful transaction. We agree with Beehr's (1987) suggestion that the term 'stress' be used to denote the general process linking stressors, strain and coping, rather than to describe specific elements.

In the early 1950s Lazarus, Deese and Osler (1952) initiated an influential line of research on stress and coping which led to the development of a

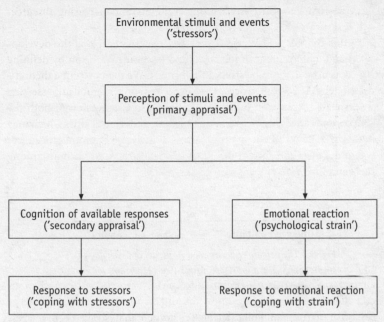

Fig. 8.1 Variables in the stress-coping process

comprehensive model depicting stress as a *transaction* process between the individual and the environment. This perspective views stress as arising from environmental demands which exceed a person's resources and capacity, when the outcomes are important for the person. This recognition of the interaction between the individual and the environment was formalized in the person–environment (P–E) fit model of stress developed by French, Caplan and Harrison (1982). In their view, 'strain can result from the mismatch between the person and the environment on dimensions important to the well-being of the individual' (p. 58). French *et al.* (1982) described the relationship between P–E misfit and strain as a U-shaped curve (Figure 8.2). For each individual's capabilities there are optimal levels of environmental demands. When these optimal levels are reached, strain will be minimal; with too little or too much demand, strain increases.

Today there is widespread acceptance of the notion that strain is jointly determined by environmental factors and characteristics of the

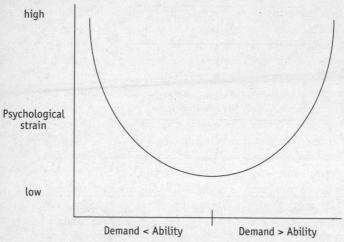

Psychological
strain

low

Demand < Ability   Demand > Ability

Fig. 8.2 The person–environment fit model of psychological
strain (adapted from French, Caplan and Harrison, 1982, p. 29,
with permission from J. Wiley and Sons)

person. Lazarus and Folkman (1984) argued that strain occurs when
environmental demands or constraints are judged by the individual to
exceed his or her resources or capacities. The critical variable is *cognitive
appraisal*, of which there are three types: primary, secondary, and reappraisal. Primary appraisal occurs when the person evaluates the significance of an environmental demand or event for his or her well-being:
does the environment threaten well-being (physical or psychological)?
Secondary appraisal follows, when the person assesses how he/she can
deal with the situation: what coping behaviours can be utilized to reduce
stress? Finally, reappraisal entails an evaluation of whether or not attempts
at coping have been successful. This formulation is important because it
focuses attention on processes of coping with stress, which we discuss later.

Another general model of the stress process is the cybernetic (or
control) theory articulated by Edwards (1998), which extends concepts
implicit in earlier approaches. The cybernetic theory is illustrated in
Figure 8.3. It postulates that stress not only has an impact on individual
well-being, but also stimulates coping responses, which in turn affect the
original sources of strain. For example, in a work environment a person
may be experiencing role ambiguity (lack of clarity in task goals or

procedures). In response to this, the employee might approach the supervisor to seek clarification of his or her duties. Not only does this behaviour reduce the immediate uncertainty experienced, but it may also change the supervisor's behaviour such that the source of ambiguity is removed (e.g., the supervisor may provide clearer directions for the subordinate).

One specific form of strain which has received considerable attention in recent years is *burnout*, which may be defined as an extreme form of strain experienced under certain conditions, particularly when the person is confronted by on-going pressures and demands which are (seemingly) irresolvable. The term 'burnout' was used in 1974 by Freudenberger to reflect his observations on the extreme stress often experienced by workers in the helping professions, such as social work, nursing, and teaching. There have been many studies of burnout, primarily among human

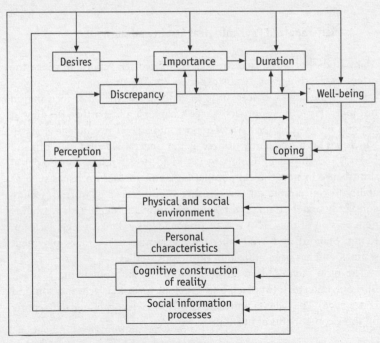

Fig. 8.3 The cybernetic theory of stress, coping and well-being (Edwards, 1998, p. 128, used with permission from J. Edwards and Oxford University Press)

service professionals, but also increasingly in other areas of employment (e.g., managers in general). Burnout is, therefore, a chronic affective response to very extreme demands (Ganster and Schaubroeck, 1991), especially pressures and conflicts arising from contact with and responsibility for the performance or well-being of other people.

MEASURES OF JOB-RELATED STRAIN

In this section, we briefly outline more commonly used approaches to assessing stress in work environments. Our focus here is on strain itself (both physical and psychological), not the stressors which induce strain or burnout, which are discussed later.

Self-reported Psychological Strain and Burnout

Many studies of workplace stress have utilized self-reports to gauge the extent of psychological strain experienced. We present two examples, one assessing psychological strain in general, and the other focusing on burnout. (For other approaches, see Chapter 1 and Further Reading at the end of this chapter.) A self-report measure of psychological strain which has been frequently utilized is the General Health Questionnaire (GHQ), developed by Goldberg (1978) to detect minor psychological disturbance in non-clinical populations. This focuses on issues such as ability to concentrate on tasks, losing sleep because of worries, feeling constantly under strain, and feeling unhappy and depressed. A twelve-item version of the GHQ was recommended by Banks, Clegg, Jackson, Kemp, Stafford and Wall (1980) for assessing strain in employment settings, and has been utilized in numerous studies.

The most commonly used device to assess burnout is the Maslach Burnout Inventory (Maslach and Jackson, 1986; Maslach, Jackson and Leiter, 1996). The 1986 version of this instrument incorporated self-reports on three components of burnout:

- *Emotional exhaustion*: a depletion of emotional energy and a feeling that one's emotional resources are inadequate to deal with the pressures encountered;

- *Depersonalization*: excessive detachment from the people with whom one works, treating individuals in the work setting (e.g., clients or patients) as objects rather than people;
- *Reduced personal accomplishment*: evaluating one's performance negatively, leading to feelings of incompetence and inability to achieve goals.

While the original MBI was designed primarily for assessing burnout in human service professionals, the revised MBI–General Survey (1996) is more applicable to non-service occupations. Emotional exhaustion remains the primary component, but depersonalization was replaced with *cynicism*, which reflects 'indifference or a distant attitude towards work . . . as a way of coping with exhausting demands' (Maslach *et al.*, 1996, p. 21). Similarly, reduced personal accomplishment was renamed *reduced professional efficacy*, to encompass a broader array of performance indicators.

Physiological Measures of Strain

Most research on strain has been psychologically-orientated, hence measurement of physiological strain has been less common. However, indicators such as elevated heart rate, blood pressure, serum cholesterol and urinary catecholamines have been examined. Typically these measures are collected concurrently with other indices of strain, such as self-reports (Hendrix, Ovalle and Troxler, 1985). Unfortunately, however, evidence for the correspondence between self-reports and physiological indices has been inconsistent (Pennebaker and Watson, 1988), and further research is needed to confirm their comparability. Fox, Dwyer and Ganster (1993) examined the relationship of job demands and physiological outcomes, using both subjective and objective assessments, and found that blood pressure and cortisol levels vary with changes in environmental pressures on the individual.

Studies exploring physiological components of strain have typically focused on one or more of the following indicators: cardiovascular symptoms (especially increased heart rate and blood pressure), biochemical reactions (such as blood cholesterol), and gastrointestinal symptoms (e.g., peptic ulcers). There is mounting evidence that stressors arising from excessive physical demands or psychological pressures can influence these physiological reactions (Fox *et al.*, 1993). Given this, tapping into physiological responses holds promise as a viable complementary method of assessing workplace stress.

Objective physiological assessments offer several advantages. They are not subject to the potential biases of self-reports, since they do not rely upon respondent recall and subjective description of strain. Also, they may enable more precise discriminations between levels of strain experienced by different individuals. In some cases, however, physiological indices are assessed via self-reports (simply asking individuals about their health), which may contain the same biases that are found in other types of self-report (Jex and Beehr, 1991).

Behavioural Indicators of Strain

Behavioural reactions to work-related stressors have been the least explored of all strain indicators (Cooper, Dewe and O'Driscoll, 2001). As noted by Jex and Beehr (1991), this is 'ironic since, at least from an organizational point of view, these may be the most important' (p. 337). Costs to the organization of behavioural responses to stress can be quite substantial.

Several behavioural indicators have been examined by researchers. Jex and Beehr (1991) distinguished between those which have significance for the organization (for example, job performance, turnover and absenteeism) and those which are more salient for individuals (such as substance abuse and destructive behaviours). Kahn and Byosiere (1992) identified fifteen behavioural reactions and classified them into five categories, which they labelled *work role disruptions* (e.g., errors, accidents), *job flight* (e.g., absenteeism, turnover), *aggressive behaviour* (e.g., vandalism, rumour spreading), *disruptions to non-work life* (e.g., interference with marital relationship), and *self-damaging behaviours* (e.g., substance abuse). Caution needs to be exercised in inferring that the above behaviours are necessarily caused by work-related stressors. They may be due, for instance, to off-the-job factors or even dispositional tendencies. Similarly, the assessment of stress-related behaviours can be quite difficult. Nevertheless, the measurement of behavioural indicators of strain is becoming increasingly relevant for developing effective stress management interventions.

SOURCES OF STRAIN

Considerable knowledge has accumulated about factors which produce job-related strain among employees. Determinants of strain can be grouped into three general categories: job-specific sources, organizational sources, and individual (personal) sources. Within the first two of these categories (job-specific sources and organizational sources), six primary stressors can be differentiated (Cartwright and Cooper, 1997): intrinsic characteristics of the job; roles in the organization; relationships at work; career development; organizational structure and climate; home–work interface.

Intrinsic Job Characteristics

These stressors are associated with the performance of specific tasks that comprise an individual's job, and are sometimes called 'task content' factors (Kahn and Byosiere, 1992). They include the level of job complexity, the variety of tasks performed, the amount of discretion and control individuals have over the pace and scheduling of their work, and even the physical environment in which the job is performed. Numerous studies have demonstrated that lack of variety, monotonous work, and an absence of discretion and control are predictors of job-related strain (Kahn and Byosiere, 1992). Similarly, poor working conditions (for instance, excessive noise and temperature) can have detrimental effects on employee psychological well-being and physical health (Cooper et al., 2001).

Work schedules (such as shiftwork) have also been explored by stress researchers. While shiftwork in general may have an effect on well-being (see Chapter 3), there is considerable variation in reactions to shiftwork, with some workers adapting more readily than others to changes in their work hours. Some of the difficulties associated with shiftwork may be alleviated by compressed shift schedules (e.g., working four twelve-hour days), which can better match job and off-the-job (e.g., family) activities (Pierce and Dunham, 1992).

Finally, the sheer amount of work is a significant stressor for many people. Having to work under time pressures to meet deadlines is a major stressor (Narayanan, Menon and Spector, 1999), and has been associated with high levels of strain, anxiety and depression (Westman and Eden, 1992). On the other hand, work which is repetitive, routine and provides little challenge for the individual can also be stressful if engaged in over long periods (Cooper and Kelly, 1993).

Organizational Roles

Around the same time that French and his colleagues were developing their person–environment fit model, Kahn, Wolfe, Quinn and Snoek (1964) began to explore the effects of role conflict, role ambiguity and role overload. Role *ambiguity* refers to unpredictability of the consequences of one's role performance, along with a lack of information needed to perform the role. Research has demonstrated a consistent link between role ambiguity in the job and high levels of psychological strain and burnout (O'Driscoll and Beehr, 2000; Zohar, 1997).

Similarly, role *conflict*, when the person experiences incompatible demands, can induce negative emotional reactions due to perceived inability to be effective on the job (King and King, 1990). Several studies have confirmed this detrimental effect, on both self-reported strain (O'Driscoll and Beehr, 1994) and physiological indicators (Kahn and Byosiere, 1992). Typically, however, the association between role conflict and psychological strain is not as strong as that between ambiguity and strain (Jackson and Schuler, 1985), although role conflict may be especially salient in the development of the emotional exhaustion component of burnout (Schaufeli and Buunk, 1996).

A third role variable is *overload*, which refers to the number of different roles a person has to fulfil and the amount of work required. Role overload can lead to excessive demands on an individual's time and may create uncertainty about one's ability to perform these roles adequately. Along with role ambiguity and conflict, overload has been found to be a major correlate of job-related strain and burnout (Cooper *et al.*, 2001).

An explanation for the negative effects of these role variables on physical and psychological well-being is that they lead to uncertainty, which is psychologically distressing and can induce emotional disturbance. Beehr (1987) adapted the expectancy theory of motivation to explain the diverse forms of uncertainty which may arise from role stressors. Ambiguity, conflict and overload may be linked with reduced effort-to-performance ($E \rightarrow P$) expectancy because they create uncertainty among employees that their efforts will lead to satisfactory job performance, and with reduced performance-to-outcome ($P \rightarrow O$) expectancy because employees are unsure of the link between rewards and successful job performance. For instance, O'Driscoll and Beehr (1994) found that these forms of uncertainty were significantly related to psychological strain and job dissatisfaction.

Work Relationships

Interpersonal relationships at work have been explored as sources of psychological strain. As we discuss shortly, there has been considerable debate over the role of social support as a moderator (or 'buffer') of the impact of stressful environments. It is clear, however, that negative interpersonal relations and the absence of support from colleagues or superiors can be significant stressors for many employees (O'Driscoll and Beehr, 1994). Conversely, having access to social support from other people in the organization can directly reduce psychological strain (Beehr and McGrath, 1992) and alleviate emotional exhaustion (Greenglass, Burke and Konarski, 1998).

Career Development

This category of potential stressors includes job insecurity, under- and over-promotion within the organization, and lack of achievement of one's goals (Cooper et al., 2001). In many countries the level of unemployment has escalated in recent years (Hanisch, 1999). Coupled with the introduction of new technologies which often result in a deskilling of the workforce (Korunka, Weiss, Huemer and Karetta, 1995), the threat of redundancy has heightened stress levels in many occupational groups (Burke and Cooper, 2000). In fact, job insecurity may be one of the single most salient sources of stress for employees today. Even when individuals believe their job is (relatively) secure, lack of promotion or career advancement is cited as a major source of dissatisfaction and strain (Jewell, 1998). There is also evidence that, despite changes in societal attitudes concerning equal employment opportunities, women and minority groups still encounter organizational barriers to their career development (Burke, 1993), which can lead to higher strain for these employees.

Organizational Structure and Climate

Psychological strain is often due to the culture and management style adopted within an organization (Cartwright and Cooper, 1997). Hierarchical, bureaucratic organizational structures allow little employee participation in decisions affecting their work and lack adequate communication, especially between managerial and non-managerial levels. The 'politics' which occur in work organizations can also have a substantial impact on employees. A climate characterized by communications focusing on negative attributes of other personnel, cynicism regarding leadership and management of the organization, and attempts by employees to further their own interests at the expense of others, will induce feelings of unsupportiveness and mistrust, which in turn increase the stressfulness of work conditions (Cropanzano, Howes, Grandey and Toth, 1997).

The Home–Work Interface

Managing the relationship between job demands and off-the-job responsibilities is another source of strain and burnout which has been studied in recent years (Cooper and Lewis, 1998). Changes in family structures and increased participation by women in the workforce, along with technological changes (such as portable computers and cellular phones) which enable job tasks to be performed outside the actual work setting, have blurred the boundaries between the job and life off the job, and can create conflict between job and off-job roles. This inter-role conflict has consistently been linked with increased psychological strain, and is especially prevalent among women and dual-career couples (O'Driscoll, 1996). Flexitime, on-site childcare facilities and other 'family-supportive' programmes are some of the initiatives which have been developed to alleviate job–family conflict and strain (Kramar, 1997).

MODERATORS OF THE STRESSOR–STRAIN RELATIONSHIP

Attention has also been given to variables which may moderate the impact of the above factors on strain experienced by employees. Research has looked for variables which might protect or buffer the individual from the negative effects of stressful work conditions. These potential moderators can be grouped into three categories: personal variables, job-related variables, and organizational variables.

Personal Moderators

Individual differences may play a major role in the relationship between work-related stressors and psychological strain. A number of studies have examined personality differences; here we focus on three which have received considerable attention. One of these is the *Type A behaviour* style, which is characterized as aggressive, ambitious, hard-driving, impatient, seeking to control, and expressing time urgency (Cooper and Bramwell, 1992). The Type A behaviour pattern is an interesting dispositional characteristic, since it may lead to both positive (e.g., high performance) and negative (e.g., high strain and possibly burnout) outcomes. Since it was first identified as a possible risk factor for coronary disorders, several studies have shown that persons demonstrating Type A characteristics are more likely than their Type B counterparts to experience negative effects from job demands (Ganster and Schaubroeck, 1991). For instance, Froggatt and Cotton (1987) illustrated that Type A individuals create more strain for themselves by increasing the volume of their workload. Nevertheless, there is still debate about the mechanism by which the Type A behaviour style affects levels of psychological strain. While it is possible that Type A people subject themselves to more stressful work conditions, it is also feasible that they appraise events as being more stressful than do Type Bs, or that they utilize different methods for coping with strain. Overall, research suggests that the Type A behaviour pattern does not necessarily have across-the-board negative consequences, but certain elements of the disposition (especially hostility) may increase proneness to strain.

Another dispositional variable which may have a significant bearing on the stressor–strain relationship is *negativity affectivity* (NA), a construct which overlaps to some extent with neuroticism, and which reflects a relatively stable tendency to experience low self-esteem and negative emotional states (Watson and Clark, 1984; see also Chapter 1). Individuals who are very high in NA are more susceptible to stressors and experience more strain than their low-NA counterparts. Spector, Zapf, Chen and Frese (2000) have outlined various explanations for the effects of NA, including that high NA individuals have a gloomy 'view of the world' and may be more sensitive to stressful conditions. It is also possible that negative feelings about life may spill over into a person's verbal and non-verbal behaviours, hence inducing negative reactions from colleagues and leading to a conflictual social environment.

A third personality moderator of stressor–strain linkages is *self-esteem* or *self-efficacy* (SE). For instance, Brockner (1988) argued that individuals low on SE tend to react more to external events because they experience more uncertainty about the correctness of their perceptions and emotional reactions (hence rely more on social cues), seek social approval by conformity with others' expectations, and tend to allow negative feedback on one area of their behaviour to generalize to other dimensions of their self-concept. Ganster and Schaubroeck (1995) noted that self-esteem might influence the coping strategies used to combat stressors, with low SE persons selecting less effective coping behaviours.

Job-related Moderators

Although there are many features of the job itself which may act as moderators of the association between work-related stressors and strain, one which has received particular attention is perceived *situational control*: the extent to which individuals believe they can exert control over specific aspects of their job, such as the pace of work, procedures for task completion and scheduling of tasks. Karasek (1979) proposed that strain develops from the combined influence of job demands (workload) and the extent of control over important decisions in the workplace (decision latitude). Where individuals have the capacity to influence decisions relevant to the completion of their job tasks, the level of strain due to a high workload is likely to be diminished. In other words, decision latitude is predicted to serve as a moderator of the impact of job demands.

Despite the intuitive appeal of this argument, research findings on the role of control in stressor–strain relationships are very mixed, and some studies (e.g., O'Driscoll and Beehr, 2000) have not demonstrated a moderator effect. Two recent studies illustrate that clearer specification of the control variable is needed. Wall, Jackson, Mullarkey and Parker (1996) found a moderator effect for perceived job control only when that was explicitly tailored to the job demands experienced by employees. Similarly, Sargent and Terry (1998) observed a moderator effect for control over central areas of one's work, but not for more peripheral areas of control, suggesting that control over particularly important aspects of the work environment may be a critical factor in reducing strain.

Organizational Moderators

Earlier we mentioned that the structure and climate of an organization can influence the degree of strain and burnout experienced by employees. Numerous studies have been conducted on social relationships in the workplace, especially the *social support* employees receive within their organization. There is consistent evidence that employees with more support from others (e.g., their boss, colleagues) experience lower levels of strain and burnout (Lee and Ashforth, 1996). Also, where an individual is faced with potentially stressful demands, conflicts and problems in the job, having support from others may reduce the impact of these pressures on that person's well-being. Social support is therefore expected to buffer or protect the individual from the negative consequences of work-related stressors.

Unfortunately, evidence for the mollifying influence of social support in work situations is very mixed. Moyle and Parkes (1999) found that managerial support reduced the amount of strain experienced by supermarket employees as a result of a forced relocation to another store, and Greenglass, Fiksenbaum and Burke (1996) observed that support from colleagues and supervisors had a significant buffering influence on teacher burnout. Other studies, however, have found no evidence of buffering and yet others have obtained a 'reverse' buffering effect, in which the presence of social support exacerbates the amount of strain experienced by employees (Ganster, Fusilier and Mayes, 1986). The type of buffering which occurs may depend on the nature of support provided. Practical and emotional support which assists the individual to cope with difficult circumstances may have a mitigating influence on strain. In contrast, where communication serves to reinforce the difficulties and problems a person is experiencing in the workplace, this is likely to increase, rather than reduce, the degree of strain reported (Fenlason and Beehr, 1994).

MANAGING STRESS

We now turn to how people and organizations can deal with job-related strain and burnout. In this section we look at coping strategies which individuals might use, and in the next section we discuss possible organizational stress management interventions. Dewe, Cox and Ferguson (1993) defined *coping* as 'cognitions and behaviors adopted by the individual following the recognition of a stressful encounter, that are in some way designed to deal with that encounter or its consequences' (p. 7). Coping refers to the cognitive, behavioural and physiological responses which individuals engage in to (1) eliminate or reduce stressors, (2) alter their appraisal of the potential harmfulness of these stressors, or (3) minimize the extent of strain which they experience.

The coping process is a transaction between the individual and the environment. According to Lazarus and Folkman's (1984) transactional model of stress, there are four main components in coping:

- primary appraisal (perception of a 'threat' to well-being);
- secondary appraisal (identifying possible coping strategies);
- implementation of a coping response;
- evaluation of whether the response was effective in enabling the person to deal with the stressor(s).

Primary and secondary appraisals determine the significance of an event or occurrence for the individual and what, if anything, can be done to minimize its impact.

Lazarus and Folkman distinguished between problem-focused and emotion-focused strategies, and this typology has served as a popular framework for understanding the diversity of stress-coping behaviours. *Problem-focused* strategies involve direct action to remove the stressor or to reduce its impact, while *emotion-focused* behaviours attempt to minimize the emotional effects of a stressor, for instance by downplaying the importance of an event, a process known as cognitive restructuring. Another form of coping, separate from either problem-focused or emotion-focused strategies, occurs when individuals endeavour to enhance their well-being via regular exercise, diet, or use of relaxation techniques, in order to avoid the negative effects of stressful work conditions. This is sometimes referred to as *symptom management*.

Many instruments have been developed for studying coping processes (see Dewe *et al.*, 1993). One popular approach is Lazarus and Folkman's (1984) Ways of Coping questionnaire, which categorizes specific coping behaviours, such as planning and problem-solving, escape/avoidance, distancing oneself from the sources of stress, and altering one's emotional response to stressful situations. Other methods are frequently based upon this instrument. However, research on stress-coping has been plagued by conceptual and methodological difficulties which have impeded progress toward a complete understanding of coping behaviours. A major concern is that many existing measures of coping were not developed from observations of how people actually respond in stressful situations, but were based rather on researchers' own assumptions about possible coping strategies (Dewe *et al.*, 1993). This criticism has been levelled in particular at instruments which provide respondents with a predetermined list of coping responses and ask them to select those which they would use to counter stressors in their work environment. In some cases, the relevance (to the respondent) of the coping responses provided is questionable.

Another issue is whether individuals have preferred *styles of coping* which are stable across time and situations, or whether they adopt *specific strategies* in response to different stressors (Terry, 1994). A few studies have attempted to explore the relationship between coping behaviours and specific stressors. For example, Wiersma (1994) used critical incident analysis to identify sources of work–home role conflicts among dual-career couples, and then link these to coping behaviours. Conflict due to role overload was handled most often by obtaining support from non-family members, dividing tasks among family members, setting priorities and cognitive reappraisal of the situation.

Because they attempt to deal with the actual source of strain, problem-focused approaches could be more helpful in the longer term than emotion-focused coping, which attempts to change a person's evaluations of stressors but may have no direct effect on the environment itself. However, there is no clear consensus on which modes of coping are consistently effective. Furthermore, there are situations in which the individual has little control or influence over environmental variables. For example, in assembly line operations the pace of work is normally determined by machine technology, and workers themselves have little control over this process. Under these circumstances, pressures and demands arising cannot be countered by individual action alone, and, unless organizations modify work technologies and processes, a reduction in psychological strain is unlikely.

ORGANIZATIONAL STRESS MANAGEMENT INTERVENTIONS

Organizational stress management interventions can be targeted either at the individual him/herself (for instance, developing more effective coping behaviours) or at the work conditions (for example, reducing workload). Murphy (1988) identified three levels of organizational stress management intervention:

- primary: reduction of stressors in the workplace;
- secondary: assisting individuals to cope with workplace stressors;
- tertiary: providing support to individuals who are experiencing the effects of job-related strain or burnout.

Primary interventions are typically developed following assessment of the specific strain-inducing factors in a work setting. Examples include reducing individuals' workloads or redesigning jobs to remove ambiguity and conflict. Secondary interventions focus on training individuals to develop more effective coping strategies, while tertiary interventions (often referred to as employee assistance programmes) provide support and counselling for workers whose well-being or job performance has been negatively influenced by workplace stress. Most stress management programmes are predominantly secondary or tertiary level interventions, and may be conducted by stress management consultants or counsellors who assist employees either to reappraise the stressfulness of their work conditions or to cope with job-related stressors. Often more attention is given to modifying employee cognitive appraisals and coping (secondary level interventions) or offering programmes which provide training and counselling for employees experiencing stress (tertiary level interventions), than to eliminating or reducing the actual stressors themselves (Kahn and Byosiere, 1992).

Evidence for the efficacy of secondary interventions, in particular, is inconsistent (Cartwright and Cooper, 1997). Stress management training is often generic in nature, rather than targeting specific work-related stressors, and there may be little preliminary diagnosis of the needs of employees or the organization (Ivancevich, Matteson, Freedman and Phillips, 1990). Employee assistance programmes, which typically incorporate counselling and support services for employees, have shown somewhat more promise as an approach to dealing with stressors, although empirical evidence on their effectiveness is again limited (Cooper and Sadri, 1991). Training and counselling employees to tolerate or cope with poorly designed jobs or organizations may yield short-term gains, but have questionable benefits for long-term mental health and well-being.

Strategies which entail changes at the broader organization level include: redesigning tasks, redesigning the physical work environment, role clarification, establishing more flexible work schedules, participative management, providing feedback and social support for employees, and more equitable reward systems. Many of these approaches are directed toward increasing worker autonomy, participation and control, which we discussed earlier as potential moderators of the stressor–strain relationship, and can be regarded as preventative measures (primary interventions).

Few studies assessing organizational changes have been published. For instance, Ivancevich et al. (1990) found only four evaluations where organizational interventions had been targeted, one on participative decision making, one which studied the effects of more flexible work schedules, a third investigating changes in work design which increased levels of autonomy, and finally one on the effects of introducing an employee representative committee whose function was to develop recommendations on stress management. Reductions in employee strain resulted from all these interventions. Burke (1993) also summarized research on several stress management programmes, including (in addition to those reviewed by Ivancevich and his associates): goal setting (to enhance role definition and clarity), use of problem-solving to resolve work-related difficulties, reducing the amount of conflict between job demands and family responsibilities, and increasing communication and information sharing between management and employees. Burke concluded that, overall, these interventions yielded positive benefits. However, this conclusion has been questioned by Briner and Reynolds (1999), who suggested that the studies reviewed by Burke varied in methodological rigour and contained mixed outcomes.

An illustration of a well-conducted stress management evaluation is a field experiment conducted by Ganster, Mayes, Sime and Tharp (1982). The intervention was a stress management training programme delivered over an 8-week period, and comprised 8 two-hour group training sessions in which employees were taught to recognize and modify their perceptions of stressful working conditions (a procedure known as 'cognitive restructuring'), coupled with training in progressive relaxation. Ganster *et al.*'s evaluation included random assignment of employees to either a treatment or control group (who did not receive the training). Three strain responses were assessed: psychological (anxiety, depression and irritation), physiological (levels of urine epinephrine and norepinephrine), and somatic complaints. These measures were collected at three points in time: pre-training, post-training, and a four-month follow-up to assess (relatively) long-term effects of the training programme. Ganster *et al.* found that employees who underwent the stress management training exhibited significantly lower post-training levels of epinephrine and depression than did control group employees. Effects of the training on other indices of strain were less definitive. Moreover, these effects were not replicated when the control group also underwent the training, suggesting a lack of generalizability. Ganster *et al.* concluded that the evidence was not sufficiently clear-cut to recommend the use of stress management training to alleviate the impact of workplace stressors.

From a managerial standpoint, it may be more convenient to target individual coping than to change organizational structures or redesign jobs. Not only might stress management training and employee assistance programmes be viewed as less costly and more readily implemented than long-term restructuring or major changes in work practices and procedures, but they may also deflect management from accepting responsibility for excessive strain experienced by their employees. However, as noted by Burke (1993), among others, removal or reduction of stressors is 'the most direct way to reduce stress since it deals with the source' (p. 85). There is mounting evidence that job redesign interventions (especially those which increase employee control and autonomy) (see also Chapter 11), adoption of more consultative or participative management styles, development of clearer role descriptions, and utilization of more effective goal-setting and performance feedback systems can all enhance employee well-being and alleviate work-related strain. While these approaches may entail immediate costs for the organization and require greater commitment and effort from management, those may be offset by long-term benefits for individual employees and for the organization as a whole.

There is increasing acknowledgement that some environmental stressors cannot be effectively dealt with solely at the individual level, and that responsibility for stress management must be shared by all constituents of an organization. Individuals need to assume personal responsibility for their appraisal of situations and for the behaviours they engage in to cope with the demands and pressures which are an inevitable element of worklife. On the other hand, management has responsibility for designing jobs and organizations which enhance, rather than detract from, employee physical and mental health. A collaborative approach to dealing with stress and burnout will result in work environments which are often both more productive for organizations and more healthy for the people who work within them.

SUMMARY

Work-related strain and burnout are costly, for organizations and individuals, so there has been considerable investigation of how stress is manifested and methods for dealing with it. In this chapter we have discussed forms of workplace strain and how it might be assessed, some of the major sources of strain and burnout, along with factors which might moderate (buffer) the impact of stressors on well-being. It is clear that there are numerous factors in people's jobs and their work settings which may create both psychological (emotional) and physical strain. Some of these stressors can be managed by individual coping strategies (such as problem-focused and emotion-focused coping), but others require some form of organizational intervention (such as redesigning jobs, reducing workloads, and providing direct assistance to employees experiencing strain). Stress management is a joint responsibility of both individual employees and managers in organizations.

FURTHER READING

Cooper and Quick (1999) provide further information on the effects of stress on health and illness, as does the book by Dunham (2000). Another important topic is the identification of workplace stressors and strain, which is discussed in Sutherland and Cooper (1999). For further coverage of theory and research on occupational stress and burnout, see Cooper (1997) and Schaufeli, Maslach and Marek (1993). Murphy and Cooper (2000) overview various approaches to stress management, especially organizational-level interventions. Finally, a comprehensive review and critique of theory, research and applications is given in Cooper, Dewe and O'Driscoll (2001).

REFERENCES

Banks, M., Clegg, C., Jackson, P., Kemp, N., Stafford, E. and Wall, T. (1980). The use of the General Health Questionnaire as an indicator of mental health in occupational studies. *Journal of Occupational Psychology*, 53, 187–94.

Beehr, T. (1987). The themes of social-psychological stress in work organizations: From roles to goals. In A. W. Riley and S. J. Zaccaro (Eds.), *Occupational Stress and Organizational Effectiveness* (pp. 71–101). New York: Praeger.

— and Franz, T. (1987). The current debate about the meaning of job stress. *Journal of Organizational Behavior Management*, 8, 5–18.

— and McGrath, J. (1992). Social support, occupational stress and anxiety. *Anxiety, Stress and Coping*, 5, 7–20.

Briner, R. and Reynolds, S. (1999). The costs, benefits and limitations of organizational level stress interventions. *Journal of Organizational Behavior*, 20, 647–64.

Brockner, J. (1988). *Self-Esteem at Work: Research, Theory and Practice*. Lexington, MA: Lexington Books.

Burke, R. (1993). Organizational-level interventions to reduce occupational stressors. *Work and Stress*, 7, 77–87.

— and Cooper, C. (2000). *Organizations in Crisis: Downsizing, Restructuring and Privatizations*. Oxford: Blackwell Publishers.

Cartwright, S. and Cooper, C. (1997). *Managing Workplace Stress*. London: Sage Publications.

Confederation of British Industry (2000). *Focus on Absence: Absence and Labour Turnover Survey*, London: CBI.

Cooper, C. (Ed.) (1997). *Theories of Organizational Stress*. Oxford: Oxford University Press.

— and Bramwell, R. (1992). A comparative analysis of occupational stress in managerial and shopfloor workers in the brewing industry: Mental health, job satisfaction and sickness. *Work and Stress*, 6, 127–38.

—, Dewe, P. and O'Driscoll, M. (2001). *Organizational Stress: A Review and Critique of Theory, Research and Applications*. Thousand Oaks, CA: Sage.

— and Kelly, M. (1993). Occupational stress in head teachers: A national UK study. *British Journal of Educational Psychology*, 63, 130–43.

— and Lewis, S. (1998). *Balancing Career, Family and Life*. London: Kogan Page.

— and Quick, J. (1999). *Stress and Strain*. Oxford: Health Press.

— and Sadri, G. (1991). The impact of stress counseling at work. *Journal of Social Behavior and Personality*, 6, 411–23.

Cropanzano, R., Howes, J., Grandey, A. and Toth, P. (1997). The relationship of office politics and support to work behaviors, attitudes and stress. *Journal of Organizational Behavior*, 18, 159–80.

Dewe, P., Cox, T. and Ferguson, E. (1993). Individual strategies for coping with stress at work: A review. *Work and Stress*, 7, 5–15.

Dunham, J. (2000). *Stress in the Workplace: Past, Present and Future*. London and Philadelphia: Whurr Publications.

Edwards, J. (1998). Cybernetic theory of stress, coping and well-being. In C. Cooper (Ed.), *Theories of Organizational Stress* (pp. 122–52). Oxford: Oxford University Press.

Fenlason, K. and Beehr, T. (1994). Social support and occupational stress: Effects of talking to others. *Journal of Organizational Behavior*, 15, 157–75.

Fletcher, B. (1988). The epidemiology of occupational stress. In C. Cooper and R. Payne (Eds.), *Causes, Coping and Consequences of Stress at Work* (pp. 3–50). New York: Wiley.

Fox, M., Dwyer, D. and Ganster, D. (1993). Effects of stressful job demands and control on physiological and attitudinal outcomes in a hospital setting. *Academy of Management Journal*, 36, 289–318.

French, J., Caplan, R. and Harrison, V. (1982). *The Mechanisms of Job Stress and Strain*. Chichester: Wiley.

Freudenberger, H. (1974). Staff burnout. *Journal of Social Issues*, 30, 159–64.

Froggatt, K. and Cotton, J. (1987). The impact of Type-A behavior pattern on role overload-induced stress and performance attributions. *Journal of Management*, *13*, 87–98.

Ganster, D., Fusilier, M. and Mayes, B. (1986). Role of social support in the experience of stress at work. *Journal of Applied Psychology*, *71*, 102–10.

—, Mayes, B., Sime, W. and Tharp, G. (1982). Managing occupational stress: A field experiment. *Journal of Applied Psychology*, *67*, 533–42.

— and Schaubroeck, J. (1991). Work stress and employee health. *Journal of Management*, *17*, 235–71.

— and Schaubroeck, J. (1995). The moderating effects of self-esteem on the work stress–employee health relationship. In R. Crandall and P. Perrewe (Eds.), *Occupational Stress: A Handbook* (pp. 167–77). Washington, DC: Taylor and Francis.

Goldberg, D. (1978). *Manual of the General Health Questionnaire*. London: Oxford University Press.

Greenglass, E., Burke, R. and Konarski, R. (1998). Components of burnout, resources and gender-related differences. *Journal of Applied Social Psychology*, *28*, 1088–106.

—, Fiksenbaum, L. and Burke, R. (1996). Components of social support, buffering effects and burnout: Implications for psychological functioning. *Anxiety, Stress, and Coping*, *9*, 185–97.

Hanisch, K. (1999). Job loss and unemployment research from 1994 to 1998: A review and recommendations for research and intervention. *Journal of Vocational Behavior*, *55*, 188–220.

Hendrix, W., Ovalle, N. and Troxler, R. (1985). Behavioral and physiological consequences of stress and its antecedent factors. *Journal of Applied Psychology*, *70*, 188–201.

Ivancevich, J., Matteson, M., Freedman, S. and Phillips, J. (1990). Worksite stress management interventions. *American Psychologist*, *45*, 252–61.

Jackson, S. and Schuler, R. (1985). A meta-analysis and conceptual critique of research on role ambiguity and role conflict in work settings. *Organizational Behavior and Human Decision Processes*, *36*, 16–78.

Jewell, L. (1998). *Contemporary Industrial/Organizational Psychology* (third edition). Pacific Grove, CA: Brooks/Cole.

Jex, S. and Beehr, T. (1991). Emerging theoretical and methodological issues in the study of work-related stress. *Research in Personnel and Human Resources Management*, *9*, 311–65.

Kahn, R. and Byosiere, P. (1992). Stress in organizations. In M. Dunnette and L. M. Hough (Eds.), *Handbook of Industrial and Organizational Psychology* (second edition, vol. 3, pp. 571–650). Palo Alto, CA: Consulting Psychologists Press.

—, Wolfe, D., Quinn, R. and Snoek, J. (1964). *Organizational Stress: Studies in Role Conflict and Ambiguity*. New York: Wiley.

Karasek, R. (1979). Job demands, job decision latitude, and mental strain: Implications for job redesign. *Administrative Science Quarterly*, 24, 285–308.

King, L. and King, D. (1990). Role conflict and role ambiguity: A critical assessment of construct validity. *Psychological Bulletin*, 107, 48–64.

Korunka, C., Weiss, A., Huemer, K-H. and Karetta, B. (1995). The effects of new technologies on job satisfaction and psychosomatic complaints. *Applied Psychology: International Review*, 44, 123–42.

Kramar, R. (1997). Developing and implementing work and family policies. *Asia Pacific Journal of Human Resources*, 35, 1–18.

Lazarus, R. and Folkman, S. (1984). *Stress, Appraisal and Coping*. New York: Springer Publications.

—, Deese, J. and Osler, S. (1952). The effects of psychological stress on performance. *Psychological Bulletin*, 48, 293–315.

Lee, R. and Ashforth, B. (1996). A meta-analytic examination of the correlates of the three dimensions of job burnout. *Journal of Applied Psychology*, 81, 123–33.

Maslach, C. and Jackson, S. (1986). *The Maslach Burnout Inventory*. Palo Alto, CA: Consulting Psychologists Press.

—, Jackson, S. and Leiter, M. (1996). *Maslach Burnout Inventory* (third edition). Palo Alto, CA: Consulting Psychologists Press.

Moyle, P. and Parkes, K. (1999). The effects of transition stress: A relocation study. *Journal of Organizational Behavior*, 20, 625–46.

Murphy, L. (1988). Workplace interventions for stress reduction and prevention. In C. L. Cooper and R. Payne (Eds.), *Causes, Coping and Consequences of Stress at Work* (pp. 301–39). New York: Wiley.

Murphy, L. and Cooper, C. (Eds.) (2000). *Healthy and Productive Work: An International Perspective*. London: Taylor and Francis.

Narayanan, L., Menon, S. and Spector, P. (1999). Stress in the workplace: A comparison of gender and occupations. *Journal of Organizational Behavior*, 20, 63–74.

O'Driscoll, M. P. (1996). The interface between job and off-job roles: Enhancement and conflict. In C. L. Cooper and I. T. Robertson (Eds.), *International Review of Industrial and Organizational Psychology 1996* (vol. 11, pp. 279–306). Chicester: Wiley.

— and Beehr, T. (1994). Supervisor behaviors, role stressors and uncertainty as predictors of personal outcomes for subordinates. *Journal of Organizational Behavior*, 15, 141–55.

— (2000). Moderating effects of perceived control and need for clarity on the relationships between role stressors and employee affective reactions. *Journal of Social Psychology*, 140, 151–9.

Olson, E. (2000). UN warns of 'alarming' rise in depression at work. *Herald Tribune*, Paris, 11 October.

Pennebaker, J. and Watson, D. (1988). Self-reports and physiological measures in the workplace. In J. Hurrell, L. Murphy, S. Sauter and C. Cooper (Eds.), *Occupational Stress: Issues and Developments in Research* (pp. 184–99). New York: Taylor and Francis.

Pierce, J. and Dunham, R. (1992). The 12-hour work day: A 48-hour, eight-day week. *Academy of Management Journal*, 35, 1086–98.

Sargent, L. and Terry, D. (1998). The effects of work control and job demands on employee adjustment and work. *Journal of Occupational and Organizational Psychology*, 71, 219–36.

Schaufeli, W. and Buunk, B. (1996). Professional burnout. In M. Schabracq, J. Winnubst and C. Cooper (Eds.), *Handbook of Work and Health Psychology* (pp. 311–46). Chichester: Wiley.

—, Maslach, C. and Marek, T. (Eds.) (1993). *Professional Burnout: Recent Developments in Theory and Research*. Washington, DC: Taylor and Francis.

Selye, H. (1936). A syndrome produced by diverse noxious agents. *Nature*, 138, 32.

Sethi, A. and Schuler, R. (1984). *Handbook of Organizational Stress Coping Strategies*. Cambridge, MA: Ballinger.

Spector, P., Zapf, D., Chen, P. and Frese, M. (2000). Why negative affectivity should not be controlled in job stress research: Don't throw the baby out with the bath water. *Journal of Organizational Behavior*, 21, 79–95.

Sutherland, V. and Cooper, C. (1999). *Strategic Stress Management*. London: Macmillan Books.

Terry, D. (1994). Determinants of coping: The role of stable and situational factors. *Journal of Personality and Social Psychology*, 66, 895–910.

Wall, Jackson, P., Mullarkey, S. and Parker, S. (1996). The demands–control model of job strain: A more specific test. *Journal of Occupational and Organizational Psychology*, 69, 153–66.

Watson, D. and Clark, L. (1984). Negative affectivity: The disposition to experience negative aversive emotional states. *Psychological Bulletin*, 96, 465–98.

Westman, M. and Eden, D. (1992). Excessive role demand and subsequent performance. *Journal of Organizational Behavior*, 13, 519–29.

Wiersma, U. (1994). A taxonomy of behavioural strategies for coping with work–home role conflict. *Human Relations*, 47, 211–21.

Zohar, D. (1997). Predicting burnout with a hassle-based measure of role demands. *Journal of Organizational Behavior*, 18, 101–15.

9

The Experience, Expression and Management of Emotion at Work

Rob B. Briner and Peter Totterdell

Emotions are intrinsic to everyday experience inside and outside work, both colouring experience and shaping behaviour. Three key aspects of emotion that influence well-being and behaviour at work will be considered here: the ways in which people experience emotions (such as feeling angry, embarrassed, excited or proud), the ways in which they express their emotions, and the ways in which they manage their own and other people's emotions.

Psychologists and others concerned with work behaviour have long been interested in employees' feelings in terms of outcomes such as satisfaction, stress and fatigue. There have also been sporadic attempts to understand those feelings, including emotions, in more detail. For example, Hersey (1931) conducted a study in which employees were asked to rate their feelings regularly, including anger, disgust, and sadness. Likewise, Herzberg, Mausner and Snyderman (1959) asked people to describe in detail how they felt at work, including emotions such as pride and shame. However, this field has received concerted attention only in the past ten years, and sociology and management researchers have been more active than psychologists. Nevertheless, the topics of emotion at work and emotional intelligence have now begun to attract considerable interest from practitioners, managers and the general public, as well as from psychologists.

THE NATURE AND IMPORTANCE OF EMOTIONS

What Are Emotions?

While examples of emotion such as envy, hate, joy, admiration, gloating, guilt, pity, and disappointment can readily be provided, and we all know what these emotions feel like, systematic definition has proved more elusive. A useful way of considering what emotions are is to examine elements found across definitions. Parkinson (1995) has identified five such elements: situational cognitive appraisal (e.g., an evaluation of threat or harm in the situation); change in action tendencies (e.g., approach or avoidance); bodily reactions (e.g., heart rate); expressive movements (e.g., facial expression, posture); and a goal structure (e.g., progress towards or thwarting of a personal plan). In other words, most definitions of emotion incorporate cognitive and behavioural elements. However, not all of these elements must be present before we can define an experience as an emotion.

Some of these aspects are particularly relevant to work. First, changes in action tendencies are one of the ways in which emotions lead to behaviour. For example, if employees feel shame they are likely to withdraw and avoid drawing attention to themselves. Second, expressive movements are the means by which emotions are communicated. For example, if a colleague looks worried or a customer looks angry, other people may change the way they approach him or her. Third, the goal structure in which emotions are produced helps us to understand how work events provoke specific emotions. For example, if employees feel proud and delighted, it is likely that they have achieved some important goal.

Emotions are part and parcel of most aspects of work psychology – from training and careers to team working and change. For this reason, other chapters in this book also deal with how people feel. Stress, job satisfaction and affective well-being all involve feelings or affect, so where does emotion fit in? Different kinds of affect can be compared on dimensions such as their intensity, their time course, and their focus (see Parkinson, Totterdell, Briner and Reynolds, 1996). Viewed on these dimensions, emotions are usually intense, rapid in onset, dissipate quickly, and are directed at specific events. Stress and satisfaction, on the other hand, are much broader feelings that tend to be somewhat less intense (though they may, of course, sometimes contain intense emotions), slower in onset, longer lasting, and are not directed at specific events. Affective well-being (see Chapter 1) also normally refers to less intense, less variable, and less directed feelings than emotions. An additional concept to consider is that of mood, which lies somewhere between affective well-being and emotions on the dimensions considered.

Why Are Emotions Important?

There is little doubt that emotions are interesting, particularly when we are actually experiencing them, but how is emotion important to psychologists? The most direct way is that emotion is a central part of the broader domain of well-being. Some approaches to well-being (for a review see Diener, Suh, Lucas and Smith, 1999) suggest a bottom-up approach, such that daily experiences of affect, including emotion, collectively lead to more general feelings of well-being. It would be surprising, for example, if people regarded themselves as fairly happy but experienced relatively few positive emotions on a daily basis.

Emotions are also important because they are causes of behaviour. Different emotions are likely to lead to particular kinds of behaviours depending on other aspects of the person and the situation. Behaviours may come about not only as a consequence of an emotion but also because behaviour may be directed towards achieving or avoiding certain anticipated emotions. For example, we may work hard towards a deadline in order to achieve the pride and satisfaction of completing the task or to avoid the embarrassment of failing to meet the deadline. In addition, emotional displays are directly related to performance where the job requires the display of particular emotions (discussed later).

EMOTIONS EXPERIENCED AT WORK

It seems reasonable to suppose that any emotion could be experienced at work. Perhaps the only exceptions would be for those people who work alone who may be less likely to experience emotions that are more social or interpersonal in nature such as love, hatred, or envy. In contrast to research on the expression of emotion, research on the experience of emotion is relatively underdeveloped. Nevertheless, studies of the experience of different emotions, such as anger (see below), shame (Poulson, 2000; Walsh, 1999), and boredom (Fisher, 1998), do exist (see Briner (1999) for further examples).

Different methods have also been used to study emotional experience at work. For example, Fisher (2000) used experience-sampling methodology, in which participants are interrupted by a signal from a programmed alarm watch and then required to answer a series of questions, to investigate the relationship between specific emotions and general job satisfaction. Fitness (2000) asked people to provide a description of an occasion at work when they felt angry with someone and then analyzed the narratives (or stories) that participants told. Another example is provided by Hahn (2000) who used a quantitative daily diary method, in which participants completed a series of rating scales every day, to examine emotional responses to interpersonal stressors. Numerous studies have also adopted qualitative methods, involving detailed observation and in-depth interviewing (see Fineman (2000) for examples).

The Causes of Emotion

The causes of emotion have long been of interest to psychologists and others (see Parkinson, 1995). While numerous theoretical approaches exist, a number seem particularly useful for considering the causes of emotion at work. Perhaps the best-known approach to emotion causation considers them to be caused by the way in which people perceive or appraise an event or situation. An early proponent of this view was Lazarus (1966), who suggested roles for both primary appraisal, in which the significance or otherwise of an event is evaluated, and secondary appraisal where options for what can be done in response are considered. In general, such cognitive approaches dominate thinking about emotion causation.

Social approaches (see Parkinson, 1996) suggest that the causes and functions of emotion are primarily social, even though we tend to view emotions as internal, private, and physiological experiences. According to Parkinson (1996), emotions are ways of communicating personal concerns to an audience (which may in some instances be an imagined rather than an actual audience). This communicative function of emotions is seen as central to understanding their interpersonal and fundamentally social role.

Goal-based approaches (e.g., Carver and Scheier, 1990; Oatley and Johnson-Laird, 1987) suggest that emotions are produced through cognitive appraisal, but that events and situations are given meaning in such appraisals because they are linked to people's goals or what they are trying to do. Thus, individuals may get angry because they have something they are currently trying hard to do (an active goal) but someone or something gets in the way of their ability to achieve that goal.

Another explanation of the causes of emotion can be found when we consider the role of individual differences. Some dispositional differences, such as in positive and negative affectivity (people's tendency to experience pleasant or unpleasant emotional states), are thought to have an influence on mood states and are also likely to play a role in the experience of emotions. Other differences, such as in Type-A personality (which characterizes individuals who tend to rush and are anger-prone), have a direct impact on the experience of emotion.

Unfortunately there are few studies that provide evidence of the causes of specific emotions experienced at work. Chapters elsewhere in this book describe features of the work environment that are known to affect stress and affective well-being. In some ways, it would be surprising if the set of causes of emotion at work were completely different or could not somehow be incorporated into these existing frameworks. However, one key difference would be that, as indicated earlier, the concepts of stress or affective well-being do not incorporate some specific emotions such as remorse, guilt, hope or gratification and hence it may be that other features of work may be causes of these specific kinds of feelings. A second key difference, as emphasized in all approaches to emotion and indeed incorporated in most definitions of emotion, is that emotions are thought to be caused by specific events. Reasoning about other kinds of affective phenomena at work, such as job satisfaction, does not usually incorporate the notion of events as causes, but rather considers as possible causes broader aspects of the environment or the person or continuing job characteristics. Weiss and Cropanzano (1996), in their Affective Events Theory (discussed later), have emphasized the centrality of specific events when considering emotion causation in the work context.

While systematic evidence about the causes of specific emotions at work has yet to be published, the available studies do provide illustrations of the kinds of research that can be done. A study by Fitness (2000), for example, analyzed people's accounts of an occasion at work when they felt angry with someone. She found that a common theme underlying these accounts of anger was some sort of violation or thwarting of an expectation about how people 'ought' to behave. Particularly relevant to the work context was that when the person who had made the participant angry was either a co-worker or a subordinate, the anger tended to focus around behaviours interpreted by the participant as demonstrating incompetence, dishonesty or laziness. However, when the person was a superior in the organization, the anger tended to focus around behaviours that were viewed as showing unfairness.

Basch and Fisher (2000) asked respondents to think of each of ten specific emotions at work and then describe the kind of event which had caused the emotion. They found that different emotions were reported as being caused by different kinds of events. For example, embarrassment was caused most frequently by making mistakes, whereas disgust was caused most frequently by acts of management.

The Effects of Emotion

The effects of emotion can be very widespread indeed and impact not only on overt behaviours but also on cognition and on subsequent emotion. Imagine the sequence of events that might occur when a supervisor experiences compassion towards a work colleague who is having difficulties. The supervisor may physically move towards the colleague to offer comfort and support, and may perhaps revise some negative opinions held about the colleague or suddenly perceive the colleague in a different light, and, through attempts to display compassion, the supervisor may start to feel sad or distressed. The effects of emotion are thus likely to be both broad and complex. Some of the ways people have thought about the effects of emotion are considered here, along with some examples of research.

As indicated earlier, behavioural responses tend to be part of what emotions are considered to be. In the case of the five so-called basic emotions (happiness, sadness, anxiety, anger, disgust), the behavioural tendencies have been described as follows (Oatley and Johnson-Laird, 1987). If subgoals are being achieved, the person experiences happiness and will tend to continue with the plan. A failure or loss of active goal will result in sadness that in turn is likely to lead to inactivity or the search for a new plan or goal. Where there is some threat to the attainment of some personally important goal, the person will experience anxiety and will tend to stop what he or she is doing, look for possible dangers, and/ or escape the situation. When an active plan is frustrated, anger is felt which results in increased effort or aggression towards whatever is frustrating the attainment of the goal. Finally, if a goal connected with taste or some kind of moral standard is violated, the person experiences disgust and will reject whatever is causing the feeling or try to withdraw.

Clearly this same kind of reasoning could also be applied to other emotions and would apply in any context where emotions are experienced. However, some approaches have been developed to aid understanding of the effects of emotion in specifically work settings. In particular, Affective Events Theory (Weiss and Cropanzano, 1996) represents the very first attempt to provide a comprehensive account of the causes, consequences (attitudinal and behavioural) and structure of affective experiences such as moods and emotions at work. As such, it represents an important development in the field, even though it draws heavily on existing theories of emotion and has not been comprehensively tested. Here we focus in particular on how the theory accounts for the behavioural consequences of emotion.

According to the theory, behaviours at work are either direct responses to affective experiences (affect-driven behaviours) or they are indirect responses mediated by work attitudes such as job satisfaction (judgement-driven behaviours). Affect-driven behaviours (such as coping responses) are thus more spontaneous and require less cognitive processing before they occur, whereas judgement-driven behaviours (such as absence and lateness) require more careful consideration of the situation followed by a decision to behave in a particular way. This distinction leads to the prediction that emotions will be less correlated with judgement-driven behaviours (because they are mediated by work attitudes) than with affect-driven behaviours.

The theory also focuses on the role of episodes of emotion and how they unfold over time. In other words, there is less concern with a simple stimulus-response approach to emotions and their effects and rather more concern with on-going processes. In essence, therefore, the context in which emotions occur and what happens next in an emotion episode will strongly determine the medium- or longer-term effect of any specific emotion.

The effects of mood on many aspects of behaviour and cognition are pervasive (see Parkinson *et al.*, 1996). For example, in relation to job behaviour, employees who experience more positive moods are more likely to receive higher ratings of their job performance (Staw, Sutton and Pelled, 1994), more likely to help customers (George, 1991), and less likely to be absent from work (George, 1989). Some associations between affective well-being and behaviour at work, such as discretionary behaviour, have also been discussed in Chapter 1, but what is known about the effects of emotion on work behaviours? At the present time there is very little evidence on which to draw. However, given the behavioural tendencies associated with emotion, discussed above, we would expect that there would be significant behavioural consequences of experienced emotions. It is likely that such effects will be found in both task-related and other work behaviours. For example, if employees feel angry towards their supervisor, it is possible they will exert less effort and also communicate their anger to work colleagues. Employees may also start to perceive their job differently and perhaps think about changing jobs if the same events and feelings are repeated. There are clearly many causes and consequences of the experience of emotion at work. Next we consider the causes and consequences of the way emotion is expressed at work.

THE EXPRESSION OF EMOTION AT WORK

Employees use a combination of facial, postural, and vocal communication to express emotions to colleagues and customers. Sometimes employees try to express the emotions that are being experienced, but they may also choose to express different or modified emotions. For example, an employee may feel angry with a customer but have to act pleasantly. Mann (1999), for example, found that employees reported hiding their true feelings and faking emotions in about 60 per cent of workplace communications.

Employees select particular emotional displays because of personal preference, general social norms, or because their job has particular requirements concerning which emotions are expressed, how they are expressed, and in what situations they are expressed. When a job has such requirements, employees are engaging in what has come to be known as 'emotional labour'.

Emotional Labour

The concept of emotional labour was first defined by Hochschild (1983, p. 7), in her pioneering research on flight attendants, as 'the management of feeling to create a publicly observable facial and bodily display; emotional labor is sold for a wage and therefore has exchange value'. Management of emotional expression (also known as emotion work) is of course also required in other social situations outside the workplace, but what makes emotional labour different is that it is exchanged for a wage.

All but the most solitary jobs involve some emotional labour, because employer-sanctioned rules regarding emotional expression are likely to exist whenever there is social interaction. Most jobs involve emotional labour because most jobs are likely to be done better when employees use appropriate emotional expressions. For example, leaders may display enthusiasm in order to motivate others, and team members may suppress negative feelings, such as contempt, to maintain team harmony. However, emotional expression is central in some jobs involving high levels of interaction with clients or customers and, unsurprisingly, most research on emotional labour has focused on such jobs. Emotional expression has been studied in a range of service roles, including flight attendants (Hochschild, 1983), supermarket cashiers (Rafaeli and Sutton, 1990), bill (debt) collectors (Sutton, 1991), hairdressers (Parkinson, 1991), fast-food workers (Leidner, 1991), criminal interrogators (Rafaeli and Sutton, 1991), and environmental regulatory inspectors (Fineman and Sturdy, 1999).

Two of these studies are noteworthy because the researchers gained temporary employment in order to use participant observation as their research method: Anat Rafaeli worked as a supermarket cashier and Robert Sutton as a debt collector. The supermarket cashier study (Rafaeli and Sutton, 1990) collected observational ratings of cashiers' use of smiling, thanking and other emotional expressions during customer transactions. Cashiers were less likely to display positive emotions during busy periods because positive emotions encouraged customers to prolong interactions. However, positive emotions were more likely to be used when customers were more demanding, because positive emotions also provoked greater compliance from customers. Sutton (1991) found that the appropriate emotional expression for debt collectors depended on the emotional state of the debtor on the other end of the telephone. Irritation or anger was expressed to debtors who seemed indifferent, friendly, or sad because they were considered under-aroused or unmotivated, but warmth or calm was expressed to anxious or angry debtors because they were considered too aroused to process information about their debt. These and similar studies demonstrate that emotional expression at work is not merely about being pleasant, but also about using different emotions in different circumstances to achieve specific job-related goals.

The Determinants of Employee Expression

The choice of which emotions to express at work is probably determined, as it is in other social situations, by general rules or norms. However, in jobs involving emotional labour there are often specific and explicit rules which are shaped by more occupation-specific norms. For example, norms specify that nurses should express concern, funeral directors solemnity, and sales clerks friendliness.

Ashforth and Humphrey (1993) distinguished between 'feeling rules', that specify the range, intensity, duration, and object of emotions that employees should experience, and 'display rules' that specify what emotions should be expressed. The public nature of display rules makes them easier to enforce. Display rules can match or clash with people's experienced feelings.

One reason why employees comply with display rules is that they can personally benefit from doing so (described in more detail below). Pressure of social conformity is another reason for compliance. However, employees may also comply because they identify with their job and therefore agree with its norms. Ashforth and Humphrey (1993) have suggested that employees who strongly identify with their job role will feel more authentic in complying with display rules and hence are likely to find it less effortful to display the required emotion.

The Effects of Expression on Organizations and Employees

The expression of emotion at work can affect organizational performance in a number of ways. Rafaeli and Sutton (1987) identified three types of gains (or losses). Immediate gains are instant effects, such as positively influencing a customer to buy. Encore gains refer to return visits which result from making a favourable impression on customers. Contagion gains refer to indirect effects, such as obtaining additional business because customers have told others how much they enjoyed the service. Another potential gain for the organization is that employees may undertake their tasks more effectively. For example, transactions may proceed more smoothly if employees express affiliative emotions.

The expression of emotion can also result in organizational losses if employees display inappropriate emotions. For example, business may be lost due to surly or rude customer service. While there is at present little empirical evidence that demonstrates that emotional expression has positive or negative effects on organizations as a whole, it seems highly plausible.

Turning now to individual employees, emotional expression at work can result in a mixture of gains and losses in a number of areas. Parkinson's (1991) study of emotional expression in trainee hairdressers nicely illustrates some of these mixed effects. Trainees who were more emotionally expressive and open in customer interactions received bigger tips. However, some trainees also reported using deceptive impression management strategies. For example, one trainee commented, 'You've got to be nice to them, instead of telling them what you really feel like, like kicking them or drowning them' (p. 430). Trainees who used such deceptive strategies reported lower job satisfaction and reduced well-being.

The relationships between emotional labour and health are complex, and may partly depend on the variety, duration and intensity of emotions required (see Morris and Feldman, 1996). For example, Zapf, Vogt, Seifert, Mertini and Isic (1999) found that the requirement to express positive emotions was associated with feelings of both personal accomplishment and emotional exhaustion. Similarly, Schaubroeck and Jones (2000) found that the requirement to express positive emotions was associated with symptoms of ill health but mainly among employees who did not identify with their job.

Adverse effects are more likely to occur when there is a mismatch between the emotions required, emotions expressed, and emotions felt. One type of mismatch, known as emotional deviance, occurs when the requirements or display rules are disregarded (Rafaeli and Sutton, 1987). Deviance may be particularly harmful if the employee still accepts the display rules, for example a nurse who can no longer express empathy due to burnout. Another mismatch, known as emotional dissonance, occurs when there is a discrepancy between what a person expresses and what he or she feels. Emotional dissonance has consistently been found to be associated with negative consequences for the employee, such as emotional exhaustion, physical symptoms, and lower job satisfaction (e.g., Zapf et al., 1999).

EMOTION MANAGEMENT

The Management of Experience

The previous sections may have given the impression that feelings are experiences that happen to people rather than processes over which they have some control. However, people can and do make active attempts to manage their emotional experiences using affect regulation, which involves applying cognitive or behavioural strategies to change or maintain emotion.

Unlike coping strategies, affect regulation strategies are not only used in response to negative events. Nevertheless, the most common purpose of affect regulation is to get out of an unpleasant emotional state such as feeling unhappy or miserable (by using upward regulation strategies to reduce negative and increase positive feelings). There are, however, also sometimes good reasons to inhibit pleasant states or even maintain unpleasant states (Parrott, 1993). For example, highly pleasant states, such as joy and elation, are less conducive for doing tasks that require concentration and may be inappropriate if expressed during a formal situation such as an interview or negotiation.

Parkinson and Totterdell (1999) identified over 160 distinct strategies people use to terminate unpleasant emotions. They then asked a group of trainee teachers to rate their moods and their use of different regulation strategies every two hours during two school weeks (Totterdell and Parkinson, 1999). Although cognitive distraction (thinking of pleasant things) was most commonly used, the most effective strategies were behavioural diversion (pleasant, relaxing or energetic activities) and reappraisal (looking at things differently). Venting feelings and avoiding thinking about things were generally ineffective. An important feature of affect regulation is that it consumes resources that are required by other tasks involving mental control, leading to performance decrements on those tasks (Muraven and Baumeister, 2000) (see also Chapter 2). This includes performance decrements in tasks requiring physical stamina, problem-solving and emotional expression, which may have implications for job performance when those are involved.

People can also influence other people's emotional experiences as well as their own. Two processes are important here. The first is non-conscious and known as primitive emotional contagion (Hatfield, Cacioppo and Rapson, 1994), in which people automatically mimic the expressive displays of others and, through somatic feedback, experience similar emotions. The second is a conscious process of emotional comparison in which people evaluate the feelings of others to determine their own feelings.

Although there has been surprisingly little research on this topic in work psychology, some progress has been made in the areas of leadership, teams, and customer service. It is generally assumed that leaders use emotions to influence their audience. Transformational leaders in particular (see Chapter 12) are thought to express strong emotions in order to motivate followers, and to display emotions that tell followers what to feel. Lewis (2000) found that observers of a chief executive leader felt more nervous when the leader expressed anger, and less enthusiastic when the leader expressed sadness. The leader was also rated as more effective when he or she displayed a neutral emotional tone.

A small set of studies has provided evidence that members of work teams influence each other's moods in such a way that their moods tend to converge and influence work performance. An observational study of work teams (Bartel and Saavedra, 2000) and a survey study of sales teams (George, 1990) both demonstrated that mood can be sufficiently consistent within a team to be treated as a collective property of the team (as well as the property of individuals). Furthermore, the collective mood of teammates can influence team members' moods, as shown by field studies of nursing, accountancy and professional sports teams (Totterdell, Kellett, Teuchmann and Briner, 1998; Totterdell, 2000). These studies have found that emotional contagion in teams is greater when team members are older (in samples between nineteen and sixty years), in more positive moods, more sensitive to others' feelings, and more committed to the team, and when teams are working on highly interdependent tasks. This set of studies has also discovered that the transfer of positive emotions within teams is associated with reduced absenteeism, more helpful behaviour, better interpersonal relations, and enhanced task perform-ance. In addition, a study by Pugh (2001) has shown that displays of positive emotion by bank tellers enhance the positive affect of customers, which in turn influences customers' ratings of service quality.

The Management of Expression

Hochschild (1983) identified two main ways in which individuals control their emotional expression: surface acting and deep acting. Surface acting involves displaying emotions that are not felt and is achieved by focusing on the display of emotion rather than inner experience. However, surface acting may lead to an inauthentic display, because the emotions are not felt and the person's actual feelings may also leak out. In contrast, deep acting involves trying to experience the emotions that are going to be displayed by using thoughts, images, or memories that evoke the emo-tions. Deep acting is more likely to produce an authentic display and requires a greater effort. The analogy with acting has also led to a distinction between 'onstage' (dealing with customers and clients) and 'offstage' (with coworkers only) emotional expression at work.

One of the main methods used to manage employee emotion is through training. In particular, jobs involving high levels of emotional labour usually train employees to follow display rules. For example, flight attendants in Hochschild's (1983) study were instructed by a trainer, 'Now girls, I want you to go out there and really smile. Your smile is your biggest asset' (p. 4). Other methods include monitoring and giving explicit feedback on emotion performance, the use of rewards and sanctions, and providing role models. Some organizations, such as call centres, use scripts specifying exactly what employees must say to customers and how it should be expressed.

Organizations can also manage emotional expression by recruiting employees who already have an appropriate style. A potential pitfall, however, is that interviewees who convey positive emotions are more likely to be hired (e.g., Fox and Spector, 2000), even though displaying positive emotions may not be the main job requirement. Some employers have also started selecting people on the basis of emotional competencies because of claims (examined below) that emotional intelligence and job performance are linked (e.g., Goleman, 1998).

Emotional Intelligence

The concept of intelligence is often equated only with cognitive intelligence (as traditionally measured by intelligence quotient or IQ), whereas numerous researchers suggest that general intelligence incorporates different intelligences, including social intelligence (see Mayer and Salovey, 1993). Placed within this framework, emotional intelligence (also known as emotional quotient or EQ, by analogy with IQ) is a type of social intelligence that applies to emotions in the self and others. It is particularly relevant to the management of emotion at work, but is only one of many individual difference variables that are likely to play a role.

Salovey and Mayer (1990) originally defined emotional intelligence as 'the ability to monitor one's own and others' feelings and emotions, to discriminate among them, and to use this information to guide one's thinking and actions' (p. 189). A later definition covered abilities in four areas, and applies to emotions in the self and others: perception, appraisal, and expression of emotion; emotional facilitation of thinking; understanding emotion and emotion knowledge; and the reflective regulation of emotions to promote emotional and intellectual growth (Mayer and Salovey, 1997). Other writers have presented similar models of emotional intelligence but have included different emotion abilities (e.g., Goleman, 1998). Proponents of the concept of emotional intelligence are in general agreement that it is an ability that is learned and therefore develops with age, experience and appropriate training.

A number of approaches to the measurement of emotional intelligence have been used. Some studies have used self-report measures of overall emotional intelligence or its components (e.g., Schutte, Malouff, Hall, Haggerty, Cooper, Golden and Dornheim, 1998). Other studies employ multiple independent raters to assess emotional competencies, which are the behavioural manifestations of emotional intelligence (e.g., Goleman, 1998). However, both these approaches suffer from the fact that people are not always good judges of their own or other people's abilities. A third approach uses ability tests, for example asking individuals to identify the emotions portrayed in pictures or stories (e.g., Mayer and Geher, 1996). However, scores on these tests are not entirely objective, because they are based on agreement with the consensus of a group of independent judges or with the report of the person portrayed.

Some scholars have raised questions concerning the psychometric status of emotional intelligence. Mayer and Salovey (1993, 1997) argued that emotional intelligence involves a set of abilities (measured in terms of maximum possible attainment) rather than a behavioural preference (measured as typical rather than maximum behaviour) and is therefore an intelligence rather than a personality trait. Schutte *et al.* (1998) found that emotional intelligence was associated only with the Openness to Experience trait of the big five personality dimensions (see Chapter 5). However, Davies, Stankov and Roberts (1998) found that self-report measures of emotional intelligence were indistinguishable from the Extroversion, Agreeableness and (lack of) Neuroticism dimensions of the big five, and that available objective ability measures in this area did not satisfy accepted psychometric standards.

Concerning the relationship between emotional intelligence and job performance, Goleman (1998) analyzed the competencies required for many job roles and concluded that emotional competencies, such as understanding and influencing others, are essential for job effectiveness. Goleman (1998) also reported that a group of financial advisors who went through an emotional competence training programme had significantly greater subsequent sales gains than comparison groups. However, the evidence concerning the relationship with job performance is very slim at present. It is also the case that different jobs are likely to require different strengths across the dimensions of emotional intelligence (e.g., Bar-On, Browne, Kirkcaldy and Thome, 2000).

Emotional intelligence has also been considered to be an important determinant of leadership (e.g., George, 2000), team cohesion (e.g., Abraham, 1999), innovation (e.g., Huy, 1999) and other organizational processes. However, the empirical evidence is again lacking at present. There is also a division emerging between scientific and popular conceptions. Mayer (1999), for example, suggests that popular accounts make sensational and unjustified claims about emotional intelligence and stretch its meaning to include other personality characteristics.

IMPLICATIONS AND FUTURE DIRECTIONS

Ethical and Practical Implications

While there is a broad acceptance that employers have a right to ask employees to perform physical behaviours (e.g., in manual labour) or engage in cognitive activities (e.g., in knowledge work), emotional behaviour might be considered to be outside what employers can reasonably demand. Emotions are often regarded as intensely personal experiences and hence attempts by employers to manage employee emotion might be seen as interfering in something personal to the employee. In contrast, Smith (1999) argues that the skill involved in displaying particular emotions should be regarded and valued in exactly the same way as any other employee skill, and proper training and rewards should be offered.

While we may be concerned about the ethics of attempts to control employee emotions, manipulating and controlling emotion is not easily achievable. For example, one way of trying to make employees feel a certain way about the organization and its products is through culture change programmes, but it is not clear that such initiatives work. Indeed, telling people how they should feel may actually be counterproductive (van Maanen and Kunda, 1989). In the case of emotional labour, it is not always the case that employees follow prescribed display rules and they may resist attempts to control their displays of emotion (Ashforth and Humphrey, 1993).

Selection and training are two major areas in which practical implications seem most relevant. Given that the ability to display particular emotions is influenced by various individual characteristics, including perhaps emotional intelligence, one implication is to ensure that individuals selected for emotionally demanding jobs have attributes which facilitate their performance. Another obvious application would be to train emotion skills.

A further area of potential application concerns job design. This may be particularly important where there are high demands for emotional displays and low levels of control, such as in the intensive emotion work undertaken by employees in call centres. It is also likely to be important in work such as nursing and teaching which likewise make high emotional demands. A key issue therefore is how jobs which do contain high levels of emotional demand can be designed so employees can do them effectively and safely.

Last, as mentioned earlier, employee well-being has usually been thought of in terms of features such as stress, satisfaction and fatigue. Looking at well-being in terms of emotion may provide ideas for other kinds of intervention to enhance well-being. This approach has great promise because it provides a more focused way of assessing employee feelings. For example, knowing that employees feel contempt or are angry is likely to help focus interventions more precisely than knowing they are 'stressed'. In addition, because the causes and consequences of emotion are more specific, we are more likely to know what type of intervention will be effective for changing levels of specific emotions.

Future Directions

In a rapidly developing field, future directions are often difficult to predict. There do, however, seem to be a number of empirical and theoretical gaps. In empirical terms, for example, we lack even the simplest descriptive data about who experiences which emotions and in which jobs and roles. While work on emotional labour is more advanced, the dynamics of emotional labour are not well understood, nor are the situations in which it may be harmful or beneficial.

The kinds of theoretical development needed have already started with Affective Events Theory (Weiss and Cropanzano, 1996). At the simplest level, studying emotion provokes critical examination of existing constructs such as stress and satisfaction. At other levels, studying emotion is particularly conceptually challenging because it places on-going events and people's responses to those events at the heart of understanding emotional experience. It is how these events and reactions unfold over time that is difficult to characterize in simple cause–effect terms. Lazarus' early work on transactions (1966) or his later work (1999) on emotional narratives and core relational themes may offer useful frameworks.

There will be many as yet unknown directions in which psychologists and others will take the study of emotion other than those described briefly here. More certain, however, is that considering emotion as part of work psychology enriches and enhances our understanding of work experience and behaviour.

SUMMARY

Emotion at work is a relatively new topic within work psychology. Emotions are different from other kinds of feeling states such as stress and satisfaction in a number of important ways. In particular, they are brief and directed at specific events. A wide range of emotions is experienced at work and relatively little is known about such experiences. A number of theoretical approaches to understanding how emotions arise at work exist, and most of these emphasize the importance of specific events and their interpretation as causes of particular emotions.

Considerably more work has been conducted on the expression of emotion at work and in particular on jobs which involve emotional labour, where the employee is required to display certain kinds of emotions to customers and clients. There are a number of ways in which organizations encourage displays of particular emotions in jobs that involve emotional labour. Emotional displays have costs and benefits for both organizations and employees.

How employees and organizations manage the experience and expression of emotion is a key consideration. Individuals attempt to regulate both their own and others' feelings in a variety of ways. Likewise, employees use a number of strategies in order to display the appropriate emotion. Emotional intelligence is likely to be an important factor in the management of both experience and expression of emotion.

Important ethical implications concern the extent to which it is reasonable for employers to demand that their employees display and experience specific emotions. For work psychology a number of practical implications are also apparent particularly in the areas of selection, training, and job design.

FURTHER READING

The first book on emotion at work, *Emotion in Organizations* edited by Fineman (1993), now has a second edition (2000). These volumes represent the largest collections of articles on emotion at work and both draw heavily on sociological and ethnographic rather than psychological approaches to the study of emotion. Other edited collections include *Emotions in the Workplace: Research, Theory and Practice* (Ashkanasy, Hartel and Zerbe, 2000), *Managing Emotions in the Workplace* (Ashkanasy, Zerbe and Hartel, 2002) and *Emotions at Work: Theory, Research and Applications in Management* (Payne and Cooper, 2001), which contain a mixture of psychological and other approaches.

There are also a number of special issues of journals, including *European Journal of Work and Organizational Psychology* (1999, Volume 8, Issue 3), *Journal of Organizational Behavior* (2000, Volume 21, March Issue), *Organizational Behavior and Human Decision Processes* (2001, Volumen 86, Issue 1) and *Advances in Developing Human Resources* (2002, Volume 4, Issue 1). A special issue of the *Annals of the American Academy of Political and Social Science* (1999, 561) focuses on emotional labour in the service economy. There is also a website *http://www.uq.net.au/emonet/* dedicated to the study of emotion in organizational settings.

REFERENCES

Abraham, R. (1999). Emotional intelligence in organizations: A conceptualization. *Genetic Social and General Psychology Monographs*, 125, 209–24.

Ashforth, B. E. and Humphrey, R. H. (1993). Emotional labor in service roles: The influence of identity. *Academy of Management Review*, 18, 88–115.

Ashkanasy, N. M., Hartel, C. E. J. and Zerbe, W. J. (Eds.) (2000). *Emotions in the Workplace: Research, Theory and Practice*. Westport, Conn.: Quorum Books.

Ashkanasy, N. M., Zerbe, W. J. and Hartel, C. E. J. (Eds.) (2002). *Managing Emotions in the Workplace*. Armonk, NY: M. E. Sharpe.

Bar-On, R., Brown, J. M., Kirkcaldy, B. D. and Thome, E. P. (2000). Emotional expression and implications for occupational stress: An application of the Emotional Quotient Inventory (EQ-i). *Personality and Individual Differences*, 28, 1107–18.

Bartel, C. A. and Saavedra, R. (2000). The collective construction of work group moods. *Administrative Science Quarterly*, 45, 197–231.

Basch, J. and Fisher, C. D. (2000). Affective events–emotions matrix: A classification of work events and associated emotions. In N. M. Ashkanasy, C. E. J. Hartel and W. J. Zerbe (Eds.), *Emotions in the Workplace: Research, Theory and Practice* (pp. 36–48). Westport, Conn.: Quorum Books.

Briner, R. B. (1999). The neglect and importance of emotion at work. *European Journal of Work and Organizational Psychology*, 8, 323–46.

Carver, C. S. and Scheier, M. F. (1990). Origins and functions of positive and negative affect: A control-process view. *Psychological Review*, 97, 19–35.

Davies, M., Stankov, L. and Roberts, R. D. (1998). Emotional intelligence: In search of an elusive construct. *Journal of Personality and Social Psychology*, 75, 989–1015.

Diener, E., Suh, E. M., Lucas, R. E. and Smith, H. L. (1999). Subjective well-being: Three decades of progress. *Psychological Bulletin*, 125, 276–302.

Fineman, S. (Ed.) (1993). *Emotion in Organizations*. London: Sage.

— (Ed.) (2000). *Emotion in Organizations: Second Edition*. London: Sage.

— and Sturdy, A. (1999). The emotions of control: A qualitative exploration of environmental regulation. *Human Relations*, 52, 631–63.

Fisher, C. D. (1998). Effects of external and internal interruptions on boredom at work: Two studies. *Journal of Organizational Behavior*, 19, 503–22.

— (2000). Mood and emotions while working: Missing pieces of job satisfaction? *Journal of Organizational Behavior*, 21, 185–202.

Fitness, J. (2000). Anger in the workplace: An emotion script approach to anger episodes between workers and their superiors, co-workers and subordinates. *Journal of Organizational Behavior, 21,* 147–62.

Fox, S. and Spector, P. E. (2000). Relations of emotional intelligence, practical intelligence, general intelligence, and trait affectivity with interview outcomes: It's not all just 'G'. *Journal of Organizational Behavior, 21,* 203–20.

George, J. M. (1989). Mood and absence. *Journal of Applied Psychology, 74,* 317–24.

— (1990). Personality, affect and behavior in groups. *Journal of Applied Psychology, 75,* 107–16.

— (1991). State or trait: Effects of positive mood on prosocial behaviors at work. *Journal of Applied Psychology, 76,* 299–307.

— (2000). Emotions and leadership: The role of emotional intelligence. *Human Relations, 53,* 1027–55.

Goleman, D. (1998). *Working with Emotional Intelligence.* London: Bloomsbury.

Hahn, S. E. (2000). The effects of locus of control on daily exposure, coping and reactivity to work interpersonal stressors: A diary study. *Personality and Individual Differences, 29,* 729–48.

Hatfield, E., Cacioppo, J. T. and Rapson, R. L. (1994). *Emotional Contagion.* Cambridge: Cambridge University Press.

Hersey, R. B. (1931). Emotional cycles in man. *Journal of Mental Science, 77,* 151–69.

Herzberg, F., Mausner, B. and Snyderman, B. B. (1959). *The Motivation to Work.* New York: John Wiley and Sons.

Hochschild, A. R. (1983). *The Managed Heart: Commercialization of Human Feeling.* Berkeley: UCP.

Huy, Q. N. (1999). Emotional capability, emotional intelligence, and radical change. *Academy of Management Review, 24,* 325–45.

Lazarus, R. S. (1966). *Psychological Stress and the Coping Process.* New York: McGraw-Hill.

— (1999). *Stress and Emotion: A New Synthesis.* London: Free Association Books.

Leidner, R. (1991). Serving hamburgers and selling insurance: Gender, work, and identity in interactive service jobs. *Gender and Society, 5,* 154–77.

Lewis, K. M. (2000). When leaders display emotion: How followers respond to negative emotional expression of male and female leaders. *Journal of Organizational Behavior, 21,* 221–34.

Mann, S. (1999). Emotion at work: To what extent are we expressing, suppressing, or faking it? *European Journal of Work and Organizational Psychology, 8,* 347–69.

Mayer, J. D. (1999). Emotional intelligence: Popular or scientific psychology? *American Psychological Association Monitor,* September, p. 50.

— and Geher, G. (1996). Emotional intelligence and the identification of emotion. *Intelligence, 22,* 89–113.

— and Salovey, P. (1993). The intelligence of emotional intelligence. *Intelligence, 17,* 433–42.

— and Salovey, P. (1997). What is emotional intelligence? In P. Salovey and

D. Sluyter (Eds.), *Emotional Development and Emotional Intelligence* (pp. 3–31). New York: Basic Books.

Morris, J. A. and Feldman, D. C. (1996). The dimensions, antecedents, and consequences of emotional labor. *Academy of Management Review*, 21, 986–1010.

Muraven, M. and Baumeister, R. F. (2000). Self-regulation and depletion of limited resources: Does self-control resemble a muscle? *Psychological Bulletin*, 126, 247–59.

Oatley, K. and Johnson-Laird, P. N. (1987). Towards a cognitive theory of emotions. *Cognition and Emotion*, 1, 29–50.

Parkinson, B. (1991). Emotional stylists: Strategies of expressive management among trainee hairdressers. *Cognition and Emotion*, 5, 419–34.

— (1995). *Ideas and Realities of Emotion*. London: Routledge.

— (1996). Emotions are social. *British Journal of Psychology*, 87, 663–83.

—, Totterdell, P., Briner, R. B. and Reynolds, S. (1996). *Changing Moods: The Psychology of Mood and Mood Regulation*. London: Longman.

— and Totterdell, P. (1999). Classifying affect regulation strategies. *Cognition and Emotion*, 13, 277–303.

Parrott, W. G. (1993). Beyond hedonism: Motives for inhibiting good moods and maintaining bad moods. In D. M. Wegner and J. W. Pennebaker (Eds.), *Handbook of Mental Control* (pp. 278–305). Englewood Cliffs, NJ: Prentice Hall.

Payne, R. L. and Cooper, C. L. (Eds.) (2001). *Emotions at Work: Theory, Research and Applications in Management*. Chichester: Wiley.

Poulson, C. F. (2000). Shame and work. In N. M. Ashkanasy, C. E. J. Hartel and W. J. Zerbe (Eds.), *Emotions in the Workplace: Research, Theory and Practice* (pp. 250–71). Westport, Conn.: Quorum Books.

Pugh, S. D. (2001). Service with a smile: Emotional contagion in the service encounter. *Academy of Management Journal*, 44, 1018–27.

Rafaeli, A. and Sutton, R. I. (1987). Expression of emotion as part of the work role. *Academy of Management Review*, 12, 23–37.

— and Sutton, R. I. (1990). Busy stores and demanding customers: How do they affect the display of positive emotion? *Academy of Management Journal*, 33, 623–37.

— and Sutton, R. I. (1991). Emotional contrast strategies as means of social influence: Lessons from criminal interrogators and bill collectors. *Academy of Management Journal*, 34, 749–75.

Salovey, P. and Mayer, J. D. (1990). Emotional intelligence. *Imagination, Cognition and Personality*, 9, 185–211.

Schaubroeck, J. and Jones, J. R. (2000). Antecedents of workplace emotional labor dimensions and moderators of their effects on physical symptoms. *Journal of Organizational Behavior*, 21, 163–84.

Schutte, N., Malouff, J. M., Hall, L. E., Haggerty, D. J., Cooper, J. T., Golden, C. J. and Dornheim, L. (1998). Development and validation of a measure of emotional intelligence. *Personality and Individual Differences*, 25, 167–77.

Smith, S. L. (1999). The theology of emotion. *Soundings*, 11, 152–8.

Staw, B. M., Sutton, R. I. and Pelled, L. H. (1994). Employee positive emotion and favourable outcomes at the workplace. *Organization Science*, 5, 51–71.

Sutton, R. I. (1991). Maintaining norms about expressed emotions: The case of bill collectors. *Administrative Science Quarterly*, 36, 245–68.

Totterdell, P. (2000). Catching moods and hitting runs: Mood linkage and subjective performance in professional sport teams. *Journal of Applied Psychology*, 85, 848–59.

—, Kellett, S., Teuchmann, K. and Briner, R. B. (1998). Evidence of mood linkage in work groups. *Journal of Personality and Social Psychology*, 74, 1504–15.

— and Parkinson, B. (1999). Use and effectiveness of self-regulation strategies for improving mood in a group of trainee teachers. *Journal of Occupational Health Psychology*, 4, 219–32.

van Maanen, J. and Kunda, G. (1989). 'Real feelings': Emotional expression and organizational culture. *Research in Organizational Behavior*, 11, 43–103.

Walsh, S. (1999). Shame in the workplace. *The Psychologist*, 12, 20–22.

Weiss, H. M. and Cropanzano, R. (1996). Affective events theory: A theoretical discussion of the structure, causes and consequences of affective experiences at work. *Research in Organizational Behavior*, 18, 1–74.

Zapf, D., Vogt, C., Seifert, C., Mertini, H. and Isic, A. (1999). Emotion work as a source of stress: The concept and development of an instrument. *European Journal of Work and Organizational Psychology*, 8, 370–400.

10 | Occupational Safety

Julian Barling, E. Kevin Kelloway and
Anthea Zacharatos

Most workers in developed countries generally assume that their organizations will take all steps necessary to ensure that they return home safely at the end of the workday. Yet work-related injuries and fatalities continue at an alarming and unacceptable rate. In 1995 in the United States, there were 6210 fatal work injuries and approximately 3.6 million disabling injuries. These injuries resulted in an estimated 225 million production days lost for that year alone, and almost 455 million days in future years because of the debilitating, long-term consequences in many cases (United States Bureau of the Census, 1997). In the United Kingdom, approximately 1.1 million employed people were injured at work each year between 1993 and 1996 (Health and Safety Executive, 1997), with the corresponding annual financial cost to the British economy of £4–9 billion. In 1993 alone, there were 758 work-related fatalities in Canada. In the same year, 423,184 Canadian workers suffered injuries serious enough to be compensated either for wages lost due to time off work or for a permanent disability (Statistics Canada, 1994).

Taken in isolation, however, these data do not show the social meaning of occupational safety. Reasons, Ross and Paterson (1981) noted that a worker is twenty-eight times more likely to be injured or to die on the job than to suffer the same fate at the hands of a criminal. The salience of occupational safety is further apparent because the annual number of fatalities attributable to workplace injuries and illness in the USA exceeds the annual death rate due to several illnesses and other causes that attract more public attention and sympathy, such as breast, prostate or colorectal cancer, vehicular-related deaths, firearms and AIDS (Leigh, Markowitz, Fahs, Shin and Landrigan, 1997; Sauter, Hurrell, Fox, Tetrick and Barling, 1999).

Table 10.1 *Comparison of productivity losses in terms of days not worked as a function of occupational injuries (lost-time accidents) and strikes in Canada, 1993–6*

	1993	1994	1995	1996
Strike	1,516,640	1,606,580	1,583,061	3,345,220
Lost-time accident	15,807,748	17,639,363	16,593,260	14,470,574

While cries about the dire consequences of strikes for organizations in terms of days of work lost are frequently heard, the importance of occupational safety for productivity can be appreciated by comparing the numbers of work days lost as a function of strikes to that of occupational injuries. As can be seen from Table 10.1, the situation in Canada is clear. Over a four-year period, organizations lost approximately fifteen million work days per year to occupational injuries. During the same period, the number of workdays lost as a function of strikes never exceeded five million. Clearly, the number of people being injured or killed at work is unacceptable, and this issue is deserving of sustained research attention from psychologists.

Surprisingly, therefore, occupational or workplace safety has attracted very little research by industrial and organizational (I/O) psychologists or management scholars. In their quantitative review of the extent to which research has addressed different topics in I/O psychology, Campbell, Daft and Hulin (1982) showed that occupational safety attracted less than 1 per cent of the relevant research. To assess whether this situation has changed since that earlier study, which is possible given the occurrence of several high-profile industrial disasters (e.g., the tragedies at Bhopal and Chernobyl) we examined all articles published in several mainstream journals (the *Academy of Management Journal, Academy of Management Review, Administrative Science Quarterly, Journal of Organizational Behavior* and the *Journal of Occupational and Organizational Psychology*) between 1990 and 1999. Our analysis shows that the proportion of articles directly addressing occupational safety remains less than 1 per cent. While we acknowledge that occupational safety is covered in other academic journals (e.g., *Accident Analysis and Prevention, Human Factors,* the *Journal of Safety Research* and *Safety Science*), our central point remains: occupational safety has not attracted the attention of I/O psychologists or management scholars. This situation cannot continue; the number of workplace accidents and fatalities is unacceptable.

In this chapter we will first consider how occupational safety is conceptualized and operationalized. We will then discuss three major themes (ergonomics, leadership and human resources) through which psychological research has provided a body of knowledge that can now serve as the basis for understanding and enhancing occupational safety. Lastly, we will address several remaining challenges, notably young workers' occupational safety, new forms of work organization, and the need for intervention studies.

HOW SHOULD WE CONCEPTUALIZE AND OPERATIONALIZE OCCUPATIONAL SAFETY?

Most discussions about occupational safety, whether in the academic literature or in workplaces, typically focus on 'accidents' and/or fatalities. Thus, debate, discussions and research about occupational safety revolve around the number of accidents, the amount of time off work required following such an event (frequently taken as an indicator of severity), and the number of workers that have been killed.

Several factors limit the reliability and utility of accident and fatality measures for organizational research and practice. First, accidents and especially fatalities occur relatively infrequently and are not normally distributed, introducing challenges into the analysis of such data. Second, there are substantial definitional differences as to what constitutes an occupational injury across different jurisdictions. For example, what one state in the United States, or province in Canada, might accept as evidence of a back injury requiring time off work might be refused by other states or provinces. This renders any comparisons of injury rates across jurisdictions hazardous at best.

Psychologists have traditionally expended considerable efforts on obtaining accurate data. This leads to a third problem in assessing the number of occupational accidents, because there are realistic concerns that organizations' databases on accidents and fatalities may underestimate the actual prevalence of the problem. Recent analyses show that there is a tendency for accidents to be under-reported. In 1987, the Bureau of Labor Statistics in the United States initiated a pilot project to assess the accuracy of accident and injury data. Two hundred randomly selected manufacturing sites, each with more than ten employees, were visited by inspectors from the Occupational Safety and Health Administration (OSHA) (Eisenberg and MacDonald, 1988). Data for each of these establishments were also obtained from OSHA-mandated employer records of injuries and illnesses, medical records, workers' compensation reports and other relevant workplace records.

Evidence of both under-reporting and over-reporting of incidents occurred (Eisenberg and MacDonald, 1988), and several of the findings are noteworthy. First, almost all cases of over-reporting were associated with incidents that required no time lost from work, whereas under-reporting involved incidents both with and without lost work time. Second, the total number of injuries and illnesses was under-reported by about 10 per cent, and the number of lost workdays was under-reported by about 25 per cent. Very few establishments were responsible for the under-reporting, indicating that this is a systematic rather than a random phenomenon. A follow-up study of 250 construction establishments some 10 years later replicated this pattern (see Conway and Svenson, 1998).

How can this inaccuracy be avoided? While psychologists and behavioural scientists decry the sole use of self-report measures of behaviour, self-reported measures of occupational events and injuries may be more accurate than compulsory reports by the organization to government agencies. As Grunberg, Moore and Greenberg (1996) note: 'We cannot think of any compelling reason or incentives for workers to deliberately misreport their accidents and injury experiences to independent researchers' (p. 226). Conway and Svenson (1998) suggest that we make use of multiple sources or records in identifying the 'real' rates of incidents and injuries. This is worth serious consideration, and is also the recommended methodology for psychological research in general.

Zohar (2000) has focused attention on micro-accidents (those incidents requiring some first aid but no time away from work) and 'near misses' (Hemingway and Smith, 1999). These may be more useful indicators, because they occur with greater frequency than accidents. Also, the difference between a 'near miss' and an actual accident may be no more than luck. Including near misses and micro-accidents is important for a more complete picture of safety-related incidents.

Focusing on near misses, micro-accidents and accidents requiring time off work, however, provides only a limited picture of issues important in occupational safety. Instead, as will become apparent throughout this chapter, other factors critical to predicting safety-related incidents must also be considered.

Waiting for the incident or injury to occur will provide little useful information for future interventions. Instead, information about factors that immediately precede safety incidents will enable researchers and practitioners to predict injuries and incidents and to construct interventions that are more likely to enhance safety. Other issues of considerable interest are safety climate, safety compliance and safety initiative, safety knowledge, and safety-related leadership, inasmuch as they provide the motivation and skills that enable employees to perform safely.

Employees' perceptions of the safety climate in the organization has been of interest for some time (see Zohar, 1980). Perceived safety climate reflects employees' shared perceptions with respect to safety in their work environment, and employee behaviours are dependent on these perceptions. Research confirms that perceived safety climate is a substantial predictor of safe performance (Hofmann and Stetzer, 1996; Zohar, 2000). For example, based on data from fifty-three different work groups, employing a total of 534 production workers, Zohar (2000) showed that perceived safety climate predicted the number of micro-accidents five months following the measurement of safety climate. The fact that Zohar (2000) obtained data on perceived safety climate and micro-accidents from separate sources (namely, individual employees and company records, respectively) and also used a longitudinal design generates considerable confidence in these results.

Safety compliance and safety initiative reflect two additional aspects of occupational safety (Griffin and Neal, 2000; Neal, Griffin and Hart, in press; Williams, Turner and Parker, 2000). When employees follow safety-related rules and work in a safe manner, they are exhibiting safety compliance (Griffin and Neal, 2000; Simard and Marchand, 1994; Thompson, Hilton and Witt, 1998; Williams et al., 2000), which is expected to reduce injuries and safety incidents. In contrast, safety initiative refers to employee behaviours that go beyond simply working within established safety standards. Instead, they involve behaving proactively to help the organization improve occupational safety. For example, proactive employees engage in such behaviours as volunteering to participate in safety audits and pushing their supervisors to take action to improve safety (Griffin and Neal, 2000; Simard and Marchand, 1994; Williams *et al.*, 2000). Both safety compliance and safety initiative are components of safety performance, and in addition to measures of actual safety incidents provide a more thorough conceptualization of workplace safety.

Perceived safety climate, safety compliance and safety initiative all reflect aspects of the motivation to perform safely. It would avail little, however, for employees to be motivated to perform safely if they did not have the skills or knowledge to do so. Because of this, safety training is critical, and is discussed later in this chapter. Where safety training is effective, employees' knowledge of how to perform safely would be enhanced. Griffin and Neal's (2000) studies in manufacturing and mining organizations document the extent to which safety knowledge is central to occupational safety.

Lastly, we conclude this section with a comment on the use of the term 'accident'. 'Accidents happen!' is a frequent explanation offered in organizations following serious safety infractions. Why is this important? Terminologically, 'accident' implies that the event in question is random, and beyond the control of those involved. Yet subsequent examinations of most safety-related incidents reveal just the opposite: the overwhelming majority are both predictable and preventable. Were this just a terminological issue, we would dutifully relegate the term 'accident' to the status of a footnote. However, routinely using the word 'accident' presumably implies the users' agreement with this implicit meaning. In that sense, if these events were indeed random, managers might be forgiven for believing that they have less control over safety issues in the workplace than they actually do. Hence, no blame could be assigned, a comforting thought given possible legal and moral ramifications. In contrast, we argue that 'accidents don't just happen'; instead, they are predictable *and* preventable events over which all actors in the system, both management and employees, can exert control. Wherever possible, therefore, we will refrain from using the term 'accident'.

ERGONOMICS

Ergonomics or human factors engineering* is generally concerned with the design of a work system in which the work methods, layout, machines, equipment, and physical environment (e.g., lighting, noise, heat, vibration) are compatible with the physical and behavioural characteristics of the worker (Laing, 1992). One of the basic ergonomic texts reflects this orientation in its title, *Fitting the Task to the Human* (Kroemer and Grandjean, 1997). Thus, in contrast to traditional human resource practices that emphasize 'fitting' the human to the task (i.e., through selection and training), ergonomic approaches focus on the design of the work and task environment to ensure compatibility with human abilities.

There are at least three ways in which ergonomists attempt to achieve this fit, and these correspond to the principal subfields of ergonomics. First, physical ergonomics focuses on the design of the physical workplace. Drawing on fields such as physiology, biomechanics and anthropometry, the goal of physical ergonomics is to ensure that work is designed to fit the physical capabilities of the individual. In recent years, health and safety applications of physical ergonomics have focused on the prevention of musculoskeletal disorders and repetitive strain injuries.

Second, cognitive ergonomics draws on research in memory, decision-making and perceptual processes to ensure that the mental requirements of work suit human abilities. For example, cognitive ergonomists have devoted a great deal of attention to the design of process control mechanisms (e.g., gauges, switches) in order to ensure that displays are easily understood and controls easily operated. The design of computer-based technology draws increasingly on cognitive ergonomic research; see Chapter 4.

Finally, organizational ergonomics (sometimes called macro-ergonomics) considers issues of the broader socio-technical environment. Researchers interested in larger issues of system design frequently focus on the notion of 'system-risk', the suggestion that many factors (both

---

* The term 'human factors' is more common in North America, where 'ergonomics' refers to purely physical design. In Europe and the United Kingdom, the term 'ergonomics' is used more generally.

technical and human) operating in a complex system contribute to the riskiness of a system. Disasters such as the meltdown at Three Mile Island and the explosion in Bhopal are attributed to systems failure rather than a single cause (Kletz, 1998). Reducing risk means understanding how physical and human factors interact.

Drawing on principles of ergonomic design, LaBar (1996) identifies four key areas that may lead to safety problems in workplaces: process control, automation, maintenance, and operating procedures. Ergonomic design principles related to process control should ensure that displays and switches conform to individual expectations. For example, use of a green light to indicate danger instead of the more traditional red light would violate expectations. It is important to note that these expectations may not be universal. For North Americans, the 'up' position of a switch means 'on' or 'start', whereas for Europeans the 'down' position typically means 'on'. Gauges and displays should also be suited to their purpose. Numeric dials can be read and interpreted quickly, but digital displays are required for precision.

As the use of technology in workplaces increases, it becomes increasingly important that the design of automated systems take human limitations into account (see also Chapters 2 and 4). The principal concern here is to ensure that both humans and machines do the tasks they are best suited for. Humans are best suited for tasks that require active involvement, judgement and decision-making. Machines are best suited for repetitive motions and material handling.

Safety experts typically attribute a high percentage of workplace accidents to maintenance issues. Equipment and machines that do not allow easy access or that have hard-to-replace components discourage active maintenance. Conversely, equipment should be designed so as to allow only one method of re-assembly following routine maintenance procedures.

Finally, creating a safe working environment means establishing clear procedures on how jobs are to be completed. These procedures should detail the best method of doing the work, for example in clear guidelines for proper lifting techniques. Supplemented by clear policies and procedures on use of supplementary lifting devices, procedures to ensure that individuals lift properly can dramatically reduce the incidence of lower back injuries in the workplace.

Implementing a comprehensive ergonomics programme in the workplace requires considerable commitment from both management and employees. Typically such programmes consist of primary, secondary, and tertiary interventions (Montgomery and Kelloway, 2001). Primary interventions focus on prevention, and attempt to redesign the workplace or work procedures so as to minimize or eliminate potential hazards. Secondary interventions attempt to protect workers from hazards through, for example, the design of personal protective equipment or the formulation of policies dealing with the length of time one can be exposed to a hazard. Finally, tertiary interventions involve providing treatment for those individuals who are injured in the workplace and ensuring their safe return to work through efforts at accommodation and rehabilitation. Clearly, tertiary interventions by themselves are insufficient as they allow injuries to occur first. Secondary interventions, such as wearing personal protective equipment, have been criticized because they focus on the individual rather than the source of the problem. As Montgomery and Kelloway (2001) suggest, secondary and tertiary interventions are best viewed as complements to, rather than replacements for, primary interventions.

LEADERSHIP

It is usually held as axiomatic in organizations that 'leadership makes a difference': research findings over several decades consistently show that high quality leadership is associated with a host of positive organizational outcomes, including greater employee morale (Pillai, Schriesheim and Williams, 1999), individual sales performance (Barling, Weber and Kelloway, 1996), and branch-level financial performance (Howell and Avolio, 1993). (See also Chapter 12.) Similarly, union shop stewards' leadership is associated with rank and file members' participation in the union (Kelloway and Barling, 1993), and coaches' leadership in sports teams predicts team success (Charbonneau, Barling and Kelloway, 2001). Given these broad effects, the possible role of leadership in understanding, predicting and preventing safety infractions is intriguing, and three streams of research collectively point to its importance.

First, research has generally shown that organizations in which leaders pay attention to occupational safety enjoy higher levels of employee motivation to work safely, as well as better organizational safety records (Cohen, 1977; Hofmann, Jacobs and Landy, 1995; Smith, Cohen, Cohen and Cleveland, 1978). Simard and Marchand (1995) investigated the effect of senior management commitment on employees' willingness to take safety initiatives. Based on responses from approximately 23,000 employees, they found that senior management commitment to occupational safety was the strongest predictor of supervisors using a participative style in the management of occupational safety. In turn, this participative style was the most significant predictor of employees' safety initiative.

While there is a growing understanding of the central role of management in organizational safety performance, little research has examined precisely what a 'strong commitment to occupational safety' means in terms of managerial action. Zohar (1980) claimed that management commitment to occupational safety can be expressed in the following different ways: safety matters receive high priority at meetings, safety officers enjoy high status positions, safety training is emphasized, open channels of communication exist between workers and employers to discuss safety issues and new ideas for enhancing safety, and there is a stable workforce. Griffiths (1985) adds to this list: a comprehensive safety policy, clear safety-related objectives, and extensive training and employee involvement.

A second stream of research has focused on leader–member exchange theory, which involves a pattern of reciprocated behaviours or social exchanges between leaders and followers (Hughes, Ginnett and Curphy, 1999). With respect to safety, it is assumed that when leaders engage in behaviours that benefit subordinates, subordinates will feel obligated to respond with behaviours that would benefit the leader. In this respect, it is assumed that occupational safety would be perceived to be important to leaders and thus a means of benefiting leaders.

Hofmann and his colleagues have conducted two studies to assess the utility of leader–member exchange to occupational safety. First, Hofmann and Morgeson (1999) studied 49 supervisor-group leader dyads in a manufacturing facility producing commercial heating and air conditioning systems, and showed that leader–member exchange was indirectly associated with the number of accidents that had occurred over a one-year period. Specifically, positive leader–member exchanges resulted in higher quality safety communication between supervisors and group leaders. In turn, the greater the safety communication, the more group leaders were committed to occupational safety, and it was their commitment to occupational safety that directly affected the number of accidents.

In the second study, Hofmann, Morgeson and Gerras (2000) extended this notion to the military context, and studied 118 military teams required to transport heavy equipment (e.g., tanks, artillery vehicles, forklifts and cranes). Each team consisted of approximately five members and one supervisor. The supervisors' jobs included ensuring safety, which was an integral part of their performance evaluation. The results of this study replicate and extend Hofmann and Morgeson's (1999) research on leader–member exchange and occupational safety. Again, there was an indirect relationship between leader–member exchange and occupational safety. Positive leader–member exchange resulted in what Hofmann *et al.* (2000) called high safety citizenship behaviours. Safety citizenship behaviours then resulted in occupational safety. Thus, Hofmann *et al.*'s (2000) results showed that the relationship between leadership and occupational safety is indirect, and identified safety citizenship behaviour as an additional mediator of this relationship.

In the third research stream, transformational leadership (Bass, 1998) has been used as an organizing framework for understanding occupational safety for several reasons. First, transformational leadership has received extensive empirical scrutiny (Avolio, 1999; Bass, 1998; see Chapter 12), more than all other leadership theories combined since 1990 (Judge and Bono, 2000). Second, its validity is supported in a variety of contexts (e.g., Lowe, Kroeck and Sivasubramanian, 1996), including unions (Kelloway and Barling, 1993), where the availability of formal rewards by leaders is limited and the importance of personal influence is magnified accordingly. Each of the four factors comprising transformational leadership (idealized influence, inspirational motivation, intellectual stimulation and individualized consideration) lends itself to the possibility of enhancing safety performance. Leaders high in idealized influence would convey how they value employee safety through their personal behaviours. Those high in inspirational motivation would convince their followers that they could attain levels of safety not previously considered possible. The potential benefits of intellectual stimulation for enhancing safety performance are considerable. Providing intellectual stimulation for followers to confront safety issues would add knowledge about new ways of achieving high safety levels. Individualized consideration would be evident through leaders' personal concern about their followers' physical safety at work, far beyond what would normally be required to satisfy the minimal requirements of government regulations or a collective agreement.

A further reason supporting the appropriateness of transformational leadership is that controlled-outcome research shows that transformational leadership can be taught to managers (Barling, Weber and Kelloway, 1996). While the focus of most safety training is on employees, training managers in the use of transformational leadership to enhance the occupational safety of others is just as important, and presents an innovative research challenge for scholars in the areas of both safety and leadership.

Williams *et al.* (2000) studied the role of transformational leadership in the occupational safety of a group of production technicians in a chemical processing plant. They showed that transformational leadership predicted employees' safety compliance and proactive behaviours to enhance safety. Barling, Loughlin and Kelloway (2000) examined the predictors of occupational injuries among a heterogeneous group of employees in two separate studies. They showed that transformational leadership was significantly and indirectly associated with occupational injuries. Specifically, transformational leadership predicted perceived safety climate, which significantly predicted employees' safety consciousness (their safety knowledge and safety behaviours). In turn, safety behaviours were significantly associated with safety-related events (having the potential for harm), and it was the occurrence of these safety-related events that resulted in occupational injuries. As in other studies of transformational leadership, however, it was not possible to isolate the differential role of the four components of leadership because they are so highly correlated (Bycio, Hackett and Allen, 1995).

HUMAN RESOURCES

Together with safety training, personnel selection has traditionally been one of the two most frequent techniques used to achieve occupational safety within a human resources model. To date, however, the use of selection has focused mainly on the utility of personality screening questionnaires to differentiate between potential employees in terms of characteristics such as current or former drug addiction or alcoholism, and the extent to which they had been involved in accidents in prior jobs, which would presumably predict their susceptibility to occupational accidents. These strategies typically screen for personality characteristics, and several different questionnaires have been used (e.g., Jones, 1991; Borofsky, Bielema and Hoffman, 1993; Borofsky and Smith, 1993; Borofsky, Wagner and Turner, 1995).

To gain an appreciation of how these questionnaires are used, an examination of some of the research using this approach is useful. In one study, Borofsky and Smith (1993) compared the safety records in a mid-sized manufacturing facility of fifty-three employees *before* and another fifty-three employees *after* the introduction of pre-employment screening based on the Employee Reliability Inventory. This questionnaire assesses seven personality factors, namely freedom from disruptive alcohol and substance use, courteous job performance, emotional maturity, conscientiousness, trustworthiness, long-term job commitment and intelligent job performance. Borofsky and Smith's (1993) data show that the number of employees who had accidents after the use of pre-employment screening began was significantly lower than that within the group prior to the screening process. In a second study (Borofsky *et al.*, 1995), they focused on the safety records in a resort hotel employing approximately 3800 people, and again showed that the number of accidents and the accident rate as a percentage of the total workforce was lower after screening had been implemented.

Despite this, several methodological flaws in these studies preclude the inference that the screening procedures caused a decrease in the safety-related incidents. First, any study that lacks a control group leaves us with what Cook and Campbell (1979) refer to as 'uninterpretable results', because other plausible, alternative hypotheses could just as easily explain the increase in safety in these studies. For example, it is possible the employees in the two groups held different jobs or performed different work; perhaps data gathered before the introduction of screening were obtained from people engaged in more hazardous work? Second, because of the absence of any control group, we cannot rule out the possibility that the apparent changes were simply a part of a pre-existing trend toward increased safety, because the very factors that motivated the organization to introduce the prescreening program in the first instance may have resulted in other changes in the organization that could also have accounted for the changes.

Even if we could accept the validity of the findings from these studies, ethical problems are raised in the extent to which this approach places primary responsibility for inappropriate behaviours on vulnerable individual employees, and then aims to exclude such individuals from the organization. Parenthetically, this approach allows management to abdicate responsibility, despite the evidence in this chapter that managers' behaviour does indeed influence occupational safety.

The second human resource approach intended to influence occupational safety is safety training. Safety training is one of the major organizational interventions used in this field. The need for its even greater emphasis is illustrated by Murray, Fitzpatrick and O'Connell's (1997) survey of fifty-five individuals involved in commercial fishing off the coast of Newfoundland. They found that fifteen of these individuals (27 per cent of their sample) could not swim!

In general, the results of well-designed studies show that employees who have undergone safety training suffer fewer work-related injuries than their untrained counterparts (Hale, 1984). In addition, some aspects of training (e.g., active learning, or behaviourally-based training) are more effective than others (Cohen and Jensen, 1984). The role of perceived safety climate is again salient, because organizations in which safety training is perceived to be offered because of management commitment, rather than because of compliance with external regulations or collective agreements, enjoy better safety records (Zohar, 1980). Of course, safety training is especially important when work is inherently more dangerous. In many 'normal' work situations, learning can occur through direct job-related experience. In the case of inherently hazardous work, however, the potential human cost of errors is far too high, making training an especially important aspect of any programme to improve occupational safety.

SOME REMAINING CHALLENGES

Several issues deserve some attention because of the challenges they will present to occupational safety. These include occupational safety for young workers, the effects of new forms of work organization on occupational safety, and the need for well-controlled intervention studies.

Young Workers

Society generally approves of young people being employed because of the opportunities offered for acquiring responsible behaviour patterns (Barling and Kelloway, 1999). Employment among teenagers and young adults (i.e., below the age of twenty-five) is thus customary. For example, approximately 50 per cent of full-time university students are employed on a part-time basis in both Canada (Krahn, 1991) and the United States (Manning, 1990). There are also indications that such employment may be on the rise, because the opportunities for part-time work have increased steadily (Barling, 1999; Barling and Gallagher, 1996), and teenagers' allowances have probably not increased sufficiently to keep pace with their discretionary purchases (Waldman and Springen, 1992).

Why is this pattern so significant? Examining non-fatal workplace accidents and injuries across the life span shows that adolescence is the age group with the highest risk. As Castillo (1999) notes, based on US data, adolescents' injuries are common, indeed more so than for adults, and the injuries they incur can exert a substantial effect on their lives. The pattern is not restricted to non-fatal injuries: approximately seventy people younger than eighteen years old, predominantly males, die each year from work-related injuries in the United States.

Given this, there is a paucity of psychological research investigating the predictors of work injuries among adolescents. Frone's (1998) study of 319 young workers, aged between sixteen and nineteen, uncovered five variables that predicted work injuries. Not surprisingly, the extent of physical hazards at work was positively associated with work injuries, as was job tenure. One explanation for the relationship between job tenure and work injuries is that adolescents with greater job experience are likely to be placed in jobs that require more skills and that are more hazardous. There are three other predictors of greater interest in terms of the psychology of the workplace. On-the-job substance abuse rather than substance abuse in general predicted occupational injuries, which may cast doubt on the usefulness of questions about general drug use in a selection interview. Second, like others (Hofmann and Stetzer, 1996) Frone showed that work overload was associated with job injuries, as was boredom on the job. The findings relating to these latter two variables are interesting, as job design may be an appropriate intervention for occupational safety. Specifically, research should now focus on whether improvements in job design, for example increasing job-related autonomy that enhances productivity and mental health, might also influence occupational safety (Parker and Wall, 1997; see also Chapter 11).

New Forms of Work Organization

The last decade has witnessed substantial changes in the nature and pace of work and in the employment relationship (Barling, 1999; Tetrick and Barling, 1995). We now turn our attention to two of these changes which have considerable bearing on occupational safety, namely the move toward lean production, and the increase in the use of contract or contingent workers.

The goal of lean production is to increase efficiency by abolishing activities that add little or no value to the organization, thereby ensuring that the appropriate amount and quality of goods will be available when needed for the next stage of the production process. Landsbergis, Cahill and Schnall (1999) used the job demands framework of Karasek and Theorell (1990) to understand the possible effects of lean production. They speculated that, because lean production intensifies the pace and demands of work while mostly reducing the amount of decision latitude available to the individual employee, lean production methods will have a negative effect on occupational safety.

Jackson and Mullarkey's (2000) study focused on health rather than safety, but the central lesson to be learned from their findings would presumably apply to occupational safety as well. They contrasted the effects of lean production with a traditional manufacturing system for garment making, and showed that the effects of lean production were not uniform. To the extent to which greater decision latitude was experienced as a result of lean production, health was better. In contrast, where autonomy and latitude were compromised by lean production, employee health suffered. Interestingly, these results parallel Frone's (1998) finding that boredom is associated with more injuries. Clear ramifications for work design seem to follow.

Another consequence of changes in forms of work organization has been the increased use of contingent or contract workers. The link between their use and aspects of occupational safety is important. When organizations do not make a long-term investment in their employees, they are unlikely to provide extensive training (Pfeffer, 1998), and this association extends to safety-specific training. More specifically, Rebitzer (1995) notes that host organizations rely mostly on contractors to provide safety training for their employees, despite the fact that they are less effective at doing so.

There are some initial indications that occupational safety is compromised by introducing contingent workers. First, following a workplace disaster in which twenty-three workers were killed and 232 injured, the United States Occupational Safety and Health Administration conducted a study, and the US Congress held hearings, part of which focused on occupational safety (see Kochan, Smith, Wells and Rebitzer, 1994). They concluded that contractor firms, especially non-unionized ones, provided less safety training, and that the widespread use of contract labour may well compromise safety. Second, Collinson (1999) reached a similar conclusion in his qualitative study of occupational safety in North Sea oil rigs. He showed that contingent workers are often treated less favourably than employees with fixed-term contracts, for example in terms of the quantity and quality of safety equipment available.

The Need for More Intervention Studies

To date, research has focused mostly on identifying those workplace factors and employee experiences that are associated with occupational safety. For example, Zohar (2000) shows convincingly that perceived safety climate is linked to a lower rate of micro-accidents. Similarly, Hofmann and Morgeson (1999) show that certain leader–member exchanges are associated with accidents. However, it would be premature to assume that changing the safety climate or enhancing the quality of leader–member exchanges will necessarily result in higher levels of occupational safety. We conclude this section, therefore, by calling for well-designed intervention studies that apply existing knowledge from psychological research to enhance occupational safety.

SUMMARY

The state of occupational safety remains a major social and economic concern, yet psychologists have been remiss in not directing their energies, methodologies and talents at this issue. The literature that does exist suggests that a knowledge of traditional workplace approaches in the areas of leadership, human resources and ergonomics could be applied usefully to understand, predict and perhaps control occupational safety. In addition, special challenges in this field include the level of occupational safety experienced by young workers and contract workers. These present a research agenda in which psychologists could be involved for a long time to come.

RECOMMENDED READING

In *Normal Accidents: Living with High-Risk Technologies*, Perrow (1984) argues that, as a result of recent technological innovations, major accidents in the workplace may now be viewed as normal, and thus to be expected. Walker (1991) vividly portrays the safety hazards involved in a high-risk occupation in *Working on the Edge*, in which he tells the story of his seasonal work in the off-shore fishing industry.

An increasing number of web-sites are helpful in the area of this chapter. For example, *http://www.ccohs.ca/resources/www.html* (maintained by the Canadian Centre for Occupational Health and Safety), aims to promote occupational safety by providing information and advice, and permits an extensive internet search of occupational safety. *http://www.cdc.gov/niosh/homepage.html* (home page of the National Institute for Occupational Safety and Research in the USA) has the facility for downloading recent articles on occupational safety and contains an extensive database for information on funding, training, special events and programmes. An extensive set of current and historical data pertaining to all aspects of occupational safety and health is available from *http://www.bls.gov* (web-site of the Bureau of Labor Statistics in the United States), which also provides access to articles from the journal *Monthly Labor Review*.

The British Health and Safety Executive can be accessed at *http://www.hse.gov.uk*. This site provides national information on legislation, training, research and practice, and describes the joint initiative on occupational safety between the European Union, United Kingdom and United States of America. *http://www.nohsc.gov.au* is the web-site of the National Occupational Health and Safety Commission in Australia. It is an excellent resource for information on research, training, legislation, practice and small business initiatives in Australia. Extensive national statistics and reports are provided.

REFERENCES

Avolio, B. J. (1999). *Full Leadership Development: Building the Vital Forces in Organizations*. Thousand Oaks, CA: Sage.

Barling, J. (1999). Changing employment relations: Empirical data, social perspectives, and policy options. In D. B. Knight and A. E. Joseph (eds.), *Restructuring Societies* (pp. 59–82). Ottawa: Carlton University Press.

— and Gallagher, D. G. (1996). Part-time employment. In C. L. Cooper and I. T. Robertson (eds.), *International Review of Industrial and Organizational Psychology* (pp. 243–77). London: John Wiley & Sons.

— and Kelloway, E. K. (eds.) (1999). *Young Workers: Varieties of Experience*. Washington, DC: American Psychological Association.

—, Loughlin, C. A. and Kelloway, E. K. (in press). Development and test of a model linking transformational leadership and occupational injuries. *Journal of Applied Psychology*.

—, Weber, T. and Kelloway, E. K. (1996). Effects of transformational leadership training on attitudinal and fiscal outcomes: A field experiment. *Journal of Applied Psychology, 81*, 827–32.

Bass, B. M. (1998). *Transformational Leadership: Industry, Military and Educational Impact*. Mahwah, NJ: Erlbaum.

Borofsky, G. L., Bielema, M. and Hoffman, J. (1993). Accidents, turnover, and use of a pre-employment screening inventory. *Psychological Reports*, 73, 1067–76.

— and Smith, M. (1993). Reductions in turnover, accidents, and absenteeism: The contribution of a pre-employment screening inventory. *Journal of Clinical Psychology*, 49, 109–16.

—, Wagner, J. and Turner, S. (1995). Sustained reductions in turnover and accidents associated with the ongoing use of a pre-employment screening inventory: Results of a three-year longitudinal study. *Psychological Reports*, 77, 195–204.

Bycio, P., Hackett, R. D. and Allen, S. J. (1995). Further assessment of Bass' (1985) conceptualization of transactional and transformational leadership. *Journal of Applied Psychology*, 80, 468–78.

Campbell, J. P., Daft, R. L. and Hulin, C. L. (1982). *What to Study: Generating and Developing Research Questions*. Thousand Oaks, CA: Sage.

Castillo, D. N. (1999). Occupational safety and health in young people. In J. Barling and E. K. Kelloway (eds.), *Young Workers: Varieties of Experience* (pp. 159–200). Washington, DC: American Psychological Association.

Charbonneau, D., Barling, J. and Kelloway, E. K. (2001). Transformational leadership and sports performance: The mediating role of intrinsic motivation. *Journal of Applied Social Psychology*, 31, 1521–34.

Cohen, A. (1977). Factors in successful occupational safety programs. *Journal of Safety Research*, 9, 168–78.

Cohen, H. H. and Jensen, R. C. (1984). Measuring the effectiveness of an industrial lift truck safety program. *Journal of Safety Research*, 15, 125–35.

Collinson, D. L. (1999). 'Surviving the rigs': Safety and surveillance on North Sea oil installations. *Organization Studies*, 20, 579–600.

Conway, H. and Svenson, J. (1998). Occupational injury and illness rates, 1992–1996: Why they fell. *Monthly Labor Review*, 121(11), 36–58.

Cook, T. D. and Campbell, D. T. (1979). *Quasi-experimentation: Design and Analysis for Field Issues*. Boston, Mass.: Houghton Mifflin.

Eisenberg, W. M. and McDonald, H. (1988). Evaluating workplace injury and illness records: Testing a procedure. *Monthly Labor Review*, 111(4), 58–60.

Frone, M. R. (1998). Predictors of work injuries among employed adolescents. *Journal of Applied Psychology*, 83, 565–76.

Griffin, M. A. and Neal, A. (2000). Perception of safety at work: A framework for linking safety climate to safety performance, knowledge, and motivation. *Journal of Occupational Health Psychology*, 17, 347–58.

Griffiths, D. K. (1985). Safety attitudes of management. *Ergonomics*, 28, 61–7.

Grunberg, L., Moore, S. and Greenberg, E. (1996). The relationship of employee participation to workplace safety. *Economic and Industrial Democracy*, 17, 221–41.

Hale, A. R. (1984). Is safety training worthwhile? *Journal of Occupational Accidents*, 6, 17–33.

Health and Safety Executive (1997). *The Cost of Accidents at Work*. Sudbury, UK: HSE Books.

Hemingway, M. and Smith, C. S. (1999). Organizational climate and occupational stressors as predictors of withdrawal behaviours and injuries in nurses. *Journal of Occupational and Organizational Psychology*, 72, 285–99.

Hofmann, D. A., Jacobs, R. and Landy, F. (1995). High reliability process industries: Individual, micro and macro organizational influence on safety performance. *Journal of Safety Research*, 26, 131–49.

— and Stetzer, A. (1996). A cross-level investigation of factors influencing unsafe behaviors and accidents. *Personnel Psychology*, 49, 307–39.

— and Morgeson, F. P. (1999). Safety-related behavior as a social exchange: The role of perceived organizational support and leader–member exchange. *Journal of Applied Psychology*, 84, 286–96.

—, Morgeson, F. P. and Gerras, S. J. (2000). When is safety my job? The moderating effect of leader–member exchange and leader safety commitment on subordinate role definition and behavior. Revised manuscript submitted for publication.

Howell, J. M. and Avolio, B. J. (1993). Transformational leadership, transactional leadership, locus of control and support for innovation: Key predictors of consolidated-business-unit performance. *Journal of Applied Psychology*, 78, 891–902.

Hughes, R. L., Ginnett, R. C. and Curphy, G. J. (1999). *Leadership: Enhancing the Lessons of Experience*. Boston, MA: Irwin McGraw Hill.

Jackson, P. R. and Mullarkey, S. (2000). Lean production teams and health in garment manufacture. *Journal of Occupational Health Psychology*, 5, 231–45.

Jones, J. W. (1991). A personnel selection approach to industrial safety. In J. W. Jones (ed.), *Pre-employment Honesty Testing* (pp. 185–94). New York: Quorum.

Judge, T. A. and Bono, J. E. (2000). Five-factor model of personality and transformational leadership. *Journal of Applied Psychology*, 85, 751–65.

Karasek, R. A. and Theorell, T. (1990). *Healthy Work: Stress, Productivity and the Reconstruction of Working Life*. New York: Basic Books.

Kelloway, E. K. and Barling, J. (1993). Member's participation in local union activities: Measurement, prediction, replication. *Journal of Applied Psychology*, 78, 262–79.

Kletz, T. A. (1998). *What Went Wrong? Case Histories of Process Plant Disasters*. Woburn, Mass.: Gulf Professional Publishing Company.

Kochan, T. A., Smith, M., Wells, J. C. and Rebitzer, J. B. (1994). Human resource strategies and contingent workers: The case of safety and health in the petrochemical industry. *Human Resource Management*, 33, 55–77.

Krahn, H. (1991). Youth employment. In R. Barnhorst and L. C. Johnson (eds.). *The State of the Child in Ontario* (pp. 139–59). Toronto: Oxford University Press.

Kroemer, K. H. E. and Grandjean, E. (1997). *Fitting the Task to the Human: A Textbook of Occupational Ergonomics* (fifth edition). New York: Taylor and Francis.

LaBar, G. (1996). Can ergonomics cure 'human error'? *Occupational Hazards*, 58(4), 48–62.

Laing, P. (1992) (ed.) *Accident Prevention Manual for Business and Industry: Engineering and Technology.* Washington, DC: National Safety Council.

Landsbergis, P. A., Cahill, J. and Schnall, P. (1999). The impact of lean production and related new systems of work organization on health. *Journal of Occupational Health Psychology*, 4, 108–30.

Leigh, J. P., Markowitz, S. B., Fahs, M., Shin, C. and Landrigan, P. J. (1997). Occupational injury and illness in the US: Estimates of costs, morbidity and mortality. *Archives of Internal Medicine*, 157, 1557–68.

Lowe, K., Kroeck, K. G. and Sivasubramanian, N. (1996). Effectiveness correlates of transformational and transactional leadership: A meta-analytic review. *Leadership Quarterly*, 7, 385–425.

Manning, W. D. (1990). Parenting employed teenagers. *Youth and Society*, 22, 184–200.

Montgomery, J. and Kelloway, E. K. (2001). *Management of Occupational Health and Safety* (second edition). Toronto: Nelson Canada.

Murray, M., Fitzpatrick, D. and O'Connell, C. (1997). Fisherman's blues: Factors related to accidents and safety among Newfoundland fisherman. *Work and Stress*, 11, 292–7.

Neal, A., Griffin, M. A. and Hart, P. M. (in press). The impact of organizational climate on safety climate and individual behavior. *Safety Science*.

Parker, S. K. and Wall, T. D. (1997). *Job and Work Design: Organizing Work to Promote Well-being and Effectiveness.* Thousand Oaks, CA: Sage.

Perrow, C. (1984). *Normal Accidents: Living with High-Risk Technologies.* New York: Basic Books.

Pfeffer, J. (1998). *The Human Equation: Building Profits by Putting People First.* Boston, MA: Harvard Business School Press.

Pillai, R., Schriesheim, C. A. and Williams, E. S. (1999). Fairness perceptions and trust as mediators for transformational and transactional leadership: A two-sample study. *Journal of Management*, 25, 649–61.

Reasons, C., Ross, L. and Paterson, C. (1981). *Assault on the Worker: Occupational Safety and Health in Canada.* Toronto: Butterworth.

Rebitzer, J. B. (1995). Job safety and contract workers in the petrochemical industry. *Industrial Relations*, 34, 40–57.

Sauter, S. L., Hurrell, J. J., Fox, H., Tetrick, L. E. and Barling, J. (1999). Occupational health psychology: An emerging discipline. *Industrial Health*, 37, 199–211.

Simard, M. and Marchand, A. (1994). The behavior of first-line supervisors in accident prevention and effectiveness in occupational safety. *Safety Science*, 17, 169–85.

— and Marchand, A. (1995). A multilevel analysis of organizational factors related to the taking of safety initiative by work groups. *Safety Science*, *21*, 113–29.

Smith, M. J., Cohen, H. H., Cohen, A. and Cleveland, R. J. (1978). Characteristics of successful safety programs. *Journal of Safety Research*, *10*, 5–15.

Statistics Canada (1994). *Work injuries 1991–1993* (Cat. No. 72-208). Ottawa, Canada.

Tetrick, L. E. and Barling, J. (1995). *Changing Employment Relations: Behavioral and Social Perspectives*. Washington, DC: American Psychological Association.

Thompson, R. C., Hilton, T. F. and Witt, L. A. (1998). Where the safety rubber meets the shop floor: A confirmatory model of management influence on workplace safety. *Journal of Safety Research*, *29*, 15–24.

United States Bureau of the Census (1997). *Statistical Abstract of the United States*, 117th edition. Washington, DC.

Waldman, S. and Springen, K. (1992). Too old, too fast? *Newsweek* (16 November), 80–82, 87, 88.

Walker, S. (1991). *Working on the Edge*. New York: St Martin's Press.

Williams, H., Turner, N. and Parker, S. K. (2000). The compensatory role of transformational leadership in promoting safety behaviors. Paper presented in August at the Academy of Management meeting, Toronto.

Zohar, D. (1980). Safety climate in industrial organizations: Theoretical and applied implications. *Journal of Applied Psychology*, *65*, 96–102.

— (2000). A group-level model of safety climate: Testing the effect of group climate on microaccidents in manufacturing jobs. *Journal of Applied Psychology*, *85*, 587–96.

11

Designing Jobs to Enhance Well-being and Performance

Sharon K. Parker

Consider the case of Paul, who works in a call centre. Paul's job is to respond to incoming calls, typically about 500 per day. Paul cannot leave his telephone unless his supervisor has agreed. His calls are closely monitored to ensure he responds in the most efficient way, and to check that he follows a script of what he should say. He is told by his supervisor several times a day how much time he has spent on calls.

Now contrast this with the case of Anita, who works in a different call centre. Anita answers a similar number of calls per day, but she works as part of a self-managing team. She and her colleagues decide when to take breaks from work, and what they will say to the clients. They exchange roles amongst each other, so that on some days Anita works as a sales consultant and on other days she responds to queries about technical support. Anita and her team monitor their own performance, tracking their team's call times as well as issues such as customer satisfaction. The team meets each morning to allocate tasks, to discuss performance and to anticipate problems.

These hypothetical scenarios illustrate differences in *work design*. Although Paul and Anita carry out the same core tasks, their jobs differ in how they have been organized, such as in the degree of autonomy afforded to them and the style of supervision. The way jobs are designed has important consequences for individual outcomes such as job satisfaction and stress, as well as for organizational outcomes such as customer satisfaction. If you ask yourself which of Paul's or Anita's job you would prefer and why, most of you would probably opt for Anita's job because she has control over important aspects of her work as well as variety in her tasks. Research would suggest that, compared to Paul, Anita will have greater job satisfaction and lower work stress, as well as higher motivation to go out of her way to help customers and colleagues.

Because of its impact on individual and organizational outcomes, work design can have significant implications for social, health, and economic policy. Indeed, in some countries, work design is taken so seriously it is part of government legislation. For example, in an effort to promote productivity and employee health, the Swedish Work Environment Legislation (*http://www.av.se/english/legislation/chapter2.shtm*) includes the following types of statutory requirements for work design:

- Technology, work organization and job content shall be designed in such a way that the employee is not subjected to physical or mental strains which can lead to ill-health or accidents . . . Closely controlled or restricted work shall be avoided or limited.
- Efforts shall be made to ensure that work provides opportunities of variety, social contact and co-operation, as well as coherence between different tasks.

Implicit in this legislation is the assumption that employers can influence the design of work in their organization. Put another way, work can be 'redesigned' to achieve particular outcomes for employees and/or organizations. Research in this area is exciting because the findings can influence the nature of work activities and hence enhance the quality of people's lives and the success of organizations. In this chapter I describe specific ways that individual jobs and groups of jobs can be designed, or redesigned, for greater effectiveness. I then review the evidence concerning whether work redesign achieves its goals. Finally, I look at developments occurring within today's workplace and some of their potential implications for work design theory and practice.

A natural starting point for this chapter, however, is to examine the principles of job simplification which dominated work organization earlier in the twentieth century and which, to some extent, still dominate today. It is the practice of job simplification which spurred interest in the psychological aspects of work design and redesign.

EARLY TYPES OF WORK DESIGN: JOB SIMPLIFICATION

Prior to the industrial revolution, which took place from about 1760 to around the mid 1830s, most jobs were called 'trades' or 'crafts', and workers mostly acquired their skill through lengthy learning-by-doing apprenticeships. Decisions about how tasks were allocated and performed were based on tradition, rules of thumb, and the recommendations of craft guilds. Management was a personal style of leadership based on the know-how of highly skilled crafts-people.

Then came the industrial revolution, with large numbers of people moving to cities to operate machines in large factories. Factory work was vastly different to craft work, and questions arose about how best to manage the various activities. One solution, reflected in proposals by Adam Smith, was to break down complex jobs into simpler and narrower ones, so that workers would become more proficient in those tasks and time would be saved through their not having to move to different activities. An added advantage of this 'horizontal division of labour' was that the approach required less skilled, and hence cheaper, labour.

Early in the twentieth century, Frederick W. Taylor was influential in advocating his complementary ideas of 'scientific management'. The basic principle was for engineers to identify the 'one best way' of carrying out particular tasks (e.g., eliminating all slow or unnecessary movements) and then to reconstitute the job according to those best ways. This meant a 'vertical division of labour' in which engineers and managers were responsible for determining how to do the work, or the thinking aspects, whilst employees were to focus on the doing, with little or no autonomy over decisions.

Associated with scientific management was the use of time-and-motion studies, in which tasks were timed to find the most efficient way of doing them and then linked to wages to motivate a high rate of production. From here it was but a short step to control workers' activities further with the use of a moving assembly line. Introduced by 1914 by Henry Ford at his automobile factory in Michigan in the United States, the system involved using transporters and conveyors to move the product between stages, thereby removing 'unproductive' time spent in carrying products and tightly controlling the speed of work. By the mid 1900s, job simplification was well entrenched in the USA and Europe (Davis, Canter and Hoffman, 1955), and was applied in both manufacturing and administrative domains (Braverman, 1974).

The new machinery of the industrial revolution thus did much more than reduce the physical toil required of workers. It also changed jobs and the way people thought about them in profound ways. A belief emerged that jobs had to be as narrow and simplified as possible. These beliefs are very strong, even today. For example, Campion and Stevens (1991) showed that naive participants (college students) in work design simulations typically choose job simplification rather than other work design options.

As it became more widespread, some people began to question the consequences of job simplification for both employees and organizations. In Britain, the Industrial Research Fatigue Board showed that repetitive work was dissatisfying, tiring, and boring (Wyatt and Ogden, 1924) as well as potentially damaging for mental health (Fraser, 1947). Research from the USA also found negative effects of job simplification, such as increased absenteeism, turnover, and dissatisfaction (Walker and Guest, 1952).

One limitation of this early research, however, was that studies focused on the negative effects of routine and repetitive tasks, with much less attention given to the removal of autonomy and discretion from jobs. Neither were the effects of work content on productivity systematically considered, and few recommendations were made for changes that might improve the situation. As time progressed, these limitations were addressed. Psychologists began to talk about 'redesigning' Tayloristic jobs, a movement that gave rise to, and became increasingly based on, theoretical models of work design. I describe these developments next, looking at work designs for individual and group jobs in turn.

DESIGNING INDIVIDUAL JOBS

Early Work Redesigns: Job Rotation and Horizontal Job Enlargement

Two early forms of work redesign were job rotation and horizontal job enlargement. Job rotation is self-explanatory from its title: employees move at regular intervals to perform jobs typically carried out by others, either on an obligatory or on a voluntary basis. For example, a hotel receptionist might go from answering telephone enquiries to welcoming customers on the front desk. Another form of rotation is when managerial and professional employees transfer temporarily among different jobs, as a form of orientation or career development (Campion, Cheraskin and Stevens, 1994).

Horizontal job enlargement (or more simply 'job enlargement') involves broadening the actual job content to include additional tasks at the same level of responsibility. Ideally, the job includes all of the tasks required to complete a product or service job from start to finish (e.g., a waiter's job would include not just bringing customers their food, but also seating customers, taking orders, and sorting out the bill). Horizontal job enlargement became popular during the 1940s and 1950s, particularly in manufacturing plants where machine operators' jobs were enlarged to include setting up machines and quality inspection as well as machine operation. Walker (1950) reported how this type of job enlargement in a plant of the American company IBM resulted in improved product quality, reduced scrap, decreased machine idle time, and a reduction by 95 per cent in set-up and inspection times.

From an employee perspective, job rotation and job enlargement can make work more interesting by increasing the variety of tasks, and they can alleviate the physical strain that can arise when doing the same task over and over. Job rotation for managers and professionals, in the form of longer-term departmental transfers, can also lead to benefits such as a broader perspective on the business and an increased network of contacts (Campion *et al.*, 1994). However, a limitation of job rotation and horizontal job enlargement is that these practices typically do not affect the amount of autonomy and decision-making authority present in a job. If all tasks are completely specified for a worker, moving between them does not increase his or her opportunity to influence what happens.

Job Enrichment

Job enrichment is a type of work redesign that does address the vertical division of labour by adding some thinking and planning elements to the job. Essentially, job enrichment (also sometimes referred to as 'vertical job enlargement') involves enhancing the autonomy and discretion people exercise in their work. One way is to give employees responsibility for decisions traditionally made by supervisors or managers (for example, allowing nurses to decide on how and when they do their tasks). A second possibility is to upgrade jobs to include additional skilled tasks that are not necessarily elements of supervisory work (e.g., allowing nurses to carry out tasks that would usually be performed by doctors).

An example of job enrichment amongst bank staff was reported by Griffin (1991). Management redesigned bank tellers' jobs at the same time as installing new computer technology. Tellers were trained to carry out all banking transactions, rather than (for example) having to refer commercial and travellers' cheque customers to specialist tellers. They were able to make decisions that previously required the supervisor's authority. For example, tellers could permit customers to withdraw money after checking that the information system showed adequate funds in their account. The new technology was designed so that tellers could monitor their errors and transactions at all times. Finally, customers were informed as to the name of the teller who performed their transaction so that the customer could contact this person if he or she later had queries. Using a longitudinal research design, Griffin (1991) showed that the job enrichment had short-term positive effects on tellers' job satisfaction and organizational commitment, and a long-term positive effect on performance. Interestingly, the gains in job satisfaction and commitment were not sustained in the long term, perhaps because employees can develop higher expectations for their jobs after work redesign.

Although popular, job enrichment in the mid to late 1990s did not replace job simplification on a large scale; the latter practice was too deeply embedded within most organizations. However, there has been a resurgence of interest in job enrichment in recent years. Current practices referred to as empowerment, high involvement and high performance work systems (e.g., Bown and Lawler, 1992; Lawler, 1988) are all underpinned by principles of job enrichment.

Herzberg's Two-Factor Theory and the Job Characteristics Model

One of the early work design theories responsible for putting job enrichment on the agenda is the Two-Factor (or Motivation–Hygiene) Theory (Herzberg, 1966; Herzberg, Mausner and Snyderman, 1959). Herzberg and colleagues asked people to make causal attributions for occasions when they had been either satisfied or dissatisfied at work. They found that satisfaction was typically attributed to aspects intrinsic to the work itself (e.g., the freedom to decide what to do next), which they called 'motivator factors', whereas dissatisfaction was mostly attributed to extrinsic aspects (e.g., company policy) referred to as 'hygiene factors'. The first set of factors was viewed as being particularly important for employee satisfaction and behaviour. Overall, however, interest in the theory has declined in the light of subsequent studies that failed to replicate the original results (e.g., Wall and Stephenson, 1970).

A theory of job enrichment that largely replaced Herzberg's Two-Factor Theory is the Job Characteristics Model (Hackman and Oldham, 1976). This model identified five *core job characteristics* as important for promoting motivational outcomes. These characteristics were:

- skill variety (requiring different skills; SV)
- task identity (completing a whole piece of work, TI)
- task significance (having an impact on other people, TS)
- autonomy (having choice and discretion, A)
- feedback (obtaining feedback about performance from the job, F).

The core job characteristics were suggested to result in three *critical psychological states*: skill variety, task identity and task significance leading to *experienced meaningfulness* of the work; autonomy promoting *experienced responsibility*; and feedback determining *knowledge of results* of work activities. In turn, the critical psychological states were suggested collectively to promote work satisfaction, internal work motivation, and work performance, and to reduce absence and turnover. A particular formula was applied to obtain a single index of the overall potential of a job to promote work motivation, or the *Motivating Potential Score* (MPS). This formula [MPS = (SV + TI + TS)/3 × A × F)] weights autonomy and feedback more heavily than the other core job characteristics. An additional feature of the model was the recognition that not all individuals would respond to job enrichment in the same way. It was proposed that individuals with higher *growth need strength* (i.e., a desire for challenge and personal development) would respond more favourably to enriched jobs than others.

The Job Characteristics Model was an important development. The main proposition – that the core job characteristics can be important determinants of outcomes such as job satisfaction – has been supported. In addition, it has sometimes been found that growth need strength moderates the relationship between job characteristics and outcomes such as job satisfaction in the expected way (e.g., Champoux, 1991). Nevertheless, other reviews and studies have not supported that moderating role of the growth need strength (e.g., Johns, Xie and Fang, 1992) or other more specific predictions of the model, such as the link between the job characteristics and the critical psychological states (e.g., Fried and Ferris, 1987). Similarly, a simple additive score of the five job characteristics has proved to be as strongly related to outcomes as the complex MPS score, if not more so. Other criticisms that have been made of the model are that it considers only a narrow range of work characteristics and outcomes, and that, as described later, the predicted performance benefits of enriched job content have not always been obtained.

Further Theoretical Contributions to Job Enrichment

There have been other important theoretical developments that inform job enrichment (see Parker and Wall, 1998). For example, the range of job characteristics has been expanded beyond those suggested by Hackman and Oldham (1976), to include features such as the level of physical demands, the physical context (e.g., the design of office conditions), the degree of role clarity, the level of cognitive demand, and the degree of social support (see also Chapter 1). The possibility of an interactive effect of job characteristics has also been explored, enquiring whether job demands and job control combine synergistically, more than merely being added together (Karasek, 1979). Thus job demands might be less harmful when they are accompanied by high levels of job control. Although findings regarding such an interactive effect are mixed, the possibility remains of interest because the implication is that, as long as job control is enhanced, increased job demands do not necessarily incur detrimental effects for employee well-being.

Other contributions take a different approach from that of linking job characteristics to outcomes. For example, the social information processing approach proposes that social cues such as other people's views determine reactions to job characteristics (Salancik and Pfeffer, 1977). Another approach is Campion and colleagues' interdisciplinary perspective (e.g., Campion and Berger, 1990) expands our understanding of work design by summarizing different approaches that vary in their derivation, recommendations, and anticipated costs and benefits. Thus, over and above the motivational approach to work design (focused on in this chapter), they describe a *mechanistic approach* that focuses on efficiencies (i.e., based on scientific management principles), a *biological approach* that focuses on physical comfort and health, and a *perceptual-motor approach* that focuses on reliability and usability.

One contribution that has gained popularity in recent years is psychological empowerment theory (e.g., Spreitzer, 1995). This distinguishes empowerment practices (such as job enrichment) from empowerment in psychological terms, the cognitive-motivational states that arise from these practices. Psychological empowerment involves individuals having a sense of 'competence' or self-efficacy that they can perform the tasks; believing that the goals to be accomplished have 'meaning'; feeling a sense of self-determination and 'choice' over work tasks; and believing that their actions have an 'impact' or make a difference. These four cognitive motivational states – competence, meaning, choice, and impact – are proposed to mediate the link between objective work conditions and psychological outcomes in broadly the same way that the Job Characteristics Model (above) proposed that critical psychological states would mediate the link between job characteristics and outcomes. Indeed, impact and meaningfulness are similar to that model's critical psychological states of 'knowledge of results' and 'experienced meaningfulness' respectively, and choice overlaps with the work characteristic of autonomy (although the former is a psychological sense of self-determination, whereas autonomy is an actual feature of work).

Nevertheless, although there are some similarities with the Job Characteristics Model, the psychological empowerment approach is additionally helpful. First, it highlights to a greater extent than traditional work design theory the potential link between job characteristics and employee self-efficacy (see Parker, 1998, for more on this topic). Second, and more generally, its focus is on measuring and promoting the cognitive motivational states that constitute 'psychological empowerment' rather than on merely changing objective work conditions. As such, determinants of empowerment beyond work design have been investigated, such as leadership and relationships with co-workers.

DESIGNING GROUP WORK

Frequently in organizations, groups of employees need to co-ordinate their activities to provide a service or to make a product. In such cases (see also Chapter 13), it is more sensible to think about redesigning a group of interdependent jobs rather than focusing on individual people's jobs. The most influential theory guiding group work design is the sociotechnical systems approach.

Socio-technical Systems Approach and Autonomous Work Groups

The socio-technical systems approach originated at the Tavistock Institute of Human Relations in London during the 1950s. In particular, two consultants, Trist and Bamforth (1951) studied 'long-wall' coal mining methods in Durham, England. The long-wall method largely arose because of the recent introduction of large-scale machinery. Groups of forty or fifty people were now divided into specialized groups, each group focusing on one specific stage of mining, each person typically carrying out a single fragmented task. This approach contrasted negatively to the previous 'short-wall' method in which small groups of people worked together as a team to remove coal from one section of the coal face. Trist and Bamforth observed that, to improve the working conditions of the 'long-wall' miners, some pits had spontaneously developed a form of mining in which multiskilled, self-selected and self-led groups were responsible for the whole coal-getting cycle on any one shift. Compared to the conventional long-wall method, this 'composite method' produced higher output and less absenteeism and worked to about 95 per cent of its potential (whereas the long-wall method worked to only about 78 per cent of its potential).

Out of these observations, and observations of similar practices in an Indian textile mill (Rice, 1958), the Tavistock consultants developed the concept of jointly optimizing social and technical systems when designing work, rather than focusing on only one or the other system. (Usually most attention is paid to the technical system.) Other socio-technical systems principles were articulated (Cherns, 1976), such as that methods of working should be minimally specified and that variances in work processes should be handled at the source. 'Autonomous work groups' in which groups decide on their own methods of working were advocated as a key way of simultaneously satisfying social and technical requirements, as well as conforming to other socio-technical systems principles.

An example of autonomous work groups was reported by Wall, Kemp, Jackson and Clegg (1986) in a study of a confectionery manufacturer. Before the redesign, each person worked within a specific part of the process carrying out a limited task. After the redesign, employees worked in groups of eight to twelve people, and were expected to carry out several tasks including new activities such as quality inspection and analyzing performance data. Groups were responsible for their own decision-making and reaching their targets. They had no supervisor, but reported directly to a manager, who was also responsible for three or more other groups. A longitudinal analysis showed clear benefits of autonomous work groups for employee satisfaction and reduced supervisory costs, but no demonstrable effect on work motivation or the volume of production. Interestingly, staff turnover was higher amongst the autonomous work groups, leading the authors to conclude that work group autonomy had specific, rather than universal, positive effects on employee well-being and behaviour. Some staff were unhappy with the added responsibilities and interdependence, and left the company.

The socio-technical systems approach to work design is one of enduring value. Autonomous work groups (also often called self-managing teams) are widely advocated within the modern management literature. For example, self-managing teams are argued to be one of the seven key features of 'high performance' organizations (Pfeffer, 1998), and autonomous work groups can be seen in many successful organizations around the world. Nevertheless, the socio-technical systems approach has not been immune to criticism. One issue concerns the rather vague recommendations about which work characteristics are important for which outcomes. Models that offer more specific guidance about how specific group features link to outcomes have been put forward (e.g., Cohen, Ledford and Spreitzer, 1996), and these are described next.

Group Effectiveness Models

Models that include factors not built into traditional job enrichment theory consider, for instance, the broader organizational context, the role of group processes and the importance of leadership style. An illustrative model is that suggested by Hackman (1987), which is an example of an input–process–output model (see also Chapter 13). The 'output' is an effective group (i.e., a group that meets its organizational standards, that can continue working together, and that meets its members' needs for satisfaction). Increases in various 'process' features (effort, knowledge, and appropriateness of task performance strategies) are proposed to lead to greater effectiveness as long as the group has the necessary material resources. The three levers to change the process criteria, or the 'inputs' to the model, are:

- *Group design*, which is partly about structuring tasks so that people have variety, autonomy, etc., but also involves making appropriate decisions about the composition of the group (e.g., a suitable number of people) and ensuring the group has appropriate norms about performance.
- *Organizational context* refers to having the appropriate reward, education, and information systems to support and reinforce team performance.
- *Group synergy* is concerned with features that help the group to interact effectively.

Although research investigating these types of models is still limited in quantity, there is support from cross-sectional studies for a wider focus than just on work design. For example, Campion, Papper and Medsker

(1996) reported that team effectiveness was most strongly predicted by various process characteristics (such as the degree of social support and communication within the team) as well as job design features (the degree of group self-management, variety, etc.). Contextual characteristics and the level of interdependence were predictive to a lesser extent, and various composition characteristics (such as group heterogeneity) were inconsistently related to team effectiveness.

HOW EFFECTIVE IS WORK REDESIGN?

Work design theory proposes that job enrichment and autonomous group working will have benefits for employees and the organizations in which they work. Is this the case? Answering this question is not as straightforward as it might seem because many relevant studies suffer from methodological inadequacies.

Methodological Considerations

One of the best ways to investigate the effects of work redesign is to collect information on outcomes (e.g., employee well-being or perform-ance) before and after the redesign, comparing any change against a similar group of employees that has not undergone the same work redesign. Unfortunately, such longitudinal field studies with control groups are relatively rare. More common are cross-sectional surveys in which employees' perceptions about task characteristics are related to outcomes such as their well-being. These studies offer more external validity than laboratory studies, but they do not allow conclusions to be made about the direction of causality. For example, they do not allow the researcher to assess whether job autonomy leads to job satisfaction, whether more satisfied employees perceive their jobs as being more autonomous, or whether both processes are at work.

A further criticism that has historically been made, but is now largely resolved, concerns the assessment of job characteristics by asking for employee's ratings of those. Can employees accurately describe their job content, or are perceptions of job content affected more by other factors, such as peers' views and employees' general affective state? Many years of research and debate on this issue suggest that perceptions of job characteristics correspond sufficiently closely to objective job characteristics to be considered as valid indicators (Oldham, 1996). Perceptions of job content also have the advantage of reflecting different meanings specific to individual workers, rather than assuming that a job is experienced identically by everyone.

Different Effects for Different Outcomes

Despite some of the methodological pitfalls of single studies, a consensus has emerged from the many reviews of studies investigating the link between work design and outcomes. The widely agreed conclusion is that the effects of job enrichment and autonomous group working are stronger and more consistent for well-being and attitudinal outcomes, such as job satisfaction and work motivation, than they are for behavioural outcomes such as work performance, absence and turnover. (See reviews by, for example, Beekun, 1989; Fried and Ferris, 1987; Kelly, 1992; Pasmore, Francis, Haldeman and Shani, 1982.) An example serves to demonstrate. In a longitudinal investigation of the implementation of self-managing teams in a new and an established mineral processing plant, Cordery, Mueller and Smith (1991) found the expected positive benefits of autonomous work groups for job satisfaction and organizational commitment. However, absence and staff turnover levels were higher for autonomous work groups in the new plant, although (because of other differences) this was not necessarily due to the work design.

Moderators, Mediators and Additional Outcomes to Consider

The finding that there is no universal or automatic positive effect of work redesign on behavioural outcomes calls for a differentiated and more sophisticated approach. This must seek to ascertain when work redesign does or does not have particular effects (i.e., investigate 'moderators'), as well as why it has the effects it does (i.e., investigate 'mediators'). I describe these approaches next, and also point to the value of considering an expanded set of outcomes of work design.

Moderators (additional influences)

One proposed moderator is the degree of uncertainty within the environment. Thus, job enrichment and autonomous work groups may be most likely to enhance performance if there is a high level of uncertainty, such as in settings of frequent product design change or unreliable technology. Consistent with parallel arguments made within general organizational theory (Burns and Stalker, 1961), it has been suggested that, if uncertainty is high, decision-making is better devolved to the employees concerned (Wall and Jackson, 1995). For example, such variable circumstances mean that rules and procedures cannot be specified for all the uncertainties that arise, nor can a supervisor oversee all of the many decisions.

A study by Wall, Corbett, Martin, Clegg and Jackson (1990) supports this proposition. These researchers compared the effect of enhanced operator autonomy over complex technology characterized by different levels of operational uncertainty. For machines with low uncertainty, there were no performance benefits of greater control by the operatives. In contrast, where machines were liable to frequent operational problems (e.g., because of the delicacy of the product they dealt with), an increase in operator control led to substantial performance gains. An investigation of autonomous group working within water treatment plants showed similar results (Cordery, Wall and Wright, 1997).

Another factor that is likely to influence the success of group work design is task interdependence. It is commonly accepted that teams are appropriate only if tasks are interdependent, but organizations do not always follow advice to this effect. Sprigg, Jackson and Parker (2000) described a wire manufacturing company that introduced a common model of team working within its wire-mills and roperies section. Positive performance and well-being outcomes arose in the roperies section but not in the wire-making section. Analysis of the data indicated that the difference in well-being could be accounted for by contrasting levels of interdependence in the two areas. Thus, team working was a success only in the roperies, where interdependence was high and there was a need for employees to co-operate to make the product. An individual work redesign (i.e., job enrichment) was suggested to be more appropriate for employees in the wire-mills.

Team dynamics (interrelationships between members) are also likely to impinge on the effectiveness of autonomous work groups. This was suggested in a longitudinal study of high performance work teams by

Banker, Field, Schroeder and Sinha (1996). These researchers found that quality and labour productivity improvements associated with group working mostly occurred within a team that was most cohesive. The group with the least performance benefits was one that had persistent conflict among team members throughout the implementation of group work.

Uncertainty, interdependence and group dynamics are just some of the factors that are likely to influence the effect of work redesign on performance. There are also other candidates, such as how the work redesign is implemented and whether supporting changes are made to human resource systems (see Parker and Wall, 1998). The key point to make is that universal positive effects of work redesign on performance cannot be assumed. Organizations contemplating work redesign should analyze their situation carefully to check that it is appropriate for the particular work redesign.

Mediators (mechanisms)

Considering mechanisms means moving beyond knowing *that* work design can affect behaviour and well-being at work to trying to ascertain *why* that is the case. Traditional work design theory has concentrated on mechanisms of a motivational kind. Thus, the Job Characteristics Model essentially proposed that employees perform better as a result of job redesign because they are more motivated. However, a key development in recent years has been a focus on cognitive mechanisms linking work design and outcomes. For example, studies by Wall, Jackson and Davids (1992) and others have shown that enhanced job autonomy can promote the acquisition and application of knowledge, such as learning to prevent machine faults from occurring, which in turn leads to enhanced performance (e.g., reduced machine downtime).

If we know more about why work characteristics affect outcomes, it will be easier to judge the circumstances under which a particular form of work design will and will not be effective. For example, the finding that job enrichment can promote the use and development of knowledge suggests that job enrichment will be a good solution in complex and uncertain situations where employees require considerable knowledge to work effectively. Wall and Jackson (1995) have made precisely this argument, conceptually linking the mediating role of knowledge with the moderating role of organizational uncertainty.

Expanded outcomes

Another development in work design research has been to consider the effects of work redesign on outcomes over and above those proposed by the Job Characteristics Model. For example, researchers have begun to take more seriously the possible link between work design characteristics and safety (see also Chapter 10). Studies have shown an association between job autonomy and safety outcomes such as a reduction in lost-time per injuries (Shannon, Mayr and Haines, 1997) and higher employee adherence to safety procedures (Parker, Axtell and Turner, 2001).

A growing number of studies have investigated how work redesign can promote employee learning and development. Over and above knowledge (as described above), learning-related outcomes of work redesign that have been documented include: the development of a more flexible role orientation (e.g., Parker, Wall and Jackson, 1997), increased self-efficacy (Parker, 1998), greater personal initiative (Frese, Kring, Soose and Zempel, 1996) and enhanced cognitive complexity (Kohn and Schooler, 1978). For instance, Parker, Wall and Jackson (1997) showed that the introduction of autonomous work groups resulted in employees moving away from a narrow 'that's not my problem' mentality to a more flexible, proactive role orientation in which they felt responsibility for a wide range of production issues. Considering these sorts of expanded outcomes is likely to be especially important in today's work place, where high levels of initiative and flexibility are often expected from employees.

DESIGNING WORK IN THE FUTURE

The work design theories described earlier in the chapter were developed in the mid to late 1900s, largely in response to the practice of job simplification within manufacturing. However, a global market place, more demanding customers, new flexible and internet-based technologies, and various economic and political developments have spurred fundamental change in many organizations. This change is occurring at the level of industry (e.g., a growth in service work), organization (e.g., more flexible organizational designs), work place (e.g., virtual team working, telecommuting), and employee (e.g., an ageing workforce). What do all of these changes mean for work design research and practice?

In addressing this question, Parker and Wall (2001) highlighted first of all the need for continued attention to job simplification. Several researchers have pointed to the deskilling effects of flexible production technologies (e.g., Braverman, 1974; see also Chapter 4) as well as related initiatives such as just-in-time and total quality management practices (e.g., Delbridge and Turnbull, 1992). Job simplification concerns have also arisen in relation to the fast-expanding world of call centres. Employees' job autonomy can be severely restricted by tight and constant electronic monitoring of agents' time, as well as by the need for agents to respond to customer enquiries on the basis of standard scripts. However, in contrast to these somewhat pessimistic views, other researchers are highly optimistic about the effects of modern changes on work design. For example, it has been suggested that because information technology increases employees' access to information (e.g., about customer data bases), they are able to act more autonomously and make decisions at the point of action (Mohrman and Cohen, 1995).

The reality is that the pessimists and the optimists are both right. There is likely to be both job simplification and job enrichment as a result of modern changes; the precise effect will depend on the nature of the systems involved, the organizational context, and the choices made in organizing the work. The question, therefore, is probably less usefully phrased in terms of whether job simplification occurs, and more usefully phrased as 'under what circumstances does job simplification arise and when is it more or less effective for different outcomes?'

In this respect, level of uncertainty in a job setting is likely to continue to be an important contingency variable. Uncertainty is likely to increase in modern organizations (for example, as flexible technologies enable the production of more varied products), which is one reason why job enrichment and self-management initiatives are advocated as recipes for future work design. Nevertheless, uncertainty will not increase in all organizations or all areas within organizations, and some practices will reduce uncertainty. It is also the case that work designs will sometimes be introduced that are not in tune with circumstances (most often, simplified work designs are retained or introduced in spite of highly uncertain contexts). All of this means that considering operational uncertainty as a contingency variable will continue to be essential for the foreseeable future.

As well as continuity with previous research, the modern context also requires the expansion of work design theory (Parker and Wall, 2001).

Specific practices raise particular issues. For example, the growth of temporary contract working highlights to a greater extent than before the importance of job security; and expanding work loads combined with the pressures of juggling family commitments highlight the importance of people's autonomy over their working hours. Telecommuting, or working from home, raises some old work design issues and some new ones. For example, it might be assumed that telecommuters have more autonomy over their work, especially their working hours, because there is no supervisor directly watching over them. However, evidence from a British study suggests that many telecommuters' work time is tightly controlled by employer deadlines (Huws, Podro, Gunnarsson, Weijers, Arvanitaki and Trova, 1996). Moreover, in some cases autonomy can be severely restricted because the telecommuter's performance is monitored electronically. A further aspect of work that has so far not received much attention in work design research is social contact, yet this might become an increasingly desired aspect for those regularly working at home in isolation from colleagues.

More generally, changes occurring in the work place are likely to increase the cognitive, social, and emotional demands on staff. Increasingly, physical or manual work and what is referred to as 'routine knowledge work' (such as processing accounts), are absorbed by new technology, leaving to employees the complex problem-solving or 'nonroutine knowledge work' (Mohrman and Cohen, 1995). The greater uncertainty, and the increasing number of roles that front-line workers are expected to play (for instance, providing information, selling, and performing an intelligence-gathering role; Frenkel, Korczynski, Shire and Tam, 1999), can also increase cognitive demands. Work designs are required that support the development of expertise and the sharing of knowledge between staff. Managing the social and emotional demands of work is also likely to be an important work design issue. In front-line customer service work, employees need to be 'on stage' emotionally (Hochschild, 1989; see also Chapter 9), displaying resilience and flexibility in the face of frequent uncertainties (Frenkel et al., 1999).

SUMMARY

Interest in the psychological aspects of work content, and the practice of work redesign, largely arose in response to job simplification, which grew to be the dominant way of organizing jobs after the industrial revolution. Job enlargement and job rotation are two forms of individual job redesign that aim to counter the horizontal division of labour inherent in job simplification. Job enrichment (applied to individual jobs) and autonomous work groups (applied to groups of interdependent jobs) are theoretically-derived forms of work redesign that aim to counter the vertical division of labour by enhancing job autonomy. Both types of work redesign have consistently been shown to enhance employee job satisfaction and motivation, although their effects on behavioural outcomes such as work performance and absence are less clear cut.

In recent years, research concerning the effects of work redesign has become more sophisticated, being concerned with identifying when and how work design affects outcomes. For example, work redesign has been suggested to be most beneficial to performance in highly uncertain contexts. Nevertheless, work design research needs to become even more sophisticated in the light of vast transformations in the work place. Some aspects of work design that are already established will remain so, such as job simplification and the role of uncertainty as a contingency, but other factors (e.g., emotional or cognitive demand) will increasingly distinguish between different forms of work and their consequences.

FURTHER READING

A summary of work design theory and research, ways to develop work design theory in the light of the changing work place, and some important practical issues associated are covered in Parker and Wall's (1998) *Job and Work Design: Organizing Work To Promote Well-Being and Effectiveness*. A detailed account of job design principles is given in Hackman and Oldham's (1980) *Work Redesign*. Several papers and chapters that integrate and critique established job design research and theory have been referred to throughout the chapter (also Kelly, 1992). A special issue on team working in *Human Relations* (2000, vol. 53, no. 1) covers the history of autonomous work groups as well as recent perspectives on team working. Readable practitioner-oriented articles include those by Bowen and Lawler (1992) on the empowerment of service workers and by Lawler (1988) on high involvement. There are also numerous websites on the topics of 'job design' and 'work design', such as the following, which describes a practical example of work redesign: *http://www.ifla.org/IV/ifla64/135-96e.htm*.

REFERENCES

Banker, R. D., Field, J. M., Schroeder, R. G. and Sinha, K. K. (1996). Impact of work teams on manufacturing performance: A longitudinal field study. *Academy of Management Journal*, 39, 867–90.

Beekun, R. I. (1989). Assessing the effectiveness of sociotechnical interventions: Antidote or fad? *Human Relations*, 10, 877–97.

Bowen, D. E. and Lawler, E. E. (1992). The empowerment of service workers: What, why, how, and when. *Sloan Management Review*, Spring, 31–9.

Braverman, H. (1974). *Labour and Monopoly Capital: The Degradation of Work in the Twentieth Century*. New York: Monthly Review Press.

Burns, T. and Stalker, G. M. (1961). *The Management of Innovation*. London: Tavistock.

Campion, M. A., Cheraskin, L. and Stevens, M. J. (1994). Career-related antecedents and outcomes of job rotation. *Academy of Management Journal*, 37, 1518–33.

— and Berger, C. J. (1990). Conceptual integration and empirical test of job design and compensation relationships. *Personnel Psychology*, 43, 525–53.

—, Papper, E. M. and Medsker, G. J. (1996). Relations between work team characteristics and effectiveness: A replication and extension. *Personnel Psychology*, 49, 429–52.

— and Stevens, M. J. (1991). Neglected questions in job design: How people design jobs, task–job predictability, and influence of training. *Journal of Business and Psychology*, 6, 169–91.

Champoux, J. E. (1991). A multivariate test of the job characteristics theory of motivation. *Journal of Organizational Behavior*, 12, 431–46.

Cherns, A. B. (1976). The principles of socio-technical design. *Human Relations*, 29, 783–92.

Cohen, S. G., Ledford, G. E. and Spreitzer, G. M. (1996). A predictive model of self-managing work team effectiveness. *Human Relations*, 49, 643–76.

Cordery, J. L., Mueller, W. S. and Smith, L. M. (1991). Attitudinal and behavioural effects of autonomous group working: A longitudinal field study. *Academy of Management Journal*, 43, 464–76.

—, Wall, T. D. and Wright, B. M. (1997). Towards a more comprehensive and integrated approach to work design: Production uncertainty and self-managing team performance. Paper presented at the Society of Industrial and Organizational Psychologists Annual Conference, St Louis.

Davis, L. E., Canter, R. R. and Hoffman, J. (1955). Current job design criteria. *Journal of Industrial Engineering*, 6, 5–11.

Delbridge, R. and Turnbull, P. (1992). Human resource maximisation: The management of labour under just-in-time manufacturing systems. In P. Blyton and P. Turnbull (Eds.), *Reassessing Human Resource Management*. London: Sage.

Fraser, R. (1947). *The Incidence of Neurosis Among Factory Workers* (Report No. 90. Industrial Health Research Board). London: HMSO.

Frenkel, S. J., Korczynski, M., Shire, K. A. and Tam, M. (1999). *On the Front Line: Organization of Work in the Information Economy*. London: Cornell University Press.

Frese, M., Kring, W., Soose, A. and Zempel, J. (1996). Personal initiative at work: Differences between East and West Germany. *Academy of Management Journal*, 39, 37–63.

Fried, Y. and Ferris, G. R. (1987). The validity of the job characteristics model: A review and meta-analysis. *Personnel Psychology*, 40, 287–322.

Griffin, R. W. (1991). Effects of work redesign on employee perceptions, attitudes and behaviours: A long-term investigation. *Academy of Management Journal*, 34, 425–35.

Hackman, J. R. (1987). The design of effective work teams. In J. Lorsch (Ed.), *Handbook of Organizational Behaviour*, pp. 316–41. Englewood Cliffs, NJ: Prentice-Hall.

— and Oldham, G. (1976). Motivation through the design of work: Test of a theory. *Organizational Behaviour and Human Performance*, 16, 250–79.

— and Oldham, G. R. (1980). *Work Redesign*. Reading, Mass.: Addison-Wesley.

Herzberg, F. (1966). *Work and the Nature of Man*. Cleveland, OH: World Publishing.

—, Mausner, B. and Snyderman, B. (1959). *The Motivation to Work*. New York: Wiley.

Hochschild, A. (1989). *The Second Shift*. New York: Viking.

Huws, U., Podro, S., Gunnarsson, E., Weijers, T., Arvanitaki, K. and Trova, V. (1996). *Teleworking and Gender*. Institute of Employment Studies Report 317. Grantham: Grantham Book Services Ltd.

Johns, G., Xie, J. L. and Fang, Y. (1992). Mediating and moderating effects in job design. *Journal of Management*, *18*, 657–76.

Karasek, R. A. (1979). Job demands, job decision latitude and mental strain: Implications for job redesign. *Administrative Science Quarterly*, *24*, 285–308.

Kelly, J. E. (1992). Does job re-design theory explain job re-design outcomes? *Human Relations*, *45*, 753–74.

Kohn, M. L. and Schooler, C. (1978). The reciprocal effects of the substantive complexity of work on intellectual complexity: A longitudinal assessment. *American Journal of Sociology*, *84*, 24–52.

Lawler, E. E. (1998). Choosing an involvement strategy. *The Academy of Management Executive*, *11*, 197–204.

Mohrman, S. A. and Cohen, S. G. (1995). When people get out of the box: New relationships, new systems. In A. Howard (Ed.), *The Changing Nature of Work*, pp. 265–410. San Francisco: Jossey-Bass.

Oldham, G. R. (1996). Job design. In C. L. Cooper and I. T. Robertson (Eds.), *International Review of Industrial and Organizational Psychology* (pp. 33–60). Chichester: John Wiley & Sons.

Parker, S. K. (1998). Role breadth self-efficacy: Relationship with work enrichment and other organizational practices. *Journal of Applied Psychology*, *83*, 835–52.

—, Axtell, C. M. and Turner, N. (2001). Designing a safer workplace: Importance of job autonomy, communication quality and supportive supervisors. *Journal of Occupational Health Psychology*, *6*, 211–28.

—, Wall, T. D. and Jackson, P. R. (1997). 'That's not my job': Developing flexible employee work orientations. *Academy of Management Journal*, *40*, 899–929.

— and Wall, T. D. (1998). *Job and Work Design: Organizing Work To Promote Well-Being and Effectiveness*. London: Sage.

— and Wall, T. D. (2001). Work design: Learning from the past and mapping a new terrain. In N. Anderson, D. S. Ones, H. K. Sinangil and C. Viswesveran (Eds.), *Handbook of Industrial, Work and Organizational Psychology*, Vol. 1. (pp. 90–109). London: Sage.

Pasmore, W., Francis, C., Haldeman, J. and Shani, A. (1982). Socio-technical systems: A North American reflection on the empirical studies of the seventies. *Human Relations*, *35*, 1179–204.

Pfeffer, J. (1998). Seven practices of successful organizations. *California Management Review*, *40*, 96–124.

Rice, A. K. (1958). *Productivity and Social Organization*. London: Tavistock.

Salancik, G. R. and Pfeffer, J. (1977). A social information processing approach to job attitudes and task design. *Administrative Science Quarterly*, *23*, 224–53.

Shannon, H. S., Mayr, J. and Haines, T. (1997). Overview of the relationship between organizational and workplace factors and injury rates. *Safety Science*, *26*, 201–17.

Spreitzer, G. M. (1995). Psychological empowerment in the workplace: Dimensions, measurement, and validation. *Academy of Management Journal, 38,* 1442–65.

Sprigg, C. A., Jackson, P. R. and Parker, S. K. (2000). Production team-working: The importance of interdependence for employee strain and satisfaction. *Human Relations, 53,* 1519–43.

Trist, E. L. and Bamforth, K. W. (1951). Some social and psychological consequences of the long-wall method of coal-getting. *Human Relations, 4,* 3–38.

Walker, C. R. (1950). The problem of the repetitive job. *Harvard Business Review, 28,* 54–8.

— and Guest, R. (1952). *The Man on the Assembly Line.* Cambridge, Mass.: Harvard University Press.

Wall, T. D., Corbett, M. J., Martin, R., Clegg, C. W. and Jackson, P. R. (1990). Advanced manufacturing technology, work design and performance: A change study. *Journal of Applied Psychology, 75,* 691–7.

— and Jackson, P. R. (1995). New manufacturing initiatives and shopfloor work design. In A. Howard (Ed.), *The Changing Nature of Work* (pp. 139–74). San Francisco: Jossey-Bass.

—, Jackson, P. R. and Davids, K. (1992). Operator work design and robotics system performance: A serendipitous field study. *Journal of Applied Psychology, 77,* 353–62.

—, Kemp, N. J., Jackson, P. R. and Clegg, C. W. (1986). An outcome evaluation of autonomous work groups: A long-term field experiment. *Academy of Management Journal, 29,* 280–304.

— and Stephenson, G. M. (1970). Herzberg's two-factor theory of job attitudes: A critical evaluation and some fresh evidence. *Industrial Relations Journal, 1,* 41–65.

Wyatt, S. and Ogden, D. A. (1924). *On the Extent and Effects of Variety and Uniformity in Repetitive Work* (Report No. 26, Industrial Fatigue Research Board). London: HMSO.

12

Leadership

Beverly Alimo-Metcalfe and
Robert J. Alban-Metcalfe

Although it has been suggested that there are as many definitions of leadership as persons who have tried to define it, four common themes have typically been emphasized. These are that leadership is a process, involves influencing others, occurs within a group context, and involves goal attainment (Northouse, 2001). More recently, definitions of leadership have also drawn attention to the role of leaders in 'defining organizational reality' (Bryman, 1996).

Formal studies of leadership, which date back to the beginning of the twentieth century, have sought to identify those factors that make certain individuals particularly effective in influencing the behaviour of other individuals or groups, and in making things happen that would not otherwise occur or preventing undesired outcomes (Rosenbach and Taylor, 1993).

Early investigations, which focused on the personal characteristics or the behaviours of individuals who emerge as leaders, were followed by those that considered the influence of situational factors on leadership behaviour. More recent research interest has centred on relationships between leaders and followers, with some writers stressing the need to study 'followership'. This has been argued as important, not only because all leaders are also followers, but also because modern notions of leadership place considerable emphasis on the power and importance of followers in ultimately legitimizing and enabling leadership (e.g., Lee, 1993; De Pree, 1993). This last period saw the growth of attention to differences between 'leaders' and 'managers'.

Varying use of the terms 'manager' and 'management', and 'leader' and 'leadership', has long been a source of confusion in the literature.

The position adopted here is that a manager is a person who takes on a management role, which comprises activities such as planning, organizing, setting objectives, creating and monitoring systems, and ensuring that standards are met. In contrast, a leader is someone who takes on a more proactive role, with activities such as creating a vision for an organization, helping the organization to develop by adapting to changing circumstances, and encouraging innovative practices.

Thus, management can be thought of as an essentially static, 'closed-ended' activity of dealing effectively and efficiently with day-to-day events, and maintaining the *status quo*, while leadership is essentially dynamic and 'open-ended' – challenging the current practice and dealing creatively with the way in which an organization can utilize its potential to move forward and deal successfully with the future. While managers and management are essential for creating order and efficiency in organizations, particularly in highly complex ones, they are not sufficient for enabling organizations to cope successfully with change. Leadership and management can best be regarded as distinct but complementary. Unfortunately, much research into the nature of leadership has failed to draw this distinction.

A further source of confusion in the leadership literature is the frequent lack of distinction between two kinds of studies: those which have focused on individuals who hold formal leadership positions in organizations and those which have focused on individuals (who may or may not occupy formal leadership positions) who emerge as having a particularly positive effect on the performance and motivation of others. In the former case, a leader or leadership is regarded as an *independent* variable, and in the latter a *dependent* variable. We would urge readers to be mindful of this further distinction.

EARLIER APPROACHES TO STUDYING LEADERSHIP

Trait Approach

This approach, which analyzes the attributes of leaders, has also been referred to as the 'great man' approach, because such individuals were often the focus of attention (Northouse, 2001; Wright, 1996). The approach was predicated on a general acceptance that what differentiated leaders from non-leaders, or followers, was their enduring personal characteristics or 'traits'. Thus, 'leadership' was attributed to the possession of characteristics such as energy, dominance or intelligence, which were considered largely in-born and enduring. These characteristics, it was asserted, could be used to predict effectiveness in a variety of situations. Other early studies looked at factors such as birth order, child-rearing practices and early socialization, as well as at the socio-economic status of parents or guardians.

Two important reviews of the literature, by Mann (1959) and Stodgill (1948), were widely interpreted as concluding that there were no consistent findings in relation to the personality characteristics that differentiated leaders from non-leaders, or more effective from less effective leaders, where a 'leader' was sometimes defined as an individual who emerged as such in a group with no appointed leader. Thus, for example, Mann reported ninety-one studies which showed a significant positive relationship between leadership status and intelligence, but a further ninety studies where no such relationship was detected, and one study which revealed a negative relationship (Wright, 1996). The most consistent findings arose from twenty-three studies indicating that the average leader surpassed the intelligence of the average member of the leader's group (or 'follower'); five studies which found no significant differences; and five studies which indicated that an extremely large difference between leader and followers was detrimental to leadership (Lord, De Vader and Alliger, 1986).

Stodgill concluded that the qualities, characteristics and skills needed by a leader are to a large extent determined by demands of the situation in which he (or she) is to function. However, he later wrote that, while both personal and situational factors are involved, it is possible to identify a number of relatively consistent personal characteristics associated with appearing leader-like. These include: a strong drive for responsibility and task completion, venturesomeness and originality, self-confidence and sense of personal identity, and ability to influence others' behaviour and to structure social interaction systems (Wright, 1996). It is, however, the combination of characteristics that is important: the possession of certain characteristics in abundance, if in the absence of certain other characteristics, may be a recipe for failure.

Consistent with this perspective, other recent studies have investigated personality as a moderating variable in determining leadership behaviours (e.g., Zaleznik, 1993). Indeed, Bass (1998) suggested that, in certain combinations, personality traits may account for as much as 35 per cent of variation. This view was supported by the findings of Church and Waclawski (1995), who looked at the relationship between personality-orientation, as measured by the Myers–Briggs Type Indicator (MBTI) and the Kirton Adaptor–Innovator measure (KAI), and the use of 'enabling behaviours' of leadership. No significant differences were detected between the subordinates' and managers' perceptions of the extent to which they showed enabling behaviour, but there were between-manager differences in the *type* of enabling behaviours used. Thus, managers classified as 'motivators' were seen as more likely to encourage risk-taking, to maintain a challenging and motivating work environment, and to take time to celebrate accomplishments. On the other hand, 'inventors' were significantly better at innovating, setting direction, and establishing a sense of mission about their work, but were only average at influencing followers by arousing their hopes, enthusiasm, and energy.

The value of this study has been to increase understanding of the relationship between personality and the process of leadership. Unlike earlier attempts at investigating the relationship between personality and appearing leader like to observers, studies such as the one just described determined 'leadership' by taking into account the views and experiences of those most affected by leadership, namely the followers. In other words, they focused on leadership as a dependent variable. The study was, however, limited in that it concerned only one aspect of leadership, albeit one that is crucial to the effectiveness of the process, namely the feelings of subordinates of being 'enabled' in their activities.

Although one of the strengths of the trait approach was that it focused on the leader (rather than management) component of leadership, it can be criticized for failing to take into account the effect of situational factors. Traits that may make a person an effective leader in one situation may not do so in another. Two further criticisms are that, in spite of it being intuitively appealing to identify 'leadership traits', the list of such traits is almost unending, and that the approach did not offer possible avenues for training and development.

Behavioural Approach

The attention of psychologists investigating leadership next switched to behaviours that might differentiate effective from ineffective leaders, that is, to the behaviour of individuals who are effective in influencing the actions of 'followers'. Typically, such behaviour was described as the 'leadership or managerial style' adopted by the leader. Commonly, the style was envisaged as a dimension of leadership behaviour, along which individuals could be measured. Although well over thirty different models have been devised, most can be described in terms of four styles: (1) concern for task – also called 'task-orientated' or 'production-centred'; (2) concern for people – also called 'person-orientated' or 'employee-centred'; (3) directive leadership – also called authoritarian or autocratic; (4) participative – also called democratic.

In some studies, styles such as directive and participative were represented as discrete types of leadership; in others they were regarded as opposite poles of a single dimension. The justification for identifying opposite poles was that leaders rarely act in ways that are simultaneously directive and participative. However, an individual may be highly participative in certain situations, but highly directive in others (Wright, 1996). In other studies, only concern for task and concern for people were investigated, either as discrete types of leadership or as opposite ends of one dimension.

A third approach, adopted in the Ohio State University studies, used two composite dimensions, consideration (concern for people merged with participative) and initiating structure (concern for task merged with directive), which they regarded as independent of each other. A further approach was to collapse all four styles into a single leadership dimension, which ranged from participative and person-centred to directive and task-centred, from which a single 'leadership score' was calculated.

A small number of studies sought to establish cause–effect relationships between leadership style and outcome (or 'criterion') variables, such as productivity, errors made, labour turnover, absenteeism, stress and job satisfaction, but the results were inconsistent. Reasons for this inconsistency may include a failure to take account of the influence of subordinate behaviour; leadership style may vary according to the behaviour of subordinates. Other factors likely to determine whether or not one style is identified as superior to another are the nature of the criterion variables examined and the extent to which two or more criterion variables interact with one another.

The results of correlational studies of leadership behaviour were also inconsistent. For example, a survey by Stodgill (1974) reported positive relationships between follower-orientated styles and group productivity in forty-seven studies, and a zero or negative correlation in forty-six, while work-orientated styles were associated with group productivity in forty-seven cases, with zero or negative relationships in thirty-three. The findings point to the need to study situational variables, which can moderate the impact of specific leadership styles.

A meta-analysis (in which correlation coefficients from a number of studies are averaged) was conducted on scales used to measure consideration and initiating structure by Fisher and Edwards (1988). Two versions of the Leadership Behavior Description Questionnaire (LBDQ and LBDQXII) produced similar results. Low to moderate positive correlations with job performance were found for both consideration and initiating structure, high positive correlations were observed between leaders' consideration and measures of satisfaction, and moderate positive correlations occurred between leaders' initiating structure and subordinate satisfaction.

Blake and Mouton (1964) devised a Managerial Grid, in which leadership styles were described in relation to two independent dimensions: concern for results and concern for people. A low–low score was categorized as 'impoverished management', a low–high score as 'country club management', a high–low score as 'authority-compliance management', and a high–high score as 'team management'. The last of these, which was seen as involving sound participation, effective integration of people and production, and staff involvement in determining conditions and strategies of work, was regarded as the best style. Subsequently, two further styles were identified, paternalism and opportunism, plus a third motivational dimension.

In common with the trait theorists, advocates of the behavioural approach assumed that one combination of behaviours would lead to successful leadership, regardless of the situation. This assumption has been found to lack consistent empirical support. Nevertheless, the approach was valuable in that it broadened the focus of research to include leader behaviour and how leaders act in different situations, and in that distinctions were drawn between task-related behaviour and relationship-related behaviour. It also provided a tool for self-analysis, which had the potential for informing training and development. It was not, however, able to show how leadership behaviours are linked to performance outcomes, nor did it succeed in identifying a universal style that would be effective in most situations.

Situational and Contingency Approaches

Other theorists argued that different situations require different kinds of leadership, and that effective leaders are those that are sensitive to subordinates' needs, adapting their behaviour to the demands of different situations. Thus, Hersey and Blanchard (1982) devised their situational leadership model (SLII) to assess both leadership style and subordinates' developmental level. Leadership style was defined with reference to two dimensions: directive behaviours, and supportive behaviours. Combinations of high versus low scores were used to identify four styles, which were labelled as directing (high–low), coaching (high–high), supporting (low–high) and delegating (low–low).

Similarly, subordinates were categorized into one of four groups in terms of two dimensions – commitment and competence – but with explicit recognition that employees can move backward as well as forward along a developmental continuum. The SLII model sought to specify which leadership style is appropriate for each developmental level.

Fiedler's (1967) contingency theory suggested that leadership performance can only be understood in relation to the context in which it occurs, and that success is achieved when there is a good leader–situation match. The theory provides a framework for analyzing styles and situations. Leadership style is measured using the Least Preferred Co-Worker (LPC) scale (in which a manager rates his or her least-preferred colleague on a range of characteristics). Individuals who view their LPC in relatively positive terms are described as relationship motivated, while those whose ratings of that person are low are identified as task motivated. Situational factors are measured in terms of: (a) leader–member relations – group atmosphere, and confidence in and loyalty towards the leaders; (b) task structure – clarity of tasks set; (c) position power – amount of leader's authority to reward or to punish.

The LPC and situational scores were used to predict whether or not a leader would be effective in a particular setting, though the inner workings of the theory are unclear (Northouse, 2001).

In path–goal theories, the emphasis is on the relationship between leadership style and the characteristics of both the subordinates and the work setting. The underlying assumption was that subordinates' motivation would be greater if they (a) thought themselves capable of doing their work, (b) believed that a certain outcome would result from their effort, and (c) regarded the payoffs as worthwhile. Although path–goal theory is conceptually complex, it is essentially concerned with the way in which leader behaviour, subordinate characteristics and task characteristics affect the path between subordinate activity and organizational goals. Four types of leadership behaviour have been examined – directive, supportive, participative, and achievement-orientated. Subordinates were seen to have relevant needs in the areas of affiliation, preference for structure, desire for control, and self-perceived ability to perform a task, which would determine the extent to which they found the leader's behaviour a source of satisfaction. Thus, for example, it was predicted that directive leadership would be suited to subordinates who were dogmatic and authoritarian and had to work in situations of uncertainty, because that provided desired psychological structure and task clarity.

Task characteristics in path-goal theories included the design of the task, the organization's formal authority structure, and the nature of the work. Where tasks were clearly structured, group norms were explicit, and an established authority system existed, the paths to goals would be evident, and little leadership intervention necessary. Leadership intervention would, however, be required for tasks that were unclear or ambiguous, or where the task was repetitive and thus de-motivating. A leader should, therefore, choose a leadership style that is suited to subordinates' needs and task requirements.

The approaches discussed so far tend to treat subordinates in a collective way, considering a group as a whole, and suggest the use of a single, stable leadership style. In contrast, leader–member exchange (LMX) theory advocates recognition of individual differences, and an emphasis on dyadic relationships between a leader and each of her/his subordinates. Early studies focused on the quality of leader–subordinate interaction, and led to the distinction between 'in-group' and 'out-group' communication, between a leader and favoured or disapproved followers respectively. In-group communication would characteristically be richer in content, resulting in negotiation of role responsibilities, whereas out-group communication would be more formal and lead to more closely defined roles (Graen and Uhl-Bien, 1995). The quality of the leader–subordinate relationship, and thus membership of one or other type of group, depends partly on the personal characteristics of both persons, and partly on (a) the subordinates wishing to increase their range of responsibilities and (b) the leader doing more for these subordinates. In-group subordinates would tend to receive more information, influence, confidence, and concern from their leader than would those in the out-group.

Later studies of LMX theory focused on organizational effectiveness, in particular the positive outcomes for leaders, followers, groups, and organizations of the quality of leader–member exchanges. The effects of high-quality leader–member exchanges were seen in low employee turnover, high performance evaluations, frequency of promotion, organizational commitment, desirable work assignments, job attitudes, attention and support from the leader, opportunities for participation, and good career progress (Graen and Uhl-Bien, 1995).

The Vroom-Yetton (1973) normative model was concerned with subordinates' participation in decision-making and the effectiveness of such decisions, and in the relationship between amount and form of participation. Two types of decision process were involved: decisions affecting the entire team, and decisions affecting only one subordinate. In each case, five methods for allocating decision-making responsibility were identified. These ranged between situations in which a leader makes a decision alone, through those in which a leader chairs a meeting and is willing to implement any solution that has the support of the group, to situations in which a leader delegates a problem to a subordinate with full authority to solve the problem alone. Problems were analyzed with reference to twelve attributes, with each rated on a five-point scale. The attributes included quality requirements, commitment requirements, subordinate conflict and time constraint. On the basis of a mathematical formula, suggestions for leader behaviour were made.

Situational models have proved to be of practical value in training and development, particularly because of their emphasis on the need for adaptability and flexibility on the part of the leader, and on the need to interact differently with subordinates according to the nature of the task. General criticism centres on the paucity of research to justify some of the assumptions made and on the ambiguity of some prescriptions made. This is reflected in a failure to define precisely some of the terms used.

Contingency theory is supported by much empirical research, and has broadened understanding of the impact of situations on leaders. While recognizing that not all leaders will be effective in all situations, the theory has predictive value, and leads to the production of 'leadership profiles'. On the other hand, it fails to explain fully why some styles are more effective than others, and the validity of measures such as the LPC scale has been called into question. Another general criticism of situational and contingency models is that their complexity sometimes makes them difficult to understand and apply.

CURRENT APPROACHES

Following the major recession of the 1970s, Peters and Waterman (1982) provided an analysis of North America's most 'successful' companies, in which they emphasized the role of the 'transforming leader'. This kind of person was seen, first and foremost, as articulating a vision for the organization, communicating this vision by his/her passion and charisma, and as a consequence defining a meaning for the organization, and, typically, transforming its culture.

Bryman (1996) described the models that emerged from this analysis as the 'new paradigm'. This was because he, in common with other major leadership writers, argued that earlier situational models are more to do with 'management' of organizations in times of relative stability than with leadership, which is inherently concerned with handling change. He identified a range of new models that emerged, mainly in the 1980s, as falling into this category. These included the models of charismatic leadership of House (1977) and Conger (1989), Sashkin's (1988) notion of visionary leadership, and several transformational leadership models, of which Bass's is the most famous. These were seen as revealing a conception of the leader as someone who, by defining an organization's mission and the values which will support it, makes explicit organizational reality and prioritizes some features above others. Thus, Bryman asserts that in the 'new paradigm' approach leaders are seen as managers of meaning, rather than merely in terms of their influence on subordinates.

A four-stage charismatic model was devised by Conger and Kanungo (1988), in which each stage was seen as requiring differing leadership behaviour and skills. The extent to which a leader is viewed as charismatic is determined by the number of such behaviours, their intensity, and their relevance to followers. The stages comprise: (1) detecting deficiencies and opportunities and formulating a strategic vision, (2) communicating a vision; articulating its appropriateness; motivating followers, (3) building trust, based on expertise, success, self-sacrifice, personal risk-taking and unconventional behaviour, and (4) demonstrating how to achieve the vision using empowerment, modelling and unconventional tactics. Leadership behaviour is assessed along six dimensions – vision and articulation, environmental sensitivity, unconventional behaviour, personal risk, sensitivity to member needs, and not maintaining the *status quo* (Hunt, 1996).

Transformational Leadership

One of the most popular models of this 'new paradigm' era was developed by Bass (1985, 1998). He uses the term 'transformational', because of his belief that an essential distinguishing feature of leaders is their ability to transform followers 'to perform beyond expectations'. Bass's model was based on the distinction drawn by Burns (1978) between 'transformational' and 'transactional' leadership in the political world. Burns argued that transformational politicians move people beyond their self-interest to work for the greater good by engaging their higher needs. Such politicians were contrasted with others who trade promises for votes, that is who influence followers by transactions of exchange.

Bass translated a model of leadership ascribed to politicians so that it applied to managers in organizations. He also questioned Burns' assertion that transformational and transactional leadership are at opposite ends of a single continuum of leadership. The two approaches were subsequently found to be independent of each other and complementary in their value (Bass, 1998).

Transformational leaders are characterized by being able to motivate colleagues and followers to:

- view their work from new perspectives,
- be aware of their team's and organization's mission or vision,
- attain higher levels of ability and potential, and
- look beyond their own interests toward those that will benefit the group (Bass, 1985).

However, transformational leadership is not seen as being sufficient for effective organizations. Rather, for an organization to be successful, transformational leadership must be accompanied by effective management – or 'transactional leadership' as it is now commonly labelled. Transactional leadership entails an exchange between leader and follower in which the leader rewards the follower for specific behaviours and for performance that meets with the leader's wishes, and criticizes, sanctions or punishes non-conformity or lack of achievement (Bass, 1998).

In order to measure leadership behaviour, Bass developed the Multifactor Leadership Questionnaire (MLQ) (Bass and Avolio, 1990), which identified the following four transformational components:

- Idealized influence: transformational leaders behave in ways that result in them being admired, respected and trusted, such that their followers wish to emulate them. They are extraordinarily capable, persistent, and determined;
- Inspirational motivation: transformational leaders behave such that they motivate and inspire those around them by providing meaning, optimism and enthusiasm for a vision of a future state;
- Intellectual stimulation: transformational leaders encourage followers to question assumptions, reframe problems and approach old solutions in new ways, and to be creative and innovative. At times, their followers' ideas may differ from those of the leader, who may solicit or encourage their views;
- Individualized consideration: transformational leaders actively develop the potential of their followers by creating new opportunities for development, coaching, mentoring, and paying attention to each follower's needs and desires. They know their staff well, as a result of listening, communicating, and encouraging rather than monitoring their efforts.

The MLQ also has two transactional components:

- Contingent reward: approved follower actions are rewarded, disapproved actions are punished or sanctioned.

● Management by exception (active) and management by exception (passive): corrective transactional dimensions. The former involves monitoring performance and intervening when judged appropriate; the latter involves correction only when problems emerge.

In addition, the questionnaire measures:

● Laissez-faire: a style of leadership that is, in fact, an abrogation of leadership, since there is an absence of any transaction. This style is deemed to be most ineffective.

Subsequent analyses (Avolio, Bass and Jung, 1999) led to a revision of the model of the transformational components of leadership, in which the first two dimensions became combined into one, referred to as 'charismatic-inspirational'.

The Multifactor Leadership Questionnaire (MLQ) has been widely used in different settings. In reviewing findings, Bass concluded that, in general, transformational leadership is more effective and satisfying than transactional leadership, and cited considerable evidence for the superiority of the transformational style over the transactional style alone (Bass, 1998). He argues that, while context and other contingencies are a source of variance, the fundamental transformational phenomena transcend organizations and countries (Bass, 1997).

Criticism and extension of the Bass model
Transformational leadership has been criticized for having poorly defined parameters (Northouse, 2001), for treating leadership as a personal predisposition, rather than a behaviour that can be learnt (Bryman, 1992), and for being based primarily on qualitative data. Despite the fact that instruments that measure transformational leadership have been applied in several countries and cultures (e.g., Bass, 1997), it is possible that the items might not reflect the perceived content of leadership in those diverse settings (Alimo-Metcalfe and Alban-Metcalfe, 2001). Research by Den Hartog and associates (1999) indicated that, while certain aspects of transformational leadership generalize over a wide range of cultures, others do not (Alban-Metcalfe and Alimo-Metcalfe, 2000a, b).

Although there is undoubted respect for Bass's model of leadership and his contributions to the literature, his work has not been without its critics. Hunt (1996) cites three criticisms: (1) that the Multifactor Leadership Questionnaire (MLQ) was developed before substantial data had been gathered on the nature of transformational leadership from interviews and observations; (2) that the MLQ includes both descriptions of leader behaviour and outcomes of behaviours; (3) that the individualized consideration scale contains items reminiscent of those included in previous leadership scales developed some decades earlier, with the descriptions of transactional leadership implying an ineffective leader; (4) that the model gives insufficient attention to the two-way aspects of leader–follower relations. Bass and Avolio (1993) have addressed these and other criticisms.

A further observation about the methodology adopted in the major models of transformational leadership – and in earlier models – is that they have been developed from studying white males, with findings extrapolated to people in general. The MLQ, for example, was based on interview data from seventy South African executives – sixty-nine of whom were white, and all of whom were men – augmented by descriptions of transformational and transactional leadership in the literature.

Gronn (1995), in expressing concerns about what he regards as a current obsession with transformational leadership, asserted that the notion of 'heroic' leadership has long been discredited and is virtually defunct. Bryman (1996) pointed out that the 'new paradigm' leadership studies were based on samples that differ significantly from those of the early researchers, which focused on individuals at supervisor level and middle-level managers. In contrast, more recent studies examined very senior managers in large North American corporations. A further source of difference from earlier research, which applied standardized questionnaires, was the use of case studies of senior executives of world-leading companies. Thus, apart from the nature of the sample, there have been differences in the method of data collection used.

The choice of sample has also been examined by Alimo-Metcalfe and Alban-Metcalfe (2001), who pointed out that the published charismatic, visionary, and transformational models derived from the USA were based on observations of 'distant leaders', such as chief executives, religious leaders, and politicians, rather than 'close' or 'nearby leaders', such as individuals' immediate bosses. Two issues are relevant here. Firstly, Shamir (1995) has shown that 'social distance' affects notions of leadership. When Israeli students were asked to describe the characteristics of a 'close' and a 'distant' leader whom they regarded as charismatic, both similarities and significant differences were detected. 'Distant' charismatic leaders were characterized as having rhetorical skills, an ideological orientation and sense of mission, as being persistent and consistent, and as not conforming to social pressures – descriptions which are typically reflected in the 'new paradigm' models. In contrast, 'close' charismatic leaders were more frequently viewed as sociable, open and considerate of others, with a sense of humour and high level of expertise in their field, as being highly dynamic and active, having an impressive physical appearance and perceived as intelligent, as setting high performance standards for themselves and their followers, and as original or unconventional in their behaviour. In the main these characteristics are not emphasized in 'new paradigm' models.

Secondly, Alimo-Metcalfe and Alban-Metcalfe (2001) point out that one important aspect of new paradigm models is an emphasis on the importance of followers' attitudes and feelings towards the leader. However, these have usually been ignored in studies of leader characteristics. Since leadership is ultimately a social process (Bass, 1998; Conger, 1998), followers' perceptions of leadership might be a better arbiter of what constitutes leadership in a boss, rather than researchers' observations of distant leaders.

Thus, Alimo-Metcalfe and Alban-Metcalfe (2001) elicited over 2000 constructs of 'nearby' leadership from over 150 managers (approximately equal numbers of males and females) at middle to top levels in two principal public sector organizations in the United Kingdom, using the repertory grid interviewing technique. These constructs formed the basis of a questionnaire, distributed to over 600 organizations, with individuals asked anonymously to rate their current or a previous boss in terms of leadership behaviours. Analysis of over 1450 responses led to the development of the Transformational Leadership Questionnaire (TLQ), which revealed a conception of transformational leadership very different from that in current US transformational models. Table 12.1 describes the dimensions in the instrument.

One major difference is that the single most important factor to emerge was 'genuine concern for others' well-being and development'. Although in some ways resembling the dimension labelled 'individualized consideration' in the Multifactor Leadership Questionnaire (MLQ), it emerged as the first, rather than the last factor in analyses of the UK questionnaire. A second notable difference was an emphasis in the British data on 'connectedness' with stakeholders, internal and external to the

Table 12.1 *The Transformational Leadership Questionnaire© scales and alpha coefficients of internal reliability*

Genuine Concern for Others	Genuine interest in staff as individuals (17 items; alpha = .97).
Stakeholder Sensitivity and Skills	Understands, and is sensitive to, the different needs and agenda of various internal and external stakeholders (6 items; alpha = .93).
Decisive, Determined, Self-confident	Is decisive when required; self-confident (8 items; alpha = .90).
Integrity, Trusted, Honest and Open	Is trusted; makes decisions based on moral and ethical principles (9 items; alpha = .93).
Empowers, Delegates, Develops Potential	Trusts staff to take decisions/initiatives on important matters (8 items; alpha = .91).
Inspirational Networker, Promoter, Communicator	Has a wide network of links to external environment; is able to communicate effectively the vision of the organization/team (10 items; alpha = .93).
Accessible, Approachable	Is accessible to staff at all levels (6 items; alpha = .85).
Clarifies Boundaries, Keeps Others Informed, Involves Others In Decisions	Makes clear the boundaries of responsibility (5 items; alpha = .85).
Encourages Critical and Strategic Thinking	Encourages the questioning of traditional approaches to the job (7 items; alpha = .89).
Intellectual Versatility	Has the capacity to deal with a wide range of complex issues (10 items; alpha = .93).
Manages Change Sensitively and Skilfully	Maintains a balance between stability and change (7 items; alpha = .89).
Risk-taker/Entrepreneurial	Is prepared to take calculated risks to achieve important outcomes (3 items; alpha = .81).

organization. For example, creating the organization's vision is characterized in the UK research by behaviours of engaging others in the process, as opposed to the actions of a single individual. Other qualities identified are the approachability and accessibility of the leader, her/his integrity, and the importance placed by a leader on the development of leadership in others by empowering and encouraging the questioning of approaches to one's job. Whilst these latter characteristics are reflected in the MLQ, North American models tend to create a strong sense of the leader as a role model to emulate. The TLQ also portrays the leader as someone to respect and trust, but it combines these features with a sense of her/his own humanity, humility and vulnerability, which are to a large extent absent from US models. A further significant difference is the greater complexity of the range of factors that emerged. Nine scales were identified in the TLQ, compared with three factors in Bass's model. Finally, a different tenor emerges from the UK conception of transformational leadership. It is far less 'heroic' in flavour than US models; indeed, it resembles more closely the notion of 'leader as servant', espoused several decades ago by Greenleaf (1970).

It is not clear to what extent differences between US models of leadership and the model represented by the Transformational Leadership Questionnaire are attributable to differences between cultures or in the methodology employed. In the latter respect, the British study is characterized by: (1) adoption of a grounded theory approach; (2) being based on followers' perceptions of their immediate boss, rather than the perceptions of researchers and others; (3) use of data collected from managers and professionals in middle to top positions; (4) involvement of a significant proportion of females, as well as males, in the research; and (5) being conducted in the public sector. Research currently underway to develop a private-sector version of the TLQ may answer at least the question of generalizability.

Thus, while the TLQ study reinforces the notion that there are cultural differences as well as similarities in notions of leadership, the 'new paradigm' has led to a revitalization of research interest in the field. It serves to emphasize the importance of followers' perspectives of leadership far more than was the case in earlier research.

Leadership versus Management Revisited

The distinction between transformational and transactional leadership relates directly to the distinction drawn earlier between leaders and managers (Hunt, 1996). Thus, transformational leadership is coming to be equated with leadership itself; transactional leadership with closed-ended, relatively static management. The complementarity of leadership and management is illustrated in Table 12.2, based on Kotter (1990).

Consistent with this kind of distinction, some writers, notably Zaleznik (1993), have maintained that leaders and managers are different kinds of people; indeed, that they are of a 'different psychological type' from each

Table 12.2 *Comparison of leadership and management (adapted from Kotter, 1990)*

Activity	Leadership	Management
Agenda creation	*Establishing direction:* Developing future vision. Articulating the vision in a way to inspire others.	*Planning-budgeting:* Developing detailed strategic plans. Allocating resources.
Human resource development for achievement	*Aligning people:* Enthusing others to join in achieving the vision. Creating teams that understand and are engaged in developing the vision and means to achieve it.	*Organizing/staffing:* Developing planning and staffing structures, aims and objectives. Providing policies and procedures for guidance, and monitoring systems.
Execution	*Motivating/inspiring:* Energizing staff to overcome barriers to change by inspiring, maintaining positive expectations, valuing and developing.	*Controlling/ problem-solving:* Detailed monitoring of results. Identifying deviations, organizing corrections.
Outcomes	*Tends to produce:* Change, often dramatic. Potential for effective change.	*Tends to produce:* Order/predictability, efficiency. Results expected by stakeholders.

other and have different orientations to work. Zaleznik argued that managers tend to view work as an enabling process involving people and ideas interacting to establish strategies and to make decisions, through negotiating and bargaining coupled with use of rewards and punishments. In contrast, he wrote that, whereas managers act to limit choices, leaders work in the opposite direction, to develop fresh approaches to long-standing problems and to open issues for new options. Thus, the leader needs to project her/his ideas into images that excite people, and then develop choices that give substance to the projected images. As a consequence, leaders create excitement in work, but they also work from high-risk positions, and are often temperamentally disposed to seek out risk and danger, especially where opportunity and reward appear high. Zaleznik also believed that managers and leaders have different orientations in their relations with others, with managers relating to people according to their role in sequences of events or in decision-making, while leaders are more concerned with ideas and relate to other people in more intuitive and empathetic ways. In essence, the distinction is between a manager's attention to *how things get done*, in contrast to a leader's attention to *what events and decisions mean* to participants.

Gender and Leadership

Historically, the study of leadership has been the study of men's perceptions of the phenomenon. As a consequence, the approaches and models that have emerged have been models of leadership as construed and exhibited by men, which have then been superimposed on women, with the assumption that no differences exist. However, in reviewing the history of leadership, a number of writers have concluded that there has been a distinct masculine gender bias in its construction (Alimo-Metcalfe, 1995; Bass, 1990; Schein, 1994) and in the interpretation of findings which have compared men's and women's approaches (Jacobson and Jacques, 1990). Prior to the 1970s and equal opportunities legislation in the USA and the United Kingdom, there was little interest in the question of whether gender differences occur in the area of this chapter.

Few, if any, significant differences were found (Powell, 1993), and where found they were relatively minor, though they suggested that women were more likely to be participative and democratic in decision-making

(Eagly and Johnson, 1990) and more team-orientated (Ferrario, 1994). However, Gilligan (1982) made the point that the differences identified were a consequence of women being compared to a male norm, as opposed to a study of differences in which each gender was viewed in its own right.

It was only in the 1990s that major significant differences with respect to gender and leadership style began to emerge. Adopting the MLQ, Rosener (1990) published the findings from a US survey of female and male executives' descriptions of their leadership approach. This revealed significant differences with respect to the managers' perceived use of transformational behaviours, with women scoring higher on the use of transformational behaviours, apart from intellectual stimulation which showed no significant difference. Since Rosener's findings were based on self-report data, they might be interpreted as reflecting merely differences in what men and women perceive to be appropriate leadership behaviour. However, two independent British studies which investigated constructs of leadership held by senior female and male managers (Alimo-Metcalfe, 1995; Sparrow and Rigg, 1993) support Rosener's findings, with women in general identifying transformational components, and men in general identifying transactional ones.

Alimo-Metcalfe (1994, 1995) argued that, if the findings from these studies can be generalized to wider populations of managers, then there are very important implications for leadership selection, assessment, and development practices in organizations. Furthermore, a number of studies which have examined leadership behaviours rated anonymously by co-workers of managers as part of a 360-degree feedback process have revealed a consistent pattern. In general, women are perceived as significantly more transformational in leadership style than men, and men in general are rated as more likely to adopt a transactional or *laissez-faire* style of leadership (Bass, Avolio and Atwater, 1996).

FROM THE PRESENT TO THE FUTURE

There has been confusion about the definition of leadership, in part due to the enormous wealth of studies and the wide range of methodologies adopted. Some studies are about the characteristics of individuals who occupy formal leadership positions, while others have investigated the characteristics of those who display leadership, irrespective of whether they occupy a formal position. It is important to be aware of the distinction between the two when studying the literature.

It is also important to note from whose perspective leadership is being defined or construed. For example, in our study of transformational leadership (above) we elicited constructs of leadership from recipients of the process, emphasizing the notion of leadership as a dependent variable. Other contemporary leadership researchers have focused on studying the characteristics of those in very senior positions, who are deemed as displaying leadership by virtue of the success they have achieved (or influenced) in terms of their organization's success. In some studies, leadership is defined by a positive impact on workplace colleagues, in others by some measure of organizational success.

We have argued that it is important to distinguish between studies of 'distant' and 'nearby' leadership, but this is not to say that either is more valuable or valid than the other. Caution should be exercised in extrapolating from the findings of one kind of study to another, and in applying data from either source in personnel selection processes and in the development of leadership at all levels in an organization. Caution should also be exercised when applying a model of leadership derived from one population to different ethnic and cultural groups (Den Hartog *et al.*, 1999). The literature will be enriched by investigating leadership from the perspective of diversity, rather than by judging a closeness of fit to a predetermined 'norm'.

Further research is needed in relation to moderators of leadership effectiveness (Gronn, 1999), such as organizational context, and the personality and attitudes of 'followers', as well as their race, ethnicity, gender and age. Attention should also be paid to the combination of leader and follower characteristics, as factors influencing leadership effectiveness.

SUMMARY

Leadership is traditionally described as a goal-directed process, which occurs within a group context and involves influencing others. It is essentially open-ended in nature, and enables organizations not only to cope with change but also to be proactive in shaping their future. In contrast, management, with which leadership is sometimes confused, is essentially closed-ended, and aims at the perpetuation of existing structures and processes. Leadership and management are both necessary if an organization is to succeed, and may best be regarded as complementary to each other.

Research into leadership focused initially on personal traits, before moving on to study behaviours and then to examine ways in which leadership behaviour can be affected by situational factors. In more recent approaches, a distinction has been drawn between 'transformational leadership', which corresponds to leadership as such, and 'transactional leadership' which corresponds to management. Models of transformational leadership place emphasis on the role of the leader as someone who 'manages meaning' and defines organizational reality by articulating an organization's mission and the values which will support it.

The literature in general lacks clarity in defining 'leadership', sometimes employing the term in studies of people in leadership roles and at other times defining it as an outcome measure of effectiveness. Leadership research has been based almost exclusively on samples of white, male managers, with conclusions generalized to the whole population, irrespective of gender or cultural or ethnic background. A new, gender-inclusive instrument is available to measure transformational leadership, reflecting a 'leader as servant' rather than an 'heroic' model of leadership.

FURTHER READING

It is particularly important to adopt a critical approach to reading in this area and to question some of the generalizations that are made. We would recommend that, as far as possible, primary sources be obtained, or at least texts which provide details of original studies. Wright's (1996) book deserves special mention here, together with those of Hunt (1996) and Northouse (2001) and the writings of Bryman (1992, 1996). All of those provide full and readable summaries of leadership research and the development of thinking, as well as introducing a healthy critical perspective. Finally, the collections of writings edited by Rosenbach and Taylor (1993) and Davidson and Burke (1994) contain some interesting chapters, including the rarely discussed, yet increasingly important, subject of between-individual diversity in leadership. Interested readers may also wish to consult the journal *Leadership Quarterly* and *www.leadershipfoundationsuk.com*, *www.tlq360.com*, *www.lrdl.co.uk* and *www.shlgroup.com*.

REFERENCES

Alban-Metcalfe, R. J. and Alimo-Metcalfe, B. (2000a). An analysis of the convergent and discriminant validity of the Transformational Leadership Questionnaire. *International Journal of Selection and Assessment, 8*, 158–75.

— and Alimo-Metcalfe, B. (2000b). The Transformational Leadership Questionnaire (TLQ-LGV): A convergent and discriminant validity study. *Leadership and Organization Development Journal, 21*, 280–96.

Alimo-Metcalfe, B. (1994). Gender bias in the selection and assessment of women in management. In M. J. Davidson and R. Burke (Eds.), *Women in Management: Current Research Issues*. London: Paul Chapman.

— (1995). An investigation of female and male constructs of leadership and empowerment. *Women in Management Review, 10*, 3–8.

— and Alban-Metcalfe, R. J. (2001). The development of a new transformational leadership questionnaire. *Journal of Occupational and Organizational Psychology, 74*, 1–27.

Avolio, B. J., Bass, B. M. and Jung, D. I. (1999). Re-examining the components of transformational and transactional leadership using the Multifactor Leadership Questionnaire. *Journal of Occupational and Organizational Psychology, 72*, 441–62.

Bass, B. M. (1985). *Leadership and Performance Beyond Expectations*. New York: The Free Press.

— (1990). *Bass and Stodgill's Handbook of Leadership: Theory, Research and Applications* (third edition). New York: The Free Press.

— (1997). Does the transactional–transformational leadership paradigm transcend organizational and national boundaries? *American Psychologist, 52*, 130–39.

— (1998). *Transformational Leadership: Industrial, Military, and Educational Impact*. Mahwah, NJ: Erlbaum.

— and Avolio, B. J. (1990). *Transformational Leadership Development: Manual for the Multifactor Leadership Questionnaire*. Palo Alto, CA: Consulting Psychologists Press.

— and Avolio, B. J. (1993). Transformational leadership: A response to critiques. In M. M. Chemers and R. Ayman (Eds.), *Leadership Theory and Research*. London: Academic Press.

—, Avolio, B. J. and Atwater, L. (1996). The transformational and transactional leadership of men and women. *International Review of Applied Psychology*, 45, 5–34.

Blake, R. R. and Mouton, J. S. (1964). *The Managerial Grid*. Houston, TX: Gulf.

Bryman, A. (1992). *Charisma and Leadership in Organizations*. London: Sage.

— (1996). Leadership in organizations. In S. R. Clegg, C. Hardy and W. R. Nord (Eds.), *Handbook of Organizational Studies* (pp. 276–92). London: Sage.

Burns, J. M. (1978). *Leadership*. New York: Harper & Row.

Church, A. H. and Waclawski, J. (1995). The effects of personality orientation and executive behaviour on subordinate perception of workgroup enablement. *The International Journal of Organizational Analysis*, 3, 20–51.

Conger, J. A. (1989). *The Charismatic Leader: Behind the Mystique of Exceptional Leadership*. San Francisco, CA: Jossey-Bass.

— (1998). Qualitative research as the cornerstone methodology for understanding leadership. *Leadership Quarterly*, 9, 107–21.

— and Kanungo, R. N. (1988). Behavioural dimensions of charismatic leadership. In J. A. Conger and R. N. Kanungo (Eds.), *Charismatic Leadership: The Elusive Factor in Organizational Effectiveness* (pp. 78–97). San Francisco, CA: Jossey-Bass.

Davidson, M. J. and Burke, R. J. (1994). *Women in Management: Current Research Issues*. London: Paul Chapman Publishing.

De Pree, M. (1993). Followership. In W. E. Rosenbach and R. L. Taylor (Eds.), *Contemporary Issues in Leadership Research* (pp. 137–40). Oxford: Westview Press.

Den Hartog, D. N., House, R. J., Hanges, P. J., Ruiz-Quintanilla, S. A., Dorfman, P. W. and Associates (1999). Culture specific and cross-culturally generalizable implicit leadership theories: Are attributes of charismatic/transformational leadership universally endorsed? *Leadership Quarterly*, 10, 219–56.

Eagly, A. H. and Johnson, B. T. (1990). Gender and leadership style: A meta-analysis. *Psychological Bulletin*, 108, 233–56.

Ferrario, M. (1994). Women as managerial leaders. In M. J. Davidson and R. J. Burke (Eds.), *Women in Management: Current Research Issues* (pp. 110–25). London: Paul Chapman.

Fiedler, F. E. (1967). *A Theory of Leadership Effectiveness*. New York: McGraw-Hill.

Fisher, B. M. and Edwards, J. E. (1988). Consideration and initiating structure and their relationships with leadership effectiveness: A meta-analysis. Best papers proceedings, Academy of Management. Anheim, CA. 201–5.

Gilligan, C. (1982). *In a Different Voice*. Cambridge, MA: Harvard University Press.

Graen, G. B. and Uhl-Bien, M. (1995). Relationship-based approaches to leadership: Development of leader–member exchange (LMX) theory over twenty-five years: Applying a multi-level multi-domain perspective. *Leadership Quarterly*, 6, 219–47.

Greenleaf, R. K. (1970). *The Servant as Leader*. San Francisco, CA: Jossey-Bass.

Gronn, P. (1995). Greatness re-visited: The current obsession with transformational leadership. *Leading and Managing*, 1, 14–27.

Gronn, R. (1999). Substituting for leadership: The neglected role of the leadership couple. *Leadership Quarterly*, 10, 41–62.

Hersey, P. and Blanchard, K. H. (1982). *The Management of Organizational Behavior: Utilizing Human Resources* (fourth edition). Englewood Cliffs, NJ: Prentice-Hall.

House, R. J. (1977). A 1976 theory of charismatic leadership. In J. G. Hunt and L. L. Larson (Eds.), *Leadership: The Cutting Edge* (pp. 189–207). Carbondale, IL: Southern Illinois University Press.

Hunt, J. G. (1996). *Leadership: A New Synthesis*. Newbury Park, CA: Sage.

Jacobson, S. W. and Jacques, R. (1990). Of knowers, knowing and the known: A gender framework for revisioning organizational and management scholarship. Presentation to the Academy of Management Annual Meeting, 10–12 August, San Francisco.

Kotter, J. P. (1990). *A Force for Change*. London: The Free Press.

Lee, C. (1993). Followership: The essence of leadership. In W. E. Rosenbach and R. L. Taylor (Eds.), *Contemporary Issues in Leadership Research* (pp. 113–21). Oxford: Westview Press.

Lord, R. G., De Vader, C. L. and Alliger, G. M. (1986). A meta-analysis of the relation between personality traits and leadership perceptions: An application of validity generalization procedures. *Journal of Applied Psychology*, 71, 402–10.

Mann, R. D. (1959). A review of the relationships between personality and performance in small groups. *Psychological Bulletin*, 56, 4, 241–70.

Northouse, P. (2001). *Leadership: Theory and Practice* (second edition). London: Sage.

Peters, T. and Waterman, R. (1982). *In Search of Excellence*. London: Harper Row.

Powell, G. (1993). *Women and Men in Management* (second edition). Newbury Park, CA: Sage.

Rosenbach, W. E. and Taylor, R. L. (Eds.) (1993). *Contemporary Issues in Leadership*. Oxford: Westview Press.

Rosener, J. (1990). Ways women lead. *Harvard Business Review*, November/December. 119–25.

Sashkin, M. (1988). The visionary leader. In J. A. Conger and R. N. Kanungo (Eds.), *Charismatic Leadership: The Elusive Factor in Organizational Effectiveness* (pp. 122–60). San Francisco, CA: Jossey-Bass.

Schein, V. (1994). Managerial sex typing: A persistent and pervasive barrier to women's opportunities. In M. J. Davidson and R. J. Burke (Eds.), *Women in Management: Current Research Issues* (pp. 41–52). London: Paul Chapman.

Shamir, B. (1995). Social distance and charisma: Theoretical notes and an exploratory study. *Leadership Quarterly*, 6, 19–47.

Sparrow, J. and Rigg, C. (1993). Job analysis: Selecting for the masculine approach to management. *Selection & Development Review*, 9, 2, 5–8.

Stodgill, R. M. (1974). *A Handbook of Leadership: A Survey of Theory and Research*. New York: Free Press.

— (1948). Personal factors associated with leadership: A survey of the literature. *Journal of Psychology*, 25, 35–71.

Vroom, V. H. and Yetton, P. N. (1973). *Leadership and Decision Making*. Pittsburgh, PA: University of Pittsburgh Press.

Wright, P. L. (1996). *Managerial Leadership*. London: Routledge.

Zaleznik, A. (1993). Managers and leaders: Are they different? In W. E. Rosenbach and R. L. Taylor (Eds.), *Contemporary Issues in Leadership* (pp. 36–56). Oxford: Westview Press.

13

Team Working

John Cordery

Recent accounts of success and failure in organizations point to the importance of teamwork in promoting organizational effectiveness (e.g., O'Reilly and Pfeffer, 2000). The rapid rise in the popularity of teams in work organizations (Lawler, Mohrman and Ledford, 1995; Gittleman, Horrigan and Joyce, 1998; Devine, Clayton, Philips, Dunford and Melner, 1999) has, in turn, resulted in psychologists devoting an increasing amount of effort to studying the factors that shape their effectiveness (Ilgen, 1999). Within work organizations, the term 'team' is used to refer to a group of people organized around an interdependent set of tasks, and who share responsibility for achieving particular outcomes (Guzzo and Dickson, 1996). More than that, a team and its members interact with others (e.g., clients, customers, suppliers, or other members of the organization), in ways that reflect the perspectives, interests and goals of the team as a whole. Given this definition, this chapter seeks to provide an introductory overview of current knowledge about the causes of effectiveness in teams.

TYPES OF TEAM

The first point to note is that not all teams in organizations serve the same purpose. A useful taxonomy covering different types of teams is provided by Cohen and Bailey (1997) who identify four broad team types. *Work teams* are teams that are charged with the responsibility for performing tasks associated with core activities of an organization, such as manufacturing products, delivering services or technical maintenance. Membership of such teams tends to be relatively stable and the role of the team is clearly defined in terms of a set of formal operational responsibilities. Examples of this type of team would be a mining crew or a customer service unit within airline reservations. *Parallel teams*, on the other hand, are teams which operate alongside the formal organizational structure. They typically draw their membership from a range of work areas (and from formal work teams), and are used for on-going problem-solving and innovation, such as required by total quality management and continuous improvement strategies, or as a mechanism for employee involvement in organizational decision-making. Examples of parallel teams include quality circles (Griffin, 1988), process improvement teams (Fairfield-Sonn, 1999) and employee involvement teams (Magjuka and Baldwin, 1991).

Project teams, sometimes called task forces, are created for a specific purpose and are time-delimited. Once they have generated their specific output (e.g., a plan for the development of a new product, or the implementation of an organizational change programme), they cease to be. Members then either return to their more permanent organizational units, or become part of another project team. Project teams are generally composed of people with a range of expertise, and this cross-functionality increases their capacity to respond to complex problems under time pressure.

The fourth category of teams are *management teams*. Such teams include all those responsible for the overall performance of a business unit, and so there may be several management teams within the one organization. At the top of the organization, the executive management team is that which is responsible for developing corporate strategy, and for the overall performance of the organization.

POTENTIAL BENEFITS OF TEAM WORKING

Why create teams in the first instance? In theory, working in teams may be seen as offering a range of advantages over working alone (Katzenbach and Smith, 1993). From a performance perspective, a team can frequently bring a greater range and depth of knowledge and expertise to bear on a complex task than any individual team member. Furthermore, teams encourage flexibility in responding to rapidly shifting task demands, as members are required to co-operate (e.g., in adjusting to fluctuations in workflows or to member absences). Teams encourage members to work for the collective good, as opposed to their own self-interest, and, to the extent that they are cross-functional and externally focused, can help foster a climate of collaboration across organizational boundaries. Teams also provide the opportunity for synergistic outcomes; innovative and creative decisions that result from bringing together a diversity of ideas and experience. To the extent that they provide increased opportunities for direct participation by employees in decision-making, teams can also improve the implementation of decisions, improve task motivation, and enhance work involvement and organizational commitment. From the perspective of employee well-being, teams provide the opportunity for satisfaction of a range of important needs, by means of increased participation in decision-making and valued social engagement (within the team, and across organizational boundaries). Both social support and the opportunity for involvement in decision-making provided by team work may help enhance job satisfaction and reduce occupational stress.

This is the plus-side of team working. However, it is worth pointing out that teams frequently fail to realize these potentials in organizational settings (Hackman, 1990). To understand why this is the case, it is necessary to examine the specific aspects that contribute to and detract from team effectiveness.

FACTORS INFLUENCING TEAM EFFECTIVENESS

Our way of thinking about team effectiveness has been greatly influenced by the work of McGrath (e.g., McGrath, 1984), whose Input–Process–Output (IPO) perspective on team functioning underpins most models of team effectiveness developed over the past two decades (e.g., Herold, 1978; Gladstein, 1984; Hackman, 1987; Sundstrom, DeMeuse and Futrell, 1990; Cohen and Bailey, 1997), and which provides a useful diagnostic framework for identifying potential causes of team effectiveness (or the lack thereof). Within this framework, *inputs* to team functioning include such factors as task characteristics (e.g., autonomy) and interdependence, the composition of the group, and the organizational context. Because they can frequently be directly manipulated by the organization, input variables are sometimes referred to as 'team design' variables. *Process* refers to the sorts of interactions that occur within the team, and between team members and other groups, customers and the like; for example, communication, conflict, decision-making, and problem-solving. Finally, team inputs and processes give rise to a range of *outputs*. Outputs may be conceptualized as performance outcomes (e.g., levels of output or quality), member affective reactions (e.g., job satisfaction, commitment, stress) and behavioural outcomes (e.g., absenteeism, turnover). It is important to distinguish between these different team outputs, because the underlying causes of each may be different. For example, a team may generate high levels of output, but its members may also experience high levels of workload-related stress. Team outputs may also have a reciprocal influence on inputs. For example, a team that performs poorly may attract closer supervision and a reduction in team autonomy.

Five main 'clusters' of input and process factors have been found to predict team effectiveness (Campion, Medsker and Higgs, 1993), and these are depicted in Figure 13.1.

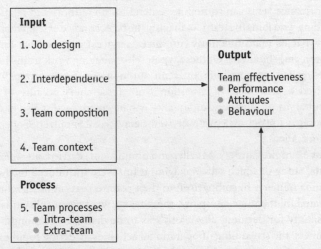

Fig. 13.1 *Clusters of variables influencing team effectiveness*

Job Design

The first of the input variables, 'job design', includes a range of features of jobs that have been shown to have a positive impact on employee motivation and satisfaction (e.g., Hackman and Oldham, 1980). These include how varied the tasks are, whether the tasks performed impact significantly on others, whether the team is involved in producing or delivering a complete product or service, and whether continuous direct feedback on performance is available to the team. However, the job design feature most referred to in the team effectiveness literature is autonomy, the opportunity a team is given to make its own decisions (Banker, Field, Schroeder and Sinha, 1996; see also Chapter 11). Campion and colleagues' (1993) study of financial services teams found that reported autonomy exhibited the most consistent correlation with measures of productivity and employee satisfaction, as well as with managerial judgements of team effectiveness. Work teams at the low end of the autonomy continuum are given little influence in decision-making about the work process, whilst 'self-managing teams' and 'self-designing teams' are given high levels of discretion in relation to the 'what, how and when' of work performance. This can sometimes extend to full authority in relation to deciding who joins the team, managing the performance of team members and what its main functions (products, services) and external linkages (customers) should be. Of these types, self-managing work teams (sometimes called autonomous or semi-autonomous work groups) have received a great deal of attention from researchers because of their potential for productivity and quality enhancement, whilst also having a favourable impact on employee well-being (e.g., Spreitzer, Cohen and Ledford, 1999).

For example, Cordery, Mueller and Smith (1991) carried out an experimental study in which self-managing teams were introduced into a new alumina refinery. In comparison to their counterparts at other refineries operated by the same company, these teams were given substantial responsibility for deciding how work was to be distributed amongst team members, the scheduling of operational activities, ordering supplies, and training other team members. Over a period of twelve months it was found that team members reported higher levels of job satisfaction and organizational commitment than employees in more traditional working arrangements. Paradoxically, levels of absenteeism and staff turnover were also higher for the self-managing teams, an outcome explained in terms of the particular demands associated with getting used to high levels of self-management in a new plant.

A useful illustration of the potential for productivity gains arising out of self-managing work teams is provided by a study by Batt (1999). She looked at the performance of 330 customer service representatives in a large telecommunications company that trialled the use of self-managing teams. She found that participation in self-managing teams was associated with sustained improvements of nearly 10 per cent in sales per employee, though this advantage increased to 17 per cent where self-managing teams operated with the support of advanced information systems that encouraged group goal setting, problem solving and learning.

The finding that job design factors exert a powerful influence on motivation and job satisfaction within teams has led to the notion of team empowerment. An empowered team (Kirkman and Rosen, 2000) is one in which the work performed by the team is designed to provide high levels of self-management to the team (*autonomy*), work that is perceived as valuable and worthwhile (*meaning*), as well as providing timely and accurate knowledge of the impact of the work on others (*impact*). A fourth characteristic of empowered teams, *potency*, is defined as the extent to which the team has a positive collective belief in its own performance capabilities. Teams that feel empowered in this way have been shown to experience positive outcomes, in terms of team member intrinsic job satisfaction and performance (Kirkman and Rosen, 1999).

Interdependence

The second category of 'input' variables that predict team effectiveness are those that reflect varying types of interdependence amongst members of the team. *Task interdependence* is the extent to which team members are required to interact in the performance of the task, whilst *outcome interdependence* is the extent to which important outcomes such as rewards received by one individual are dependent on the performance of others in the group. In a study of teams of service technicians, Wageman (1995) found that task and outcome interdependence were associated with different aspects of team effectiveness, the former influencing cooperation amongst team members, whilst the latter influenced task motivation. This research suggests that interdependence between tasks performed by those making up the team is a prerequisite for effective team working. Some jobs (for example, an airline reservations clerk) require little collaboration with others for the job to get done effectively and efficiently. The study also suggests that one way to increase effort expenditure within a team is to ensure that rewards relate to the performance of the team as a whole, not just individuals within it.

Team Composition

The make-up of the team is another important contributor to team effectiveness. (See the overview in Figure 13.1.) Not surprisingly, studies have demonstrated that teams composed of members with high levels of technical knowledge and skill tend to perform better than those with less well qualified members (Tannenbaum, Salas and Cannon-Bowers, 1996). However, researchers have also identified a range of knowledge, skills and abilities (KSAs) that contribute to effective functioning within team roles, namely conflict resolution, collaborative problem-solving, communication, goal setting and performance management, and planning and task coordination KSAs (Stevens and Campion, 1994; 1999).

In addition to ability factors, it appears that the personality make-up of the team affects its performance (Neuman and Wright, 1999). For example, it has been found that the more team members rate highly on the personality dimensions of agreeableness and conscientiousness, the better the team as a whole seems to perform (Barrick, Stewart, Neubert and Mount, 1998). With respect to some traits, having a balance of personalities in a team appears important. For example, too many highly extroverted team members may impact negatively on performance (Neuman, Wagner and Christiansen, 1999).

This notion of balance and complementarity in team composition is at the core of Belbin's team role theory (Belbin, 1981; 1993). This theory identifies a number of possible team roles, with team effectiveness enhanced to the extent that (a) these roles are strongly represented amongst the various team members, and (b) an appropriate mix of roles exists. For example, two of the possible team roles are those of 'plant' (someone who is creative, imaginative and unorthodox and who solves difficult problems) and 'monitor/evaluator' (someone who is sober and strategic, who sees all options, and judges accurately). Belbin (1993) would argue that the roles of plant and monitor/evaluator are complementary and counterbalancing within teams. For example, the plant helps the team generate new ideas and options for dealing with problems, while the monitor/evaluator helps the team when it must decide which ideas and options are best to pursue. Other complementary and counter-balancing roles (Fisher, Hunter and Macrosson, 1998) are those of 'chairman' (a good communicator and delegator) and 'shaper' (someone who thrives on pressure, challenging and driving the team).

One of the most researched aspects of team composition relates to the demographic characteristics of team members. Three main perspectives exist on how demographic diversity might influence group performance (Williams and O'Reilly, 1998). The first of these holds that, as team membership becomes more heterogeneous, so the amount and availability of information that the group can draw on in decision-making and problem-solving will also increase (an additive resources view). This would suggest that the impact of demographic diversity on performance is positive, particularly when it comes to innovative and creative problem-solving.

A second perspective on the impact of demographic composition on team effectiveness draws on the work of social identity/self-categorization theorists (Hogg and Terry, 2000). In contrast to the additive resources view, this perspective suggests that increasing the diversity of demographic characteristics within teams may be associated with conditions where perceived differences between sub-groups (e.g., those based on categories of gender, ethnicity) are exaggerated by individual team members, leading to increased conflict, communication problems, less cohesiveness, and increased member dissatisfaction.

The final paradigm for examining the impact of demographic composition on team effectiveness involves looking at similarity/attraction processes (Pfeffer, 1983). The essence of this approach is the principle of 'homophily', the tendency for individuals to like and be attracted to those others who share similar backgrounds, attitudes, values, and other demographic values (Ibarra, 1993). These processes of attraction are proposed to have positive impacts on communication and cohesiveness within groups whose members share demographic characteristics (Tsui, Egan and O'Reilly, 1992).

So what has research been able to conclude about the impact of demographic diversity on team effectiveness? In general, the conclusion must be that diversity in teams frequently has negative effects on team effectiveness. Of the various demographic variables studied, including age, gender, ethnicity and job tenure, only functional diversity (the extent to which a group possesses diverse knowledge, skills and abilities) has consistently been found to be positively related to both performance and satisfaction (Williams and O'Reilly, 1998).

Finally, how does the team size influence effectiveness? Unfortunately, research indicates that there is no clear cut answer to this question (Hill, 1982). On the one hand, increasing the number of people in a team is likely to increase the range of resources (KSAs) available to the team. However, one might also expect that communication and coordination would become more difficult as the team becomes larger. These counter-vailing forces may, in turn, result in an inverted U-shaped relationship between size and performance (Cohen and Bailey, 1997).

Team Context

The fourth set of determinants of team effectiveness (see Figure 13.1) arises out of the context within which the team operates. Hyatt and Ruddy (1997) carried out round-table discussions with members of customer service teams and their managers to establish the main factors that teams saw as facilitating or blocking their performance. They then designed a survey-based instrument to measure these factors, and administered it to 100 other work teams. They found that the extent to which groups reported receiving support, in the form of resources, information, feedback and recognition from their manager and the organization, was the most powerful predictor of how quickly the teams responded to a · customer request. In another study of manufacturing and service teams across four different organizations, Kirkman and Rosen (1999) found that levels of empowerment experienced by teams (i.e., autonomy, impact, meaning and potency) were also dependent on the existence of a range of supportive human resource management practices. These included the extent that the team was permitted to select new members, was rewarded as a team (rather than as individuals), evaluated the performance of its own team members, and was cross-trained. Cross-training occurs when a team member is trained to take on the tasks, roles and responsibilities of other team members. One way in which cross-training improves team functioning is by facilitating the development of shared mental models (see later), which helps coordination and communication within teams (Cannon-Bowers, Salas, Blickensderfer and Bowers, 1998).

Kirkman and Rosen (1999) also found a significant correlation between levels of empowerment experienced by a team and behaviours exhibited by the team's external leader. Most teams, even those classified as self-managing, have a manager or supervisor outside the team with formal authority to direct the team and its members. Such leaders have considerable opportunity to regulate inputs to the team. For example, they are in a position to directly control how much autonomy team members are given (Manz and Sims, 1987), and may resist transferring responsibility for decision-making to teams because of concerns about the impact on their own job security and performance (Stewart and Manz, 1997). First-level supervisors and managers also play an important boundary-management role in helping the team gain access to resources and rewards, thereby shaping the context for team performance. They may also intervene directly to help teams deal with conflict, to coach performance, and to provide reward and recognition to team members.

The context for teamwork may also include broader features of the organizational environment, such as the degree of turbulence or uncertainty associated with its product-market and the technological systems it operates. Studies indicate that the potential for teams to be given autonomy is greater in more uncertain or turbulent industries (Haleblian and Finkelstein, 1993), and it can also be argued that self-managing work teams are likely to be maximally effective where production systems are characterized by high levels of operating uncertainty; for example where advanced manufacturing technology is deployed (Wall, Cordery and Clegg, 2002). Similarly, team effectiveness has been found to vary with the complexity and newness of the product being developed in project teams (Emmanualides, 1993), and the climate of the organization to influence inputs such as autonomy (Gupta, Dirsmith and Fogarty, 1994).

Team Processes

Referring back to Figure 13.1, the fifth category of influences on team effectiveness relates to what actually goes on within the team. Interactions between team members and between members and individuals/groups external to the team are strongly predictive of both team performance and member satisfaction (Guzzo and Dickson, 1996). Of those process variables traditionally studied, cohesiveness is an overarching term used to describe levels of interpersonal attraction and liking within the team (West, Borrill and Unsworth, 1998). Although strong cohesion can be dysfunctional for teams (it may, for example, encourage groupthink, a phenomenon discussed later in the chapter), generally speaking cohesiveness is positively associated with both performance and member satisfaction (Mullen and Copper, 1994). However, as Xie and Johns (2000) found, cohesiveness potentially interacts with other aspects of team functioning to impact on behaviour. In their study of absenteeism amongst manufacturing employees in the People's Republic of China, they observed that highly cohesive work groups had lower absenteeism rates than low cohesive groups where there were weak group norms regarding absence behaviour. Norms are standards or rules of behaviour which are applied to team members (Feldman, 1984). Xie and Johns (2000) found that where these norms were strong, absenteeism was higher for the high cohesive group. They explained this in terms of highly cohesive work groups colluding in maintaining levels of absenteeism in order to balance both production demands and the needs of individual members for days off.

The power of a cohesive team to increase the salience of norms and adherence to them is well illustrated in Barker's (1993) study of self-managing work teams. In the teams he studied, strong values-based behavioural norms developed that were enforced by the team through peer pressure, rewards and sanctions. Barker (1993) referred to the process of enforcing adherence to those norms as concertive control, observing that, whilst such processes could be beneficial as far as team performance was concerned, the consequences of resisting that control for individual team members could involve humiliation and a reduction in individual autonomy.

Related to the concept of cohesiveness is the concept of trust (Fukuyama, 1995; Kramer, 1999). Kirkman, Jones and Shapiro (2000) found that concerns about whether other team members could be trusted provided some of the most powerful reasons for employees resisting entering into teamwork arrangements. An employee's trust in other team members is likely to be related to perceptions of their benevolence and integrity but also to perceived competence (Mayer, Davis and Schoorman, 1995). Thus, it is possible to like other team members, but not to be willing to risk putting one's faith in their technical ability to carry out the task effectively. Recent research has indicated that the likelihood of productive group processes is enhanced by high levels of interpersonal trust amongst team members (Dirks, 1999).

Decision-making processes within teams have been subject to considerable scrutiny over the years (Guzzo and Salas, 1995). In general, decision-making by groups is improved when they develop constructive norms regarding problem solving. That is, they do not shy away from raising and discussing problems. Alper, Tjosvold and Law (1998) have identified the importance of constructive controversy, the willing consideration of opposing positions, as a precursor to team effectiveness. Thus, although too much intra-group conflict can hinder team effectiveness, conflict can also give rise to beneficial outcomes. Effective decision-making is also related to the extent to which groups go about scanning and reviewing their environment in order to identify and classify problems (West et al., 1998).

Another set of process variables that has been found to exercise considerable influence on team performance is related to motivational processes occurring within teams. Two main strands of research exist. The first deals with collective efficacy beliefs, the aggregate belief of team members that their team can be effective in performing their overall job (Prussia and Kinicki, 1996). This construct has also been referred to as group potency (Guzzo, Yosst, Campbell and Shea, 1993) and group efficacy (Gibson, 1999), and has been found to be a significant predictor of performance in work teams (Little and Madigan, 1997). As noted earlier, a team's belief in its own capabilities is one of the elements contributing to team empowerment.

Motivation in teams has also been linked to cultural differences in self concept, and in particular to the degree to which team members possess individualistic or collectivistic cultural values. For example, it has been found that people from countries where individualistic values predominate will tend to resist teamworking more (Kirkman, Jones and Shapiro, 2000), and will be less influenced by group-focused training (Earley, 1994) than those from societies characterized by more collectivistic values. In a study that focused on psychological well-being at work, Schaubroeck, Lam and Xie (2000) compared the effects of job demands on job-related anxiety, depression, absenteeism and turnover intentions for teams of bank tellers in the United States of America and Hong Kong. It was found that a strong collective belief in the team's ability reduced the impact of job demands on stress for team members with more collectivistic values (Hong Kong) but not for those possessing more individualistic values (USA).

Much as it does at the individual level, group goal-setting is held to have a motivating influence on team performance (O'Leary-Kelly, Martocchio and Frink, 1994). Teams who have set collective goals will tend to expend more effort, persist longer in pursuit of that goal, and achieve higher levels of performance than groups without goals. This effect is enhanced by the team's commitment to that goal, and by the provision of feedback on team performance (Sawyer, Latham, Pritchard and Bennett, 1999). Goal acceptance has also been found to moderate the relationship between cohesiveness and team performance (Podsakoff, MacKenzie and Ahearne, 1997).

A recent development in the study of intra-team processes has involved the study of shared mental models. These are knowledge structures that the team as a whole uses in order to help it understand and react to its operating environment. Mathieu, Heffner, Goodwin, Salas and Cannon-Bowers (2000) have identified four types of shared mental model. The first of these is related to technology and equipment, and represents knowledge that team members share about the operating characteristics of equipment and systems, and associated procedures. Second, there is shared knowledge related to the job or task, such as the best way to approach given tasks, or likely constraints on effective task performance. Third, team members can have shared cognitions relating to the way the team interacts, such as an understanding of the various member roles and responsibilities, patterns of interaction, and information flows. Finally, there is team-specific shared knowledge about the values, attitudes, knowledge, and skills of team members. The importance of such shared models is that they can exert a positive impact on performance under demanding and dynamic task conditions (Cannon-Bowers, Salas and Converse, 1993). For example, knowing who possesses particular information or technical skill within the team can optimize the allocation of tasks. It can also mean that employees know where to seek information and advice when they encounter a particular problem.

Finally, whilst the majority of research into leadership and teams has focused on external leadership (see later), the importance of leadership processes *within* teams is increasingly being recognized. Emergent leaders are those who are not vested with formal authority, but who nevertheless exert considerable influence over other team members' behaviour. Taggar, Hackett and Saha (1999) found that teams performed best when all team members exhibited leadership behaviours and that leadership emergence within a team was related to the general cognitive ability and personality characteristics (conscientiousness, extroversion and emotional stability) of individual team members. The emergence of leaders within groups has also been linked to the composition of the group, in particular group gender composition (Eagly and Karau, 1991), with men tending to emerge as leaders in groups more often than women (Karakowsky and Siegel, 1999).

Whilst many intra-team processes contribute positively towards team effectiveness, there are a number of common process 'pathologies' that may arise within teams and which will have a negative impact. One of the most commonly referred to phenomena associated with team decision-making is that of *groupthink* (Janis, 1982; Esser, 1998), a term used to denote poor decision-making by groups that can arise when the group is highly cohesive, where there is strong leadership, where decision-making procedures are unstructured, where pressure to find a solution is intense, where member homogeneity is high, and where the group is insulated or closed off from external sources of information or influence.

It has been argued that design factors associated with self-managing teams will mean that they are particularly prone to groupthink (Moorhead, Neck and West, 1998). For example, such teams are typically insulated from experts, are homogeneous in terms of skills, and may lack formal impartial leadership. Ways of avoiding groupthink within teams include the development of effective normative rules for decision-making, fostering open and participative leadership practices, rotating team members to increase external contact, investing in technical and self-leadership training, and ensuring that individual autonomy is encouraged by group norms and selection procedures (Moorhead *et al.*, 1998).

A second frequently observed process pathology associated with teams is that of *social loafing*, where some individuals are observed to reduce their work effort when members of a group. Researchers have observed that where it is difficult to isolate an individual's contribution to the group task, as in many teams, motivation to expend effort is typically reduced below levels that would have been observed where an individual's performance contribution can be directly identified (Karau and Williams, 1993). There appears to be a growing consensus that social loafing is best understood within an expectancy-values framework of motivation (Shepperd and Taylor, 1999), such that its control will depend on ensuring that individuals value the outcome(s) of team performance (valence), perceive a relationship between their own performance and that of the team (expectancy), and also believe that performance is linked to those valued outcomes (instrumentality).

It is commonly believed that the likelihood of extreme or risky decisions is increased within a team environment, a phenomenon referred to as *risky shift* or group polarization (Isenberg, 1986). Risky shift arises partly through processes of social comparison, where moderate members of the group feel motivated to accept more socially attractive extreme positions held by others in the group (Friedkin, 1999), and partly as a result of a team developing a strong belief in its ability (Whyte, 1998).

It must also be recognized that teams do not necessarily develop effective processes immediately on formation, nor are the same processes important at all stages in the performance of the team task. The work of Tuckman (Tuckman, 1965; Tuckman and Jensen, 1977) suggests that groups progress through five stages of development. In the first, called 'forming', team members become oriented to each other, the team task, and the nature of their dependence on other team members. Next comes 'storming', a stage characterized by intragroup conflict, where team members begin to assert themselves in an attempt to shape the goals and functioning of the team. In the third stage, 'norming', rules for regulating team functioning are agreed on, paths to performance agreed, and the group begins to develop effective team processes, such as cohesion, communication and collaboration. Next, there is 'performing', where team members carry out their respective components of the overall team task. Finally, for temporary teams at least, comes 'adjourning', where members of the group disengage from each other and from the collective task.

A contrasting perspective on team development sees group progress towards task completion as a 'punctuated equilibrium', rather than an orderly progression through stages (Gersick, 1988; 1989). Gersick (1988) studied project teams, those formed for a specific purpose and operating for a fixed time period. She found that, no matter the history of the team or the length of time allocated it to complete its task, all groups spent precisely half the time allotted in a state of *inertia*. In this first phase, very little work progress was made. However, at the halfway point in the team's life, a *transition* took place with a dramatic alteration to internal and external patterns of activity. This halfway point was then followed by a second period of equilibrium, in which plans that were developed at the transition were executed. Finally, approaching deadlines brought about another transitional burst of activity, referred to as *completion*, during which behaviour patterns within the group shifted once more as the group struggled to complete its task on time.

Gersick's work is interesting, because it helps us understand the important role played by time in team functioning. For example, effective completion of the group task may depend on team members developing a shared expectation concerning deadlines for task completion (in terms of team mental models). It may also be that the most effective point at which to place team development interventions that require a major shift in group functioning, the point at which they will be resisted least, might be the mid-point of the team's life-span. Gersick's work is also useful in pointing out that group processes (norms, routines, etc.) change as the group gains experience and as it encounters different problems over time (McGrath, 1991; Weldon, 2000).

Finally, researchers have begun to examine the way in which teams interact with their environment. Extra-team processes are interactions between team members and other groups and individuals (external agents) outside the team. Teams that are responsible for performing complex/uncertain tasks and which are dependent on people outside the team for resources, information and support are held to perform better when they develop processes for facilitating interactions with those external agents (Ancona and Caldwell, 1992). In a study of high technology manufacturing teams, Bailey (2000) found that the quality of extra-team processes (external communication, external conflict, and external task dependence), largely involving interactions with supervisors and engineers, predicted team performance.

OVERVIEW OF THE INPUT–PROCESS–OUTPUT MODEL

The input–process–output model that was outlined earlier in this chapter has at its core the assumption that certain inputs (e.g., team composition, job design, interdependence, and context) and processes (e.g., motivation, constructive controversy) determine a team's overall effectiveness. The model has stimulated a great deal of research, thereby advancing considerably our understanding of the main contributors to effectiveness.

However, it should also be pointed out that there are a number of deficiencies associated with the model. In the main, these relate to its breadth and lack of specificity. As a result, it is hard to test the model in its entirety, and one is never entirely sure that the subset of variables measured in any particular study are those actually responsible for observed team effectiveness. The model is also low on specificity about relationships amongst input and process variables. Some inputs, for example autonomy, may influence team performance and member satisfaction through their impact on group processes (e.g., motivation or decision-making), but they may also conceivably influence these outcomes directly. The model offers no clear indication as to which input factors influence outputs directly and which have their impact indirectly through group processes. Such criticisms have led to calls for the development of more 'fine-grained' models of team effectiveness, where relationships between factors of interest (e.g., inputs and processes) are specified with greater precision (Goodman, Ravlin and Schminke, 1987).

Finally, there is a need for studies which evaluate the utility of the theory in a predictive sense, for example by assessing the impact of controlled changes to inputs in real organizational settings. The most comprehensive studies using the framework (e.g., Campion *et al.*, 1993) have all been correlational, a design factor that severely limits the extent to which causal relationships can be inferred.

IMPLICATIONS FOR PRACTICE

Despite the model's limitations, the body of research carried out by psychologists under its auspices is such that we can now offer some fairly specific guidelines for creating high performing teams in organizations, teams whose members are likely to feel empowered to perform well and who are also satisfied in their work (e.g., Katzenbach and Smith, 1993; Wageman, 1997). First, teams need to have a clear and engaging direction, a shared understanding of what they exist to achieve. Next, teams function better in situations where the tasks they perform represent a real team task. That is, each member is necessarily dependent on others in the team in order to be able to perform their own job effectively and to achieve valued rewards, and they are held collectively responsible for team outputs. Third, teams must be given sufficient authority to make meaningful decisions as a team about the way work is performed and to vary work strategies as they see fit. A high performing team needs to have in place processes that lead to it setting specific and challenging goals for the performance of the team as a whole.

It is also important to build a range of skills and competencies into the team, and to cross-train team members in order to encourage co-operative and helping behaviour. Teams must be large enough to generate flexibility in task allocation and to encompass a diversity of knowledge and skills, but not so large as to make it difficult for team members to communicate and coordinate their activities. An effective team is likely to have a significant proportion of rewards distributed on the basis of the performance of the team as a whole, rather than the performance of individuals. High performing teams will also have developed a constructive set of strategy norms that encourage open-ended discussion, experimentation with new ideas and active problem-solving. Finally, teams require a supportive organizational context, such that team excellence is recognized and rewarded, and information needed for planning teamwork, material resources and technical advice and training are available when needed.

SUMMARY

The proliferation of teams in organizations has created a sense of urgency in the quest to discover more about the factors that underlie their effectiveness. Whilst many benefits can be proposed for teamwork, the experience of many organizations is that these are either difficult to achieve or hard to sustain. In studying team effectiveness in organizations, researchers have been guided by a framework that distinguishes between inputs to the team and interactive processes within the team as antecedents of team effectiveness. In this way, many powerful influences on team effectiveness have been identified, a good number of which lie within the ambit of managerial control. It is thus possible to develop prescriptive guidelines for practice when implementing teams. However, many questions still remain unanswered, such as the precise psychological mechanisms that give rise to observed relationships between team inputs and team outputs, and how teams function in different organizational settings. Increasingly, researchers are looking to develop more complex models of team functioning, models that take greater account of the organizational environment within which teams operate and which are able to guide more precisely their design and implementation.

FURTHER READING

A useful starting point for developing a more in-depth understanding of factors influencing team effectiveness is Hackman's (1987) chapter entitled 'The design of effective work teams'. This could be supplemented by reading the influential study by Campion, Medsker and Higgs (1993) and Ilgen's (1999) article in *American Psychologist*. Comprehensive overviews of the research literature on team effectiveness are provided by Guzzo and Dickson (1996), Cohen and Bailey (1997) and in the *Handbook of Work Group Psychology* (West, 1996). A more practical perspective on team effectiveness is provided by Katzenbach and Smith (1993) in *The Wisdom of Teams* and Mohrman, Cohen and Mohrman in *Designing Team-based Organizations: New Forms for Knowledge Work* (1995). Kirkman and Rosen's (2000) article provides an excellent overview of contemporary approaches to team empowerment. More information on how self-managing work teams operate can be found in Wageman's (1997) article on introducing self-managing teams in Xerox, and in the studies by Cordery, Mueller and Smith (1991) and Batt (1999).

REFERENCES

Alper, S., Tjosvold, D. and Law, K. (1998). Interdependence and controversy in group decision making: Antecedents to effective self-managing teams. *Organizational Behavior and Human Decision Processes*, 74, 33–52.

Ancona, D. G. and Caldwell, D. F. (1992). Bridging the boundary: External activity and performance in organizational teams. *Administrative Science Quarterly*, 37, 634–65.

Bailey, D. E. (2000). Modelling work group effectiveness in high-technology manufacturing environments. *IIE Transactions*, 32, 361–8.

Banker, R. D., Field, J. M., Schroeder, R. G. and Sinha, K. K. (1996). Impact of work teams on manufacturing performance: A longitudinal field study. *Academy of Management Journal*, 39, 867–90.

Barker, J. R. (1993). Tightening the iron cage: Concertive control in self-managing teams. *Administrative Science Quarterly*, 38, 408–37.

Barrick, M. R., Stewart, G. L., Neubert, M. J. and Mount, M. K. (1998). Relating member ability and personality to work-team processes and team effectiveness. *Journal of Applied Psychology*, 83, 377–91.

Batt, R. (1999). Work organization, technology and performance in customer service and sales. *Industrial and Labor Relations Review*, 52, 539–64.

Belbin, R. M. (1981). *Management Teams: Why They Succeed or Fail*. London: Heinemann.

— (1993). *Team Roles at Work*. Oxford: Butterworth Heinemann.

Campion, M. A., Medsker, G. J. and Higgs, A. C. (1993). Relations between work group characteristics and effectiveness: Implications for designing effective work groups. *Personnel Psychology*, 46, 823–50.

Cannon-Bowers, J. A., Salas, E., Blickensderfer, E. and Bowers, C. A. (1998). The impact of cross-training and workload on team functioning: A replication and extension of initial findings. *Human Factors*, 40, 92–101.

—, Salas, E. and Converse, S. A. (1993). Shared mental models in expert team decision making. In N. J. Castellan (Ed.), *Current Issues in Individual and Group Decision Making* (pp. 221–46). Hillsdale, NJ: Erlbaum.

Cohen, S. G. and Bailey, D. E. (1997). What makes teams work: Group effectiveness research from the shop floor to the executive suite. *Journal of Management*, 23, 239–90.

Cordery, J. L., Mueller, W. S. and Smith, L. M. (1991). Attitudinal and behavioural effects of autonomous group working: A longitudinal field study. *Academy of Management Journal*, 34, 464–76.

Devine, D. J., Clayton, L. D., Philips, J. L., Dunford, B. B. and Melner, S. B. (1999). Teams in organizations: Prevalence, characteristics, and effectiveness. *Small Group Research*, 30, 678–711.

Dirks, K. T. (1999). The effects of interpersonal trust on work group performance. *Journal of Applied Psychology*, 84, 445–55.

Eagly, A. H. and Karau, S. J. (1991). Gender and the emergence of leaders: A meta-analysis. *Journal of Personality and Social Psychology*, 60, 685–710.

Earley, P. C. (1994). Self or group? Cultural effects of training on self efficacy and performance. *Administrative Science Quarterly*, 39, 89–117.

Emmanualides, P. A. (1993). Towards an integrative framework of performance in product development projects. *Journal of Engineering and Technology Management*, 10, 363–92.

Esser, J. K. (1998). Alive and well after 25 years: A review of groupthink research. *Organizational Behavior and Human Decision Processes*, 73, 116–41.

Fairfield-Sonn, J. W. (1999). Influence of context on process improvement teams: Leadership from a distance. *Journal of Business and Economic Studies*, 5, 47–66.

Feldman, D. C. (1984). The development and enforcement of group norms. *Academy of Management Review*, 9, 47–53.

Fisher, S. G., Hunter, T. A. and Macrosson, W. D. K. (1998). The structure of Belbin's team roles. *Journal of Occupational and Organizational Psychology*, 71, 283–8.

Friedkin, N. E. (1999). Choice shift and group polarization. *American Sociological Review*, 64, 856–75.

Fukuyama, F. (1995). *Trust: The Social Virtues and the Creation of Prosperity*. New York: Free Press.

Gersick, C. J. G. (1988). Time and transition in work teams: Toward a new model of group development. *Academy of Management Journal*, 31, 9–41.

— (1989). Marking time: Predictable transitions in task groups. *Academy of Management Journal*, 32, 274–309.

Gibson, C. B. (1999). Do they do what they believe they can? Group efficacy and group effectiveness across tasks and cultures. *Academy of Management Journal*, 42, 138–52.

Gittleman, M., Horrigan, M. and Joyce, M. (1998). 'Flexible' work practices: Evidence from a nationally representative survey. *Industrial and Labor Relations Review*, 52, 99–115.

Gladstein, D. L. (1984). Groups in context: A model of task group effectiveness. *Administrative Science Quarterly*, 29, 499–517.

Goodman, P. S., Ravlin, E., and Schminke, M. (1987). Understanding groups in organizations. In B. M. Staw and L. Cummings (Eds.), *Research in Organizational Behavior* (vol. 9, pp. 121–73). Greenwich, CT: JAI Press.

Griffin, R. W. (1988). Consequences of quality circles in an industrial setting: A longitudinal assessment. *Academy of Management Journal, 31*, 338–58.

Gupta, P. P. Dirsmith, M. W. and Fogarty, T. J. (1994). Coordination and control in a government agency: Contingency and institutional theory perspectives on GAO audits. *Administrative Science Quarterly, 39*, 264–84.

Guzzo, R. A. and Salas, E. (Eds.) (1995). *Team Effectiveness and Decision Making in Organizations*. San Francisco: Jossey-Bass.

—, Yost, P. R., Campbell, R. J. and Shea, G. P. (1993). Potency in groups: Articulating a construct. *British Journal of Social Psychology, 32*, 87–106.

— and Dickson, M. W. (1996). Teams in organizations: Recent research on performance and effectiveness. *Annual Review of Psychology, 47*, 307–38.

Hackman, J. R. (1987). The design of effective work teams. In J. W. Lorsch (Ed.), *Handbook of Organizational Behavior* (pp. 316–41). Englewood Cliffs, NJ: Prentice-Hall.

— (Ed.) (1990). *Groups that Work (and those that Don't)*. San Francisco: Jossey-Bass.

— and Oldham, G. R. (1980). *Work Redesign*. Reading, MA: Addison-Wesley.

Haleblian, J. and Finkelstein, S. (1993). Top management team size, CEO dominance, and firm performance: The moderating roles of environmental turbulence and discretion. *Academy of Management Journal, 36*, 844–63.

Herold, D. M. (1978). Improving the performance effectiveness of groups through a task-contingency selection of intervention strategies. *Academy of Management Review, 3*, 315–25.

Hill, G. W. (1982). Group versus individual performance: Are n + 1 heads better than one? *Psychological Bulletin, 91*, 517–39.

Hogg, M. A. and Terry, D. J. (2000). Social identity and self-categorization processes in organizational contexts. *Academy of Management Review, 25*, 121–40.

Hyatt, D. and Ruddy, T. M. (1997). An examination of the relationship between work group characteristics and performance: Once more into the breach. *Personnel Psychology, 50*, 553–85.

Ibarra, H. (1993). Personal networks of women and minorities in management: A conceptual framework. *Academy of Management Review, 18*, 56–87.

Ilgen, D. (1999). Teams embedded in organizations: Some implications. *American Psychologist, 54*, 129–39.

Isenberg, D. J. (1986). Group polarization: A critical review and meta-analysis. *Journal of Personality and Social Psychology, 50*, 1141–51.

Janis, I. L. (1982). *Groupthink: A Study of Foreign Policy Decisions and Fiascos* (second edition). Boston, Mass.: Houghton Mifflin.

Karakowsky, L. and Siegel, J. P. (1999). The effects of proportional representation and gender orientation of the task on emergent leadership behavior in mixed-gender work groups. *Journal of Applied Psychology*, *84*, 620–31.

Karau, S. J. and Williams, K. D. (1993). Social loafing: A meta-analytic review and theoretical integration. *Journal of Personality and Social Psychology*, *65*, 681–706.

Katzenbach, J. R. and Smith, D. K. (1993). *The Wisdom of Teams: Creating the High Performance Organization*. Boston, MA: Harvard Business School Press.

Kirkman, B. L., Jones, R. G. and Shapiro, D. L. (2000). Why do employees resist teams? Examining the 'resistance barrier' to work team effectiveness. *International Journal of Conflict Management*, *11*, 74–92.

— and Rosen, B. (2000). Powering up teams. *Organizational Dynamics*, *28*, 48–66.

— and Rosen, B. (1999). Beyond self-management: Antecedents and consequences of team empowerment. *Academy of Management Journal*, *42*, 58–75.

Kramer, R. M. (1999). Trust and distrust in organizations: Emerging perspectives, enduring questions. *Annual Review of Psychology*, *50*, 569–88.

Lawler, E. E., III, Mohrman, S. A. and Ledford, G. E. (1995). *Employee Involvement and Total Quality Management: Practices and Results in Fortune 1000 Companies*. San Francisco: Jossey-Bass.

Little, B. L. and Madigan, R. M. (1997). The relationship between collective efficacy and performance in manufacturing work teams. *Small Group Research*, *28*, 517–34.

McGrath, J. E. (1984). *Group Interaction and Performance*. Englewood Cliffs, NJ: Prentice-Hall.

— (1991). Time, interaction, and performance (TIP): A theory of groups. *Small Group Research*, *22*, 147–74.

Magjuka, R. J. and Baldwin, T. T. (1991). Team-based employee involvement programs: Effects of design and administration. *Personnel Psychology*, *44*, 793–812.

Manz, C. C. and Sims, H. P., Jr. (1987). Leading workers to lead themselves: The external leadership of self-managing work teams. *Administrative Science Quarterly*, *32*, 106–28.

Mathieu, J. E., Heffner, T. S., Goodwin, G. F., Salas, E. and Cannon-Bowers, J. A. (2000). The influence of shared mental models on team process and performance. *Journal of Applied Psychology*, *85*, 284–93.

Mayer, R. C., Davis, J. H. and Schoorman, F. D. (1995). An integrative model of organizational trust. *Academy of Management Review*, *20*, 709–34.

Mohrman, S. A., Cohen, S. G. and Mohrman, A. M. (1995). *Designing Team-based Organizations: New Forms for Knowledge Work*. San Francisco: Jessey Bass.

Moorhead, G., Neck, C. P. and West, M. S. (1998). The tendency toward defective decision making within self-managing teams: The relevance of groupthink for the 21st century. *Organizational Behavior and Human Decision Processes*, *73*, 327–51.

Mullen, B. and Copper, C. (1994). The relation between group cohesiveness and performance: An integration. *Psychological Bulletin*, 115, 210–27.

Neuman, G. A., Wagner, S. H. and Christiansen, N. D. (1999). The relationship between work-team personality composition and the job performance of teams. *Group and Organization Management*, 24, 28–45.

— and Wright, J. (1999). Team effectiveness: Beyond skills and cognitive ability. *Journal of Applied Psychology*, 84, 376–89.

O'Leary-Kelly, A. M., Martocchio, J. J. and Frink, D. D. (1994). A review of the influence of group goals on group performance. *Academy of Management Review*, 37, 1285–1302.

O'Reilly, C. A. and Pfeffer, J. (2000). *Hidden Value: How Great Companies Achieve Extraordinary Results with Ordinary People*. Boston, MA: Harvard Business School Press.

Pfeffer, J. (1983). Organizational demography. In B. Staw and L. Cummings (Eds.), *Research in Organizational Behavior* (vol. 5, pp. 299–357). Greenwich, CT: JAI Press.

Podsakoff, P. M., MacKenzie, S. B. and Ahearne, M. (1997). Moderating effects of goal acceptance on the relationship between group cohesiveness and productivity. *Journal of Applied Psychology*, 82, 974–83.

Prussia, G. E. and Kinicki, A. J. (1996). A motivational investigation of group effectiveness using social cognitive theory. *Journal of Applied Psychology*, 78, 61–72.

Sawyer, J. E., Latham, W. R., Pritchard, R. D. and Bennett, W. R. (1999). Analysis of work group productivity in an applied setting: Application of a time series panel design. *Personnel Psychology*, 52, 927–67.

Schaubroeck, J., Lam, S. and Xie, J. L. (2000). Collective efficacy versus self-efficacy in coping responses to stressors and control: A cross cultural study. *Journal of Applied Psychology*, 85, 512–25.

Shepperd, J. A. and Taylor, K. M. (1999). Social loafing and expectancy-value theory. *Personality and Social Psychology Bulletin*, 25, 1147–58.

Spreitzer, G. M., Cohen, S. G. and Ledford, G. E. (1999). Developing effective self-managing work teams in service organizations. *Group and Organizational Management*, 24, 340–66.

Stevens, M. J. and Campion, M. A. (1994). The knowledge, skill, and ability requirements for teamwork: Implications for human resource management. *Journal of Management*, 20, 503–30.

— and Campion, M. A. (1999). Staffing work teams: Development and validation of a selection test for teamwork settings. *Journal of Management*, 25, 207–28.

Stewart, G. L. and Manz, C. C. (1997). Understanding and overcoming supervisor resistance during the transition to employee empowerment. In W. A. Pasmore and R. W. Woodman (Eds.), *Research in Organizational Change and Development* (vol. 10, pp. 169–96). Greenwich, CT: JAI Press.

Sundstrom, E., DeMeuse, K. P. and Futrell, D. (1990). Work teams: Applications and effectiveness. *American Psychologist, 45*, 120–33.

Taggar, S., Hackett, R. and Saha, S. (1999). Leadership emergence in autonomous work teams: Antecedents and outcomes. *Personnel Psychology, 52*, 899–926.

Tannenbaum, S. I., Salas, E. and Cannon-Bowers, J. A. (1996). Promoting team effectiveness. In M. A. West (Ed.), *Handbook of Work Group Psychology* (pp. 503–29). Chichester: John Wiley & Sons.

Tsui, A., Egan, T. and O'Reilly, C. A. (1992). Being different: Relational demography and organizational attachment. *Administrative Science Quarterly, 37*, 549–79.

Tuckman, B. (1965). Developmental sequence in small groups. *Psychological Bulletin, 63*, 384–99.

— and Jensen, M. (1977). Stages of small-group development. *Group and Organizational Studies, 2*, 419–27.

Wageman, R. (1995). Interdependence and group effectiveness. *Administrative Science Quarterly, 40*, 145–80.

— (1997). Critical success factors for creating superb self-managing teams. *Organizational Dynamics, 26*, 37–49.

Wall, T. D., Cordery, J. L. and Clegg, C. W. (2002). Empowerment, performance and operational uncertainty: A theoretical integration. *Applied Psychology: An International Review, 51*, 146–69.

Weldon, E. (2000). The development of product and process improvements in work groups. *Group and Organizational Management, 25*, 244–68.

West, M. A. (Ed.) (1996). *Handbook of Work Group Psychology*. Chichester: John Wiley & Sons.

—, Borrill, C. S. and Unsworth, K. L. (1998). Team effectiveness in organizations. In C. L. Cooper and I. T. Robertson (Eds.), *International Review of Industrial and Organizational Psychology* (vol. 13, pp. 1–48).

Whyte, G. (1998). Recasting Janis's groupthink model: The key role of collective efficacy in decision fiascoes. *Organizational Behavior and Human Decision Processes, 2*, 185–209.

Williams, K. Y. and O'Reilly, C. A. (1998). Demography and diversity in organizations. *Research in Organizational Behavior, 20*, 77–140.

Xie, J. L. and Johns, G. (2000). Interactive effects of absence culture salience and group cohesiveness: A multi-level and cross-level analysis of work absenteeism in the Chinese context. *Journal of Occupational and Organizational Psychology, 73*, 31–52.

14

Human Resource Management and Business Performance

Stephen Wood and Toby Wall

Human resource management (HRM) is a term used to represent that part of an organization's activities concerned with the recruitment, development and management of its employees. As such, HRM embraces many of the practices considered separately elsewhere in this book, including personnel selection (Chapter 5), learning and training (Chapter 6), career development (Chapter 7), the design of jobs (Chapter 11) and team working (Chapter 13). It also encompasses other practices such as harmonization (minimizing status differentials between employees), communication, participation, appraisal of performance and incentive payment systems.

Research on HRM has involved not only psychologists, but also management scientists, employee relations specialists and economists. This area of enquiry differs from traditional psychological work in two main ways. First it involves characterizing practices as a whole, whereas much research by psychologists has examined specific components of HRM separately. The second difference is that the unit of analysis of HRM is the organization, not the individual employee. When studying personnel selection, job design or other components of human resource management, psychologists' emphasis has been on predicting the performance of individual workers, but for others investigating HRM, the focus is the relationship of those practices to organizational-level performance. Taken together, these differences mean the field of HRM is distinctive in its concern to assess personnel practices collectively in terms of their effects on, for example, company productivity, profit or labour turnover.

Most work on human resource management, however, is driven by three more specific and stronger assumptions. The first, which came to prominence in the 1980s through the work of several popular (e.g., Peters and Waterman, 1982) and academic (e.g., Lawler, 1986; Walton, 1985) writers, is the idea that competitive advantage stems as much from developing the human as the technical side of business. As the term HRM denotes, the clear message was that employees should be considered as a resource rather than a cost. The emphasis moved towards HRM practices that could enhance the involvement of employees in their work and the organization more generally, in the belief that this would harness people's energies and commitment towards organizational goals. Various terms were coined to reflect this perspective, including high involvement (Lawler, 1986), high commitment (Walton, 1985), and high performance management (Lawler, Mohrman and Ledford, 1995; Huselid, 1995). We use high involvement management (HIM) to cover them all.

The second guiding view, as Wood (1999) makes explicit, is that the common element underlying high involvement management is the contrast with a control or Taylorist style of human resource management based on a narrow and tightly specified definition of jobs (see Chapter 11). To illustrate the difference between the two approaches, HIM assumes that gains will accrue from: investment in training and development rather than limiting training costs to meet immediate needs, as in the control model; empowering employees (through enrichment, introducing self-managing teams, and encouraging subordinate participation) rather than simplifying and closely specifying job requirements; and ensuring good communications up and down the organization rather than limiting information to a need-to-know basis. Much of the justification for the association of these practices with high involvement arises from work psychology, and in particular job redesign theory, which also took the Taylorist control model as its benchmark against which improvements would be judged.

The third assumption is that the practices comprising high-involvement management are mutually reinforcing. For example, teamworking without good communication, or empowerment without training, is expected to have little effect. The basic implication is that there are synergistic relationships between the practices, so that the whole is greater than the sum of its parts.

Following the focus on high involvement practices, a body of research emerged in the 1990s that aimed to test their assumed superior performance over the control forms of human resource management. Our aim in this chapter is to critically review that evidence and consider the issues to which it gives rise. We concentrate our review on the studies which have been most widely cited.

KEY STUDIES OF HRM AND ORGANIZATIONAL PERFORMANCE

Arthur's Steel Mill Study

Arthur (1994) conducted one of the first studies of the relationship between human resource management and organizational performance, using a sample of thirty small US steel mills. He collected data on HRM practices and organizational performance by questionnaires completed by human resource managers. Analysis proceeded in two stages. He first examined HRM in cach mill in terms of a commitment-control distinction. Those mills classified as exhibiting a 'commitment' approach were characterized by employee involvement in managerial decisions, formal participation programs, training in group problem-solving and an emphasis on skilled work. This contrasted with the mills where management used a 'control' approach, in which the above practices were less developed and whose aim Arthur (1994) saw as being to: 'reduce direct labor costs, or improve efficiency, by enforcing employee compliance with specified rules and procedures and basing employee rewards on some measurable output criteria' (p. 672). Fourteen of the mills fell into the commitment category, with the remaining sixteen being of the control type.

The second stage was to determine whether there was any difference in performance between the two types of mill. To this end three outcome measures were used: labour efficiency (average number of labour hours required to produce one ton of steel); scrap rate (tons of raw steel required to produce one ton of finished product) and labour turnover (number of shop floor workers who had left in the last year). Analyses of the data, controlling statistically for such factors as plant size and degree of trade union membership, showed that the mills identified as having commitment HRM systems had higher labour efficiency and a lower scrap rate than those with control-oriented systems. In addition they had only half as much labour turnover.

In this study then a clear link between a set of human resource management practices and mill performance was found. However, since both sets of measures were taken at the same time, the direction of causality is unclear. The results could mean the practices led to improved performance, but equally it may be that better performing mills were more able to invest in training, skilled employees and the other aspects of human resource management.

Ichniowski and Colleagues' Steel Finishing Lines Study

The study by Arthur was based on questionnaire measures of both HRM practices and performance, and looked simply at the cross-sectional relationship between the two types of measure. Ichniowski, Shaw and Prennushi (1997) investigated the same industrial sector in the USA, but in more detail since they included a longitudinal component. They focused on thirty-six steel finishing lines selected because of their similarity in terms of technology and product.

Ichniowski and colleagues obtained details of human resource management practices from site visits involving interviews with a variety of personnel, including human resource managers, operations managers, superintendents, line workers and trade union representatives, together with inspection of documents (e.g., personnel files and collective bargaining agreements). From that information they categorized the lines into four types. 'HRM system 1', the most 'innovative', corresponded to the notion of high involvement management. Mills of that kind had all of the following features: systematic personnel selection procedures, teamwork, job rotation, off-the-job training, long-term employment security, systematic communication practices and incentive schemes rewarding quality as well as quantity. In contrast, 'HRM System 4' lines had none of the above characteristics. Lines classified as 'System 2' or 'System 3' occupied intermediate positions between the two, having some but not all of the practices to different degrees, with the former having the greater proportion.

Ichniowski and colleagues obtained monthly performance data for all the steel finishing lines, resulting in a data set of 2190 observations (an average of sixty per line). Their main performance measure was 'uptime' (i.e., the amount of time the line was in operation) because this directly determines output and was comparable across lines. Additionally, they inspected each line to assess technological features likely to affect uptime, identifying up to twenty-five possible factors (e.g., age of the line, degree of computerization). They controlled for these factors in subsequent statistical analyses.

The results showed that uptime was highest for the lines with the full complement of high involvement HRM practices (System 1), progressively reduced through Systems 2 and 3, and was lowest for System 4, which had none of the practices. Moreover, the lines that changed during the period when performance data were collected showed corresponding improvements in uptime (these changes being either System 4 to 3 or 3 to 2 since none went from 2 to 1, or in the reverse direction). The difference in uptime between the HRM systems was only a few percentage points, which might at first appear inconsequential, despite being statistically significant. However, estimates of the financial implications for a sample line showed that this level of improvement could result in an annual gain of over $1 million.

Given the evidence of both a cross-sectional and change-based association between the human resource management systems and line performance, this study increases the confidence that we can place on a causal interpretation. However, it should be noted that the System 1 lines (the full high involvement ones) were all new lines that began operation with the full complement of innovative HRM practices. This confuses the issue slightly, though is compensated for by the fact that the expected gradual reduction of performance effects is evident across the lines with the other systems.

MacDuffie's Study of Car Assembly Plants

MacDuffie (1995) conducted a study of sixty-two car assembly plants from across the world, though the majority were based in the USA, Europe and Japan. Information on management practices within the plants was collected by questionnaire, supported by site visits or telephone contact. Three sets of practices were identified, each measured by its own index.

The first two indices, the Work System Index and the Human Resource

Policies Index, together can be taken as representing the high involvement management approach. The Work Systems Index was designed to reflect the nature of shop floor work in terms of: the level of shop floor participation; the number of production-related suggestions received from employees; the extent of teamwork; the extent of job rotation; and the degree of production worker involvement in quality tasks. The HRM Policies Index covered the extent to which: staff selection was based on an openness to learning, rather than on previous relevant experience; status barriers between managers and workers were minimized (i.e., harmonization across employee grades); training was provided both for new recruits and experienced production staff; and pay levels were dependent on plant performance (this representing a contrast with Arthur's treatment of incentive pay as part of the control approach).

The third measure, the Use of Buffers Index, was designed to represent the extent to which plants had adopted lean production, an American expression for the use of Japanese management methods which aim to work on a just-in-time basis using total quality management procedures (Womack, Jones and Roos, 1990). The buffers index had three components: the average number of vehicles held in work-in-progress buffers as a percentage of output; the average level of components kept in stock; and the percentage of space dedicated to final repair. The lower the scores on each of these, the more lean is the plant. The logic of the lean production approach is to make vehicles on demand, rather than for delivery into stock, and to purchase components solely for immediate use so as to minimize the amount of money tied up in materials and finished goods. Success in running such systems is held to depend on flexible and involved employees, so that when a problem arises they can deal with it themselves. The novelty of MacDuffie's study is that he tested both the effects of high involvement management and whether this affects successful lean production.

MacDuffie took two indices of plant performance: labour productivity, defined as the labour hours to build a vehicle; and quality, the number of defects per vehicle. Labour productivity was made comparable across plants by adjustments to reflect differences due to the complexity of the product (e.g., number of components and welds). Data on quality were obtained from an independent industry-wide report.

Using multivariate regression techniques to control for other possible factors affecting plant performance (e.g., degree of automation and mix of models produced), MacDuffie found that all three sets of practices were associated with productivity. Similarly, the Work System Index and the Human Resource Policies Index (the two HRM measures) were associated with superior quality, though the Use of Buffers index was not. Thus high involvement management was associated both with fewer build hours and fewer defects per vehicle.

MacDuffie addressed the hypothesis that the success of high involvement management accrues from using an appropriate combination of practices, by testing whether the relationship between the Use of Buffers Index and performance was stronger in those plants with more developed Work Systems and Human Resource Policies. The results showed there was such a synergistic effect among the three sets of practices for productivity, but not for quality.

This study adds further weight to those of Arthur and of Ichniowski and colleagues, particularly as it involves another manufacturing setting and includes plants from outside the USA. As with Arthur's study, however, it is not conclusive, in that it only shows a cross-sectional association between the two types of variable, not that the HRM and lean production practices were necessarily the reason for the performance benefits.

Huselid's Large-scale Study of HRM and Business Performance

The previous studies were relatively small-scale and each encompassed only a single business sector. Huselid's (1995) contribution extends the field by looking at a greater diversity of enterprises and by using alternative performance criteria.

Huselid studied a set of 968 organizations with over 100 employees by sampling firms from all major industries in the US private sector. He obtained information on the firms' human resource management practices by a questionnaire mailed to the senior human resources professional in each organization. Analysis of the relationships among those practices showed they fell into two groups. The first, which he labelled 'Employee Skills and Organizational Structures', covered the extent of use of a range of practices such as information sharing, formal job analysis, attitude surveys, training and selection testing, participation in quality circles or labour-management teams, and incentive payment schemes. The second group, labelled 'Employee Motivation', included performance appraisal, staff recruitment and promotion on merit (rather than on seniority).

Huselid then examined how use of these two sets of practices was related to labour turnover (measured by a single item in the questionnaire), productivity (sales per employee) and corporate financial performance. Corporate financial performance was measured in two ways: one was a capital-market index of the value of the firm (Tobin's q, reflecting current and potential profitability); the other was an accountancy-based index of gross rate of return on capital (GRATE, reflecting past profit). The considerable diversity in the sample, which covered firms from thirty-five sectors ranging from manufacturing to banking, meant that it was necessary to control statistically for a wide variety of factors that could confound the findings, such as firm size and sector.

The findings showed that Employee Motivation, but not Employee Skills and Organizational Structures, was significantly associated with productivity. Those companies placing more emphasis on staff recruitment, appraisal and promotion on merit had greater sales per employee. But neither measure of HRM practices had a significant relationship with labour turnover.

The analyses for corporate financial performance revealed that the Employee Skills and Organizational Structures index of HRM practices showed a weak relationship with the market value (Tobin's q), but a much more substantial one with the gross rate of return on assets (GRATE). Thus companies providing more employee participation and training had better performance. In contrast the Employee Motivation index showed a substantial relationship with market value, but not with gross rate of return on assets.

As the author comments, these 'results are not entirely unambiguous' (Huselid, 1995, p. 662). The observed patterns are not consistent across outcome measures, nor are they particularly impressive in terms of the strength of the statistical relationships. However, this again does not mean they are unimportant. Indeed, Huselid calculated that for this sample of companies the effect of a one standard deviation increase in both sets of HRM practices would be an increase of $18,641 in market value and $3,814 in return on capital per employee per year. Thus without being definitive, this study further reinforces the view that HRM practices affect business performance.

Huselid and Colleagues' Study of HRM and Prospective Business Performance

Using a sample of 293 US firms from ten different sectors, Huselid, Jackson and Schuler (1997) conducted a study that represents a methodological advance on previous work in two respects. First, they examined the relationship between human resource management practices and subsequent business performance in order to determine whether HRM practices in one year predict performance in the following year. This also allowed them to examine the relationship between these practices and improvements in performance across the year. Since it is difficult to imagine how subsequent performance might determine previous HRM practices, this research design strengthens the basis for causal inference. The second advance was that the study focused not simply on the use of HRM practices, but on their effective use.

Information on human resource management within firms was obtained by questionnaire completed by senior managers, 92 per cent of whom were in HRM positions. They were asked to rate their satisfaction with 'the results currently being achieved' (Huselid *et al.*, 1997, p. 175) for individual practices. Analysis of the ratings found that there were two dimensions. One, which Huselid *et al.* labelled 'Strategic HRM Effectiveness', concerned how well the HRM function developed employees in terms, for example, of: teamwork; subordinate participation and empowerment; employee–manager communications; workforce flexibility and deployment; and management development and succession planning. The other dimension they called 'Technical HRM Effectiveness', which measured how well traditional personnel tasks were carried out, including recruitment, selection, training, performance appraisal and the administration of payment systems.

Performance was measured by the same three indices used in Huselid's (1995) earlier study that we have just discussed: productivity (sales per employee); and the two measures of profit, namely gross return on assets (GRATE) and a market value index (Tobin's q). Statistical analyses controlled for a large number of factors known to relate to performance, including firm size and sector.

The analyses revealed a positive relationship between Strategic HRM Effectiveness and subsequent firm performance for productivity and both indices of profit. There was also a relationship with change in performance across the one-year period for productivity and for the GRATE index of profit. That is to say, firms reporting more success in implementing teamwork, participation, empowerment, workforce flexibility, communications and management development were those which subsequently performed better and showed most improvements in performance. For Technical HRM Effectiveness, however, there was no statistically significant relationship with any measure of performance. Estimating the financial implications of the findings, the authors calculated that the effect of a one standard deviation improvement in a measure that combined both strategic and technical effectiveness would result in an increase of: $44,380 per employee per year for productivity; $9,673 per employee per year in cash flow; and $8,882 per employee per year in market value. As in Huselid's previous study, the statistical findings for the relationship between HRM practices and business performance were modest, but the financial implications substantial.

Patterson and Colleagues' Study of Single-Site UK Businesses

Many large organizations, including those in Huselid's studies, operate across more than one site that may have different operations and types of product. Crucially, human resource management practices can also differ across sites. Economic performance, however, is usually measured for the organization as a whole. In his first study Huselid allowed for inter-site variation in the use of some of the practices by asking for information on the proportion of employees in the organization to which the practice applied. But this is not entirely satisfactory for there is no guarantee that the sites in which the practices are most used are those contributing most to overall organizational performance. Clearly, there are many uncertainties in the relationship between HRM and performance where samples include multi-site organizations. For this reason, Patterson and his colleagues (Patterson, West, Lawthom and Nickell, 1997; Patterson, West and Wall, 2000a; 2000b) focused their research on single-site organizations, reasoning that if there were an effect of HRM on performance it should be stronger in such a sample. They also took a longitudinal approach, examining how the use of HRM practices related to subsequent performance and change over time.

The sample comprised eighty UK manufacturing firms ranging from sixty to 1200 employees. The study used an intensive process of data collection for HRM practices based on multiple interviews conducted on site. These typically involved the chief executive, the production director, the finance director and the HRM director, and were supported by examinations of relevant company documents and observation of work practices. Researchers rated the 'degree of sophistication' of each company's HRM practices, having not at that stage acquired any information about company performance, so that they would not be influenced in their perception of the practices by how well the company was doing.

The analysis revealed two groups of human resource management practices that tended to go together. The first the researchers called 'Acquisition and Development of Employee Skills', because it covered selection and recruitment, induction, training and appraisal. The other they called 'Job Design', since it included skill flexibility, job variety, job responsibility and formal teams. Other practices measured and found to be independent of the two main factors were the extent of use of quality improvement teams, systematic employee communication, harmonization, comparative pay (high or low for the geographical region) and performance-related incentive pay.

Two measures of performance were taken, namely productivity (sales per employee) and profit (per employee). The data were collected from published figures after the audit of HRM practices, and covered two periods. Prior performance was for the three years before the year of the HRM audit, and subsequent performance was for the year after the audit.

As in previous studies, the data were analysed using statistical controls to remove effects of relevant background factors (e.g., sector and company size). The researchers found that both the Acquisition and Development of Employee Skills and the Job Design indices were significantly related to subsequent performance and to change in performance. Communication, harmonization, comparative pay and incentive pay, however, had no demonstrable effects. Collectively, the HRM practices accounted for 18 per cent of the variation between companies in change in productivity and 19 per cent in change in profit. This is much larger than the effect recorded in the Huselid *et al.* (1997) study that also looked at change across companies. Patterson and his colleagues also found that Acquisition and Development of Skills and Job Design had independent effects on subsequent company productivity and profits, though their effect on profits was largely the result of their positive effects on productivity.

Like MacDuffie, Patterson and colleagues considered a number of additional non-HRM practices, and in particular the use of advanced manufacturing technology, just-in-time production and total quality management. Of these only advanced manufacturing technology showed any relationship with firm performance, the association being positive and limited to company productivity. It may be that its lack of association with profit is because the productivity gains were offset by the cost of the technology.

These results are important in showing that the relationship of HRM practices to productivity and profit is more substantial than non-HRM practices that are typically introduced in the expectation of boosting company performance; and because they suggest which aspects of HRM may be most important in promoting performance. A problem, of course, is that by focusing only on single-site manufacturing companies, the findings are not generalizable to the whole economy.

Other Relevant Studies

Several other empirical studies have supported the view that high involvement practices benefit business performance. These include: Lawler, Mohrman and Ledford's (1995, 1998) study of large US manufacturing and service companies, suggesting HRM has greater effects when coupled with total quality management initiatives; Delaney and Huselid's (1996) study of both profit and non-profit US firms; Delery and Doty's (1996) work with banks; Koch and McGrath's (1996) multi-industry study; Youndt, Snell, Dean and Lepak's (1996) longitudinal study of 97 US manufacturing plants; Hoque's (1999) investigation in the UK hotel industry, which also links effective HRM to quality initiatives; Appelbaum, Bailey, Berg and Kalleberg's (2000) study of US Steel, Apparel and Medical Instruments plants; and Guthrie's (2001) cross-sectional study of New Zealand business organizations.

We have found only three studies which fail to show a positive HRM-performance link. In Guest and Hoque's (1994) investigation of 119 UK new (green-field site) organizations, effects for high involvement HRM practices were found for reduced labour turnover and fewer disputes, but not for reported productivity. Wood and de Menezes (1998), in their analysis of data from a representative sample of UK workplaces (the 1990 Workplace Industrial Relations Survey), found that high users of high involvement practices reported better financial performance than moderate users, but not than low users. Finally, and uniquely, Wright, McCormick, Sherman and McMahan (1999), in their study of US petro-chemical refineries, found a negative relationship between high involvement HRM practices and reported performance indicators. There is no obvious explanation for this anomaly.

HRM AND PERFORMANCE: TAKING STOCK

There is no doubt that there are considerable strengths in the studies that we have reviewed. The sector-specific studies have mainly concerned manufacturing, but they have been complemented by investigations using heterogeneous samples. Research has also involved different methods and alternative indicators of performance. Across this diversity, with but a few exceptions, high involvement forms of human resource management have been found to be positively associated with organizational performance. Despite that consistency, however, the evidence should not be considered better than promising, and certainly not definitive in causal terms. The studies have both methodological and conceptual limitations. While opening up an important area of management to scientific scrutiny, viewed collectively they raise more questions than they have answered. We complete this chapter by considering some of these limitations and unresolved issues.

Methodological Limitations

Most of the studies to date suffer from one or more of three limitations. First, the majority of studies, being cross-sectional, only show an association between HRM and performance at one point in time. While such an association is expected to exist if high involvement human resource management practices do promote organizational effectiveness, it is also plausible to assume that more successful enterprises will tend to use their performance gains to invest in their infrastructure, including in HRM practices of the kind examined here. Some studies do link practices to future performance (e.g., Huselid *et al.*, 1997; Patterson, *et al.*, 1997), suggesting a causal influence, but the amount of evidence of causality is limited.

A second reason for caution stems from the fact that most studies have used self-report measures of HRM practices from a single organizational representative. Such measures may be quite accurate for many practices, such as whether or not the organization has incentive pay schemes or uses psychometric selection methods. For other practices, however, such as job enrichment and teamwork, they may be less valid. The view of a senior manager on the extent to which shop floor employees are accorded autonomy over how to complete their work may not correspond closely to the experience of the employees themselves. Similarly, what appears to be teamwork to a senior manager may be less evidently collaborative to those supposedly working together. Where measures of this kind are related to measures of performance, any inaccuracies will weaken the observed relationship. In this respect, therefore, some studies may underestimate the effect of HRM practices on performance, in that the association could be stronger if better measures were available.

A third methodological issue is the 'common-method response bias' that may arise when researchers make use of self-report measures of both HRM practices and business performance from one respondent. Some respondents may take a typically rosy view of their organizations, deliberately or unwittingly over-estimating both their use of practices and their performance; while others may be systematically more pessimistic in both respects. As a result, a positive relationship between the practices and performance would be found solely because of such reporting tendencies, rather than because the relationship actually existed. Thus, if such a bias exists, the HRM–performance relationship will be over-estimated.

Although these methodological issues weaken the evidence accumulated to date, they are far from fatal criticisms of the body of evidence as a whole. This is because there are few studies to which all three apply, and some studies to which none applies. Nevertheless, there is a clear need for future work to strengthen its foundations by using longitudinal designs, obtaining evidence on HRM practices from multiple sources within organizations, and ensuring that the sources of performance data are as independent as possible from those used to characterize HRM. Particularly valuable would be well-designed change studies, mapping the short and longer-term effects of the deliberate introduction of high involvement HRM practices.

Equivalence of Human Resource Management Across Studies

So far we have treated existing empirical research as if it were investigating a uniform concept. There is justification for this in that investigators have drawn on overlapping sets of practices in developing their overall measures of HRM, and the studies are linked conceptually by the notion of high involvement management. Nonetheless, there have been important differences across studies. Some, for instance, have included empowerment or job enrichment as a core practice (e.g., Arthur, 1994; Huselid et al., 1997) whereas others have not (e.g., Huselid, 1995; Ichniowski et al., 1997). Similarly, harmonization, employment security, teamwork and performance-related pay have appeared as components of HIM in some studies (e.g., Ichniowski et al., 1997; MacDuffie, 1995) but not in others (e.g., Arthur, 1994). Moreover, in some studies a single index has been used (e.g., Arthur, 1994; Ichniowski et al., 1997), whereas in others two or more dimensions of high involvement management have been identified (e.g., MacDuffie, 1995; Huselid, 1995).

Such differences to some extent reflect diversity in the underlying concepts used by investigators, with some, for example, placing the emphasis on practices that enhance the autonomy and empowerment of non-managerial personnel, and others focusing on performance management initiatives such as appraisal and performance-related pay. Another important reason for the diversity in operationalizing HRM has been the reliance of many researchers on developing their measures on the basis of practices which tend to co-occur in their particular sample. In other words, they end up using empirical rather than conceptual grounds for developing their measures.

Whatever the reason, the outcome is that studies have operationalized HRM in different ways, and in so doing have made it more difficult to determine the overall pattern of results. For the future it is important to obtain greater consistency across studies, and this is more likely to be achieved by basing research on conceptual and theoretical considerations than on observed empirical overlap.

Identifying the Active Ingredients

Faced with the many practices held to comprise high involvement management, managers with limited resources might legitimately ask which ones are the most important in terms of promoting performance. They cannot hope to implement them all at the same time, so where should they start? This is an issue of both theoretical and methodological significance, not least because identification of the most salient component practices would help promote greater equivalence across studies.

As yet, however, research offers few answers to this question. By aggregating practices to provide an overall measure, each practice is treated implicitly as if it were equally important. With only a few exceptions (e.g., Patterson *et al.*, 1997), studies have provided insufficient information about which individual practices have the strongest effects and which may be marginal or even irrelevant. Of course, it may prove difficult to isolate the contribution of any one practice to organizational performance, and this is so for two reasons. First, the effect of a particular practice on performance is likely to be weak simply because it is such a small part of the HRM process as a whole. Second, if the use of practices is correlated, it will be difficult to disentangle their separate effects. To overcome such problems there is a need for much more detailed and intensive research than has been reported to date.

Synergy Between Practices

Taken to its extreme the argument that the impact of individual practices on performance derives from the way they reinforce one another (Becker and Gerhart, 1996; Wood, 1999) implies that all practices are potentially active but they are only activated when others are present. As we saw at the outset, this argument tends to carry the implication that individual practices 'have a limited ability to generate competitive advantage in isolation' (Barney, 1995). It can be exemplified by Huselid's (1995) assumptions that enhancing skills through personnel selection and training will not by itself be enough to have an impact on performance, but needs to be associated with other practices such as appraisal and internal promotion to realize its full potential.

This notion of synergy between practices has considerable intuitive appeal, and is one of the major justifications for investigating HRM as a whole, rather than focusing on separate components. Nonetheless its validity remains one of the main unknowns in the area. Few investigators have directly tested whether or not HRM practices operate synergistically to affect performance. Some consider they are doing this when, having identified by cluster analysis a set of firms that use all the high-involvement practices, they test those firms' performance relative to other clusters. But this is not an adequate test, as it simply compares groupings of organizations on the basis of their having particular practices, not on the strength of the interaction effect.

One of the few direct tests showing synergy is that conducted by MacDuffie (1995), who found an interaction between the measures of Work System, Human Resource Policies and Use of Buffers in predicting company productivity. Others who have directly addressed this issue (e.g., Patterson et al., 2000b) have had less success. The overall conclusion must be that we lack evidence rather than that we have contradictory findings. Future research needs to grasp this nettle.

Use or Effective Use?

The approach taken in the vast majority of studies has been to measure the presence of practices, rather than how well they are used. For example, Huselid (1995) recorded whether or not appraisals were used to determine employees' pay, but did not assess how frequently or how well the appraisal was done. We have found only two exceptions to this approach, namely: the study by Huselid et al. (1997), which addressed effectiveness in terms of respondents' satisfaction with the use of the practice; and Patterson et al.'s (1997) work, which audited the depth and sophistication of use of the practices.

The dominant approach based simply on the use of practices is plausible. Clearly, to be used effectively a practice has to be implemented, and most organizations can implement practices competently. Nonetheless there will be diversity in how well or fully practices are used, and this is likely to affect performance. Wood (1997), for instance, showed there was a tendency in the United Kingdom for Japanese-owned manufacturing plants to have better developed high-involvement practices than their UK-owned counterparts. While team briefing in Japanese manufacturing plants typically takes place at the beginning and end of each shift, in UK-owned plants it more often occurred once a month, a quarter or as considered necessary. No research to date has demonstrated whether the depth of use of a particular practice enhances the performance effects. Nor has research shown that, if a practice is designed or implemented badly, it results in worse effects on the organization than if it were not implemented at all. As research progresses, it is important that measurement is refined to take account of variations in how well HRM practices are implemented in each organization.

Mechanisms

One of the features of research on the relationship of HRM with organizational performance is the lack of detailed empirical investigation into what might account for such a link (Guest, 1997). Such research is vital if we are to understand the reasons for the association between HRM practices and performance.

In the literature we have reviewed there are many suggestions about what the mechanisms may be, but exploration of them is weak. Initial emphasis was placed on the effect of the practices on employees' commitment to the organization or to their job (Wood, 1999). Subsequently, attention has broadened to skills acquisition and the promotion of organizational learning (e.g., Appelbaum et al., 2000). For example, Huselid (1995) and MacDuffie (1995) suggest that HRM practices influence the way in which employees react to discretion in their jobs, and encourage them to expend discretionary effort for the sake of the organization. More specifically, Huselid (1995) suggests that selection and training serve to augment employee skills, that work design or empowerment initiatives provide the opportunity to use those skills, and that appraisal and internal promotion schemes give employees direction and motivation to deploy their skills towards organizational goals.

Such propositions have been tested within the narrower confines of research on work design and empowerment. Thus Parker and colleagues (1997; Parker, 2000) showed how high discretion practices are positively associated with proactive behaviour, initiative, flexible orientations and internalization of organizational strategies on the part of employees. Similarly, Parker (1998) demonstrated a link between employee empowerment and self-efficacy; and Leach, Jackson and Wall (2001; see also Wall, Cordery and Clegg, 2002) showed that empowerment is significantly associated with greater work knowledge.

Nevertheless, examination of mechanisms linking HRM as a whole to organizational performance is lacking. The kinds of question requiring answers are as follows. Are employee commitment and initiative greater in organizations with high involvement HRM systems than in other settings? Do employee self-efficacy and knowledge increase following the introduction of high involvement management? Do changes in employee commitment, self-efficacy and knowledge account for superior organizational performance? Appelbaum *et al.* (2000) and Godard (2001) addressed aspects of these questions and both found greater levels of organizational commitment in high-involvement systems, though Godard did also find higher stress levels. Appelbaum *et al.* did not, however, investigate the links between the organizational commitment and the higher organizational performance that they also observed in these systems. Their analysis of the mediating effect of these psychological states thus stopped at the halfway point. Research needs to include measures of relevant employee attitudes (see Guest, 1997), knowledge and behaviours, both as an end in itself and in order to establish the main routes through which involvement HRM approaches work. It is here that psychology can make its biggest contribution to the HRM area.

Fit with Other Factors

The final, and perhaps most significant, issue concerns the extent to which the effects of high involvement human resource management practices may be regarded as universal or contingent on other factors (Wood, 1999). Some commentators explicitly assume a universal effect, arguing that high involvement practices will outperform other systems in all contexts (e.g., Pfeffer, 1994; 1998). Thus high involvement management may be seen as 'best practice', and several reviewers of the studies we have discussed (e.g., Becker and Gerhart, 1996) have concluded that this is justified. Yet, there remains doubt about whether the effectiveness of high involvement management will be the same in all circumstances. Perhaps it is best fitted to certain contingencies. One of the more common contingencies to be proposed is that of organizational strategy. Porter (1985) distinguished between a cost-minimization and a quality-enhancement competitive strategy, the former competing on the basis of cheaper goods, the latter on better quality. Investigators drawing on this work expect that a high involvement HRM approach will be more appropriate for firms adopting the quality enhancement strategy (Beaumont, 1995). Attempts to test this directly have provided mixed findings, with studies by Youndt, Snell, Dean and Lepak (1996) and by Hoque (1999) offering some support, but Huselid's (1995) research rather less.

Other factors affecting the strength of the effect of high involvement on performance have been discussed. For example, some writers imply that its effect is strengthened where HRM is fully integrated into the strategic processes of the organization (Guest and Hoque, 1994; Becker and Huselid, 1998). Others emphasize the significance of its being part of a broader total quality management or lean production approach (Lawler *et al.*, 1995; 1998). Evidence to date on such possible moderating influences is scant and inconclusive, though MacDuffie's (1995) study could again be seen as offering support for the latter argument.

SUMMARY

The term 'human resource management' developed as an alternative to the more traditional 'personnel management' to reflect the need to harness the potential of employees more fully to enhance business performance. Subsequent elaboration led to the notion of high involvement HRM, incorporating such practices as extensive communications, harmonization (minimizing status differentials among employees), greater investment in training, and employee empowerment. The assumption is that, in contrast to traditional Taylorist approaches based on narrowly defined low discretion jobs, high involvement HRM will yield better organizational performance.

Studies of high involvement HRM have largely supported the predicted benefits. Nonetheless, research to date remains inconclusive and incomplete. This is for a variety of reasons, including: over-reliance on cross-sectional and self-report data, leaving the question of causality unresolved; inadequate evidence about whether component practices affect perform-ance individually or synergistically; neglect of the mechanism linking the practices to performance; and lack of information about the extent to which the effects are universal or contingent on other factors. The systematic study of HRM and business performance has made a promising start, and the way forward is now clear.

FURTHER READING

References to the main empirical studies of the effects of HRM systems on performance have been presented in the chapter. Wood (1999) provides a more in-depth and comprehensive overview of these studies, while Guest (1997) discusses some of the key conceptual issues. Storey's (1995; 2001) edited collections of papers cover the issues and practices in human resource management in a critical and informative way. There are several textbooks introducing students to the main areas of HRM, of which Ivancevitch (2000), Milkovitch and Boudreau (1997), Noe, Hollenbeck, Gerhart and Wright (2000) and Schuler and Jackson (1999) are good examples.

REFERENCES

Appelbaum, E., Bailey, T., Berg, P. and Kalleberg, A. L. (2000). *Manufacturing Advantage: Why High Performance Work Systems Pay Off*. Ithaca, NY: Cornell University Press.

Arthur, J. B. (1994). Effects of human resource systems on manufacturing perform-ance and turnover. *Academy of Management Journal*, 37, 670–87.

Barney, J. (1995). Looking inside for competitive advantage. *Academy of Manage-ment Executive*, 9, 49–61.

Beaumont, P. (1995). *The Future of Employment Relations*. London: Sage.

Becker, B. E. and Gerhart, B. (1996). The impact of human resource management on organizational performance: Progress and prospects. *Academy of Manage-ment Journal*, 39, 779–801.

— and Huselid, M. A. (1998). High performance work systems and firm performance: A synthesis of research and managerial implications. In G. R. Ferris (Ed.), *Research in Personnel and Human Resources* (vol. 16, pp. 53–101). Stamford, Conn.: JAI Press.

Delaney, J. T. and Huselid, M. A. (1996). The impact of human resource management practices on perceptions of organizational performance. *Academy of Management Journal, 39,* 919–69.

Delery, J. E. and Doty, D. H. (1996). Modes of theorizing in strategic human resource management: Tests of universalistic, contingency, and configurational performance predictions. *Academy of Management Journal, 39,* 802–35.

Godard, J. (2001). High performance *and* the transformation of work? The implications of alternative work practices for the experience and outcomes of work. *Industrial and Labor Relations Review, 54,* 776–805.

Guest, D. (1997). Human resource management and performance. A review and research agenda. *International Human Resource Management, 8(3),* 263–76.

— and Hoque, K. (1994). The good, the bad and the ugly: Employee relations in new non-union workplaces. *Human Resource Management Journal, 5,* 1–14.

Guthrie, J. P. (2001). High involvement work practices and, turnover and productivity: Evidence from New Zealand. *Academy of Management Journal, 44,* 180–92.

Hoque, K. (1999). Human resource management and performance in the UK hotel industry. *British Journal of Industrial Relations, 37,* 419–43.

Huselid, M. A. (1995). The impact of human resource management practices on turnover, productivity, and corporate financial performance. *Academy of Management Journal, 38,* 635–72.

—, Jackson, S. E. and Schuler, R. S. (1997). Technical and strategic human resource management effectiveness as a determinant of firm performance. *Academy of Management Journal, 40,* 171–88.

Ichniowski, C., Shaw, K. and Prennushi, G. (1997). The effects of human resource management practices on productivity. *American Economic Review, 87,* 291–313.

Ivancevitch, J. (2000). *Human Resource Management* (eighth edition). Homewood: Irwin.

Koch, M. J. and McGrath, R. G. (1996). Improving labor productivity: Human resource management policies do matter. *Strategic Management Journal, 17,* 335–54.

Lawler, E. E. (1986). *High Involvement Management.* San Francisco: Jossey-Bass.

—, Mohrman, S. A. and Ledford, G. E., Jr. (1995). *Creating High Performance Organizations.* San Francisco: Jossey-Bass.

—, Mohrman, S. A. and Ledford, G. E., Jr. (1998). *Strategies for High Performance Organizations.* San Francisco: Jossey-Bass.

Leach, D. J., Jackson, P. R. and Wall, T. D. (2001). Realising the potential of empowerment: The impact of a feedback intervention on the performance of complex technology. *Ergonomics, 44,* 870–86.

MacDuffie, J. P. (1995). Human resource bundles and manufacturing performance: Organizational logic and flexible production systems in the world auto industry. *Industrial and Labor Relations Review, 48*, 197–221.

Milkovitch, G. and Boudreau, J. (1997). *Human Resource Management* (eighth edition). Homewood, Ill.: Irwin.

Noe, R., Hollenbeck, J., Gerhart, B. and Wright, P. (2000). *Human Resource Management* (third edition). New York: McGraw Hill.

Parker, S. K. (1998). Enhancing role breadth self-efficacy: The roles of job and other organizational interventions. *Journal of Applied Psychology, 83*, 835–52.

— (2000). From passive to proactive motivation: The importance of flexible role orientations and role breadth self-efficacy. *Applied Psychology: An International Review, 49*, 447–69.

—, Wall, T. D. and Jackson, P. R. (1997). 'That's not my job': Developing flexible employee work orientations. *Academy of Management Journal, 40*, 899–929.

Patterson, M. G., West, M. A., Lawthom, R. and Nickell, S. (1997). *Impact of People Management Practices on Business Performance*. London: Institute of Personnel and Development.

—, West, M. A. and Wall, T. D. (2000a). Integrated manufacturing, empowerment and company performance. Working Paper 238, Institute of Work Psychology, University of Sheffield.

—, West, M. A. and Wall, T. D. (2000b). HRM and company performance: A critique and some UK evidence. Paper presented at Academy of Management Annual Meeting 2000, Toronto, Canada. Working paper 239, Institute of Work Psychology, University of Sheffield.

Peters, T. J. and Waterman, R. H. (1982). *In Search of Excellence*. New York: Harper Row.

Pfeffer, J. (1994). *Competitive Advantage Through People: Unleashing the Power of the Workforce*. Boston, MA: Harvard University Press.

Pfeffer, J. (1998). *The Human Equation: Building Profits by Putting People First*. Boston, MA: Harvard Business School Press.

Porter, M. (1985). *Competitive Advantage: Creating and Sustaining Superior Performance*. New York: Free Press.

Schuler, R. S. and Jackson, S. (1999). *Managing Human Resources*. Stamford, Conn.: Thomson Learning.

Storey, J. (1995). *Human Resource Management: A Critical Text*. London: Routledge.

— (2001). *Human Resource Management: A Critical Text* (second edition). London: Routledge.

Wall, T. D., Cordery, J. L. and Clegg, C. W. (2002). Empowerment, performance and operational uncertainty: A theoretical integration. *Applied Psychology: An International Review, 51*, 146–69.

Walton, R. E. (1985). From 'control' to 'commitment' in the workplace. *Harvard Business Review*, 63, 77–84.

Womack, J., Jones, D. T. and Roos, D. (1990). *The Machine that Changed the World*. New York: Rawson.

Wood, S. (1997). How different are human resource practices in Japanese 'transplants' in the UK? *Industrial Relations*, 35, 511–25.

— (1999). Human resource management and performance. *International Journal of Management Reviews*, 1, 367–413.

— and de Menezes, L. (1998). High commitment management in the UK: Evidence from the Workplace Industrial Relations Survey and Employers' Manpower and Skills Practices Survey. *Human Relations*, 51, 485–515.

Wright, P. M., McCormick, B., Sherman, W. S. and McMahan, G. C. (1999). The role of human resource practices in petro-chemical refinery performance. *International Journal of Human Resource Management*, 10, 551–71.

Youndt, M. A., Snell, S. A., Dean, J. E. and Lepak, D. P. (1996). Human resource management, manufacturing strategy, and firm performance. *Academy of Management Journal*, 39, 836–65.

15

Organizations as Psychological Environments

Roy Payne

This chapter contains some frameworks for describing different organizations so as to provide insight into the effects organizations are likely to have on people working in them. Two main concepts are used: organizational structure and organizational culture. The chapter shows the nature of the links between them. The final part focuses on cultures that lead to the kind of jobs that most people find psychologically satisfying. Dissatisfying psychological environments tend to be lacking in cultural qualities which lead to health and well-being, to positive attitudes towards the organization, and hence to motivation for achieving the organization's goals.

THE NATURE OF ORGANIZATIONS

Organizations are established to achieve outcomes: to produce things, to provide services, to govern people, to invent things, to sell things. In attempting to reach such goals, the managers who shape organizations try to create social structures that will help in their attainment. Organizational structure encompasses much more than merely the organization chart. It is also about the creation of rules and procedural systems to ensure that people carry out activities reliably and efficiently. Examination of why senior managers choose to achieve some goals rather than others is the realm of organizational strategy and culture. Strategy, structure and culture are interrelated but they tend to have somewhat separate literatures. However, Mintzberg's work on organizational structure offers a framework that can be used to indicate links amongst the three concepts.

MINTZBERG'S CONCEPTS FOR ANALYZING ORGANIZATIONS

The Five Basic Parts

Mintzberg (1983) has written an abbreviated version of his original (1979) book, called *Structure in Fives*. He divides an organization into five basic parts. At the top is the *strategic apex*, where policies are decided, plans made to execute them, resources allocated and orders given to ensure their execution. Below the strategic apex is the *middle line* of employees, who are responsible for carrying out the orders and making sure the policies are pursued. To do the actual work itself (whether it is producing goods or providing a service) there is an *operating core*. In an organization like a university this is the staff of professors and lecturers; in a hospital it is the doctors and the nurses. In other words, the operating core can in some cases consist of highly qualified individuals, though in many manufacturing organizations the role is filled by blue-collar workers, skilled and less skilled. It is worth noting that the relative size of the middle line and the operating core has changed in many organizations due to the downsizing, delayering, or 'rightsizing' that has occurred in recent years, as businesses have striven to reduce costs and improve their competitiveness. There are relatively fewer managers, and they also have more people to manage; that is, managers and supervisors have larger spans of control.

This central part of the organization's structure is assisted by two other groups. Firstly, there is what Mintzberg calls the *technostructure*. Individuals in the technostructure are analysts or technical advisers. They plan and design work, they select and train people to do the work, they decide strategies for controlling how work is done, but they do not directly produce the main output or service. A major role they have is to create standardization of products and processes and thus to improve efficiency. Included here are staff within departments of personnel, work study or systems analysis. The second group to assist the main workflow is the *support structure*. These individuals and groups service the organization's needs by looking after the buildings, keeping accounts, paying bills and wages, providing meals, distributing mail, etc. These five parts and

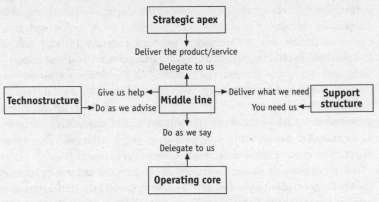

Fig. 15.1 *A simplified version of Mintzberg's (1979) five-part model of organization*

the main tensions/demands amongst them are presented in simplified form in Figure 15.1.

While there are considerable advantages in having groups of specialists providing expert services within the organization, it increases the problem of integrating those specialist groups so that they can work together. Mintzberg proposed that managers have developed five broad approaches to co-ordinate the different parts of the organization's structure so that they function as a purposeful whole.

The Five Coordination Mechanisms

The first procedure is *mutual adjustment*. This relies on people communicating regularly, so that they can adjust to each other and to changing circumstances. Much depends on their trust in each other, personal competence and commitment to each other, as well as their commitment to the organization's mission and success. Managers of a more autocratic bent, however, might prefer to use another method of coordination. They might like to keep a close eye on people, issuing instructions and monitoring employees' actions to see that the instructions have been properly carried out. Mintzberg identifies this as *direct supervision*.

If neither of these options is preferred, managers have to create some measure of control by standardizing one or more parts of people's work performance. There are three basic ways of standardizing. Firstly, one can *standardize the input* of personnel to the system. That is, senior managers can select people who are trained to produce a standard performance. For example, the training which professionals receive makes them responsible for achieving a 'professional standard'. If the task is too simple to demand the use of highly trained professionals, then the next option is to *standardize the work processes*. Systems are carefully designed, rules provided about how to make the system work, and procedures are built in to monitor the quantity and quality of work achieved. The mass production process is based on this coordination principle.

If it is not possible to standardize either the input or the work process, then managers are left with *standardizing the output*. Those in the strategic apex produce clear and precise specifications for the quantity, quality and delivery of a product or service. Put simply, standardization of input controls *who* does things, standardization of work processes controls *how* things are done, and standardization of output controls *what* gets done. The social mechanisms for controlling *when* things are done and the quality of performance vary in each of these different structures. For organizations employing standardization of input, control of timing and performance is largely dependent on trusting people to behave professionally and to provide services/products on time and to the required quality and value. Standardization of work processes depends on good design of business and operating processes. Standardization of output relies on specification of production standards and deadlines and on the establishment of sanctions associated with failure to meet them. Mintzberg uses these five basic parts and five coordinating mechanisms to create a typology of organizations. In this there are five 'ideal types'. The essential concepts are summarized in Figure 15.2, which is adapted from Mintzberg's revisions of the earlier books (Mintzberg, 1989).

Figure 15.2 gives examples of the five types. Organizations using a *simple structure* tend to be new, small and entrepreneurial, frequently governed by the owner (often also the founder) and not infrequently managed in a relatively autocratic manner. An *ad hoc structure* is often new too, for this is likely to arise in fast-changing technologies such as computer companies or other entrepreneurial or creative businesses. Adhocracies are also found in larger organizations, where they spring up as separate 'think tanks', examining what the organization ought to be

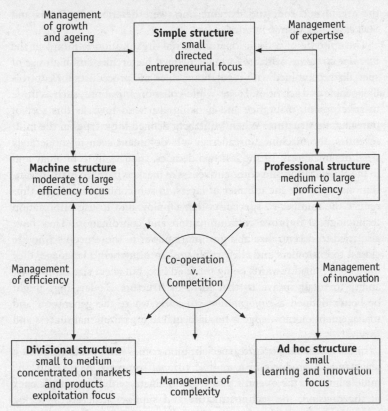

Fig. 15.2 A simplified version of Mintzberg's (1989) five types of organization

like in the more distant future. Dealing with rapid change and containing experts who are often from a range of disciplines requires people in adhocracies to put much effort into communication of a free-wheeling, informal kind, so their main co-ordination mechanism is mutual adjustment. Since there is little structure either within the company or the environment, people have to negotiate with each other to agree goals, allocate resources, and give and take responsibility. In a classic study of what makes organizations innovative, Burns and Stalker (1961) described organizations as having structures which varied along a continuum that they called the mechanistic–organismic continuum. Adhocracies are at the organismic end, and extreme ones were described by Burns and Stalker as 'organismic jungles'.

The epitome of a traditional industrial organization is found in the *machine structure*, with its formally defined hierarchies and high use of specialists, combined with regulations, rules and procedures for controlling people and activities. Large, white-collar organizations, such as those in government, insurance and banking also tend towards this sort of bureaucratic structure. When Mintzberg defined these types in the mid-seventies, the machine bureaucracy was dominant even in moderately sized organizations. In the last two decades, changes in technology and in the globalization and competitiveness of markets have led many organizations to reduce the number of layers, to sub-contract work and thus reduce the number of specialists they employ, and to use information technology to improve communication and coordination. They have also tried to decentralize and give more power to those people who are closest to customers and their problems. In Mintzberg's language, they have been pulled towards being more ad hoc, but sheer size limits their ability to totally move to that form of structure. Today, they might be better defined as *information structures* where the generation and management of knowledge is fundamental to organizational success and survival.

In the *divisional structure*, specialization comes from producing just a few standard products in a multi-divisional company. As a result, the middle line and the operating core predominate, with the strategic apex of the division, the technostructure and support structure all being relatively small. While there may still be many regulations in the divisions of large companies much control comes from the managers and supervisors in the division's middle line. The focus of divisions is on exploiting niche markets with specialized products or services.

Mintzberg called the professional structure a *professional bureaucracy*. This indicates that it is a structure found in large organizations such as government, hospitals and universities. The power structure and the values that enable it to work, however, depend a lot on the professionalism of the people in the operating core and the middle line. So the bureaucracy increasingly relates to record keeping and accounting rather than to controlling what the professionals do, for that is left to their professional integrity. In recent times, these organizations have also striven to delayer, downsize, outsource services, increase the involvement of employees, and employ information technology to improve the quality of their services to each other, and hence to their clients.

The arrows in Figure 15.2 indicate the main problems and tensions that occur within organizations. Consider a small manufacturing organization using a simple structure. As it grows, it needs larger manufacturing facilities, and to design and service them it may employ technocrats who begin to exercise their power and influence. This threatens the power of the strategic apex. If the organization's simple structure moves towards becoming a machine structure, then the occupants of the strategic apex will have to decentralize some of their power. If they do not, they lose the advantages of standardization of products and economies of scale.

The major conflict within a machine structure is between the techno-structure and the middle line. If particular products become very success-ful, then the route to exploit them may be to set up a separate division to gain the advantages of specialization and business focus. Senior managers in the middle line often benefit from such changes and therefore often press the strategic apex to make them. So, the machine structure is threatened by the diversification and growth achieved by its own success, while the divisional structure is always open to the threat of becoming over-specialized, out of date and defunct. The divisional structure comes under pressure from head office strategists, encouraging the division to maintain flexibility in response to changing environments, but the division's short-term success is often built on keeping internal change at bay to optimize the benefits of specialization and standardization.

Although Figure 15.2 summarizes some of the pulls between the five structural types, it is important to recognize that these pulls also exist within single organizations. By their very nature, organizations exist to do something that cannot be done by individuals on their own. This leads to the creation of a range of jobs and duties, and inevitably some jobs are more central to the task than others. Organizational theorists have more and more recognized the wide variety of ways in which politics and power distort the organizational designs that top decision-makers have created (e.g., Pettigrew, 1973). Pettigrew's study was one of the first to illustrate how computing departments gained power because of their control of information and their ability to use technological knowledge to pursue computing goals at the expense of the broader goals of the business. In his 1989 book Mintzberg placed *politics and cooperation* at the centre of his diagram to emphasize that these continually take place in all organizations and create the forces that bring about changes in structures and cultures.

It must be recognized that the types in Figure 15.2 are 'ideal types'. Many organizations are hybrids of more than one type. This occurs in an attempt to reduce some of the conflicts between the different parts of the organization. There are many more than the five ideal types, but Mintzberg's model captures the main forces that create such diversity.

Hamel and Prahalad (1994) have attempted to predict the strategic choices senior managers will face as a result of environmental changes, and conclude their analysis with a list of the most important questions that will influence the strategy ultimately adopted. They emphasize the importance of creating structures and cultures that are responsive to the future, not just the present. Answers chosen to these questions will make considerable differences to organizations' structures and cultures. A few key questions are:

- Does the senior management have a clear and collective point of view about how the future will or could be different?
- Does the company have a clear and collective agenda for building core competencies and evolving the customer interface?
- Do all employees share an aspiration for the enterprise and possess a clear sense of the legacy they are working to build?
- Does the firm's opportunity horizon extend sufficiently far beyond the boundaries of existing product/service markets?

Whilst senior managers have to make strategic choices, it must be recognized that as organizations get larger they get more complex, and this tends to lead to an increase in rules and procedures for managing the complexity. Just how bureaucratic organizations become depends on the values of the senior managers. If they are committed to involving workers, developing trust and rewarding people for innovation and achievement, then even large companies can create successful and enjoyable work environments. Deriving from managers' values, culture becomes the key.

ORGANIZATIONAL CULTURE

It is perhaps easiest to think of culture as a national characteristic (English versus Russian versus Chinese, etc.) or in relation to smaller tribal societies (Tuaregs versus Trobrianders). Such small societies have been studied by anthropologists, many of whom set out to identify key aspects of culture. For example, Kroeber and Kluckhohn (1952) identified 164 definitions. More recently, a number of authors have offered definitions of specifically *corporate* culture. These include:

- Smircich (1983): 'social or normative glue that holds an organization together . . . the values or social ideals and the beliefs that organization members come to share. These values or patterns of belief are manifested by symbolic devices, such as myths, rituals, stories, legends and specialized language' (p. 344);
- Cooke and Rousseau (1988): 'the shared beliefs and values guiding the thinking and behavioral styles of members' (p. 245);
- Schein (1990): '(a) a pattern of basic assumptions, (b) invented, discovered, or developed by a given group, (c) as it learns to cope with its problems of external adaptation and internal integration, (d) that has worked well enough to be considered valid, and therefore, (e) is to be taught to new members as the correct way to perceive, think and feel in relation to those problems' (p. 111).
- House, Hanges, Ruiz-Quantanilla, Dorfman, Javidan, Dickson, Gupta and GLOBE (1999): 'shared motives, values, beliefs, identities and interpretations or meanings of significant events that result from common experiences of members of collectivities and are transmitted across age generations.'

These definitions combine most of the essential components of culture. It is about values, and developing systems and symbols that reinforce and perpetuate those values, so that people behave reliably and predictably to achieve the culture's purposes. Schein (1990) would add artifacts as an important way in which culture is manifested. By artifacts he means style of buildings, dress codes, speech conventions, nature of the documentation and publicity material, the type of written records kept as well as the visual 'feel' of the place. There is a tendency for authors who write about culture to assume that all cultures are 'strong' cultures. By a strong culture it is meant that there are clear patterns of values, norms and beliefs, and that the vast majority of members of the culture all share them and are guided by them.

Martin (1995) defined a strong culture as an *integrated* culture. She has pointed out that in modern complex organizations it is very difficult to create a strong culture. This is partly due to the tensions between different parts of the organization described by Mintzberg. Such tensions often produce cohesive cultures in sub-parts of the organization but little cohesion throughout the organization as a whole. When this occurs Martin describes it as a *differential* culture. There is another cultural school that argues that the modern world is so ambiguous in terms of what is good, right, or required from people, that many organizational cultures are inevitably fragmented. In *fragmented* cultures, complexity, ambiguity and change compel people to 'muddle through' in a series of temporary coalitions in order to do what they can to ensure survival. Thus, the strength of a culture is an important determinant of its effects on people. Most of the management literature is about the effects of a strong culture, arguing that the 'right' culture creates success. Weak or ambiguous cultures present a very different psychological environment, because people are unsure what to do, how to behave, who is powerful, who is not. Fragmented cultures present threats or opportunities, depending upon how the individual construes them.

Having acknowledged the importance of cultural strength, I shall focus on strong cultures that produce positive benefits for people and the organization. As indicated at the beginning of the chapter, it is assumed that poor psychological environments for employees and customers occur when the benefits of strong, positive cultures are absent.

Measuring Culture

There have been three approaches to describing and measuring cultures. The one with the longest history is the anthropological approach. This involves living in a culture and making systematic efforts to describe and explain how it works. In terms of Schein's definition of culture, this would lead to describing the nature and role of artifacts, patterns of expected behaviours and attitudes, the myths and legends of the culture and their functions in it, as well as developing insights into beliefs and values. These beliefs may be so 'taken for granted' that many members of the culture cannot articulate them clearly themselves. There are not many examples of the anthropological approach in work organizations, but some recent ones are listed in Brannen and Kleinberg (2000).

The second approach uses questionnaires, and is embedded in the literature on 'organizational climate'. In studies of organizational climate, people from throughout the organization are asked to say whether a wide range of statements are true or false, whether they describe or do not describe their organization. The questions may cover the physical environment or the structure of the company, but more typically refer to common patterns of attitudes and behaviours. Examples might be about the formality of relationships, attitudes to customers and to risk-taking, how hard people work, the importance of innovation, and how supportive people are to each other. The advantage of measuring culture through climate questionnaires is that it is relatively cheap, can cover a wide variety of aspects of the culture, and can sample a wide variety of people. When individuals' perceptions are averaged and a score given to each organization, it is possible to show differences between organizations in their climate, but this masks a problem in climate research: people in different parts of the organization often see things very differently. In terms of the analysis of culture presented earlier, there is often low consensus, reflecting a differentiated or possibly a fragmented culture. The degree of consensus has often been ignored in studies comparing the effects of different organizational climates on variables such as job satisfaction and performance. Payne (2000) has argued that the degree of consensus can usefully be used to assess whether an organization's culture is integrated, differentiated or fragmented, thus providing a more accurate diagnosis.

The third approach to measurement falls between the methods of the anthropologist and those of climate researchers. It attempts to short-cut the anthropologist's prescription to live in and intensively study a culture. These methods attempt to redefine the relatively limited questionnaires designed to study organizational climates and to cast them more directly into cultural concepts (myths, jargon, etc.). For example, Siehl and Martin (1988) first collected qualitative information about cultural concepts such as values, company jargon, organizational stories, beliefs about practices, etc., and then designed questionnaires to assess what people knew about these.

Some writers would argue that none of these methods can ever expose the real essence of culture, which ultimately also concerns unarticulated beliefs, those that are taken-for-granted. Only a deep knowledge of history, myths and rituals, and their real meaning for membership of the culture, can fully reveal the true culture. In one sense, anything less than this, such as quantitative descriptions of attitudes, norms of behaviour, etc., might be regarded by such writers as not being culture at all. Denison (1996) reviews differences between the concepts of organizational culture and climate. He contrasts them on a number of bases. From an epistemological point of view, culture is rooted in contextualism and climate is nomothetic/comparative. Contextualism assumes knowledge is dependent on the specifics of time and place – next time things could work differently. A nomothetic approach assumes that things can be measured and compared and that this will lead to increased knowledge about them which is generalizable across time and place. Culture is studied by anthropologists from the natives' point of view but is still interpreted by the anthropologist. Climate is usually defined by the researcher but is measured through the natives' perceptions of it. Culture research is qualitative and climate is quantitative. The theoretical foundations of culture are in sociology and social constructionism and those of climate in psychology, deriving from Lewin's (1951) dictum that Behaviour is a function of the Person interacting with the Environment ($B = fP \times E$). Having contrasted the two concepts, Denison concludes that they are not as far apart as many writers have claimed. The stance adopted here is that climate is a useful way of measuring culture.

Organizational Culture and Organizational Performance

Despite the difficulties in measuring culture, all three approaches have been able to show that culture influences how well organizations perform, and, in extreme cases, whether they survive at all. It is worth noting that some strong cultures affect performance positively, while other strong cultures can be the cause of a company's failure. One of the best known examples of how a strong culture can contain the seeds of its own decay is Gibbon's classic history of the fall of the Roman Empire. At the organizational level, it has been argued that IBM's strong culture and its attachment to the importance of mainframe computers instead of personal computers was the cause of its dramatic decline as the world's leading computer company.

Wilderom, Glunk and Maslowski (2000) briefly describe nine studies carried out since 1990 that relate aspects of organizational culture to aspects of organizational performance. Two of the studies had measures of cultural strength as perceived by senior managers. In the first study, strength of culture was moderately related to short-term performance, but in the other study strength of culture was moderately related to long-term economic performance. A third study involved 674 firms from five different US industries. The researchers asked a very senior manager in each company to assess the firm's culture on four dimensions. They were *involvement* of people in the business, *consistency* of agreement about the way business is done, *adaptability* of the company to customers' needs, and the degree to which there is a shared *vision* in the company. The managers were also asked to give a subjective assessment of their firm's performance and all four aspects of culture were positively correlated to performance, with consistency correlating 0.29 and vision 0.35. When measured against an objective index of performance (return on assets over a three-year period), however, the correlations were reduced in size, with consistency being the best predictor (correlation = 0.14). It is notoriously difficult to study the performance of organizations, because two organizations rarely do exactly the same things, and rarely do them in exactly the same circumstances. However, the argument that culture plays an important role is highly plausible, and the current evidence is encouraging.

One of the most ambitious research projects on organizational culture/climate is the GLOBE project. GLOBE stands for Global Leadership and Organizational Behaviour Effectiveness. The project has developed questionnaire measures of leadership practices and dimensions of organizational culture, aiming to learn which leadership practices (strategic, cultural choices) affect which cultural dimensions. The employees who complete the questionnaires are asked to rate the items as they apply to their society/nation as well as to the organization that employs them. One aim is to see how national culture relates to organizational culture. The nine examined dimensions of organizational culture are (Dickson, Aditya and Cholar, 2000):

● *Power Distance*: The degree to which members of an organization accept distinctions between members on the basis of organizational position; includes such things as perquisites, status, and decision-making power.

● *Uncertainty Avoidance*: The degree to which members of an organization actively attempt to reduce ambiguity in organizational life by relying on norms, rules and policies.

● *Humane Orientation*: The degree to which members of an organization encourage and reward individuals for being fair and kind to other organization members.

● *Assertiveness*: The degree to which members of an organization are assertive, dominant, and demanding in their interactions with other organization members.

● *Gender Egalitarianism*: The degree to which men and women are treated equally in the organization in terms of tasks assigned and opportunities for training and advancement.

● *Future Orientation*: The degree to which an organization encourages and rewards long-term versus short-term planning.

● *Performance Orientation*: The degree to which an organization focuses on and rewards high performance and efforts to improve quality.

● *Individualism/Collectivism*: The degree to which an organization focuses on individual accomplishment versus group accomplishment.

● *Organizational Collectivism*: The degree to which organizational members take pride in being associated with the organization.

Employees are not only asked about how things *are*, but also about how they think things *should be*, thus getting at their values as well as their perceptions of their environment.

To illustrate the relationship between structure and culture, let us imagine how the values implicit in these dimensions might lead to the design of a Machine Structure as defined by Mintzberg (see Figure 15.2). A belief in the value of power distance and uncertainty avoidance are both compatible with the Machine Structure. Humane orientation could be comfortably applied in a bureaucracy, but equally it might not be. The hierarchical aspect of bureaucracy is certainly compatible with assertiveness. In principle, the bureaucratic structure should not particularly favour men or women, though in Western societies it has a strong tendency to favour men. Whether or not the organization has a strong orientation to the future will probably depend much on its goals; scientifically oriented bureaucracies may value it strongly and governmental ones may not. Likewise, performance orientation may be strong or weak, depending much on the values of the top people. Many bureaucracies encourage individualism, though recent moves to encourage team-working have generated a more collectivist spirit even in some large bureaucracies. Whilst the managers of mechanistic organizations may like to create a widespread feeling of pride, that is notoriously difficult to achieve amongst the lower levels due to a high concern for power/authority and the requirement that people obey rules and regulations. On the other hand, military organizations tend to be very mechanistic but some create a very strong sense of pride and identification. Structures and cultures influence each other, but even within organizations with the same structure culture can vary.

What Work Cultures Do People Enjoy Most?

In 1988 Levering published a book entitled: *A Great Place to Work: What Makes Some Employers So Good (and Most So Bad)*. The book was based on interviews with hundreds of workers, enabling Levering to publish another book entitled, *The Best 100 Companies to Work for in America*. Such lists of employers are now published annually in the USA, UK, Switzerland and Brazil. The listings are based on a survey of the companies to indicate the degree to which employees in a company report the existence of the conditions Levering discovered from the interviews. Table 15.1 summarizes them.

Levering defines a Great Place to Work as one generating:

- *Trust*: Credibility: The trustworthiness and competence of management.

    Respect: Recognition of employees' personal and professional worth.

    Fairness: Equitable sharing of opportunities and rewards.
- *Pride*: Value attached to one's job, work group and association with the company.
- *Camaraderie*: Friendliness and community in the workplace.

Table 15.1 *Checklist for a great place to work*

Basic terms of employment	The job	Workplace rules	Stakes in success
1. Fair pay and benefits: a. compare well with similar employers b. square with company's ability to pay	1. Maximize individual responsibility for how job is done	1. Reduced social and economic distinctions between management and employees	1. Shares rewards from productivity improvement
2. Commitment to job security	2. Flexibility about working hours	2. Right to due process	2. Shares profits
3. Commitment to safe and attractive working environment	3. Opportunities for growth: a. promotes from within b. provides training c. recognizes mistakes as part of learning	3. Right to information	3. Shares ownership
		4. Right to free speech	4. Shares recognition
		5. Right to confront those in authority	
		6. Right *not* to be part of the family/team	

Note: 'A great workplace cannot be equated with the presence or absence of a particular set of policies or practices. What's important is the quality of the relationship developed between the company and its employees. With that in mind, we can use the checklist as a way of taking the pulse of a company's workplace relationships. Great places to work tend to have most or all of the attributes listed above.' (Reprinted with permission.)

Wiley and Brooks (2000) have reviewed the relationship between work climate dimensions and customer satisfaction and business performance, finding that research supports the importance of the following features:

- Customer orientation;
- Quality emphasis;
- Involvement/empowerment of employees;
- Information or knowledge about customers and business performance provided to employees;
- Teamwork/cooperation across boundaries;
- Jobs that provide satisfaction.

Apart from the emphasis on employees benefiting from company success in Levering's framework, the two lists have much in common. The procedures and policies that bring these conditions about are derived largely from the values and beliefs of the leadership and their behavioural commitment to acting in accordance with those values and beliefs. Those are the basic requirements for developing a strong culture.

In principle, it should be possible to create 'a great place to work' culture in any organization, but Levering recognized that some types of organizations are likely to be more successful than others in that respect. He describes five types of workplace based on the relationship between managers and other employees. They are:

- Partnerships (Great places to work);
- Master/Slave relationship (Exploitative places);
- Parent/Child relationship (Paternalistic places);
- Leader/Follower relationship (Entrepreneurial places);
- Machine/Part relationship (Mechanical places).

The last one of these is directly comparable to Mintzberg's Machine Bureaucracy. Organizations that have adopted this structure have made strategic choices that make it more difficult to create a culture based on the notions of equality and partnership. Whilst they may provide reasonable job benefits, many jobs are simple and repetitive, and surrounded by workplace rules. Some companies do have profit-sharing schemes, but since output is often determined more by machines than people, they are not as common as perhaps they ought to be. In many western democracies the gap between the rewards of people at the top of organizations and those at the bottom has widened considerably over the last thirty years.

Entrepreneurial organizations are often small and managed by the owner; they appear in Mintzberg's model as Simple Structures. Their small size and simplicity should make it easy to create partnerships, but the leaders often demand that people be followers rather than partners. Work tends to be designed in the way the owner thinks it should be done. Rules are rarely laid down but are likely to be made up at the leader's whim. Job security is often low, resources scarce and not wasted on environmental design. Profits are ploughed back into the business rather than the pockets of the employees. Often, they are not 'great places to work'. They can in the extreme turn into exploitative places.

Some of what Mintzberg calls professional bureaucracies can create a paternalistic culture. Basic terms of employment are often acceptable, but people are only told what the management thinks they need to know, so jobs tend to be limited in scope and development opportunities. In many professional bureaucracies authority is not to be questioned, and rewards are determined by what the management thinks people deserve rather than on some system that is designed to provide a fair share of rewards and benefits. As pointed out earlier, as organizations get larger they are almost inevitably pulled in this bureaucratic direction. This inevitability has prompted Adler (1999) to prescribe how to go about 'Building better bureaucracies'. What he calls an 'enabling bureaucracy' should:

- Involve employees in organizational systems to encourage buy-in.
- Involve employees in designing organizational systems to ensure they support the real work tasks.
- Broaden participation by investing resources, providing training, and eliminating disincentives; poor design is too expensive.
- Test successive prototypes of the new systems with employees.
- Design systems that encourage improvement suggestions by members at every level.
- Plan to do all these things.

Once again, the need for employees to share in the organization's success (or failure) is not included here, but most of the above are compatible with many of the points made by Levering.

In sum, cultures derive from values and the actions that flow from them, but political, technological and economic circumstances can create procedures that undermine values concerned with how best to treat people. Despite the existence of a considerable literature showing that good human resources practices are associated with organizational success, Pfeffer and Veiga (1999) conclude from a review that '. . . at best 12 per cent of organizations will actually do what is required to build profits by putting people first' (p. 47). According to Pfeffer and Veiga, the reasons that prevent managers from creating cultures that are great places to work are of the following kind. Many managers get enslaved by the requirement to create short-term profits that prove they are competent and that increase shareholder value in any particular financial year. The use of financial criteria alone to assess new initiatives often inadvertently destroys wisdom and employees' competencies that are based much more on intuition and tacit knowledge. This undermines the manager's confidence and reduces the likelihood of risking new things. Another consequence is that managers learn not to delegate. They learn that they had better be in control if they are to be seen as the ones responsible for success. Pfeffer and Veiga refer to this as the 'self-enhancement bias'. The final barriers to moving towards greater employee involvement derive from beliefs about what it is to be a good manager. One belief is that a good manager is mean and tough and can implement difficult decisions, another that analytical ability will ultimately prevail. The latter is sometimes referred to as 'paralysis by analysis' and is another reason why positive employment practices frequently fail to flower.

So far this chapter has considered how organizations create different cultures and the effects they have on the psychological environment they create. The relationship of culture to organizational performance has also been examined. The next section considers the effect of culture on individuals. How do different aspects of culture affect individual well-being and performance?

Culture and Its Effects on the Individual

Most of the studies that have investigated the effect of culture on people have done so by getting people to describe the organization's climate. Conceptually 'organizational climate' refers to the organization as a whole. In empirical studies of climate an organization is allocated a score based on the average score for any aspect of climate (e.g., concern for formality). As indicated above, doing this is problematic if there is not high agreement amongst the individuals in the organization (the aggregation issue). Because of this problem, researchers have often analyzed the relationship between a single individual's perceptions of climate and other variables such as individual performance or job satisfaction. When analyzed in this way, the measure of organizational climate has been defined as 'psychological climate'. Climate measures have also been designed to assess the team climate or the job climate, and some measures have contained items that ask separately about the organization, the team/department and the job. This is not a problem if the measures are scored for those different levels of analysis, but in some studies items from different levels of analysis have been combined. This sometimes makes it difficult to compare studies, but the better investigations have avoided the problem.

Brown and Leigh (1996) provide a good example of a study that has measures of all the variables of interest. They carried out an investigation of 223 sales representatives from several companies. From these sales people they obtained perceptions of their psychological environment for six dimensions, a measure of their job involvement, a measure of self-reported effort and three measures of performance provided by the sales peoples' immediate managers. The intercorrelations amongst the six climate dimensions were so strong that they were added together to measure a single dimension that assessed the degree to which the environment is seen as personally beneficial to the person. The three measures of performance were also very highly correlated. The authors were able to show that 'an organizational environment that is seen as psychologically safe and meaningful is related directly to job involvement and indirectly to effort and work performance' (p. 365).

Parker, Young, Baltes, Altmann, Huff and LaCost (1997) reported a meta-analysis of the relationships between psychological climate perceptions and various work outcomes. In a meta-analysis one finds as many studies as one can of the relationship of interest and averages them out to give a more accurate estimate of how big the relationship is. Parker *et al.* based their estimates on 115 studies that involved 64,477 people. The authors summarize their findings as follows:

It is clear that individuals' climate perceptions have significant relationships with their job satisfaction, work attitudes, psychological well-being, motivation and performance. Each of the climate categories suggests a somewhat different pattern of relationships with the various outcomes, however. In general, employees' job and role perceptions appear to have the weakest relationships with all of the outcome variables. Interestingly, leader, work group, and organizational climate perceptions are most predictive of employees' work attitudes. A similar pattern is evident for the relationships of psychological climate with employee motivation and performance. For psychological well-being, however, job and leader perceptions provide the strongest relationships. Overall, it appears that employees' climate perceptions have stronger relationships with their work attitudes than with motivation and performance. This pattern of relationships suggests that the effects of climate on motivation and performance may depend on the employees' work attitudes.

To give some idea of the size of these relationships, the single best predictor of job satisfaction is work group climate where the correlation is 0.48. Perception of organizational climate is the best predictor of 'other work attitudes' (correlation = 0.32) and it is also the best predictor of work motivation (correlation = 0.22). The strongest predictor of well-being is the climate created by one's leader (correlation = 0.44). These are moderately strong correlations and reveal the value of organizational climate as a construct in this book.

The reader was warned in Chapter 1 that causal conclusions cannot be derived from correlations. The assumption above is that climate influences attitudes, motivation and well-being, but it could be that one's level of job satisfaction or psychological well-being influences the way one sees the climate. The more satisfied one is with one's job, the more one is likely to see other aspects of the climate positively. However, the fact that organizations that strive to create an employee-oriented culture are more successful is a compelling reason for accepting that the causal direction is probably from culture to well-being, from well-being to positive work attitudes, and from positive attitudes to positive performance.

SUMMARY

In attempting to provide a way of understanding how organizations affect people's health, well-being and performance, this chapter has relied heavily on the concepts of organizational structure and organizational culture. There are many kinds of organizational structures, and a key theme is that these emerge from the influences of the environment in which the organization is operating. The environment includes the political system, the economic system, the market and the culture in which the organization is located. With increasing globalization, the environment now includes the effects of other cultures and the effects of technological innovation and of information technology in particular. These influences combine to produce organizational cultures which ultimately determine the nature of the workplace and hence its effects on people.

Good places to work are those which encourage a culture that values trust and openness, that creates pride and a desire to belong to the organization, and that is caring and supportive of people so that they achieve good health and personal development. Another important theme is that achieving such positive cultures is difficult and many organizations fail in this respect. One of the major barriers is western culture itself, with its emphasis on short-term profits and individual success and achievement. The final theme is that research shows that both people and organizations will benefit from striving to achieve these positive cultures.

FURTHER READING

On structure one should read Mintzberg's book (1989), and Trice and Beyer's (1993) book is a classic on organizational culture. There are two recent handbooks that provide the most up to date academic work on these issues. The *Handbook of Organizational Culture and Climate* (2000) is edited by Ashkanasy, Wilderom and Peterson, and the *International Handbook of Organizational Culture and Climate* (2001) edited by Cartwright, Cooper and Earley. For the more general reader I suggest books by Charles Handy, and this website (for example) will lead you to them: *www.bol.com*. Another site that provides many fruitful leads is: *www.educationplanet.com/search/People_and_Society/Culture/Business_Culture*. The site address for a Great Place to Work is: *www.greatplace towork.com*.

REFERENCES

Adler, P. S. (1999). Building better bureaucracies. *The Academy of Management Executive*, *13*, 4, 36–49.

Ashkanasy, N. M., Wilderom, C. P. M. and Peterson, M. K. (Eds.). (2000). *Handbook of Organizational Culture and Climate*. Thousand Oaks, CA: Sage.

Brannen, M. Y. and Kleinberg, J. (2000). Images of Japanese management and the development of organizational culture theory. In N. M. Ashkanasy, C. P. M. Wilderom and M. K. Peterson (Eds.), *Handbook of Organizational Culture and Climate*. Thousand Oaks, CA: Sage.

Brown, S. P. and Leigh, T. W. (1996). A new look at psychological climate and its relationship to job involvement, effort and performance. *Journal of Applied Psychology*, *81*, 358–68.

Burns, T. and Stalker, G. M. (1961). *The Management of Innovation*. London: Tavistock.

Cartwright, S., Cooper, C. L. and Earley, C. (Eds.) (2001). *International Handbook of Organizational Culture and Climate*. Chichester: J. Wiley.

Cooke, R. A. and Rousseau, D. M. (1988). Behavioural norms and expectations: A quantitative approach to the assessment of organizational culture. *Group and Organization Studies*, *13*, 245–73.

Denison, D. R. (1996). What *is* the difference between organizational culture and organizational climate? A native's point of view on a decade of paradigm wars. *Academy of Management Review*, *21*, 619–54.

Dickson, M. W., Aditya, R. N. and Cholar, J. S. (2000). Definitions and interpretations in cross-cultural organizational research: Some pointers from the GLOBE research program. In N. M. Ashkanasy, C. P. M. Wilderom and M. K. Peterson (Eds.), *Handbook of Organizational Culture and Climate*. Thousand Oaks, CA: Sage.

Hamel, G. and Prahalad, C. K. (1994). *Competing for the Future: Breakthrough Strategies for Seizing Control of Your Industry and Creating the Markets of Tomorrow*. Cambridge, Mass.: Harvard Business School Press.

House, R. J., Hanges, P. J., Ruiz-Quantanilla, S. A., Dorfman, P. W., Javidan, M., Dickson, M., Gupta, V. and GLOBE (1999). Cultural influences on leadership: Project GLOBE. In W. Mobley, J. Gessner and V. Arnold (Eds.), *Advances in Global Leadership* (vol. 1, 171–223). Greenwich, CT: JAI.

Kroeber, A. L. and Kluckhohn, C. (1952). *Culture: A Critical Review of Concepts and Definitions*. New York: Vintage Books.

Levering, R. (1988). *A Great Place to Work – What Makes Some Employers So Good and Most So Bad?* New York: Avon Books.

Lewin, K. (1951). *Field Theory in Social Science*. New York: Harper & Row.

Martin, J. (1995). Organizational culture. In N. Nicholson (Ed.), *The Blackwell Encyclopedic Dictionary of Organizational Behaviour* (pp. 376–82). Cambridge, MA: Blackwell.

Mintzberg, H. (1979). *The Structure of Organizations*. Englewood Cliffs, NJ: Prentice Hall.

— (1983). *Structure in Fives: Designing Effective Organizations*. Englewood Cliffs, NJ: Prentice Hall.

— (1989). *Mintzberg on Management: Inside Our Strange World of Organizations*. New York: Free Press.

Parker, C. P., Young, S. A., Baltes, B. B., Altmann, R., Huff, J. and LaCost, H. (1997). A meta-analysis of the relationship between psychological climate perceptions and work outcomes. Unpublished paper, Department of Psychology, Northern Illinois University, DeKalb, Ill.

Payne, R. L. (2000). Climate and culture – how close can they get? In N. M. Ashkanasy, C. P. M. Wilderom and M. K. Peterson (Eds.), *Handbook of Organizational Culture and Climate*. Thousand Oaks, CA: Sage.

Pettigrew, A. (1973). *The Politics of Organizational Decision Making*. London: Tavistock.

Pfeffer, J. and Veiga, J. F. (1999). Putting people first for organizational success. *The Academy of Management Executive*, *13*, 2, 37–48.

Schein, E. H. (1990). Organizational culture. *American Psychologist*, *45*, 109–19.

Siehl, C. and Martin, J. (1988). Measuring organizational cultures: Mixing qualitative and quantitative methods. In M. O. Jones, M. D. Moore and R. D. Snyder (Eds.), *Inside Organizations* (pp. 45–59). Beverly Hills, CA: Sage.

Smircich, L. (1983). Concepts of culture and organizational analysis. *Administrative Science Quarterly*, *28*, 339–58.

Trice, H. M. and Beyer, J. M. (1993). *The Cultures of Work Organizations*. Englewood Cliffs, NJ: Prentice Hall.

Wilderom, C. P. M., Glunk, U. and Maslowski, R. (2000). Organizational culture as a predictor of organizational performance. In N. M. Ashkanasy, C. P. M. Wilderom and M. K. Peterson (Eds.), *Handbook of Organizational Culture and Climate*. Thousand Oaks, CA: Sage.

Wiley, J. W. and Brooks, S. M. (2000). The high performance organizational climate: How workers describe top performing units. In N. M. Ashkanasy, C. P. M. Wilderom and M. K. Peterson (Eds.), *Handbook of Organizational Culture and Climate*. Thousand Oaks, CA: Sage.

16 | Organizational Change and Development

Jean Hartley

Over the last decade we have seen a variety of changes in many organizations, including re-designed work processes, networked forms of organizing, restructuring and downsizing, total quality management, continual learning and adaption, cultural change, and technological changes in work organization. Beyond these changes in organizational forms and processes, there has also been substantial restructuring in pay and conditions and in the psychological contract between employees and their organizations.

There is a vast literature on organizational change. However, much of it is unsatisfactory from an academic perspective, because it focuses largely on *how* to undertake change (generally from a management perspective) without an underlying theoretical framework to explain *why* change occurs or not, and under what conditions. The 'how to do it' literature is susceptible to the fads and fashions of current management techniques, which may not be successful over the longer term. It has been estimated that less than 30 per cent of change initiatives are successful (Binney, 1992).

It is possible to get carried away by some of the rhetoric of organizational change. Yet organizations, by definition, are characterized by continuities over time and space. There are always some stabilities in organizations (Pettigrew, 1985). What, then, do we need to know, in order to gain a deeper understanding of organizational change? First, we need some categorization of organizational change, given that it can vary from small-scale to substantial. Then, we need to consider the causes or catalysts of change – are they external to the organization or driven by key figures in the organization? Who is influential in change – what is the role of leaders, change agents, those who implement the strategy? What change processes, including strategies, behaviours and other actions, are most effective in achieving desired outcomes? What is the impact of change in terms of outputs and outcomes? What attitudes, behaviours, actions and interactions help to promote and sustain change? How can change be evaluated? These questions are examined here.

VARIETIES OF ORGANIZATIONAL CHANGE

A valuable starting point for conceptualizing organizational change is to consider different types of change, because different dynamics, processes and actors may be at work in different types. A useful distinction has been made between episodic and continuous change (e.g., Weick and Quinn, 1999). Episodic change refers to those types of change which tend to be infrequent, discontinuous and intentional. Episodic change is often precipitated by severe external challenges to the organization, or by changes in key personnel who wish to reform the organization and/or make their mark. External change agents are often used to help support the change initiative. It is often disruptive because structures and activities are replaced rather than modified.

By contrast, continuous change refers to modifications which are developmental, ongoing, incremental and partly unplanned. Recent interest in organizational learning and aspects of total quality management fit this category. In these cases the approach is processual, based on the assumption that small, incremental changes, occurring across sub-units of the organization, will cumulatively add up to substantial change. The intention is that regular adaptation to external challenges and demands should occur through small but significant shifts in behaviours, organizational processes and organizational cultures over time. Indeed, over time the small changes may cumulatively achieve major transformation. It is also assumed that change cannot be entirely planned, so that adjustment in the light of observation of interim outcomes (emergent change) is necessary.

One sub-category of this (continuous) type of organizational change is seen in the innovative organizations described by Brown and Eisenhardt (1998). They researched twelve 'relentlessly changing organizations' in the computing industry, chosen to be prototypical of a high velocity business where managing continuous change is a key strategic challenge. The firms were chosen in six pairs, one to be a dominant player in the industry along with a very good (but not dominant) player. Differences between the firms helped to identify the processes of leading effective change. Using interviews with over eighty managers, as well as questionnaires and the study of company documents, the researchers examined how the firms reacted to, anticipated and sometimes led change. Successful change in these circumstances was associated with an approach to strategy and management which encouraged continuous adaptive change. Three important features were identified. First, change was seen to be the norm not the exception. The highly successful companies had an adaptive culture that expected changes, so that staff anticipated and recognized the need to adjust what they were doing. Second, structures and cultures emphasized a small number of rules that were closely adhered to but encouraged innovation within the rules. The rules concerned priorities, deadlines, responsibilities for major outcomes and real-time measures of performance. Third, these organizations had high levels of communications throughout the entire organization, about the business and where it was heading.

Another classification of organizational change, which partly overlaps with the above framework, is that of transformational change and incremental change (e.g., Kanter, Stein and Jick, 1992; Mohrman and colleagues, 1989). Transformational change is intended to have a fundamental or radical impact on the organization's strategy, structures, people, processes or values (or a combination of those). Incremental change is concerned with improving the efficiency or effectiveness of the organization but from within the existing general framework of strategy and ways of organizing. Transformational change is intended to be more discontinuous with the past, while incremental change tends to be evolutionary.

Although the term transformational change is widely used in the literature, we can note some problems with this classification. First, does it refer to intention or outcome? Intentions occur towards the beginning of the change process, while outcomes can only be judged at or towards the end of the change. Second, this also raises questions about whose judgements are taken into account in deciding whether change is transformational or incremental. To the new chief executive, the change may be path-breaking and radical, while to the long-serving workforce it may be perceived more cynically as just another in a series of change initiatives that have failed in the past (see also Duck, 1998).

A FRAMEWORK FOR ANALYZING ORGANIZATIONAL CHANGE

On the basis of the literature and empirical research, I argue that there are four main sets of influences on organizational change. These are illustrated in Figure 16.1 and are:

- The context in which organizational change takes place (both external and internal to the organization).
- The leadership and key agents influencing or reacting to change.
- The management of change processes.
- The outputs and outcomes of change for different stakeholders.

We will examine each of these areas in turn. The framework is based on an open systems perspective, emphasizing the importance of the organization's interactions with its environment and also the existence of feedback or course-correction processes based on observation and learning by organizational actors. The arrows between the boxes represent the processes of feedback and organizational learning.

The External Context

There is increasing recognition of the importance of the external environment in understanding organizational behaviour (Rousseau and Fried, 2001), including organizational change (Hartley, 2000; Mowday and Sutton, 1993). By external context is meant the stimuli and phenomena which exist in the environment outside the organization. The context provides pressures, constraints and opportunities for organizational change, often in combination.

Pressures and opportunities may include those which are:

- Political (for example, aspects of globalization, changes in legislation and regulation; changes in the priorities of governments; changing values about acceptable outputs and outcomes from organizations).

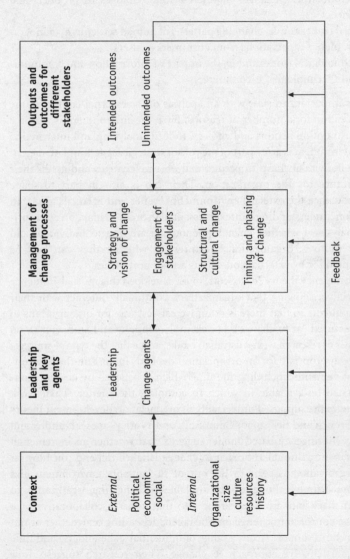

Fig. 16.1 Framework for organizational change and development

- Economic (for example, changes in economic globalization, changes in competition, changes in interest rates, changes in products and services).
- Social (for example, changing patterns of human settlement, demography, higher expectations from customers or users).
- Technological (for example, the impact of information and communication technologies, e-commerce).

It is important to start with an analysis of the external context of the organization for a number of reasons. First, the environment is a source of constraint on actions and choices. Indeed, analyzing and interpreting the environment is a key part of the role of strategic leaders and managers. These individuals have to predict and observe changes and assess their significance for the organization. Their job is also in part to shape and influence the external environment (Pfeffer and Salancik, 1978). In addition, understanding context is essential in order to make an appropriate analysis of whether change phenomena are due to individual and group motives, organizational features, or whether they can best be accounted for by external constraints and opportunities.

Contingency theory (e.g., Scott, 1992) developed this mutual-influence perspective, showing that organizations continually interact with their environments so that there is no universal best way for organizations to be structured (or to change). For example, Dunphy and Stace (1988), on the basis of research with Australian banks, argue that the type of strategic change appropriate for an organization depends in part on the environmental demands, including the time which is believed by key decision-makers to be available in which to complete the change. Their work challenges the supposed universality of organization development theory (e.g., French and Bell, 1990; Cummings and Worley, 2001). Dunphy and Stace's contingency-based model suggests that whether an incremental or a transformational approach to change is taken depends on how far the organization is seen to be 'out of fit' with its environment and how much time is thought to be available to change the organization to bring it back into fit. They argue also that either a collaborative or a coercive approach to change may be taken, depending on whether or not there is both support (from a range of influential stakeholders) and time for a participative approach to change. Their research suggests four strategies of change: participative evolution, forced evolution, charismatic

Fig. 16.2 *A typology of change strategies and conditions for their use (Dunphy and Stace, 1988)*

	Incremental change strategies	Transformational change strategies
Collaborative modes	*Participative evolution*	*Charismatic transformation*
	Use when organization is in 'fit' but needs minor adjustment, or is out of fit but time is available and key interest groups favour change.	Use when organization is out of 'fit', there is little time for extensive participation, but there is support for radical change within the organization.
Coercive modes	*Forced evolution*	*Dictatorial transformation*
	Use when organization is in 'fit' but needs minor adjustment, or is out of fit but time is available but key interest groups oppose change.	Use when organization is out of 'fit', there is no time for extensive participation and no support within the organization for radical change, but radical change is vital to organizational survival and fulfilment of basic mission.

transformation and dictatorial transformation. These are shown in Figure 16.2.

Strategic choices, as outlined by Dunphy and Stace, are mediated through perceptions. Interactions with the environment may lead to changes in perceptions and priorities. Leaders, senior managers and front-line workers may (intentionally or otherwise) act on or ignore cues in the environment. Dutton and Dukerich (1991) present a case study, based on interviews and analysis of documentation which took place over a seven-year period, of organizational change as the external context changed. They studied the image and identity of the Port Authority of New York and New Jersey, as the organization reacted to the growing numbers of homeless people who were using its bus terminals and airports as places to stay. Identity as a transport authority not as a social services organization meant that the organization initially took a very narrow view of its function (for example, in removing homeless people from premises). However, public reaction caused concern over organizational image, and, over time, a reassessment of appropriate action. The Port

Authority initiated a homelessness project team and began closer liaison with other agencies, thereby changing its approach and modifying its identity and image.

The Internal Context

Not all change is explicitly linked to the external environment. Change may be initiated by internal choices, decisions, opportunities and constraints. For example, an incoming chief executive may promote change, partly as a symbolic act of his or her purpose and power. A number of features of the internal context may be important in the initiation and trajectory of organizational change. Organizational size and structure, procedures and resources can all have impacts on change approaches and outcomes. Organization development has shown how change can be influenced (or distorted) by the existing culture of the organization and its sub-units. The recent history of change will also influence whether or not change ideas and proposals fall on fertile ground (Hartley, Cordingley and Benington, 1995). For example, Child and Smith (1987) showed, in a study of transformational change at Cadburys, that the proposals for change were shaped by understanding of the importance of continuities as well as change.

LEADERSHIP AND KEY AGENTS OF CHANGE

A useful framework for considering leadership and key agents of change is that of Kanter, Stein and Jick (1992), who argue that the experience and preoccupations of change vary according to whether the person is primarily:

- A change strategist: concerned with the connection between the organization and its environment and with the organization's overall direction and priorities. This role is often considered to be the responsibility of leaders and senior management.
- A change implementer: concerned with the detailed development of the change through project management, operational execution and continuous improvement.

• A change recipient: concerned with the effects of change because he or she is at the receiving end of change, sometimes without much opportunity to influence the change plan.

This classification is rather simple, as it appears to imply that organizational members are only in one category, whereas in practice some may move between different roles as the change develops, as van der Ven, Angle and Poole (1989) note. However, it is useful in emphasizing that change is likely to be experienced differently according to the person's location and role in the organization. We focus now on those particularly influential in change: the leadership and change agents.

Leadership

Early psychological writing tended to be rather vague about the leadership of change (and about the use of power), arguing that change initiatives needed 'the support of top management'. However, there is increasing evidence that the perceptions, cognitions and values of leaders, and the group dynamics of 'top teams' influence the analysis, choice and implementation of strategies (e.g., Sparrow, 1994).

Major change is likely to depend on the development of a vision (or sense of focus and direction about the end-point of change) which can be communicated to the rest of the organization (Bartunek, 1993; Porras and Silvers, 1991). It is particularly the role of leaders to develop and communicate vision and to energize support for change (see also Chapter 12). Nadler and Tushman (1980) argue that leadership in settings of major change requires the ability to envision the change, to energize key stakeholders by generating motivation among organizational members to act to develop the change, and to enable organizational members to act or perform even under challenging circumstances. Schein (1992) notes the symbolic role of leaders in shifting organizational cultures through their conscious choice of actions and priorities.

We must note that the strategic leadership of change is not just about rational decision-making, however persuasive the *post hoc* rationalizations of leaders! Complex change in an uncertain world can only be partially predicted and planned (Hartley, 2000). Sense-making becomes important in organizational change under conditions of uncertainty or ambiguity (Weick, 1995). Sense-making captures the idea that people (individuals or groups) make sense of confusing or ambiguous events by constructing plausible (rather than necessarily accurate) interpretations of events through action and through reinterpretation of past events.

The role of the leader, in a sense-making framework, may be less to be fully clear about the future and rational plans for shaping it (i.e., providing a 'clear vision'), and more about being able to help people understand what may be happening. Pfeffer (1981) argues that a key role for leaders is to provide 'explanations, rationalizations and legitimations for activities undertaken in organizations' (p. 4). This expresses a more interactive view of leadership than one based solely on key skills and attributes of leaders.

Leadership that is distributed between several people is particularly significant in certain types of change (Hartley and Allison, 2000; van der Ven, Angle and Poole, 1989). Instead of a 'top-down' approach, with a strategic plan communicated from senior management for middle managers and staff to implement, some research indicates the effectiveness of a different approach. This emphasizes the encouragement of innovation and creativity throughout the organization, when it is in line with the broad changes the organization is aiming to achieve. Nonaka and Takeuchi (1995) point out that innovation may sometimes begin in the middle of the organization (i.e., among team leaders, middle managers and professionals). These individuals may gain support, legitimacy and encouragement from top management, but detailed work about developing and embedding change may occur in the work teams on the front-line. A vision for change in such circumstances is likely to be 'fuzzy' rather than clear (Pettigrew and Whipp, 1991). More generally, continuous change and improvement may rely on leadership at all levels in the organization, rather than deriving merely from top leaders (Weick and Quinn, 1999).

The Role of the Change Agent

Episodic change (infrequent, discontinuous and intentional; see earlier) places considerable emphasis on the role of the change agent, whether internal or external to the organization (e.g., French and Bell, 1990; Cummings and Worley, 2001). From an organization development (OD) perspective, a change agent is someone who acts as a catalyst to the change, especially by working with people on the social processes and dynamics in the group or team and in inter-group and organizational processes. This person may work with the 'top team' to improve within-team dynamics and to clarify strategic intent, or he or she may work with parts of the organization on aspects of implementation. Change agents often draw upon behavioural science theory and frameworks to help an organization to define problems and purposes, to explore alternatives and to encourage learning.

Weick and Quinn (1999) suggest that the specific role of the change agent may depend on whether the situation is one of primarily episodic or continuous change. In episodic change, the change agent will be concerned to locate and support the prime movers of change, needing to put considerable effort into initiating activity. This is similar to the traditional role of the change agent (e.g., Cummings and Worley, 2001). However, in continuous change, the role of the change agent is to help those in the organization make sense of processes that are already under way. In this context, the change agent will seek to notice adaptive, emergent changes, make them more salient and reframe them in ways that are useful to members of the organization.

THE MANAGEMENT OF CHANGE PROCESSES

Turning now to consider the third element in Figure 16.1, we address some of the major approaches to managing change processes. There are many processes which could be addressed here, but we focus on the strategies to achieve change, the engagement of stakeholders, structural and cultural change, and the timing and phasing of change.

Strategies for Change

At the level of the whole organization, researchers often emphasize taking a systemic approach to change (e.g., Pettigrew and Whipp, 1991) so that different elements of organizational functioning are compatible with and reinforce change. Otherwise, a change can be advocated from the top of the organization but organizational processes (training, rewards, career progression, etc.) are incompatible with the objective and undermine the intended change. While change failure is sometimes interpreted as employees' 'resistance to change', viewed as a psychological attribute of individuals, there is a need to consider also the wide barriers to change, which can be structural, cultural, social or processual (Fenton-O'Creevy, 2000).

A strategy is a pattern or plan that integrates major goals, policies and action sequences into a coherent whole (Quinn, 1980). Psychologists are increasingly interested in the strategic management of change. This is seen in research into cognitive models and concepts implicitly used in strategic analysis and planning, the work of top teams and the processes of vision-creation and communication (e.g., Flood, Dromgoole, Carroll and Gorman, 2000).

We have already discussed elements of strategy in the section on leadership. The assessment of external constraints and opportunities is likely to have an impact on the strategic approach to organizational change, for example, whether to undertake episodic or continuous change, and how to engage stakeholders.

The Engagement of Stakeholders

Stakeholder analysis identifies key groups and individuals who are or will be affected by the proposed organizational changes. Internal stakeholders work within or are employed by the organization: leaders, strategic and operational managers, front-line employees, support functions. External stakeholders may be recipients of the organization's products or services, the general public, suppliers, etc. Research has primarily focused on how to engage internal stakeholders (e.g., Kanter, Stein and Jick, 1992), though some work takes a wider perspective (e.g., Jacobs, 1994).

Coercive change still does not appear in many textbooks, yet it is widely applied, with differing degrees of success. Dunphy and Stace's (1988) model indicates the structure in which it might be the primary choice. From a psychological perspective, coercive change is unlikely to increase employees' commitment to change in the short-term, because some people may feel embittered and resentful about modifications imposed on them. Control mechanisms and detailed performance management over time may be required where cooperation is absent or limited (Zaltman and Duncan, 1977). If the change requires a high degree of employee commitment and enthusiasm, a coercive approach has limitations. However, in some specific circumstances it can lead to longer-term shifts in outlook (Zaltman and Duncan, 1977), where people align their attitudes to their new imposed behaviours.

An alternative approach to managing change is to encourage stake-holders' participation in planning and implementation of the change process. A range of techniques have been advocated to engage participants in change, such as survey feedback (Nadler, 1977), process consultation (Schein, 1969), action research (Elden and Chisholm, 1993) and real-time strategic change (Jacobs, 1994). However, participation and employee involvement do not always lead to effective change in situations where the consultation is peripheral to the main changes, where it brings to the surface conflicts which are not channelled or where significant power bases prevent change. A review indicated that participation had at best a marginal effect on performance and satisfaction (Wagner, 1994). This suggests that there is a need to move away from participation as a moral imperative to a more contingent view of employee involvement. It may have significant positive impacts in some circumstances, but such impacts are not universal. However, participation can encourage the engagement of all stakeholders and ensures that problems in implementing change can be addressed through a variety of talents and experience, not only through the input of senior management. The use of a steering group as part of project management can also engage stakeholders in a participative manner.

Negotiation can be a further approach to managing change. In these cases, it is agreed that no action can be undertaken unless both parties accept it (whereas in participation settings management may still proceed without the agreement of employees). Negotiation requires the parties to have sufficient power to be able to persuade others or to have the capacity to impose sanctions. Negotiation may be formal or informal, between individuals or between groups. For example, collective bargaining with trade unions may be important where unions are recognized, and in many European countries change has been achieved in this way.

There have been assumptions, inadequately tested, that employees generally dislike or are afraid of change. This assumption is related to the notion of 'resistance to change', although the theoretical and empirical base of such a concept has been criticized on a number of grounds (Fenton-O'Creevy, 2000). If it includes any type of behaviour or non-behaviour that is opposed to change (e.g., from outright conflict to passivity or sabotage), then this is not a very meaningful concept from a psychological point of view as it is too broad and varied to operationalize. Zaltman and Duncan (1977) note that, while there can be psychological barriers to change, such as fear of change or generalized anxiety, a full picture of resistance to change needs to examine also cultural, social, institutional and organizational barriers to change.

Structural and Cultural Change

Psychologists have been particularly influential in rejecting the assumption that changing formal structures is sufficient to change the organization, arguing instead that there is a need to go beyond structures to cultures, attitudes and behaviour if sustainable change is to be achieved. Many of the change techniques in organization development are concerned to clarify feelings, cognitions and behaviours which contribute to the culture of the organization (see Chapter 15 for definitions of culture). Commentators vary in their assessment of how far the cultures of organizations can be changed (Trice and Beyer, 1993). Structural modification can have a significant impact on organizational change when informal as well as formal features are reviewed (Dawson, 1994). Kanter, Stein and Jick (1992) distinguish between 'bold stroke' and 'long march' approaches to organizational change. The first is based on primarily structural change, which can be achieved relatively quickly (though the consequences of the restructure may take some time to be realized) but where the danger is that the changes are superficial. Long march change is based on cultural change, training and organizational learning. This takes longer to achieve, with the danger that the context and needs may have changed by the time that the change is fully implemented.

Timing and Phasing of Change

The time context of organizational change is important, since it may require a number of years to implement and embed. A sense of the different phases and milestones of change can contribute to the change process (Poole, van der Ven, Dooley and Holmes, 2000). Where there is a turbulent and rapidly changing external environment, internal organizational change needs to be able to adapt to contextual events in an appropriate rhythm (Gersick, 1994).

One influential model of phased change is that of Lewin (1951) and this will be addressed in more detail in a later section. Other models have been developed, particularly from the perspective of change agents. For example, Senior (1997) outlines the phases of diagnosing the current situation, developing a vision for change, gaining commitment to the vision, developing an action plan, implementing change and assessing and reinforcing change (in a cycle which may be repeated).

Timing and phasing are also significant because different stakeholders may have varied expectations about how quickly implementation will occur. There can be tensions between managers who seek early implementation (having considered options for some time) and change implementers and recipients, for whom the possibilities are still relatively new and who have to convert broad ideas into practical on-the-ground change (Hartley, Benington and Binns, 1997).

OUTPUTS AND OUTCOMES OF CHANGE

Outputs and outcomes are addressed in the fourth box of Figure 16.1. By outputs are meant the products, services or other phenomena achieved by the organization (e.g., more or faster service, or higher quality products), whereas outcomes are the achievements in terms of the organization's goals and are based on the organization's interactions with its environment (e.g., better market share, more satisfied customers, a more adaptive organization). Outputs are often (though not always) easier to measure than outcomes (Scott, 1992). Given that any organizational change can have a range of outputs and outcomes, their investigation is often complex.

Some consequences of change can be unintended. Systems theory (Scott, 1992) indicates that these unintended outcomes are highly likely, given the complexity of interactions between different elements and processes. In addition, organizational change has a range of stakeholders with varied interests, so there may be different judgements about whether change has been effective. Stakeholder perspectives may need special attention in some circumstances. For example, the achievement of goals may be of limited value if employees found the change experience so unpleasant that they are reluctant to go through further change in the future.

Whether change is episodic or continuous, effective organizations not only evaluate how far the change has achieved its intended outcomes but also examine what else has changed simultaneously or as a consequence. Organizational learning is a process which can help this continual course correction (see later section). This is indicated in the feedback process in Figure 16.1.

There are grounds for noting that while some employees find organizational change a threat, others thrive on change and innovation (Poole *et al.*, 2000). While some employees express insecurity about change, others feel little insecurity and may even look forward to change (Hartley, Jacobson, Klandermans and van Vuuren, 1991; Hartley, 1999). Stress during change is an issue for some staff but not for others (Borrill and Parker, 2000). In some circumstances, organizational change may bring improvements in work organization and new opportunities, thus reducing stress (Parker, Chmiel and Wall, 1997). The impact of change on employees is partly dependent on how change processes are managed (Hartley, 1999; Noer, 1993).

THEORIES OF AND APPROACHES TO INDIVIDUAL AND GROUP CHANGE

Many textbooks on organizational change focus on relevant techniques, especially those to make explicit and work with the informal processes of the organization. However, this common focus on techniques has sometimes been at the expense of their conceptual underpinnings or efficacy. Here we examine possible explanations of change at the individual and group level. Psychological writing on organizational change emphasizes the importance of individual and group changes in attitudes, behaviour and learning, arguing that these are essential if changes are to be long-term and deep-rooted, rather than based merely on behavioural compliance. Individual behaviour change is thus central to organizational change to a greater or lesser degree.

Lewin's Field Theory

Lewin's (1951) field theory is an early but still influential psychological theory of change in individuals and groups. Field theory recognizes that individual and group behaviour is a function of the forces and pressures acting on the person (or group). The 'field' is the complex interplay of these forces, which may be symbolic and psychological as well as practical. This has three significant implications.

First, changing individual behaviour may best be achieved not through focus on the individual but through consideration of the group pressures, norms, values and expectations. There are a variety of diagnostic and action research techniques for learning about these group influences (e.g., Cummings and Worley, 2001), such as force field analysis, survey feedback or process consultation.

Second, Lewin's notion of the field emphasizes that the varied forces acting on individuals and groups mean that a situation is never stable but is in a continuous process of adaptation (which Lewin termed 'quasi-stationary equilibrium'): a balance of driving and restraining forces. Increasing pressures to change may only invoke increased pressures to remain stable. Instead, Lewin's approach argues for a search for ways to reduce the restraining forces on change rather than to increase the pressures for change. While there are circumstances where this is appropriate, other research suggests that a degree of discomfort or even conflict and pressure can be important to generate change, because it enforces the search for new ideas and processes (Bartunek, 1993).

Third, Lewin also developed a model of the processes of planned change, which has three stages of unfreezing, changing and refreezing. The first phase (unfreezing) consists of reducing resistance to the proposed change, and also developing perceptions of the need for change. Zaltman and Duncan (1977) describe this as the development of awareness of a performance gap (a gap between the current and the desired level of achievement). It is also identified in terms of felt need for change. The second stage involves the change itself (which account appears to imply that change is a simple and/or a single step). The third phase consists of refreezing: ensuring that the new state of the organization is stabilized, with new activities and policies assisting to maintain the modified situation.

This three-phase approach to change is schematic and general, and it has proved popular with organization development consultants, although somewhat less so with researchers. Its value lies in the indications about how to prepare for change (for example, using diagnostic techniques), and in the importance of consolidation or institutionalization of change in the refreezing phase. For example, the concept of refreezing places emphasis on training and development, on career systems and other reward systems to support rather than undermine the change. The failure to sustain change is a major weakness of many planned change programmes. The model has also been used to map the key emotional states of change (Huy, 1999).

However, Lewin's original model may be more useful for planned change of an episodic nature than for continuous change. Weick and Quinn (1999) suggest that the approach may need to be adapted for conditions of continuous change, where the problem is not one of unfreezing but of slowing down organizational shifts sufficiently so that organizational members can reflect on change. 'In the face of continuous change, a more plausible change sequence may be freeze, rebalance, unfreeze' (p. 379). To freeze an organization which is restlessly changing is to capture the current situation so that it can be analyzed. Rebalancing focuses on reinterpreting and reorganizing patterns of activity. This echoes the role of leaders and change agents in continuous change. The third stage in this view of continuous change is to unfreeze so that the organization regains its capacity to make further shifts.

Organization Development

Organization development (OD) is a general term to cover a wide range of techniques and approaches. Beckhard (1969) describes it as an approach to change which is planned, organization-wide, managed from the top, intended to increase organizational effectiveness and health, using interventions concerned with processes, and based on behavioural science knowledge. Its base in behavioural science is varied (and not often specified in detail), but is seen to derive in part from Lewin's field theory and more generally from a human relations perspective. OD has been therefore less a theory than a framework and set of values about the importance of human agency, interaction and participative management. Writers have tended to emphasize:

- Social processes, especially informal behaviours, relationships, feelings and group dynamics.
- Experiential learning: OD has developed a variety of techniques to help people learn from their own feelings and experiences, for example, in team building and in conflict management.
- The use of a change agent, acting as a catalyst for change, who brings about the change through facilitation of individual and group learning.

Where organization development has been linked with systems theory (see below), it enables individuals, groups and organizations to consider not only social processes inside the organization but also promotes consideration of the impact of the wider external environment (e.g., Weisbord, 1988; Jacobs, 1994). However, the traditional organization development movement was based solely on normative values of what organizations 'ought' to be like (openness, trust and sharing were often viewed as key values) and was isolated from issues of context, power and politics. It is now generally recognized that this traditional view is too limited in its focus. Despite that, many books on the psychology of organizational change still focus mainly on organization development techniques, providing a tool-kit for consultants rather than a conceptual treatment for researchers.

Systems Theory

Systems theory is based on the assumption that an organization can be viewed as a whole organism, composed of parts or subsystems. As an *open* system, the organization interacts with its environment, taking in information and resources as inputs, and transforming these through organizational processes, turning some of them into outputs into the environment. It is partly because of the prominence of systems theory that so many writers have pointed to the impact of the external environment on the pace and trajectory of change.

This approach can be useful in a number of ways. First, it emphasizes the role of boundary-spanners in organizational adaptation and change. So the role of strategic managers is explicitly examined; their perceptions of the environment and of the ways in which the organization may adapt to that environment (or make the environment adapt to the organization) can be important. Front-line employees in contact with customers and suppliers are also an important source of intelligence about the external environment. Second, systems theory emphasizes the need for careful diagnosis of the external environment and the appropriateness of the interlocking internal systems (for example, technological, social, human resource management, career and political systems). Third, the complexity of the external environment as well as the complexity of adaptation by the open system makes it clear that change can never be entirely planned or predictable. There will always be some emergent properties of change and some unintended consequences of change. Fourth, a systems perspective has been a significant strand in the development of theory about organizational learning, where it is argued that a changing, uncertain and unpredictable environment leads to the need for organizations to encourage a continuous process of experimentation and learning.

A specific development of systems theory is socio-technical systems theory, initially developed by the Tavistock Institute in London in the early 1950s as a result of studying changes in work organization in the coal industry (Trist and Bamforth, 1951). The approach sets out to achieve organizational change through joint optimization of the technological and social systems. This is covered in more detail in pp. 285–7.

Organizational Learning

Interest in continuous change has encouraged theory-building and writing about learning in organizations. Argyris and Schön (1996) were seminal in developing the concept of organizational learning. Starting with individuals, they make the distinction between single-loop and double-loop learning. The former involves learning from previous behaviours using feedback to adjust action. It is based on monitoring and correcting behaviour. Double-loop learning not only adjusts behaviour but also involves questioning and reflecting on the basic assumptions which underlie the behaviour. It is about 'learning how to learn'. Argyris and others argue that the capacity to examine basic assumptions is the hallmark of adaptive learning, which is necessary for continuous and emergent change, where outcomes cannot be predicted.

Weick (1996) argues that this conceptualization of organizational learning can be seen as a type of sense-making. A key theme of the organizational learning approach, then, is concerned with continual information gathering, communicating and learning so that changes in the environment and in behaviours can be interpreted and acted on.

Writers have outlined the organizational characteristics which tend to support or inhibit learning, including aspects of organizational culture (see Chapter 15). The linkage, where it exists, between individual learning and organizational learning has still to be clarified. Individuals may learn from their training and other experiences, but this does not necessarily lead to organizational learning.

A number of writers have examined how learning can spread within and between teams of people in organizations, and also in some cases between organizations (e.g., Easterby-Smith, Araujo and Burgoyne, 1999). Nonaka and Takeuchi's (1995) research on product development in Japanese companies emphasizes the dynamic nature of learning and knowledge creation in organizations. They start with the assumption that an organization which is dealing dynamically with a continuously changing environment will not only be using but also producing knowledge. Nonaka distinguishes between explicit knowledge (codified, transmittable in formal systematic language) and tacit knowledge (cannot be precisely specified, and is often deeply rooted or embodied in action in a context). Tacit and explicit knowledge are complementary in organizations, and learning between employees can occur through a variety of social interaction processes. Dixon (1999) has also drawn on the concepts of tacit and explicit knowledge in her analysis of inter-organizational learning among Canadian museum staff, arguing that both are important for effective inter-organizational learning and change.

Interest in both individual and organizational learning is growing, and psychological research can contribute substantially (see also Chapter 6). However, there are limitations. First, it is useful to distinguish between organizational learning and 'the learning organization'. The latter is widely seen to be a prescriptive approach to the ideal organization, often promulgated by consultants rather than academics (see Easterby-Smith, 1997, for a thoughtful review). Second, not all learning is beneficial to the organization. Leavitt and March (1988) note problems associated with 'superstitious' learning (making an incorrect diagnosis of the link between context and action) and also the 'competency trap' (that if an organization is adapting well, it may not be aware that other organizations are making more radical changes). Third, the assumption in some of the organizational learning literature is that sharing learning between employees is highly valued. However, power relations in organizations often mean that a person's learning is harboured not shared (Coopey, 1995).

The Evaluation of Change

There are two challenges in evaluating organizational change. The first (illustrated throughout the chapter) is that organizational change is complex: there are very many different circumstances, reasons, aims, and trajectories of organizational change. To some extent, this has encouraged idiographic research, based on detailed case study analysis of specific organizational changes. The number of research studies which are nomothetic (examining general qualities over a sample) is limited. The second difficulty is that by its nature change is not stable, so that some of the customary methodologies of psychology are not suitable. How do you study change over time, when the people may move out, the jobs may disappear, and the structures of departments or business units may be transformed almost overnight? This suggests that plans for longitudinal designs have to be carefully reviewed after a project has started, with elements of responsive adaptation of design as the change develops. It follows that, as well as quantitative studies, qualitative designs and action research (Elden and Chisholm, 1993) are also important in this field. It also means that evaluation studies are likely to have elements of formative evaluation as well as summative evaluation (see Chapter 6 for an explanation of these terms).

SUMMARY

It is helpful to distinguish between episodic change (infrequent, discontinuous and intentional) and continuous change (developmental, ongoing, incremental, emergent and cumulative). There is increasing interest in how to achieve continuous change, including through quality management and through organizational learning. Within these types of change, there are four main sets of influences (shown in Figure 16.1): the context (both external and internal), the leadership and key agents of change, the management of change processes and the outputs and outcomes of change, including the unintended outcomes (some of which are inevitable in complex change). The impact of each of these influences varies, but there are differences which relate to whether the strategic choice is to engage in change which is episodic or continuous.

Psychological writing on organizational change emphasizes the importance of individual and group changes in attitudes, behaviour and learning, arguing that these are essential if changes are to be long-term and deep-rooted. Four major explanations of behaviour change in organizations are Lewin's field theory, the organization development movement, systems theory and organizational learning theory. Each approach has its strengths and weaknesses, and none is adequate on its own.

FURTHER READING

The review article by Weick and Quinn (1999) contains a useful summary of the contrasts between episodic and continuous change, and their implications for theories of change processes and the role of leadership and change agents. Dunphy and Stace (1988) provide a valuable critique of organization development themes and strategic choices about change that is related to the external context. Kanter, Stein and Jick (1992) present a useful summary of a number of the theories and techniques of organizational change, along with case studies of change, though that book does have a focus on the USA. Burnes (2000) provides a UK equivalent, linking strategy with organization development. The text by Zaltman and Duncan (1977) remains particularly useful for its exposition of coercive and participative approaches to the engagement of stakeholders. The volume by Cummings and Worley (2001) remains the best outline of organization development frameworks, techniques and tools. Nonaka and Takeuchi's (1995) book, *The Knowledge-Creating Company* is essential reading for understanding organizational learning, in conjunction with the article by Easterby-Smith (1997).

REFERENCES

Argyris, C. and Schön, D. (1996). *Organizational Learning*. Reading, MA: Addison-Wesley.

Bartunek, J. (1993). The multiple cognitions and conflicts associated with second order organizational change. In K. Murnighan (Ed.), *Social Psychology in Organizations*. Englewood Cliffs, NJ: Prentice-Hall.

Beckhard, R. (1969). *Organization Development: Source Strategies and Models*. Reading, MA: Addison-Wesley.

Binney, G. (1992). *Making Quality Work: Lessons from Europe's Leading Companies*. London: Economist Intelligence Unit.

Borrill, C. and Parker, S. (2000). Change management and stress. In P. Flood, T. Dromgoole, S. Carroll and L. Gorman (Eds.), *Managing Strategic Implementation* (pp. 80–95). Oxford: Blackwell.

Brown, S. and Eisenhardt, K. (1998). *Competing on the Edge*. Boston, MA: Harvard Business School Press.

Burnes, B. (2000). *Managing Change: A Strategic Approach to Organizational Dynamics*, third edition. London: Pitman.

Child, J. and Smith, C. (1987). The context and process of organizational transformation – Cadbury Limited in its sector. *Journal of Management Studies*, 24, 565–93.

Coopey, J. (1995). The learning organization: power politics and ideology. *Management Learning*, 26, 193–214.

Cummings, T. and Worley, C. (2001). *Organization Development and Change* (seventh edition). St Paul, MN: West Publishing.

Dawson, P. (1994). *Organizational Change: A Processual Approach*. London: Paul Chapman Publishing.

Dixon, N. (1999). Learning across organizational boundaries. In M. Easterby-Smith, L. Araujo and J. Burgoyne (Eds.), *Organizational Learning and the Learning Organization*. London: Sage.

Duck, J. D. (1998). Managing change: The art of balancing. *Harvard Business Review on Change*, 55–81.

Dunphy, D. and Stace, D. (1988). Transformational and coercive strategies for planned organizational change: Beyond the O.D. model. *Journal of Organization Studies*, 9, 317–34.

Dutton, J. and Dukerich, J. (1991). Keeping an eye on the mirror: image and identity in organizational adaptation. *Academy of Management Journal*, 34, 517–54.

Easterby-Smith, M. (1997). Disciplines of organizational learning: Contributions and critiques. *Human Relations*, 50, 1085–113.

—, Araujo, L. and Burgoyne, J. (Eds.) (1999). *Organizational Learning and the Learning Organization*. London: Sage.

Elden, M. and Chisholm, R. (1993). Emerging varieties of action research: Introduction to the special issue. *Human Relations*, 46, 121–42.

Fenton-O'Creevy, M. (2000). In P. Flood, T. Dromgoole, S. Carroll and L. Gorman (Eds.), *Managing Strategic Implementation* (pp. 109–22). Oxford: Blackwell.

Flood, P., Dromgoole, T., Carroll, S. and Gorman, L. (2000). *Managing Strategic Implementation*. Oxford: Blackwell.

French, W. L. and Bell, C. H. (1990). *Organization Development: Behavioral Science Interventions for Organization Improvement*. Englewood Cliffs, NJ: Prentice-Hall.

Gersick, C. (1994). Pacing strategic change: The case of a new venture. *Academy of Management Journal*, 37, 9–45.

Hartley, J. F. (1999). Causes and consequences of job insecurity – and coping strategies by organizations. In M. Marmot and J. Ferrie (Eds.), *Labour Market Changes and Job Insecurity: a Challenge for Social Welfare and Health Promotion* (pp. 127–49). Copenhagen: World Health Organization.

— (2000). Leading and managing the uncertainty of strategic change. In P. Flood, T. Dromgoole, S. Carroll and L. Gorman (Eds.), *Managing Strategic Implementation* (pp. 109–22). Oxford: Blackwell.

— and Allison, M. (2000). The role of leadership in modernisation and improvement of public services. *Public Money and Management*, April, 35–40.

—, Benington, J. and Binns, P. (1997). Researching the role of internal change agents in the management of organizational change. *British Journal of Management*, 8, 61–73.

—, Cordingley, P. and Benington, J. (1995). *Managing Organizational and Cultural Change in Local Authorities*. Luton: Local Government Management Board.

—, Jacobson, D., Klandermans, B. and van Vuuren, T. (1991). *Job Insecurity: Coping with Jobs at Risk*. London: Sage.

Huy, Q. N. (1999). Emotional capability, emotional intelligence and change. *Academy of Management Review*, 24, 325–45.

Jacobs, R. W. (1994). *Real Time Strategic Change*. San Francisco, CA: Berrett Koehler.

Kanter, R., Stein, B. and Jick, T. (1992). *The Challenge of Organizational Change*. New York: Free Press.

Leavitt, B. and March, J. G. (1988). Organizational learning. *Annual Review of Sociology*, 14, 319–40.

Lewin, K. (1951). *Field Theory in Social Science*. New York: Harper and Row.

Mohrman, A., Mohrman, S., Ledford, G., Cummings, T. and Lawler, E. (1989). *Large-Scale Organizational Change*. San Francisco: Jossey-Bass.

Mowday, R. and Sutton, R. (1993). Organizational behavior: linking individuals and groups to organizational contexts. *Annual Review of Psychology*, 44, 195–229.

Nadler, D. (1977). *Survey Feedback*. Reading, MA: Addison-Wesley.

— and Tushman, M. (1980). A model for diagnosing organizational behaviour. *Organizational Dynamics*, 9, 35–51.

Noer, D. (1993). *Healing the Wounds: Overcoming the Traumas of Layoff and Revitalizing Downsized Organizations*. San Francisco: Jossey-Bass.

Nonaka, I. and Takeuchi, H. (1995). *The Knowledge-Creating Company*. New York: Oxford University Press.

Parker, S., Chmiel, N. and Wall, T. (1997). Work characteristics and employee well-being with a context of strategic downsizing. *Journal of Occupational Health Psychology*, 2, 289–303.

Pettigrew, A. (1985). *The Awakening Giant: Continuity and Change at ICL*. Oxford: Blackwell.

— and Whipp, R. (1991). *Managing Change for Competitive Success*. Oxford: Blackwell.

Pfeffer, J. (1981). Management as symbolic action. *Research in Organizational Behavior*, 3, 1–52.

— and Salancik, G. (1978). *The External Control of Organizations*. New York: Harper Row.

Poole, M. S., van der Ven, A., Dooley, K. and Holmes, M. (2000). *Organizational Change and Innovation Processes*. New York: Oxford University Press.

Porras, J. and Silvers, R. (1991). Organization development and transformation. *Annual Review of Psychology*, 42, 51–78.

Quinn, J. B. (1980). *Strategies for Change: Logical Incrementalism*. Homewood, IL: Irwin.

Rousseau, D. and Fried, Y. (2001). Location, location, location: Contextualizing organizational research. *Journal of Organizational Behavior*, 22, 1–14.

Schein, E. (1969). *Process Consultation*. Reading, MA: Addison-Wesley.

— (1992). *Organizational Culture and Leadership*. San Francisco: Jossey-Bass.

Scott, W. R. (1992). *Organizations: Rational, Natural and Open Systems*. Englewood Cliffs, NJ: Prentice-Hall.

Senior, B. (1997). Organizational change and development. In N. Chmiel (Ed.), *Work and Organizational Psychology*. Oxford: Blackwell.

Sparrow, P. (1994). The psychology of strategic management: Emerging themes of diversity and cognition. *International Review of Industrial and Organizational Psychology*, 9, 147–82.

Trice, H. M. and Beyer, J. M. (1993). *The Cultures of Work Organizations*. Englewood Cliffs, NJ: Prentice-Hall.

Trist, E. and Bamforth, K. (1951). Some social and psychological consequences of the long-wall method of coal-getting. *Human Relations*, 4, 3–38.

Van der Ven, A., Angle, H. and Poole, M. (1989). *Research on the Management of Innovation*. New York: Harper and Row.

Wagner, J. A. (1994). Participation's effects on performance and satisfaction: a reconsideration of the research evidence. *Academy of Management Review*, 19, 312–30.

Weick, K. (1995). *Sense-Making in Organizations*. Thousand Oaks, CA: Sage.

— (1996). The non-traditional quality of organizational learning. In M. Cohen and L. Sproull (Eds.), *Organizational Learning*. Thousand Oaks, CA: Sage.

— and Quinn, R. (1999). Organizational change and development. *Annual Review of Psychology*, 50, 361–86.

Weisbord, M. (1988). *Productive Workplaces: Organizing and Managing for Dignity, Meaning and Community*. San Francisco: Jossey-Bass.

Zaltman, G. and Duncan, R. (1977). *Strategies for Planned Change*. New York: Wiley.

Author Index

Authors appearing within '*et al.*' in the text are indicated here through page numbers printed in italics.

Abraham, L. M., 10, 21
Abraham, R., 245, 249
Ackerman, P. L., 161, 176, 177, 185, 199
Adams, P. H., 73
Aditya, R. N., 387, 397
Adler, P. S., 392, 397
Aggarwal, G., 140, 149
Agho, A. O., 10, 21
Ahearne, M., 338, 349
Ainsworth, L. K., 35, 49
Ajzen, I., 18, 21
Akerstedt, T., 54, 60, 62, 73
Alban-Metcalfe, R. J., 312, 313, 314, 322
Aldridge, J., 68, 73
Algera, J. A., 102, 146
Alimo-Metcalfe, B., 312, 313, 314, 318, 319, 322
Allan, C., 156, *160*, 163, *164*, *166*, *168*, 175, 177
Allen, N. J., 18, 23
Allen, S. J., 264, 272
Alliger, G. M., 168, 169, 174, 302, 324
Allison, M., 408, 423
Alper, S., 337, 345
Altmann, R., 394, 398
Amlund, J. T., 162, 176
Ancona, D. G., 341, 345

Anderson, J. R., 15, 21, 30, 48, 154, 165, 174, 175
Anderson, N., 151, 298
Andlauer, P., 74
Angle, H., 407, 409, 424
Applebaum, E., 362, 368, 369, 371
Araujo, L., 419, 423
Argyris, C., 418, 422
Arnold, J., 178, 179, 192, 193, 198, 199, 200
Arnold, V., 397
Arthur, J. B., 353, 354, 356, 357, 365, 371
Arthur, M. B., 180, 181, 188, 198, 199
Arthur, W., 128, 148, 157, 158, 175
Arvanitaki, K., 294, 297
Arvey, R. D., 10, 21
Aschoff, J., 52, 73
Ash, R. A., 105, 151
Ashforth, B. E., 17, 23, 217, 227, 238, 239, 245, 249
Ashkanasy, N. M., 249, 251, 396, 397
Association of Graduate Recruiters, 137, 146
Assouline, M., 183, 199
Atwater, L., 319, 323
Avolio, B. J., 261, 263, 271, 273, 311, 312, 313, 319, 322, 323
Axtell, C. M., 292, 298
Ayman, R., 322

Bachrach, D. G., 14, 23
Baddeley, A. D., 28, 48
Baecker, R. M., 90, 97
Bailey, D. E., 326, 328, 333, 341, 344, 345
Bailey, T., 362, 368, 369, 371
Bainbridge, L., 45, 48, 89, 97
Baldwin, T. T., 4, 5, 24, 327, 348
Baltes, B. B., 394, 398
Bamforth, K. W., 285, 299, 418, 424
Bamundo, P. J., 5, 21
Bandura, A., 156, 175
Banker, R. D., 291, 296, 330, 345
Banks, M., 208, 224
Barker, J. R., 336, 345
Barling, J., 253, 261, 263, 264, 267, 268, 271, 272, 273, 274
Barney, J., 366, 371
Baron, H., 133, 150
Bar-On, R., 245, 249
Barrick, M. R., 132, 133, 143, 146, 149, 162, 175, 332, 345
Bartel, C. A., 342, 349
Bartlett, F. C., xiii, xv
Barton, J., 68, 71, 73
Bartram, D., 105, 136, 137, 140, 144, 146, 149
Bartunek, J., 407, 415, 422
Basch, J., 234, 249
Bass, B. M., 263, 271, 303, 310, 311, 312, 313, 314, 316, 318, 319, 322, 323
Batt, R., 331, 345
Battista, M., 105, 151
Bauer, T. N., 125, 147
Baumeister, R. F., 241, 251
Baxter, P. J., 73
Beaumont, P., 370, 371
Becker, B. E., 366, 369, 370, 371
Beckhard, R., 416, 422
Beehr, T., 204, 210, 212, 213, 216, 218, 224, 225, 226, 227
Beekun, R. I., 289, 296
Beerman, B., 69, 73
Belbin, R. M., 332, 333, 345
Bell, C. H., 404, 408, 423
Benington, J., 406, 413, 422

Bennett, W. R., 157, 158, 168, 169, 174, 175, 338, 349
Bents, F. D., 33, 48
Bentson, C., 127, 148
Benyon, D., 86, 96, 98
Berg, P., 362, 368, 369, 371
Berger, C. J., 284, 296
Beyer, J. M., 396, 398, 412, 424
Bielema, M., 265, 272
Billings, C., 43, 48
Binney, G., 399, 422
Binns, P., 413, 423
Bird, M. W., 169, 177
Birdi, K. S., 4, 14, 21, 156, 160, 162, 163, 164, 166, 168, 175, 177
Bjerknes, G., 98
Blackler, F. H. M., 87, 97
Blake, R. R., 305, 323
Blanchard, K. H., 306, 324
Bleir, A., 105, 127, 152
Blickensderfer, E., 335, 345
Blundell, R., 156, 175
Blyton, P., 297
Boddy, D., 88, 97
Bongers, P. M., 8, 21
Bono, J. E., 9, 10, 12, 22, 263, 273
Bordin, E., 195, 199
Borgen, F. H., 183, 195, 199
Borman, W. C., 20, 21, 151
Borofsky, G. L., 265, 272
Borrill, C. S., 336, 337, 350, 414, 422
Bouchard, T. J., 10, 21
Boudreau, J. W., 121, 122, 147, 371, 373
Bowen, D. E., 282, 296
Bowers, C. A., 335, 345
Boydell, T., 172, 175
Bramley, P., 174, 175
Bramwell, R., 215, 225
Brannen, M. Y., 385, 397
Braverman, H., 279, 293, 296
Bray, D. W., 126, 147
Breaugh, J. A., 101, 147
Briner, R. B., 222, 224, 230, 232, 236, 242, 249, 251, 252
Broad, M. L., 171, 175
Broadbent, D. E., xiii, xiv, xv, xvi, 41, 48

Brockner, J., 216, 224
Brooks, L., 181, 198, 199
Brooks, S. M., 390, 398
Broughton, R. J., 73
Brown, C. A., 87, 97
Brown, D., 181, 198, 199
Brown, J. M., 245, 249
Brown, S., 400, 422
Brown, S. P., 394, 397
Bryman, A., 300, 309, 312, 313, 321, 323
Bryson, A., 180, 199
Buchanan, B. G., 89, 97
Buchanan, D. A., 88, 96, 97
Buckley, R., 174, 175
Bunce, D., 163, 164, 168, 177
Burger, J. M., 8, 21
Burgess, S., 180, 190, 199
Burgoyne, J., 172, 175, 419, 423
Burke, M. J., 157, 175
Burke, R, J., 213, 214, 217, 221, 222, 223,
    225, 226, 321, 322, 323, 324
Burnes, B., 421, 422
Burns, J. M., 310, 323
Burns, T., 290, 296, 379, 380, 397
Buunk, B., 212, 228
Bycio, P., 264, 272
Byham, W. C., 149
Byosiere, P., 210, 211, 212, 221, 226

Cacioppo, J. T., 241, 250
Cahill, J., 268, 274
Caldwell, D. F., 341, 345
Callinan, M., 105, 133, 134, 146, 147, 149,
    150
Campbell, D. T., 265, 272
Campbell, J. P., 114, 152, 254, 272
Campbell, R. J., 337, 347
Campion, J. E., 130, 147, 313, 348
Campion, M. A., 125, 129, 130, 147, 149,
    150, 175, 279, 280, 284, 287, 296, 329,
    330, 332, 342, 344, 345, 349
Canfield-Smith, D., 83, 97
Cannon-Bowers, J. A., 332, 335, 338, 345,
    348, 350
Canter, R. R., 279, 297
Caplan, R., 205, 206, 225

Caple, J., 174, 175
Caputi, P., 113, 147
Caranikas-Walker, F., 17, 22
Card, S. K., 82, 90, 96, 97, 98
Carey, T., 86, 96, 98
Carlson, K. D., 135, 147
Carr, L., 105, 151
Carroll, J. B., 110, 111, 147
Carroll, S., 410, 422, 423
Carskadon, M. A., 63, 74
Cartwright, S., 211, 214, 221, 225, 396,
    397
Caruso, D., 113, 149
Carver, C. S., 233, 249
Castellan, N. J., 345
Castillo, D. N., 267, 272
Cattell, R. B., 113, 147
Cavanaugh, M. A., 10, 21
Cavender, J. W., 12, 23
Caw, T-C., 73
Cesana, G., 75
Chaiken, S., 17, 20, 22
Champoux, J. E., 283, 296
Chan, A. Y. C., 113, 147
Chan, D., 146, 151
Chandhok, R., 92, 98
Chao, G. T., 192, 199
Charbonneau, D., 261, 272
Charness, N., 30, 31, 48
Chartrand, J. M., 9, 22
Chemers, M. M., 322
Chen, P., 216, 228
Cheraskin, L., 159, 175, 280, 296
Cherns, A. B., 286, 296
Child, J., 406, 422
Chisholm, R., 411, 420, 423
Chmiel, N., 41, 48, 414, 424
Cholar, J. S., 387, 397
Christiansen, N. D., 332, 349
Church, A. H., 20, 22, 303, 323
Ciarrochi, J. V., 113, 147, 313
Clapham, M. M., 128, 147
Clark, L. A., 3, 8, 25, 216, 228
Clause, C. S., 123, 151
Clayton, L. D., 236, 346
Cleary, T. A., 122, 131, 147

Clegg, C. W., 95, 97, 208, 224, 286, 290, 299, 299, 335, 350, 369, 373
Clegg, S. R., 323
Cleveland, R. J., 262, 275
Cochran, L., 194, 199
Cockcroft, A., 73
Cohen, A., 262, 272, 275
Cohen, H. H. 262, 266, 272, 274
Cohen, S. G., 287, 293, 294, 297, 298, 326, 328, 330, 334, 344, 345, 348, 349
Colligan, M. J., 67, 73, 75
Collin, A., 201, 202
Collinson, D. L., 269, 272
Colquhoun, W. P., 73, 75
Colquitt, J. A., 160, 161, 162, 166, 167
Confederation of British Industry, 203, 225
Conger, J. A., 309, 310, 314, 323, 324
Converse, S. A., 339, 345
Conway, H., 256, 272
Cook, T. D., 265, 272
Cooke, R. A., 383, 397
Cooper, C. L., 22, 24, 150, 151, 152, 177, 210, 211, 212, 213, 214, 215, 221, 225, 227, 228, 248, 251, 271, 298, 350, 396, 397
Cooper, D., 122, 146, 147
Cooper, H., 8, 9, 22
Cooper, J. T., 244, 252
Coopey, J., 220, 222
Copper, C., 336, 349
Corbett, M. J., 290, 299
Cordery, J. L., 289, 290, 297, 330, 335, 345, 346, 350, 369, 373, 406, 423
Cordingley, P., 406, 423
Cortina, J. M., 144, 147
Costa, G., 72, 73, 74, 75
Costa, P. T., 110, 114, 147
Cotton, J. L., 193, 201, 215, 226
Cox, T., 218, 219, 225
Crandall, R., 226
Cronshaw, S. F., 128, 130, 152
Crook, C. K., 93, 97
Cropanzano, R., 214, 225, 234, 235, 246, 252
Crute, V., 196, 201

Cully, M., 180, 199
Cummings, L., 347, 349
Cummings, T., 401, 404, 408, 409, 415, 421, 422
Curphy, G. J., 262, 273
CyberAtlas, 138, 147
Czeisler, C. A., 63, 74

Daft, R. L., 254, 272
Dalbokova, D. L., 68, 75
Daniels, K., 4, 21
Danna, K., 20, 21
Davids, K., 291, 299
Davidson, M. J., 321, 322, 323, 324
Davies, D. R., 28, 33, 47, 49
Davies, M., 244, 249
Davis, J. H., 337, 348
Davis, L. E., 279, 297
Davison, H. K., 144, 148
Dawis, R. V., 182, 199, 412, 422
Day, E. A., 157, 175
De Jonge, J., 8, 21
De Menezes, L., 363, 374
De Pree, M., 300, 323
De Vader, C. L., 302, 324
De Wolf, C. J., 146
Dean, J. E., 362, 370, 374
Dearden, L., 156, 175
Deary, I. J., 114, 149
Deese, J., 204, 227
Delaney, J. T., 362, 372
Delbridge, R., 293, 297
Delery, J. E., 362, 372
Delp, N. D., 163, 176
Delsen, L., xi, xvi
Dement, W. C., 63, 74
DeMeuse, K. P., 328, 350
Den Hartog, D. N., 312, 320, 323
DeNeve, K. M., 8, 9, 22
Denison, D. R., 386, 397
Department for Education and Employment, xi, xvi, 161, 174, 175
Devine, D. J., 326, 346
Dewe, P., 210, 211, 212, 213, 218, 219, 225
Dickson, M. W., 326, 336, 344, 347, 383, 387, 397

Diener, E., 3, 23, 231, 249
Digman, J. M., 110, 147
Dillon, A., 94, 97
Dinges, D. F., 63, 74
Dirks, K. T., 337, 346
Dirsmith, M. W., 335, 347
Dix, G., 180, 199
Dixon, N., 419, 422
Dobson, P., 134, 147
Docherty, N. F., 95, 97
Dolen, M. R., 125, 147
Donchin, E., 33, 48
Dooley, K., 412, 414, 424
Dorfman, P. W., 312, 320, 323, 383, 397
Dornheim, L., 244, 252
Doty, D. H., 362, 372
Downing, H., 78, 97
Downing, J., 163, 164, 177
Downs, S., 134, 150
Drakeley, R. J., 135, 148
Dreher, G. F., 127, 150
Drenth, P., 146
Dromgoole, T., 410, 422, 423
Dryden, W., 200
Duck, J. D., 402, 422
Dulewicz, V., 127, 148
Duncan, K., 97
Duncan, R., 411, 412, 415, 421, 425
Dunford, B. B., 326, 346
Dunham, J., 224, 225
Dunham, R., 211, 228
Dunnette, M., 21, 226
Dunphy, D., 404, 405, 410, 421, 422
Durso, F. T., 47, 48
Dutton, J., 405, 422
Dwyer, D. J., 17, 24, 209, 210, 225

Eagly, A. H., 17, 20, 22, 319, 323, 339, 346
Earley, P. C., 338, 346, 396, 397
Eason, K. D., 92, 94, 95, 96, 97
Easterby-Smith, M., 419, 421, 422, 423
Eden, D., 412, 428
Edwards, J., 206, 207, 225, 305, 323
Egan, T., 333, 350
Eggemeier, F. T., 34, 36, 49, 50
Ehn, P., 98

Eisenberg, W. M., 256, 272
Eisenhardt, K., 400, 422
Ekeberg, S. E., 183, 202
Elden, M., 411, 420, 423
Elliott, T. R., 9, 22
Embrey, D. E., 65, 74
Emmanualides, P. A., 335, 346
Endsley, M. R., 45, 48
Ernst, G., 68, 75
Erwin, F., 135, 147
Essrer, J. K., 339, 346
European Commission, x, xi, xvi
Eyde, L. D., 105, 151
Eysenck, H. J., 113, 148
Eysenck, M. J., 113, 148

Fabrigar, L. R., 3, 23
Fahs, M., 253, 274
Fairfield-Sonn, J. W., 346
Fang, Y., 283, 298
Farrell, D., 16, 22
Feij, J. A., 8, 24
Feldman, D. C., 240, 251
Felstead, A., 93, 98
Feltham, R., 126, 148
Fenlason, K., 218, 225
Fenton-O'Creevy, M., 410, 412, 423
Ferguson E., 218, 219, 225
Ferrario, M., 319, 323
Ferrie, J., 423
Ferris, G. R., 283, 289, 297, 371
Fiedler, F. E., 306, 323
Field, J. M., 291, 296, 330, 345
Fiksenbaum, L., 217, 226
Fineman, S., 232, 237, 248, 249
Fink, G., 47, 48
Finkelstein, S., 335, 347
Fischer, A. R., 184, 201
Fisher, B. M., 305, 323
Fisher, C. D., 232, 249
Fisher, S. G., 323, 346
Fitness, J., 232, 234, 249
Fitzpatrick, D., 266, 274
Flanagan, J. C., 104, 129, 148
Fletcher, B., 203, 225
Flood, P., 410, 422, 423

Flores, F., 96, 99
Fogarty, T. J., 335, 347
Folkard, S., 41, 48, 54, 55, 57, 58, 61, 63,
    64, 65, 66, 68, 70, 72, 73, 74, 75, 76
Folkman, S., 206, 218, 219, 227
Ford, J. K., 155, 164, 165, 166, 174, 175, 176
Forester, T., 97
Forth, J., 180, 199
Fox, H., 253, 274
Fox, M., 209, 210, 225
Fox, S., 113, 148, 243, 250
Francis, C., 289, 298
Frankenhaeuser, M., 37, 41, 48, 49
Franz, T., 204, 224
Fraser, R., 279, 297
Freedman, S., 221, 226
French W. L., 404, 408, 423
French, J., 205, 206, 225
Frenkel, S. J., 294, 297
Frese, M., 216, 228, 292, 297
Freudenberger, H., 207, 225
Fried, Y., 283, 289, 297, 402, 424
Friedkin, N. E., 340, 346
Frink, D. D., 338, 349
Froggatt, K., 215, 226
Frone, M. R., 267, 269, 272
Fukuyama, F., 336, 346
Fullerton, J., 123, 149
Fusilier, M., 217, 226
Futrell, D., 328, 350

Gaertner, S., 17, 22
Galer, M. D., 86, 98
Gallagher, D. G., 267, 271
Ganster, D. C., 43, 48, 204, 208, 209, 210,
    215, 216, 217, 222, 225, 226
Ganzach, Y., 144, 148
Gardner, C. R., 14, 21
Gates, A. I., 58, 74
Gaugler, B. B., 126, 127, 148, 151
Gechman, A. S., 13, 22
Geher, G., 244, 250
George, J. M., 9, 16, 22, 236, 242, 245, 250
Gerhart, B., 366, 369, 371, 373
Gerras, S. J., 263, 273
Gersick, C. J. G., 341, 346, 413, 423

Gessner, J., 397
Ghiselli, E.E., 119, 130, 148
Gibbons, P., 133, 150
Gibson, C. B., 327, 346
Gier, J. A., 129, 152
Gilligan, C., 319, 323
Gilliland, S. W., 144, 148
Ginnett, R. C., 262, 273
Gist, M. E., 157, 176
Gittleman, M., 326, 346
Gladstein, D. L., 328, 346
GLOBE, 383, 387, 397
Glunk, U., 387, 398
Godard, J., 369, 372
Goldberg, D., 208, 226
Golden, C. J., 244, 252
Goldstein, H. W., 182, 201
Goldstein, I. L., 174, 176
Goldstein, N. B., 144, 148
Goleman, D., 113, 148, 243, 244, 250
Gooding, R. Z., 127, 151
Goodman, M. J., 33, 48
Goodman, P. S., 342, 346
Goodwin, G. F., 338, 348
Gopher, D., 33, 48
Gorman, L., 410, 422, 423
Gottfredson, L. S., 131, 148
Graeber, R. C., 63, 74
Graen, G. B., 308, 323
Grandey, A., 214, 225
Grandjean, E., 96, 98, 259, 274
Grant, D. L., 126, 147
Gratton, L., 127, 129, 145, 150
Gray, C., 191, 201
Greenbaum, J., 95, 98
Greenberg, E., 256, 272
Greenglass, E., 213, 217, 226
Greenleaf, R. K., 316, 324
Gregg, P., 180, 199
Greuter, M. A. M., 102, 146
Griffeth, R. W., 17, 21, 22
Griffin, M. A., 257, 258, 272, 274
Griffin, R. W., 20, 281, 297, 327, 347
Griffiths, D. K., 262, 272
Gronn, R., 320, 324
Grunberg, L., 256, 272

Gruneberg, M. M., 97
Guest, D., 362, 368, 369, 370, 371, 378
Guest, R., 279, 299
Gunnarsson, E., 294, 298
Gupta, P. P., 335, 347
Gupta, V., 335, 383, 397
Guterman, H. A., 105, 127, 152
Guthrie, J. P., 362, 372
Guzzo, R. A., 326, 336, 337, 344, 346, 347

Hackett, R. D., 16, 22, 264, 272, 339, 350
Hackman, J. R., 282, 283, 287, 295, 297,
    328, 330, 344, 347
Hagberg, M., 84, 98
Haggerty, D. J., 244, 252
Hahn, S. E., 232, 250
Haines, T., 292, 298
Haldeman, J., 289, 298
Hale, A. R., 266, 272
Haleblian, J., 335, 347
Hall, D. T., 181, 198, 199
Hall, L. E., 244, 252
Hamel, G., 397, 382
Hamilton, P., 38, 49
Hammer, A. L., 183, 195, 199
Hammond, J., 99
Hanecke, K., 68, 75
Hanges, P. J., 312, 320, 323, 383, 397
Hanisch, K., 213, 226
Hansen, J. C., 183, 195, 199
Hardy, C., 323
Hardy, G. E., 16, 22
Hargie, O., 196, 201
Harker, S. D. P., 86, 94, 95, 97, 98
Harkins, S. W., 9, 22
Harmon, L. W., 183, 195, 199
Harrington, J. M., 68, 72, 74
Harrison, V., 205, 206, 225
Hart, P. M., 257, 274
Hart, S. G., 36, 48
Hartel, C. E. J., 249, 251
Hartley, J. F., 402, 406, 407, 408, 413, 414,
    416, 423
Haslett, T. K., 163, 176
Hatfield, E., 241, 250
Hawthorn, R., 200, 202

Health and Safety Executive, 253, 273
Heffner, T. S., 338, 348
Heggestad, E. D., 185, 199
Hekkens, W. Th. J. M., 73
Helander, M. G., 96, 98
Hemingway, M., 256, 273
Hendrix, W., 209, 226
Henry, S., 127, 150
Herold, D. M., 328, 347
Herriot, P., 145, 147, 148, 149, 151, 189, 199
Hersey, P., 306, 324
Hersey, R. B., 229, 250
Herzberg, F., 229, 250, 282, 297
Hesketh, B., 105, 151, 185, 199
Hicks, T. G., 35, 48
Higgins, C. A., 143, 149
Higgs, A. C., 329, 330, 342, 344, 345
Hill, G. W., 334, 347
Hill, J., 63, 64, 73
Hill, L., 195, 198, 201
Hilton, T. F., 257, 275
Hirsh, W., 184, 191, 193, 198, 200
Hochschild, A. R., 237, 242, 243, 250, 294,
    297
Hockey, G. R. J., 26, 32, 37, 38, 40, 41, 42,
    43, 48, 49, 50
Hoffman, C. C., 124, 148
Hoffman, J., 265, 272, 279, 297
Hoffman, K. E., 138, 148
Hofmann, D. A., 257, 262, 263, 268, 279,
    273
Hogg, M. A., 333, 347
Holding, D. H., 42, 49
Holland, J. L., 182–4, 185, 200
Holland, S., 86, 96, 98
Hollands, J. G., 26, 28, 33, 36, 43, 46, 47,
    50
Hollenbeck, J., 371, 373
Holmes, M., 412, 414, 424
Hom, P. W., 17, 22
Hoque, K., 362, 370, 372
Hornberger, S., 72, 73
Horrigan, M., 326, 346
Hough, L. M., 21, 115, 151, 226
House, R. J., 309, 312, 320, 323, 324, 383, 397
Houtman, I. L. D., 8, 21

Howard, A., 299
Howard, S., 90
Howell, J. M., 261, 273
Howes, J., 214, 225
Huczynski, A. A., 96, 97
Huemer, K-H., 213, 227
Huff, J., 394, 398
Huffcutt, A., 128, 130, 148
Hughes, D. G., 65, 74
Hughes, R. L., 262, 273
Hulin, C. L., 254, 272
Humphrey, R. H., 238, 239, 245, 249
Hunt, J. G., 310, 312, 317, 321, 324
Hunter, J. E., 119, 121, 130, 134, 143, 148,
    151, 161, 162, 176
Hunter, R. F., 134, 148
Hunter, T. A., 323, 346
Hurrell, J. J., 228, 253, 274
Huselid, M. A., 352, 357, 358, 359, 361,
    362, 364, 365, 366, 367, 368, 370, 372
Hutchins, E., 91, 98
Huws, U., 294, 297
Huy, Q. N., 245, 250, 416, 423
Huysman, M., 173, 176
Hyatt, D., 334, 347

Iaffaldano, M. T., 12, 22
Ibarra, H., 333, 347
Ichniowski, C., 354, 357, 365, 372
Iles, P. A., 145, 150, 191, 201
Ilgen, D., 326, 344, 347
Inkson, K., 188, 199
Institute of Personnel and Development,
    137, 149
Irby, C., 83, 97
Isenberg, D. J., 340, 347
Isic, A., 240, 252
Ivancevich, J., 221, 226, 371, 372

Jackson, C., 179, 191, 193, 198, 200
Jackson, D. N., 132, 152
Jackson, G. B., 119, 148
Jackson, N. J., 133, 150
Jackson, P. R., 208, 217, 224, 228, 268,
    273, 286, 290, 291, 292, 298, 299, 368,
    369, 372, 373

Jackson, S. E., 208, 209, 212, 226, 227, 359,
    361, 364, 365, 367, 372, 373
Jacobs, R. W., 262, 273
Jacobson, D., 414, 423
Jacobson, L., 41, 50
Jacobson, S. W., 318, 324
Jacques, R., 318, 324
Jamal, M., 13, 16, 22
Janis, I. L., 339, 347
Javidan, M., 383, 397
Jensen, M., 340, 350
Jensen, R. C., 266, 272
Jewell, L., 213, 226
Jex, S. M., 17, 24, 210, 220
Jick, T., 401, 406, 410, 412, 421, 423
Johns, G., 8, 25, 283, 298, 336, 350
Johnson, B. T., 319, 323
Johnson, L, C., 75
Johnson, V., 86, 98
Johnson-Laird, P. N., 233, 235, 251
Jones, D. T., 356, 373
Jones, J. W., 265, 273
Jones, M. O., 398
Jones, R. G., 193, 200, 240, 251, 337, 338,
    348
Jordan, J. A., 157, 175
Joseph, A. E., 271
Joyce, M., 326, 346
Judge, T. A., 5, 9, 10, 12, 20, 22, 143, 149,
    263, 273
Jung, D. I., 312, 322
Jurgens, J. C., 196, 200

Kahin, B., 149
Kahn, R., 210, 211, 212, 221, 226
Kahneman, D., 33, 37, 49
Kaliterna, L. J., 66, 71, 74, 75
Kalleberg, A. L., 362, 368, 369, 371
Kandola, R., 123, 126, 134, 149, 150
Kanfer, R., 161, 176
Kanter, R., 401, 406, 410, 412, 421, 423
Kanungo, R. N., 310, 323, 324
Karakowsky, L., 339, 348
Karasek, R. A., 7, 14, 22, 43, 49, 216, 227,
    268, 273, 284, 298
Karau, S. J., 339, 340, 346, 348

Kardash, C. M., 162, 176
Karetta, B., 213, 227
Katz, J. A., 127, 151
Katzenbach, J. R., 327, 343, 344, 348
Kaufer, D. S., 92, 98
Kavanagh, M. J., 166, 172, 177
Kehoe, C., 105, 141, 149, 151
Keller, J., 139, 149
Keller, R. T., 13, 23
Kellett, S., 242, 252
Kelloway, E. K., 261, 263, 264, 267, 271,
      272, 273, 274
Kelly, J. E., 289, 296, 298
Kelly, M., 212, 225
Kemp, N. J., 208, 224, 286, 299
Kerkhof, G. A., 73
Kidd, J. M., 184, 187, 189, 193, 194–5, 196,
      200, 202
Killeen, J., 196, 197, 200, 202
Kimball, R., 83, 97
Kinder, A., 132, 150
King, D., 212, 227
King, L., 212, 227
King, M., 95, 97
Kinicki, A. J., 337, 349
Kiris, E. O., 45, 48
Kirkcaldy, B. D., 245, 249
Kirkman, B. L., 331, 334, 335, 337, 338, 344,
      348
Kirkpatrick, D. L. 167–71, 176
Kirsch, M., 127, 151
Kirwan, B., 35, 49
Klandermans, B., 414, 423
Klayman, N., 144, 148
Klein, K. E., 56, 76
Kleinberg, J., 385, 397
Kletz, T. A., 260, 273
Kline, P., 113, 149
Kluckhohn, C., 383, 397
Kluger, A. N., 144, 148
Knauth, P., 72, 73, 74
Knight, D. B., 271
Koch, M. J., 362, 372
Kochan, T. A., 269, 274
Kogi, K., 59, 60, 74, 75
Kohn, M. L., 292, 298

Koller, M., 67, 69, 74
Kompier, M. A. J., 8, 21
Konarski, R., 213, 226
Kopelman, R. E., 5, 21, 24
Korczynski, M., 294, 297
Korunka, C., 213, 227
Kotter, J. P., 317, 324
Kozlowski, S., 174, 175, 176
Krahn, H., 267, 274
Kraiger, K., 155, 174, 175, 176
Kram, K. E., 192, 201
Kramar, R., 214, 227
Kramer, A. F., 37, 49
Kramer, R. M., 337, 348
Kring, W., 292, 297
Kroeber, A. L., 383, 397
Kroeck, K. G., 263, 274
Kroemer, K. H. E., 259, 274
Kubeck, J. E., 163, 176
Kunda, G., 245, 252
Kurz, R., 105, 149
Kyng, M., 95, 98

LaBar, G., 260, 274
LaCost, H., 394, 398
Laing, P., 259, 274
Lam, S., 338, 349
Lamberg, L., 73, 74
Landauer, T. K., 90, 96, 98
Landrigan, P. J., 253, 274
Landsbergis, P. A., 268, 274
Landy, F., 262, 273
Larson, L. L., 324
Latham, G. P., 129, 149
Latham, W. R., 338, 349
Law, B., 200
Law, K., 337, 345
Lawler, E. E., 282, 296, 298, 326, 348, 352,
      362, 370, 372, 401, 423
Lawrence, B. S., 181, 198, 199
Lawrence, S., 137, 149
Lawthom, R., 100, 150, 360, 364, 366, 367,
      373
Lazarus, R., 204, 206, 218, 219, 227, 232,
      247, 250
Leach, D. J., 369, 372

Leavitt, B., 419, 423
Ledford, G. E., 287, 297, 326, 330, 348, 349, 352, 362, *370*, 372, *401*, 423
Lee, C., 300, 324
Lee, R. T., 17, 23, 217, 227
Leggett, J., 90, 98
Leidner, R., 237, 250
Leigh, J. P., 253, 274
Leigh, T. W., 394, 397
Leiter, M., 208, *209*, 227
Lepak, D. P., 362, 374
LePine, J. A., 160, *161, 162, 166*, 175
Leplat, J., 97
Levering, R., 389, 391, 392, 397
Levin, I., 10, 23
Lewin, K., 386, 398, 413, 415, 423
Lewis, K. M., 241, 250
Lewis, S., 214, 225
Lichenfels, P. A., 128, 152
Liebert, R. M., 29, 50
Lindeman, R. H., 186, 201
Lindgaard, G., 99
Little, B. L., 327, 348
Lobban, M. C., 68, 74
Locke, E. A., 9, *10*, 22
Lofquist, L. H., 182, 199
Lord, R. G., 302, 324
Lorsch, J., 297, 347
Loughlin, C. A., 264, 271
Lowe, K., 263, 274
Lucas, R. E., 3, 23, 231, 249
Lundberg, U., 41, 49

Mabey, C., 191, 201
Macdonald, I., 55, 70, 75
MacDuffie, J. P., 355, 356, 357, 362, 365, 367, 368, 370, 373
MacIver, R., 133, 150
Mack, M. J., 121, 151
Mackenzie, S. B., 14, 23, 338, 349
Mackinnon, D. W., 126, 149
Macrosson, W. D. K., 333, 346
Madigan, R. M., 337, 348
Maertz, C. P. Jr., 125, 147
Magjuka, R. J., 327, 348
Malone, T., 90, 98

Malouff, J. M., 244, 252
Mann, R. D., 302, 324
Mann, S., 237, 250, 302
Manning, J. S., 13, 23
Manning, W. D., 267, 274
Manz, C. C., 335, 348, 349
March, J. G., 419, 423
Marchand, A., 257, 262, 274
Marek, T., 73, 228
Markowitz, S. B., 253, 274
Marmot, M., 423
Marquardt, M., 172, 176
Martin, J., 384, 385, 398
Martin, R., 8, 23, 290, 299
Martocchio, J. J., 338, 349
Maslach, C., 5, 23, 208, *209*, 227, 228
Maslowski, R., 387, 398
Mathieu, J. E., 338, 348
Matteson, M., 221, 226
Matthews, G., 28, 33, 47, 49, 114, 149
Maule, A. J., 43, 49
Maurer, S. D., 128, *146*, 149
Mausner, B., 229, 250, 282, 297
Mayer, J. D., 113, 149, 243, 244, 245, 250, 251
Mayer, R. C., 337, 348
Mayes, B., 217, 222, 226
Mayr, J., 292, 298
McCall, B. P., 10, 21
McCauley, C. D., 159, 176
McCormick, B., 363, 374
McCrae, R. R., 110, 114, 147
McDaniel, M. A., 128, 146, 149, 163, 176
McDonald, H., 256, 272
McGee, G. W., 12, 23
McGrath, J. E., 213, 224, 328, 341, 348
McGrath, R. G., 362, 372
McMahan, G. C., 363, 374
McNamara, W. J., 127, 152
McNelly, T. L., 157, 158, 175
Medsker, G. J., 287, 296, 329, *330, 342, 344, 345*
Meghir, C., 156, 175
Meir, E. I., 183, 199
Melner, S. B., 326, 346
Menon, S., 212, 227

Mertini, H., 240, 252
Meyer, J. P., 18, 23
Michel, R., 86, 98
Michelson, M., 57, 74
Midkiff, K., 68, 75
Milkovitch, G., 371, 373
Miller, R., 196, 201
Millward, N., 180, 199
Minors, D. S., 55, 58, 66, 75
Mintzberg, H., 376, 377, 378, 379, 380, 381,
    382, 384, 388, 391, 392, 396, 398
Mitler, M. M., 63, 74
Mobley, W., 397
Mohrman, A. M., 344, 348, 401, 423
Mohrman, S. A., 293, 294, 298, 326, 344,
    348, 352, 362, 370, 372, 401, 423
Monk, T. H., 55, 57, 58, 65, 68, 73, 74, 76
Montgomery, J., 261, 274
Moore, M. D., 398
Moore, S., 256, 273
Moorhead, G., 339, 348
Morgeson, F. P., 262, 263, 269, 272
Morris, J. A., 92, 98, 240, 251
Morris, N. M., 45, 48
Morrow, J. E., 159, 176
Moser, K., 116, 149
Moses, J. L., 149
Motowidlo, S. J., 13, 23
Mouloua, M., 46, 50
Mount, M. K., 132, 133, 143, 146, 149, 162,
    175, 332, 345
Mouton, J. S., 305, 323
Mowday, R., 402, 423
Moyle, P., 217, 227
Muchinsky, P. M., 12, 22
Mueller, C. W., 10, 21
Mueller, W. S., 289, 297, 330, 345, 346
Mullarkey, S., 217, 228, 268, 273
Mullen, B., 336, 349
Mullen, E. J., 154, 176
Mumford, E., 95, 98
Muraven, M., 241, 251
Murnighan, K., 422
Murphy P. J., 105, 127, 152
Murphy, K., 144, 149
Murphy, L., 220, 224, 227, 228

Murray, M., 266, 274
Myers, D. A., xi, xvi

Nachreiner, F., 68, 69, 73, 75
Nadler, D., 407, 411, 424
Narayanan, L., 212, 227
Nathan, R., 195, 198, 201
Neal, A., 257, 258, 273, 274
Neck, C. P., 339, 348
Neubert, M. J., 332, 345
Neuman, G. A., 332, 349
Neuwirth, C. M., 92, 98
Newell, A. F., 86, 98
Newell, S., 115, 149
Newstrom, J. W., 171, 175
Nicholson, N., 179, 187, 200, 201, 398
Nickell, S., 100, 150, 360, 364, 366, 367,
    373
Nielsen, J., 82, 96, 98
Noe, R. A., 127, 151, 154, 160, 161, 162, 166,
    175, 176, 371, 373
Noer, D, 414, 424
Nonaka, I., 408, 419, 421, 424
Nord, W. R., 323
Nordhaug, O., 156, 176
Norman, D. A., 43, 49, 82, 98
Northouse, P., 300, 302, 307, 312, 321, 324
Noyes, J. M., 83, 98
Nyfield, G., 133, 150

O'Connell, B. J., 7, 24
O'Connell, C., 266, 274
O'Donnell, R. D., 34, 49
O'Driscoll, M. P., 210, 211, 212, 213, 214,
    217, 225, 227
O'Leary-Kelly, A. M., 338, 349
O'Reilly, A., 180, 199
O'Reilly, C. A., 326, 333, 334, 350
Oatley, K., 230, 235, 251
Offer, M., 198, 201
Ogden, D. A., 279, 299
Ogilvie, B. D., 73
Oginska, H., 69, 73, 75
Oginski, A., 69, 75
Ognianova, V. M., 68, 75
Ohlott, P. J., 159, 176

Older-Gray, M. T., 95, 97
Oldham, G. R., 282, 283, 289, 295, 297, 298, 330, 347
Oliver, L. W., 197, 201
Olson, E., 227, 203
Olson, G. M., 90, 98
Olson, J. S., 90, 98
Ones, D. S., 12, 24, 298
Ong, C. N., 59, 75
Organ, D. W., 14, 23
Osler, S., 204, 227
Osterman, P., 161, 176
Ostroff, C., 12, 23
Oswald, A., 4, 21
Ovalle, N., 209, 226
Owens, D. S., 55, 75

Packard, J. S., 13, 23
Padgett, M. Y., 4, 5, 24
Paine, J. B., 14, 23
Palmer, D. K., 130, 147
Papper, E. M., 287, 296
Parasuraman, R., 89, 98
Parker, C. P., 394, 398
Parker, S. K., 14, 23, 217, 228, 257, 258, 264, 268, 274, 275, 283, 285, 290, 291, 292, 293, 295, 298, 299, 368, 369, 373, 414, 422
Parkes, K., 217, 227
Parkinson, B., 230, 232, 233, 236, 237, 239, 241, 251, 252
Parrott, W. G., 241, 251
Parry, J. B., 125, 152
Parsons, F., 181, 182, 194, 201
Pashler, H., 28, 49
Pasmore, W. A., 289, 298, 349
Paterson, C., 100, 150
Patrick, J., 174, 176
Patterson, M. G., 12, 23, 100, 150, 253, 274, 360, 361, 362, 364, 366, 367, 373
Patton, G. K., 12, 22
Paunonen, S. V., 133, 150
Payne, R. L., 37, 49, 225, 227, 248, 251, 385, 398
Payne, S. C., 144, 148
Payne, T., 131, 150

Pearlman, K., 105, 151
Pedler, M., 173, 175
Pelled, L. H., 236, 252
Pemberton, C., 189, 199
Pennebaker, J. W., 209, 227, 251
Perrewe, P., 226
Perrow, C., 270, 274
Pervin, L. A., 115, 150
Peters, T. J., 309, 324, 352, 373
Peterson, M. K., 396, 397
Petrie, H., 86, 98
Pettigrew, A., 381, 398, 399, 408, 409, 424
Petty, M. M., 12, 23
Pfeffer, J., 269, 274, 284, 287, 298, 326, 333, 349, 369, 373, 393, 398, 404, 408, 424
Philips, J. L., 221, 226, 326, 346
Pierce, J., 211, 228
Pillai, R., 261, 274
Pitkow, J., 140, 149
Ployhart, R. E., 125, 150
Podro, S., 294, 297
Podsakoff, P. M., 14, 23, 338, 349
Pohley, K., 126, 151
Pokorski, J., 69, 74, 75
Poole, M. S., 407, 409, 413, 414, 424
Porras, J., 407, 424
Porter, M., 370, 373
Poulson, C. F., 232, 251
Powell, G., 318, 324
Prabhu, P. V., 96, 98
Prahalad, C. K., 382, 397
Prediger, D. J., 184, 201
Preece, J., 86, 96, 98
Premack, S. L., 188, 201
Prennushi, G., 354, 357, 365, 372
Price, J. L., 10, 21
Prien, E. P., 105, 127, 151
Pringle, J. K., 188, 199
Pritchard, R. D., 338, 349
Prizmic, Z., 71, 74
Prussia, G. E., 17, 22, 337, 349
Pugh, S. D., 242, 251
Pulakos, E. D., 123, 151
Pursell, E. D., 128, 129, 149, 152

Quick, J., 225
Quinn, J. B., 226, 410, 424
Quinn, R., 212, 400, 408, 409, 416, 421, 425
Quiñones, M. A., 126, 151, 164, *165*, *166*, 176

Raab, A., 86, 98
Rackham, N., 169, 177
Radosevic-Vidacek, B., 66, 71, 74, 75
Rafaeli, A., 237, 238, 239, 240, 251
Ragins, B. R., 193, 201
Rapson, R. L., 241, 250
Rasmussen, J., 29, 50
Ravlin, E., 342, 346
Reason, J. T., 29, 31, 44, 50
Reasons, C., 253, 274
Rebitzer, J. B., 269, 274
Reddy, S., 135, 151
Rees, H., 180, 190, 199
Reichert, L., 86, 98
Reilly, R. R., 127, 150
Reinberg, A., 74
Remington, N. A., 3, 23
Rentsch, J. R., 10, 24
Reuvers, M. M. E. N., 8, 21
Reynolds, S., 222, 224, 230, 236, 251
Rice, A. K., 286, 298
Rick, J. T., 37, 49
Rietveld, W. J., 73
Rigg, C., 319, 325
Rilley, C., 68, 75
Rissler, A., 41, 50
Roberts, R. D., 244, 249
Robertson, I. T., 24, 104, 105, 117, 122, 126, 127, 129, 132, 133, 134, 145, 146, 147, 149, 150, 151, 152, 177, 227, 271, 298, 350
Robinson, S. L., 189, 201
Roe, D., 84, 98
Roe, R. A., 20, 23
Rogers, J. D., 140, 149
Rogers, Y., 86, 96, 98
Roos, D., 356, 373
Rosa, R. R., 67, 73
Rosen, B., 157, 176, 331, 334, 335, 345, 348

Rosenbach, W. E., 300, 321, 323, 324, 325
Rosenthal, D. B., 127, 148
Rosener, J., 319, 319, 324
Ross, L., 353, 374
Roth, E. M., 31, 35, 50
Rothstein, H., 135, 147
Rothstein, M. G., 132, 133, 150, 152
Rouse, W. B., 45, 50
Rousseau, D. M., 189, 201, 383, 397, 402, 424
Rout, U., 129, 150
Roxburgh, S., 8, 24
Ruddy, T. M., 334, 347
Ruderman, M. N., 159, 176
Ruiz-Quintanilla, S. A., *312*, *320*, 323, 383, 397
Ryan, A. M., 125, 150
Ryan, K., 23

Saari, L. M., 129, 149
Saavedra, R., 242, 249
Sackett, P. R., 127, 150
Sadri, G., 221, 225
Saha, S., 339, 350
Salancik, G. R., 284, 298, 404, 424
Salas E., 155, 174, 175, 176, 332, 335, 337, 338, 345, 346, 348, 350
Salgado, J. F., 132, 146, 151
Salovey, P., 113, 149, 243, 244, 250, 251
Salvendy, G., 47, 50
Sanchez, J. I., 105, 151
Sargent, L., 217, 228
Sashkin, M., 309, 324
Sauer, J., 42, 43, 48
Sauter, S. L., 228, 327, 353, 374
Sawyer, J. E., 338, 349
Scandura, T. A., 193, 201
Scerbo, M., 46, 50
Schabracu, M., 228
Schaubroeck, J., 204, 208, 215, 216, 226, 240, 251, 338, 349
Schaufeli. W. B., 8, 21, 212, 228
Scheier, M. F., 233, 249
Schein, E. H., 383, 384, 398, 407, 411, 424
Schein, V., 318, 324

Schmidt, F. L., 12, 24, 119, 121, 128, 130, 135, 143, *146*, 147, 148, 149, 151, 161, 162, 176

Schminke, M., 342, 346

Schmitt, N., 123, 127, 146, 151

Schnall, P., 268, 274

Schneider, B., 182, 201

Schneider, R. J., 115, 151

Schön, D., 418, 422

Schönpflug, W., 40, 50

Schooler, C., 292, 298

Schoorman, F. D., 337, 348

Schriesheim, C. A., 5, 24

Schroeder, R. G., 291, 296, 230, 245

Schuler, H., 116, 149

Schuler, R. S., 203, 212, 226, 228, 359, *361*, *364*, *365*, *367*, *371*, *372*, *373*

Schultetus, R. S., 30, 31, 48

Schutte, N., 244, 252

Schwoerer, C., 157, 176

Scott, W, R., 404, 413, 424

Scullen, S. E., 135, 147

Shippmann, J. S., 105, 127, 151

Segal, N. L., 10, 21

Sego, D. J., 164, *165*, *166*, 176

Seibert, S., 193, 201

Seifert, C., 240, 252

Selker, T., 84, 99

Selye, H., 204, 228

Senior, B., 413, 424

Sethi, A., 203, 228

Shamir, B., 313, 325

Shani, A., 289, 298

Shannon, H. S., 292, 298

Shapiro, D. L., 337, 338, 348

Sharf, J. C., 131, 148

Sharp, H., 86, 96, 98

Sharpley, D. A., 127, 145, 150

Shaw, K., 354, *357*, *365*, 372

Shea, G. P., 327, 347

Shepperd, J. A., 340, 349

Sheridan, T. B., 44, 50

Sherman, W. S., 363, 374

Shin, C., 353, 374

Shire, K. A., 294, 297

Shneiderman, B., 83, 98

Shortliffe, E. H., 89, 97

Shotland, A., 168, *169*, 174

Sianesi, B., 156, 175

Siegel, J. P., 339, 348

Siehl, C., 385, 398

Siffre, M., 52, 75

Silvers, R., 407, 424

Simard, M., 257, 262, 274

Sime, W., 222, 226

Simmering, M. J., 162, 175

Simon, S. J., 157, 176

Sims, H. P., 335, 348

Sinangil, H. K., 298

Sinha, K. K., 291, 296, 330, 345

Sivasubramanian, N., 263, 274

Skinner, N. F., 58, 75

Slack, A. K., 10, 25

Slane, S., 183, 202

Sluyter, D., 251

Smircich, L., 283, 298

Smith, B. A., 84, 99

Smith, C., 406, 422

Smith, C. S., 68, 75, 256, 273

Smith, D. B., 182, 201

Smith, D. K., 327, 343, 344, 348

Smith, H. L., 231, 249

Smith, L. M., 70, 75, 289, 297, 330, 345, 346

Smith, M. J., 104, 117, 147, 148, 151, 262, 265, 269, 272, 274, 275

Smith, P., 68, 73

Smith, S. L., 245, 252

Smither, J. W., 127, 150

Snell, S. A., 106, 151, 362, 370, 374

Snoek, J., 212, 226

Snow, C. C., 106, 151

Snow, R. E., 162, 177

Snyder, R. D., 398

Snyderman, B. B., 229, 250, 282, 297

Sonnentag, S., 155, 177

Sorra, J. S., 164, *165*, *166*, 176

Sparrow, J., 319, 325

Sparrow, P., 407, 424

Spector, P. E., 7, 17, 24, 113, 148, 212, 216, 227, 228, 243

Sperandio, A., 40, 50

Spettell, C. M., 29, 50
Spokane, A. R., 197, 201
Spreitzer, G. M., 284, 287, 297, 298, 330, 349
Sprigg, C., 14, 23, 290, 299
Springen, K., 267, 275
Spychalski, A. C., 126, 151
Stace, D., 404, 410, 421, 424
Stafford, E., 208, 224
Stalker, G. M., 290, 296, 379, 380, 397
Stamm, C.L., 16, 22
Stammers, R. B., 28, 33, 47, 49
Stanchez, V., 68, 75
Stankov, L., 244, 249
Stanush, P. L., 157, 175
Starke, M., 101, 147
Statistics Canada, 253, 275
Staveland, L. E., 36, 48
Staw, B. M., 236, 252, 347, 349, 351
Steel, R. P., 10, 24
Stein, B., 401, 406, 410, 412, 421, 423
Stephenson, G. M., 282, 299
Sternberg, R. J., 111, 113, 149, 151, 152, 177
Stetzer, A., 257, 268, 273
Stevens, M. J., 159, 175, 279, 280, 296, 332, 349
Stewart, G. L., 332, 335, 345, 349
Stodgill, R. M., 302, 305, 322, 325
Stokes, G. S., 135, 151
Stokes, J. P., 10, 23
Storey, J. A., 180, 191, 200, 201, 271, 274, 371, 373
Strothotte, T., 86, 98
Sturdy, A., 237, 249
Subich, L. M., 184, 201
Suchman, L., 91, 99
Suh, E. M., 3, 23, 231, 249
Sundstrom, E., 328, 350
Super, D. E., 185–7, 201
Sutherland, V., 228
Sutton, K., 140, 149
Sutton, R. I., 236, 237, 238, 239, 240, 251, 252, 402, 423
Svenson, J., 256, 272
Sytnik, N., 55, 75

Taggar, S., 339, 350
Tait, M., 4, 5, 24
Takeuchi, H., 408, 419, 421, 424
Tam, M., 294, 297
Tannenbaum, S. I., 166, 168, 169, 172, 174, 177, 332, 350
Tansley, C., 115, 149
Taris, R., 8, 24
Tattersall, A. J., 37, 50
Taubman, P., 10, 21
Taylor, K. M., 340, 349
Taylor, R. L., 300, 321, 323, 324, 325
Teachout, M., 174, 175, 176
Tellegen, A., 3, 25
Tepas, D. I., 75
Terry, D. J., 217, 219, 228, 333, 347
Tetrick, L. E., 253, 268, 274
Tett, R. P., 105, 127, 132, 152
Teuchmann, K., 242, 252
Tharp, G., 222, 226
Theorell, T., 14, 23, 43, 49, 268, 273
Thierry, H., 146
Thome, E. P., 245, 249
Thompson, A. S., 186, 201
Thompson, C. A., 24
Thompson, R. C., 257, 275
Thomson, A., 191, 201
Thoresen, C. J., 12, 22, 143, 149
Thorndike, E., 57, 75
Thornton, G. C., 124, 127, 148
Tijerina, L., 33, 48
Tinsley, H. E. A., 182, 184, 185, 200, 201
Tjosvold, D., 337, 345
Toffler, A., 77, 99
Tokar, D. M., 184, 201
Toth, P., 214, 225
Totterdell, P., 41, 48, 55, 75, 230, 236, 241, 242, 251, 252
Tracey, J. B., 166, 172, 177
Tranberg, M., 183, 202
Traver, H., 168, 169, 174
Trice, H. M., 396, 398, 412, 424
Trist, E. L., 285, 299, 418, 424
Trova, V., 294, 297
Troxler, R., 209, 226
Tsui, A., 333, 350

Tucker, P., 55, 70, 75
Tuckman, B., 340, 350
Turnbull, P., 293, 297
Turner, N., 257, 258, 264, 265, 272, 275, 292, 298
Turner, S., 93, 99
Tushman, M., 407, 424

Uhl-Bien, M., 308, 323
United States Bureau of the Census, 253, 275
Unsworth, K. L., 336, 337, 350

van der Ven, A., 407, 409, 412, 414, 424
van Maanen, J., 245, 252
van Vuuren, T., 414, 425
Veiga, J. F., 393, 398
Vernon, P. E., 125, 152
Verplank, B., 83, 97
Vicente, K., 35, 50
Vidacek, S., 66, 71, 74, 75
Vieux, N., 75
Visser, P. S., 3, 23
Viswesvaran, C., 12, 24, 298
Vogt, C., 240, 252
Volger, A., 68, 75
Vroom V. H., 308, 325

Waclawski, J., 303, 323
Wadsworth, J., 180, 199
Wageman, R., 331, 343, 345, 350
Wagner, J., 265, 272, 411, 424
Wagner, R. A., 111, 152
Wagner, S. H., 332, 349
Waldman, S., 267, 275
Walker, C. R., 279, 280, 299
Walker, S., 270, 275
Wall, T. D., 8, 16, 22, 23, 208, 217, 224, 228, 268, 274, 282, 283, 286, 290, 291, 292, 293, 295, 297, 298, 335, 350, 360, 367, 368, 369, 372, 373, 414, 424
Wallis, D., 97
Walsh, S., 232, 252
Walton, R. E., 352, 373
Wanek, J. E., 154, 176
Wanous, J. P., 188, 201

Warburton, D. M.,
Warr, P. B., 1, 4, 6, 7, 9, 12, 14, 21, 24, 156, 160, 161, 162, 163, 164, 166, 168, 169, 175, 177, 201
Wastell, D. G., 42, 43, 49
Watanabe, S., 5, 22
Waterhouse, J. M., 55, 58, 66, 75
Waterman, R. H., 309, 324, 352, 373
Waterson, P. E., 95, 97
Watson, D., 3, 8, 10, 25, 209, 216, 227, 228
Watts, A. G., 179, 180, 184, 190, 196, 197, 198, 200, 202
Weber, T., 261, 264, 271
Wedderburn, A. A. I., 59, 67, 72, 75
Weekley, J. A., 129, 152
Wegmann, H-M., 56, 76
Wegner, D. M., 251
Weick, K., 400, 407, 408, 409, 416, 418, 421, 425
Weijers, T., 294, 297
Weisbord, M., 417, 425
Weisbord. M. R., 78, 75, 99
Weisner, W. H., 128, 130, 152
Weiss, A., 213, 227
Weiss, H. M., 234, 235, 246, 252
Weizenbaum, J., 89, 99
Weldon, E., 341, 350
Wells, J. C., 269, 274
Werner, J. M., 157, 176
Wernimont, P. F., 114, 152
West, M. A., 12, 23, 100, 150, 336, 337, 344, 350, 360, 364, 366, 367, 373
West, M. S., 339, 348
Westerman, S. J., 28, 33, 47, 49
Westman, M., 212, 228
Wever, R. A., 52, 53, 73, 76
Whetzel, D. L., 128, 146, 149
Whipp, R., 408, 409, 424
White, M., 197, 200
Whitmore, M. D., 193, 200
Whyte, G., 340, 350
Wickens, C. D., 26, 28, 33, 36, 46, 47, 50
Wiener, L., 45, 50
Wiener, Y., 13, 22
Wierwille, W. W., 33, 35, 36, 48, 50
Wiggins, J. S., 126, 152

Wilderom, C. P. M., 387, 396, 397, 398
Wiersma, U., 219, 228
Wiley, J. W., 390, 398
Wilk, S. L., 154, 176
Wilkinson, L. J., 135, 152
Wilkinson, R. T., 64, 76
Williams, E. S., 261, 274
Williams, H., 257, 264, 275
Williams, K. D., 340, 348
Williams, K. Y., 333, 334, 350
Wilpon, J., 84, 98
Winnubst, J., 228
Winograd, T., 96, 99
Witt, L. A., 143, 149, 257, 275
Woehr, D. J., 130, 148
Wolfe, D., 212, 226
Wollowick, H. B., 127, 152
Womack, J., 356, 374
Wood, S., 352, 363, 366, 367, 368, 369, 371, 374
Woodland, S., 180, 199
Woodman, R. W., 349
Woodruffe, C., 126, 152
Woods, D. D., 16, 22, 31, 35, 50
Woolfe, R., 200
Woolgar, S., 94, 99,
Worley, C., 404, 408, 409, 415, 421, 424

Wright, B. M., 290, 297
Wright, J., 332, 349
Wright, P. L., 302, 304, 321, 325
Wright, P. M., 128, 152, 363, 371, 373, 374
Wroe, N., 139, 152
Wyatt, S., 279, 299

Xie, J. L., 8, 25, 283, 298, 336, 338, 349, 350

Yetton, P. N., 308, 325
Yost, P. R., 337, 347
Youndt, M. A., 362, 370, 374
Young, R. A., 201, 202
Young, S. A., 394, 398
Yu, L., 94, 97

Zaccaro, S. J., 224
Zaleznik, A., 303, 318, 325
Zaltman, G., 411, 412, 415, 421, 425
Zapf, D., 216, 228, 240, 252
Zempel, J., 292, 297
Zerbe, W. J., 249,251
Zhai, S., 84, 99
Ziegler, J., 86, 98
Zohar, D., 212, 228, 256, 257, 262, 266, 269, 27

Subject Index

Abilities, 6, 11, 20, 103, 109–13, 115, 142, 182, 184, 185, 187, 206, 244, 332, 339
see also Cognitive ability, Learning, Skill, Training

Absence from work, 15–16, 17, 20, 69, 108, 118, 172, 203, 210, 235, 242, 279, 286, 289, 295, 304, 329, 331, 336, 338

Accidents, 27, 29, 31, 44, 89, 62–6, 204, 210, 254–8, 260, 265, 267, 270, 277
see also Errors, Injuries, Safety

Adaptive behaviour, 14, 100, 105

Adrenaline, 37, 41, 53

Adverse impact, 122–5, 131–2, 139
see also Fairness

After-effects, 39, 41–2, 47

Affect regulation, 240–42, 243

Affectivity, 8–10, 185, 216, 233

Age, 69, 111, 139, 162, 163–4, 242, 292, 320, 334
see also Older workers, Young workers

Agreeableness, 109, 114, 133, 244, 332

Allocation of function, 45–6, 89

Ambiguity, see Role ambiguity, Uncertainty

Anxiety, 3, 5, 13, 14, 16, 40, 203, 212, 222, 235, 338, 412

Applied psychology, xii

Appraisal, 192, 205, 206, 218, 220, 230, 232, 243, 351, 358, 359, 361, 365, 368

Arousal, 2–4

Assessment centre, 102, 125–8, 134, 141–3, 142, 145, 193

Assessment of staff, 100–146

Attitudes, 17–18, 153–5, 168, 196, 214, 235, 308, 314, 320, 329, 338, 357, 369, 384, 386, 394–5, 412, 414, 421

Attribution theory, 329

Automation, 43–6, 88, 89, 179, 260, 356

Automatization, 15, 155, 161
see also Computers

Autonomous work groups, 286, 288–90, 292, 294, 295, 330

Autonomy, 6, 221, 223, 276–95, 328, 329, 330–31, 335, 339, 342, 364, 365
see also Control, Discretion, Participation

Bargaining, 411

Behaviour modelling, 156–7

Big five factors, 114–15, 133, 244

Biodata, 135, 143

Blindness, 86–7

Blood pressure, 5, 209
see also Cardiovascular system

Body rhythms, 51–73

Boredom, 267, 269

Boundary-spanning, 417–18

Buffering, 204, 215–18

Bureaucracy, 214, 380, 388–9, 391, 392

Burnout, 5, 17, 204, 207–8, 212, 215, 217, 220, 223–4, 240

Call centre, 79, 84, 87, 106–7, 246, 276, 293
Cardiovascular system, 46, 66, 69, 209, 215
Career, 159, 178–98, 213, 230, 308, 416
Career development, 154, 160, 185–7, 190–97, 213–14, 280, 351
Centralization, 380
Change, *see* Job design, Organization change, Training
Change agent, 400, 403, 408–9, 413, 417
Charisma, 309–10, 312–17, 404–5
Circadian rhythms, 51–73
Citizenship, 13–14, 263
Clarity, 6, 184, 221, 223
Climate, 214, 385–6, 393–5
Cognitive ability, 110–13, 130–32, 143, 157, 161–2, 164
Cognitive strategies, 155
Cohesiveness, 291, 333, 336, 338, 339, 384
Collectivism, 328, 337–8, 388, 389
Commitment, 18, 162, 166, 193, 329, 368–9
Commuting time, ix, 37, 67
Competencies, 12, 104–6, 115, 127, 132–3, 142, 193, 244, 382, 393
Complexity, 12, 292, 335, 379
Computer-supported co-operative work, 90–92, 96
Computer-based testing, 135–42
Computer-based training, 158–9
Computers, 43, 44, 59, 77–96, 135–42, 145, 157, 196, 259
Concurrent validity, 118,
Conflict, 291, 337, 415, 417
Conscientiousness, 114, 133, 162, 265, 332, 339
Consideration, 304, 305, 311, 313, 314
Construct validity, 116–20, 127, 143
Content validity, 117
Context evaluation, 170–72
Contingency theories, 306–9, 369–70, 371, 404–6
Control, 6, 7, 32, 43, 47, 78, 88, 92, 94, 184, 211, 216–17, 220, 221, 223, 277, 283–4, 336, 353, 380

see also Autonomy, Discretion, Participation
Coordination, 376–82
Coping, 71, 204–7, 215, 216, 218–19, 221, 224
Corporate culture, 383–95
see also Organization climate
Counselling, 71, 194–7, 221
Co-workers, 2, 285, 306
Criteria, 106–9, 117–19, 144, 168, 197, 304
Criterion-related validity, 117–20, 122–3, 125–35, 142–4, 145
Critical incident technique, 129, 219
Culture, 15, 115, 383–95,
Curvilinear relationships, 7–8, 143

Declarative knowledge, 15, 154, 160
see also Knowledge
Demands, 6, 27, 33, 37, 39, 44, 188, 205, 206, 208, 209, 220, 283, 336
see also Job demands
Depression, 4, 5, 13, 16, 66, 203, 212, 222, 338
De-skilling, 96, 293
see also Skill use
Development activities, 14, 154, 160, 171, 283
Development centre, 158, 193
Differential validity, 122–3, 131
Disability, 86–7, 139
Discretion, 85, 88, 211, 268, 279, 330–31, 368, 370
see also Autonomy, Control, Participation
Discretionary activities, 13–14, 20, 236
Dispositions, 8–10, 215–16, 233
Distributed cognition, 91
Diversity, 123–5, 320–21, 328, 333–4, 339, 343
Double-loop learning, 418

Electronic journals, 93–4
Emotion, 193, 219, 229–48
Emotional intelligence, 113, 229, 243–5, 246, 248
Emotional labour, 237–8, 245–7, 294

Emotional stability, 110, 114, 133, 339
  see also Neuroticism
Employability, 156, 179–80, 190
Employee assistance programmes,
  220–21
Employee-centred style, 304
Employee development centre, 158
Empowerment, 87–8, 94, 284–5, 295, 315,
  331, 334–5, 337, 343, 345, 352, 359,
  365, 366, 370, 391
Equal opportunities, 101, 122–5, 131–2,
  214, 318–19
Ergonomics, 6, 84, 96, 136, 259–61
  cognitive, 259
Errors, 26, 29–31, 33, 35, 39, 43, 47, 89,
  210, 266, 281, 304
Ethics in testing, 116
  see also Adverse impact, Equal
  opportunities, Fairness
Ethnic groups, 116, 131–2, 139, 320, 333,
  334
Evaluation of change, 414, 420
Evaluation of training, 166–72
Experience sampling, 232
Expert systems, 80, 88, 90
Expertise, 14, 26, 29–31, 155, 168, 294, 314,
  327, 379
Extroversion, 113, 114, 133, 143, 185, 244,
  332, 339

Face validity, 117
Fairness, 103, 116, 122–5, 131–2, 134, 234,
  388–9, 392
  see also Adverse impact, Equal
  opportunities
Family, x, 6, 8, 67, 69, 180, 211, 214, 222,
  294
Fatigue, 4, 5, 37, 38, 40, 41, 42, 57, 68, 69,
  246
Feedback, 6, 31, 43, 88, 127, 156–7, 158,
  161, 166, 184, 216, 221, 223, 243,
  282–4, 330, 334, 338, 403, 411, 418
Feelings, 168, 229, 241, 243, 314, 417
  see also Emotion
Fidelity of simulation, 165
Field theory, 415–16, 421

Forgetting, 158, 165
Formative evaluation, 167, 420
Full-time jobs, ix, x, xvi
Future ambiguity, 6

Gender, 5, 69, 318–19, 320, 333, 334, 339,
  388
  see also Men, Sex differences, Women
Genetic effects, 10
Goals, 6, 26–31, 38, 40, 42, 45, 106, 166,
  184, 194, 196, 213, 221, 223, 230–31,
  233, 235, 300, 307, 331, 338, 343, 379,
  413
Graphical user interface, 82
Groups, 11, 90–92, 144, 285–8, 305,
  326–45, 415
Group-think, 336, 339
Growth-need strength, 283

Happiness, 3,
  see also Well-being
Health, 8, 66, 69, 71, 72, 84–5, 94, 203,
  211, 240, 268, 270–71, 277
Heart rate, 5, 37, 53, 60, 209, 230
Heat, 6, 37, 85, 211, 259
Heredity, 10
High-involvement management, 282,
  295, 352–71
High performance organizations, 282,
  286, 352–71
Home-working, 78–9, 93
Hormones, 5, 37, 39, 222
Hours of work, ix, 51–73, 84, 221, 390
Human-centred design, 82–5, 94–5, 96
Human-computer interaction, 77–96
Human factors, see Ergonomics
Human relations, 416
Human resource management, 100, 106,
  194, 264–6, 334, 351–71, 393, 418
Hygiene factors, 282

Identity, 405–6
Ill-health, see Health
Income, 5, 6, 7, 156, 192
  see also Pay
Incremental validity, 144

Individualism, 337–8, 388, 396
Initiating structure, 304, 305
Initiative, 292, 369
    see also Proactivity
Injuries, 62–6, 253–5, 260, 261, 264, 266, 267, 292
    see also Accidents, Safety
Innovation, 179, 245, 303, 311, 327, 328, 354, 379, 382, 400–401, 408
Input-process-output model, 328–42
Integrity, 133, 315, 337
Insecurity, 213
Intelligence, 110–13, 130–32, 161–2, 243, 302
Interdependence, 288, 290, 295, 326–9, 331–2, 342, 343
Interests, 135, 182–5, 195
Internet, 96, 137–42, 145–6, 198, 290
Interpersonal contact, 6, 7, 67, 81, 93, 184, 277, 280, 294
Interview, 101, 128–30, 141, 142, 144, 145, 146
    situational, 128–9
    structure, 128–30
    training, 129
In-tray exercises, 126
Introversion, 185

Jet-lag, 56
Job
    analysis, 35, 102–6, 129, 357
    characteristics, 5–8, 9, 10, 211–12, 282–5, 287, 288–9, 291–2, 328
    complexity, 130–31, 165, 211
    demands, 6, 7, 32, 182, 184, 205, 209, 212, 215, 216, 267, 268, 276–95, 331, 338
        see also Demands
    design, 85, 87–90, 95, 96, 221–3, 246, 261, 276–95, 329, 330–31, 342, 351, 352, 361–2, 368
    enlargement, 280–81, 295
    enrichment, 88, 281–5, 287, 288, 290, 293, 352, 365
    involvement, 16, 239, 240, 265, 327, 387
    level, 4, 161, 162

    mobility, 180, 184, 197
        see also Transitions
    performance, 11–13, 113, 210, 236, 241, 242, 243, 244
        see also Performance
    previews, 141, 188
    rotation, 159, 280–81, 295, 339, 354
    satisfaction, 1–2, 3–5, 7, 9, 12, 14, 16, 17, 18, 182, 183, 193, 213, 214, 230, 234, 235, 239, 240, 246, 276, 279, 281, 283, 286, 287, 304, 305, 329, 330, 333, 334, 336, 342, 385, 391, 394, 411
    security, 180, 294, 354
    simplification, 277–9, 286, 292, 293, 294
    tenure, 108, 118, 161, 268
    transitions, 178, 184, 187–8, 236, 341
        see also Role, Work
Job characteristics model, 282–3, 291, 292
Joint optimization, 418
Just-in-time production, 293, 356, 362

Knowledge, 15, 28, 29, 31, 32, 43, 45, 89, 103, 111–13, 115, 153–5, 161, 164, 168, 173, 196, 243, 258, 287, 291, 294, 327, 332, 338, 369, 391, 393, 419
Knowledge of results, 282, 284
    see also Feedback
Knowledge work, 81, 87, 245, 294

Labour turnover, 17
Leader-member exchange, 262–3, 270, 306, 307–8
Leadership, 6, 115, 241, 245, 261–4, 269, 278, 285, 300–322, 335, 339, 387, 391–2, 395, 399–403, 406–9
    democratic, 304, 319
    personality, 301–3, 306, 308, 312, 318–19
    style, 304–9
    transactional, 311–12, 313, 317, 319, 321
    transformational, 241, 263–4, 309–17, 319, 320, 321
Lean production, 268–9, 356–7, 370
Learning, 14, 15, 43, 93, 153–74, 196, 266, 291, 292, 331, 351, 368, 379, 390, 393, 399, 414, 417–20, 421

see also Memory, Training

Learning motivation, 156, 161, 162, 163, 164, 168

Learning organization, 153, 172–3, 419

Learning strategies, 162–3

Learning transfer, 164–6

Least-preferred co-worker, 306, 309

Leisure, 67, 72

Life satisfaction, 4–5, 8,

Lighting, 85, 259

Long-term memory, 27, 28

Machine intelligence, 88–90

Management, x, 6, 11, 12, 105, 173, 174, 191, 217, 222, 223, 257, 261–4, 266, 278, 286, 300–322, 327, 334–5, 359, 376, 392–3, 405–9, 411, 416, 417

Mechanistic organization, 379–80, 389, 391

Medical diagnosis, 79–80, 89, 90

Melatonin, 70–71

Memory, 15, 27, 28, 30, 38, 40, 57–8, 64, 65, 91

Men, x, 5, 69, 313, 316, 321, 339, 388
    see also Sex differences, Women

Mental ability, 110–13, 130–32, 143, 157, 161–2, 164

Mental health, 68, 203, 221, 279, 338–9, 341

Mental models, 45, 83, 173, 335, 338–9, 341

Mentoring, 192–3

Menu structures, 82–3, 86

Minority groups, 123, 214

Mistakes, 29, 31

Mobility, 180, 192, 197
    see also Transitions

Money, xi, 6

Mood, 231, 235, 236, 242

Morning/evening types, 53, 68–9

Motivating potential score, 282–3

Motivation, 4, 18, 20, 118, 161, 163, 168, 193, 258, 262, 264, 278, 283–4, 286, 289, 291, 311, 317, 330, 332, 337–8, 340, 342, 358, 368, 394–5, 407

Movement between jobs, 178, 184, 187–8, 341

Negative affectivity, 8–10, 216, 233

Negotiation, 411

Neuroticism, 8–10, 53, 113, 114, 244
    see also Emotional stability

Night work, 59, 62, 64–6, 67, 68, 72

Noise, 6, 37, 38, 40, 41, 211, 259

Non-linear relationships, 7–8, 143

Noradrenaline, 53, 60

Norms, 6, 91, 116, 237–9, 287, 336–7, 339, 340–43, 386, 401, 415

Occupational interests, 135, 182–5, 195

Older workers, 53, 69, 161, 163–4, 242
    see also Age

Open learning, 158, 164

Openness to experience, 114, 162, 184–5, 244

Operating core, 376–7, 380

Organization, 287, 292, 375–96
    change, 193, 221, 245, 301, 384, 399–421
    climate, 214, 335, 385–6, 393–5
    culture, 15, 115, 245, 375, 383–96, 400–401, 403, 406, 407, 412, 419
    development, 399–421
    learning, 173, 368, 400, 412, 414, 418–20, 421
    performance, 12, 351–71, 386–9
    politics, 381
    size, x, 382
    strategy, 375–6, 382
    structure, 180, 214, 357, 375–82, 389, 396, 401, 412

Organizational citizenship behaviour, 13–14, 263

Organizational commitment, 18, 162, 166, 281, 289, 330

Organizational development, 399–421

Organizational learning, 173, 368, 400, 412, 414, 418–20, 421

Overtime, 13–14

Pacing, 78, 216, 220, 268

Participation, 6, 95, 214, 221, 223, 262,

Participation – *cont.*
    304–5, 307, 308, 319, 328, 351, 352,
    356–7, 358, 359, 392, 404–5, 411, 416
    see also Autonomy, Control,
    Discretion
Participation in learning, 160, 161
Participation in the labour market, x, xi,
    xvi
Part-time jobs, ix, x, xvi, 180, 267
Path-goal theory, 307
Pay, 2, 37, 38, 184, 351, 354, 356, 357, 359,
    361, 365, 390, 391
Perceptual selectivity, 28
Performance, 11–13, 20, 26–47, 62–6, 70,
    107–8, 118, 130, 133, 188, 213, 231, 239,
    261, 265, 276–95, 306, 327, 328–41,
    353–70, 385, 386–91, 401, 411
Person-environment fit, 181–5, 194, 205
Person specification, 104, 106, 110
Personality, 8–10, 69, 110, 113–16, 132–3,
    142, 143, 146, 162, 184–5, 215–16, 233,
    244, 265, 300–303, 320, 321, 332, 339
Personnel selection, 100–146
    see also Selection of staff
Physical environment, 115, 267, 283
Physiological measures, 5, 34, 37, 47, 52,
    53, 55–6, 60, 209–10, 212, 222
Positive affectivity, 8–10, 185, 233
Power, 306, 380–81, 388, 389, 406, 407,
    410–11, 420
Practical intelligence, 111–13
Practice, 30
Predictive validity, 118–19
Proactivity, 14, 257, 264, 292, 301, 368, 369
Problem-solving, 89, 111, 159
Procedural knowledge, 15, 154–5
    see also Knowledge
Process consultation, 411, 415
Promotion, 2, 108, 180, 191, 193, 213, 308,
    358, 368, 390
Psychological contract, 189, 399
Psychosomatic symptoms, 5, 68, 222, 240

Range restriction, 120, 128, 131
Reaction evaluation, 167–8, 169, 170, 171
Realistic job preview, 188

Recruiting, 101, 137–8, 141, 180, 243, 350,
    358, 359, 361
    see also Selection of staff
References, 134, 142
Rehearsal, 163
Relapse prevention, 158
Reliability of measures, 103, 116–17,
    119–20, 145
Repetitive work, 85, 212, 391
Restriction of range, 118–20, 128, 131
Retention of knowledge, 57, 157–8, 165,
    174
Retirement, xi
Risk, 63–5, 259–60, 310, 315
Risky shift, 340
Role,
    ambiguity, 6, 212, 223, 283, 306, 307
    conflict, 6, 212, 217
    transitions, 186, 187–8
    valued, 7, 184

Safety, 18, 45, 46, 62, 85, 203, 253–71, 292,
    390
    climate, 257–8, 264, 266, 269
    training, 258, 262, 264, 266, 269
    see also Accidents, Errors, Injuries
Sampling error, 119–20
Scientific management, 278
Secondary task, 32–6, 39–40, 42, 47
Security, 6, 184, 213, 365, 369, 392
Selection of staff, 71, 100–146, 243, 246,
    259, 264–6, 267, 285, 320, 334, 339,
    351, 356, 357, 359, 361, 368
Selection ratio, 121
Self-awareness, 196
Self-confidence, 156, 166, 302, 315
Self-efficacy, 9, 216, 284–5, 337, 369
Self-employment, xi, xvi, 4, 5, 179
Self-esteem, 7, 9, 156, 216
Self-managing teams, 276, 286, 288,
    330–31, 335, 339, 345, 352
Sense-making, 407–8, 418–19
Service work, x, 292, 295
Sex differences, 5, 69, 318–19, 320
    see also Men, Women
Shiftwork, 51–73, 211

Short-term jobs, 269, 294
Simulation, 165
Situational factors, 115, 153, 160, 205, 300, 302–9, 312, 369–70, 402–6
Situational interview, 128–9
Skill, xi, 14–15, 20, 26, 28–31, 84, 89, 100, 103, 115, 141, 153–5, 160, 168, 183, 196, 258, 267, 332, 338, 357–8, 361–2, 368
Skill loss, 158
Skill use, 6, 184
Sleep
   cycle, 52–7, 59, 71
   deprivation, 37–8, 40–43, 64, 70
   problems, 58, 60–62, 69, 208
Social comparison, 241, 340
Social contact, 6, 7, 67, 81, 93, 184, 277, 280, 294, 339, 389
Social information processing, 284
Social loafing, 340
Social position, 6, 184
Social support, 7, 192, 213, 217–18, 221, 283, 287, 328
Socio-technical systems, 88, 95, 259–60, 285–7, 418
Speech recognition, 84
Standardization, 376, 378, 381
Status, 7, 184
Strain, 5, 26, 204–6, 208–10, 212–20, 222–3, 259, 277, 280
   see also Stress
Strategy, 40–41, 42, 43, 69, 106, 219, 287, 315, 317, 368, 370, 376, 382, 387, 400, 401, 404–5, 407, 408, 409–10, 421
Stress, 14, 26, 32, 37–9, 41, 46, 47, 69, 100, 159, 203–24, 230, 233, 246, 276, 304, 329, 414
   management, 218–24
   see also Strain
Structure in interviews, 128–30
Structure in learning, 161–2
Structure in organizations, 180, 214, 357, 375–82, 389, 396, 401, 412
Summative evaluation, 167, 420
Supervisor ratings, 12, 107, 118, 165
Support for learning, 160–61, 166, 172, 174

Systems theories, 171, 259–60, 402, 409, 413, 417–18, 421

Tacit-knowledge, 111–3,
Task analysis, 35,
Task identity, 282
Task orientation, 304
Tasks, 27–47, 86, 236, 287, 307, 328, 341
Team roles, 332–4
Teams, 90–92, 144, 169, 230, 242, 245, 263, 276, 285–8, 290, 295, 317, 326–45, 351, 354, 356, 359, 361, 365, 368, 389, 391, 399, 410, 417, 419
Technostructure, 376–7
Teleconferencing, 80, 90
Teleworking, 78–9, 87, 93, 294
Temperature, 52–7, 60, 64
Temporal isolation, 52–3
Temporary jobs, xi, 180, 269, 293–4
Tension, 13
Tenure, 180, 118, 161, 267
Time zones, 56
Total quality management, 191, 293, 327, 356, 362, 370, 400
Trade unions, 269, 353
Trainability tests, 134
Training, 2, 108, 153–74, 180, 220–21, 222, 230, 239, 245, 246, 259, 264, 266, 269, 330, 334–5, 338, 339, 343, 351, 352, 354, 356, 357, 358, 359, 361, 368, 370, 390, 392, 412, 416
   see also Memory, Learning
Training evaluation, 166–72
Training needs, 164–5, 170
Traits, 8–10, 185
   see also Personality
Transfer of learning, 164–6, 171
Transformational change, 401, 404, 406
Transformational leadership, 241, 263–4, 309–17, 319, 320, 321
Transitions, 178, 184, 187–8, 236, 341
Travel to work, ix, 37, 67, 93
Trust, 214, 315, 336–7, 389, 418
Turnover of staff, 17, 20, 100, 197, 204, 210, 279, 286, 289, 304, 308, 329, 331, 338, 353, 358, 362

Twin studies, 10
Two-Factor Theory, 282–3
Type A, 215, 233

Uncertainty, 6, 38, 192, 212–13, 216,
    290–91, 293–5, 307, 335, 341, 388,
    407
Underload, 7
Unemployment, 17
Unfreezing, 415–16
Usability, 82, 85–8, 95
Utility analysis, 121–2, 123–4, 143

Valence, 18, 340
Validity, 103, 107, 116–20, 121, 125–36,
    145, 146
    see also Construct-validity, Criterion-
    related validity
Validity generalization, 119–20
Values, 17, 20, 91, 155, 187, 337–8, 382–9,
    392–3, 402, 415, 418
Variety, 6, 7, 85, 88, 184, 211, 277, 282, 287,
    361
Video-conferencing, 91, 93, 142
Virtual working, 77, 80, 91, 92–4, 96, 292
Visual display unit, 85
Visual search, 27, 28, 33, 39
Vocational guidance, 181
Vocational interests, 135, 182–5, 195
Voice input, 84

Well-being, 1–20, 88, 94, 96, 203, 205–7,
    211, 221, 223, 229, 230, 233, 239, 246,
    276–95, 328, 330, 338, 394–5
    see also Anxiety, Burnout, Depression,
    Job satisfaction, Life satisfaction,
    Self-esteem, Stress, Strain
Women, x, 5, 69, 139, 214, 314, 316, 339, 388
    see also Men, Sex differences
Work
    adjustment, 182
    behaviour, 10–17, 19, 129, 228, 236
        see also Job performance
    definition of, ix
    design, 221, 276–95, 368
        see also Job design
    full-time, ix, x, xvi
    load, 6, 7, 26, 32–7, 40–42, 44, 46, 47,
        164, 211–12, 215–16, 220, 268, 294, 329
    part-time, ix, x, xvi, 180, 267
    pressure, 6, 165, 172
    sampling, 126, 134, 143, 170
    simplification, 277–9, 286, 292, 293, 294
    voluntary, ix
    see also Job, Role
Working memory, 27, 28, 30–31, 38,
    40–41, 43, 57
World-wide web, 82, 137–42, 198

Young workers, 162, 164, 267–8, 270
    see also Age